Federal Justice in California

LAW IN THE AMERICAN WEST

Series Editor

John R. Wunder, University of Nebraska–Lincoln

Series Advisory Editors

Lawrence M. Friedman, Stanford University
Kermit L. Hall, University of Florida
Harry N. Scheiber, University of California, Berkeley

Volume I

CHRISTIAN G. FRITZ

Federal Justice

in California

The Court of Ogden Hoffman, 1851–1891

University of Nebraska Press   Lincoln & London

Portions of chapters 3, 6, and 7 have previously been published, in different form, as "A Nineteenth-Century 'Habeas Corpus Mill': The Chinese before the Federal Courts in California," *American Journal of Legal History* 32, no. 4 (October 1988): 347–72; "Judicial Style in California's Federal Admiralty Court: Ogden Hoffman and the First Ten Years, 1851–1861," *Southern California Quarterly* 64, no. 3 (Fall 1982): 1–25; and "Politics and the Courts: The Struggle over Land in San Francisco, 1846–1866," *Santa Clara Law Review* 26, no. 1 (Winter 1986): 127–64, and are used by permission.

The paper in this book meets the minimum requirements of American National Standard for Information Sciences— Permanence of Paper for Printed Library Materials, ANSI z39.48–1984.

Library of Congress Cataloging-in-Publication Data
Fritz, Christian G., 1953–
    Federal justice in California : the court of Ogden Hoffman, 1851–1891 / Christian G. Fritz.
        p. cm. — (Law in the American West ; v. 1)
    ISBN 0-8032-1979-2 (alk. paper)
    1. Hoffman, Ogden, 1822–1891.
    2. Judges—California, Northern—Biography. 3. United States. District Court (California : Northern District)—History.
    4. Justice, Administration of—California, Northern—History. I. Title. II. Series.
KF368.H583F75   1991
347.73′009794—dc20
[347.30709794]   90-36904
                                    CIP

For my mother and in memory of Max H. Graefe

CONTENTS

List of Illustrations, ix

Preface, xi

Chapter One

Beginnings: New York Origins and San Francisco Lifestyle, 1

Chapter Two

Ogden Hoffman's Judicial Aspirations, 29

Chapter Three

San Francisco's Court of Admiralty, 51

Chapter Four

Criminal Prosecution in the Northern District, 100

Chapter Five

California Land: The Struggle over Titles, 134

Chapter Six

The Litigious Pueblo, 180

Chapter Seven

The Chinese before the Court, 210

Conclusion: Hoffman's Judgeship, 250

Appendix, 257

List of Abbreviations, 265

Notes, 267

Index, 315

ILLUSTRATIONS

Following page 144

1. Judge Ogden Hoffman, around 1887

2. Scene of San Francisco Bay with many vessels, early 1850s

3. U.S. courthouse, San Francisco, around 1856

4. Ogden Hoffman, Sr.

5. Josiah Ogden Hoffman

6. Stephen J. Field, U.S. Supreme Court justice

7. Lorenzo Sawyer, U.S. circuit court judge

8. Matthew Hall McAllister, special circuit judge

9. Matthew P. Deady, U.S. district court judge for Oregon

10. *Diseño* of the private land grant Rancho de las Animas

11. Chae Chan Ping, who brought a test case challenging the Chinese Exclusion Act of 1888

12. A Canton certificate issued by the Chinese government in 1883 for Tung Yeong

13. Chae Chan Ping's return certificate issued by the U.S. government

At his death in 1891, Ogden Hoffman was one of the longest-serving trial judges in the history of Anglo-American law. For forty years following his appointment in 1851, Hoffman presided over the United States District Court for the Northern District of California. Simply hearing and dealing with the initial complaints of tens of thousands of litigants was an extraordinary achievement. But Hoffman's career is important apart from the staggering amount of work he accomplished and his record for judicial longevity. Hoffman's judgeship offers a special opportunity to examine the nature of the common-law tradition, the making of a trial judge, and the operation of a federal district court in the nineteenth century.

Precisely because Hoffman was a trial judge, his experience provides fresh insight into the nature of the judicial process and the workings of the common law. Since he rarely decided appeals, his judgeship is an important counterpoint to the type of judicial experience from which most of our understanding of common-law judging is drawn. Overwhelmingly, the appellate process has been the focus of studies and reflections exploring the nature of common-law adjudication.[1] Similarly, appellate judges dominate as subjects of judicial biography. It may be that appellate judges and their courts have been considered more important to the legal history of the United States, since their decisions frequently have a more general effect. Yet this scholarly emphasis has come at the cost of leaving us largely unaware of the operation of law at the trial level, where most people participate.

Hoffman's judgeship also provides a detailed picture of federal trial court practice over time. During his tenure, Hoffman exercised virtually all types of jurisdiction that a federal district court of the nineteenth century could: circuit court powers, special land jurisdiction, and proceedings in bankruptcy, as well as the traditional fare of the admiralty, criminal, and common-law and equity dockets. The judicial business of his court was subject to wide fluctuations. Indeed, an examination of the over 19,000 cases filed during his forty-year tenure reveals that Hoffman's greatest judicial labors occurred in several, somewhat overlapping, periods. Ultimately, the statistical analysis of the judicial business before Hoffman's court makes it possible to test the typicality of the northern district by comparing who used the federal trial courts for what purposes and with what results.[2]

The fundamentally different roles that trial and appellate courts play in our legal system undermine the validity of generalizing about trial courts based on the appellate experience. Trial courts are principally concerned with applying law after a determination of facts, whereas appellate courts primarily review the correctness of the law as applied.[3] These distinct functions of trial and appellate courts produce important differences in the experience of the two types of judges, both in the nineteenth century and today. Trial judges preside over the initial conflicting claims made by litigants and their lawyers and are more directly exposed to the circumstances that give rise to litigation than are appellate judges. Further, the judicial business of trial courts is readily distinguished from that of appellate courts by its far greater volume of cases, most of them routine. Moreover, in the nineteenth century, federal district judges performed their tasks largely alone, without the collegiality that both state and federal appellate judges enjoyed.

These institutional differences and the judicial experiences that they fostered clearly shaped Hoffman's judgeship. Indeed, the kind of judge Ogden Hoffman became owed much to the fact that he sat on a trial court. Although this institutional framework influenced both Hoffman's judicial character and the substance of his opinions, it hardly led to uniformity in the behavior of all federal judges. Different backgrounds, experiences, education, and political views helped shape distinctive judicial personalities within the context of a similar institutional structure.

Although the functional differences between trial and appellate courts should not be overlooked, neither should they be exaggerated. To differing degrees, both types of judges were engaged in the essential process of the common law: explaining the reasons for their decisions through written opinions. In Hoffman's day, as well as our own, judicial opinions were largely seen as the measure of a judge's contribution to law, society, and legal history. Traditionally, scholars have relied on judicial opinions as the best source for understanding the philosophy of judges and the values or ends their courts promoted.

Hoffman's opinions do offer substantial insight into his judicial attitudes, but along with other trial court judges, he left behind even more valuable sources for understanding his judgeship and his court: the case files and docket books constituting the judicial work of the northern district. Published judicial opinions are a discrete and readily accessible source. Confronting the sheer volume of archival documents in the case files, on the other hand, is a daunting task. Still, the effort is indispensable if we are to penetrate the inner workings of trial courts, assess their role in a community, and trace the relationship between the activity of judging and the development of judicial attitudes and temperament.

Moreover, combining Hoffman's judicial opinions with this additional archival source produces a comprehensive picture of a federal district court, a picture that can be compared with broader assertions about the role of law and the courts during Hoffman's period. The vast majority of cases— including those that involved or affected commerce—never went to trial, and of those that did go to trial, only a fraction were appealed. Thus, whereas legal doctrine involving such subjects as contract and tort can be traced through published opinions and treatises, day-to-day commercial litigation by and large remains an uncharted land.

Recently, legal historians have focused on two general themes: whether and to what extent judges facilitated economic and commercial development, and changes in the style and reasoning of judicial opinions. Much of this discussion of the role of law in promoting American economic development in the nineteenth century has revolved around interpretations advanced by Morton J. Horwitz and James Willard Hurst.[4] Although Horwitz, Hurst, and others discussing the subject have reached different conclusions, none of their interpretations draw on a detailed analysis of the judicial business of a nineteenth-century trial court.

Strictly speaking, this study is neither a biography nor an institutional study. Hoffman's background, education, and aspirations influenced his behavior and self-perception as a judge. This interplay between Hoffman the person and Hoffman the trial judge is the key to understanding his judgeship. How Hoffman came to comprehend his role as a federal judge and how his court was used by litigants are equally necessary in assessing the broader significance of the northern district. It is important both to appreciate the personal dimensions of Hoffman's court and to place his judicial business within a social, political, and economic context. Thus, the context of Hoffman's judgeship is first established by examining his background and judicial ambitions before analyzing the principal areas of his judicial work.

Like all authors, I have accumulated many debts in the course of writing this book. In reducing the financial kind, I am thankful to the University of California for an Ottilie R. Schubert Fellowship, to the Henry E. Huntington Library for a Post-Doctoral Fellowship, and to the American Bar Foundation for a Fellowship in Legal History.

I would also like to thank the editors of the *Southern California Quarterly*, the *Santa Clara Law Review*, and the *American Journal of Legal History* for permission to use earlier versions of portions of chapters 3, 6, and 7 that appeared in those periodicals.

This study originated as a doctoral dissertation in legal history at the University of California, Berkeley. I am most grateful to the three members of my dissertation committee: Thomas Garden Barnes for his infectious enthusiasm for archival legal history, Harry N. Scheiber for challenging me to think more broadly about the issues, and James H. Kettner, the chair of my committee, for his extraordinary conscientiousness in reading and commenting on multiple versions of every chapter. I thank Jim Kettner, particularly, for his guidance and advice.

My research was assisted by many efficient staff members of libraries, especially the staff of the Bancroft Library and the Huntington Library. Moreover, I wish to thank Henry Pomares of the Goshen Historical Society for indispensable help in using the Hoffman Papers and Dr. William Chandler of the Wells Fargo History Department for providing encouragement and many good leads.

In large measure this study owes its existence to Judge Robert F. Peckham. While Chief Judge of the U.S. District Court for the Northern District of California, Judge Peckham appointed me his historical law clerk. It was during this clerkship that I decided to write a history of the early northern district and its first judge. The enthusiastic support and help of Judge Peckham and his staff, especially Kumi Okamoto and Opal Madaris, greatly facilitated the work on this project. In addition, thanks are due to William L. Whittaker, former Clerk of Court of the Northern District, for his interest and help in gaining access to many of the court records and to Dr. Michael

Griffith, the court's Archivist-Historian, for similar help and for reading the entire manuscript.

Numerous friends and colleagues have made this a better book than it otherwise might have been. I am grateful to Gunther Barth, Malcolm Ebright, and Tony Freyer for reading portions of the manuscript and providing insightful comments. John Gordan III has shared his ideas and enthusiasm for the project in ways that have improved the book. Kermit Hall not only read the entire manuscript but also was, typically, very generous in sharing sources and ideas. Although John P. Reid may not agree with everything I have said, the manuscript is much stronger for his thorough reading, and I am most grateful for his help and interest.

Three other friends also played an important role in bringing this work to fruition: Charles Royster, who gave me a detailed critique of the entire manuscript at a critical juncture; Joseph Franaszek, who was there from the very beginning and who probably knows as much about Judge Hoffman now as I do, and Dave Greenthal, who saw little of the manuscript but whose confidence in the author also left its mark.

The most substantial revision of this work took place after I began teaching at the University of New Mexico Law School in 1987. It is my good fortune to be surrounded by dedicated and wonderfully supportive colleagues. This environment in no small measure accounts for the finished product. Three colleagues in particular deserve special thanks: Dean Theodore Parnall, for providing research grants that facilitated the revisions and the creation of the appendix, and Michael Browde and Emlen Hall, for reading and commenting on the entire manuscript. Moreover, I wish to thank Torild B. Kristiansen for her magnificent secretarial help in readying the manuscript for publication.

My greatest debt, however, is to my wife, Marlene: at once my best critic and my strongest supporter. She has seen both the valleys and the peaks of the creation of this work and shall always have my deepest gratitude.

1

Beginnings

New York Origins and San Francisco Lifestyle

Understanding Ogden Hoffman and his judgeship requires an appreciation of his extraordinary pride. One revealing comment is found in a letter he wrote in 1878, alluding to his "long descent from an historic name." Hoffman's pride in himself and in his family was both a source of strength and the cause of many hurts, real and imagined. This pride would help him cope with the disappointments he suffered later in life in his pursuit of higher judicial office.[1]

Much of Hoffman's pride came from the prominence of his grandfather and father as members of the bar and as leaders in the political life of New York. His grandfather, Josiah Ogden Hoffman, was a well-known Federalist and New York City trial lawyer who moved in the highest social and political circles of that city. During the course of his career, Josiah served in the New York Assembly, as recorder of New York City, as attorney general during John Jay's governorship of the state, and as a superior court judge for the last eight years of his life.[2]

By all accounts, Josiah was a man of fashion and a "court of last resort in the quiddities of minuets and precedence at table." He also engaged in extensive investments in land—at first successfully. In the late eighteenth century, Josiah purchased much property in upstate New York, as well as around

New York City. Unfortunately, by the 1820s he had lost all he had made. Indeed, in 1823 he wrote a confidential letter to the New York governor, Joseph Yates, requesting a judgeship because his income was "insufficient" to defray "family expenses." Being greatly "embarrassed and perplexed" by his reduced circumstances evidently drove him to drink. Although he lived until 1837, his last years were not happy.[3]

Likewise, Hoffman's father followed a similar pattern of attaining a widespread political and legal reputation but ultimately encountering financial failure. Graduating from Columbia College in 1812, Hoffman's father, Ogden Hoffman, Sr., joined the U.S. Navy when hostilities broke out with Britain. Resigning his commission in 1816, Hoffman read law in New York City and in Goshen, Orange County, New York. During this time he developed his talents as an orator by participating in a series of public debates. Toward the end of his legal apprenticeship he married Emily Burrall, whose well-to-do Orange County family would prove to be an important source of financial support for the Hoffmans.[4]

During the first years of Hoffman's legal practice in Goshen, Emily gave birth to two sons, Charles in 1821 and Ogden Hoffman, Jr., in 1822. Meanwhile, Ogden senior began to make a name for himself. In 1823 he was appointed district attorney of Orange County, and two years later the county voters elected him to the state assembly. After one term, Hugh Maxwell, the district attorney for New York City, made Hoffman his law partner. Prompted by this mark of professional advancement, Hoffman moved his family into the wider circle of opportunities presented by New York City. His association with Maxwell resulted in his appointment as the associate counsel in a number of notorious criminal cases prosecuted by the New York district attorney. After a second term in the state assembly in 1828, this time representing New York City, Hoffman succeeded his partner as the district attorney for the city in 1829. Retaining this position for seven years gave him considerable trial experience and public exposure.

During this period Hoffman's reputation grew and so did his expenditures. His wife's relatives, the Wickhams, proved to be the most important stabilizing force for the Hoffman family. By 1827, Emily insisted that the family spend the summer at Goshen with her relatives, to save money. A good deal of the financial strain on the family, however, stemmed from Hoffman's capacity to spend money. Even before his appointment as the district attorney for New York City, he moved his family to a new, more fashionable address on the west side of Broadway. Although Emily found the two-storied house "very pleasant," she objected to the annual rent of $850. On more than one occasion the Wickhams provided funds to the renowned advocate, but poor businessman, to keep his family out of debt.[5]

While Hoffman was serving as New York City's district attorney, his wife died. She had borne him five children, but only Charles and Ogden survived into adulthood. After Emily's death, her uncle, George Wickham, and his wife, Bridget, took a major part in raising Charles and Ogden. Goshen became the country haven for the two Hoffman boys, who filled the days with hunting, fishing, and watching trotter-horse racing, for which the town was well known. By the time Hoffman remarried in the late 1830s, the two boys were nearing their late teens. Hoffman's second wife, Virginia Southard, established additional connections for her husband's advancement. His new father-in-law, Samuel L. Southard, served as the secretary of the navy from 1823 to 1829 and as a Whig senator from New Jersey from 1833 until his death in 1842.[6]

Between 1820 and 1835, Hoffman continued to enhance his reputation both as a prosecutor and as a political speaker. During this time he broke from the Democratic party because of President Andrew Jackson's hostility toward the Second Bank of the United States and joined the National Republicans—the nascent Whig party. For the next twenty-five years he lent his support to the Whig cause and in 1837 entered Congress, where he served two consecutive terms. Although Hoffman shared many Whig assumptions held by men of his class, such as the benefits of an active governmental role in the economy and the natural right of educated, well-born, and wealthier men to be leaders of society, he gravitated to the most conservative wing of his party. Following in the Whig tradition of Henry Clay and Daniel Webster, these conservatives resisted and resented any discussion of issues that increased sectional tensions. Slavery, in their view, had been accommodated in a constitutional compromise that ought not to be tampered with by either the North or the South. Hoffman described the Missouri Compromise as "a holy theory, above the reach of Political Legislation." Hence it was not surprising that he was described as "one of the *National Whigs*."[7]

The calls by such Whigs for preserving the Union above all else and decrying demagogues and party spirit seem unrealistic given American political life and experience in the 1840s and 1850s. Still, their desperate efforts to cling to a mythical political past—a time of supposed apolitical stability featuring respectable and dignified leaders—formed an essential aspect of the conservative Whigs' outlook that Ogden junior inherited from his father.[8]

Hoffman's principal value to the Whig party was not as a strategist or political thinker but as a popular speechmaker. Throughout the 1830s and 1840s, Hoffman became a frequent speaker at Whig assemblies, sometimes sharing the speaker's platform with Daniel Webster and often presiding over political dinners. His forte was the seemingly extemporaneous two-to-three-hour speech. Philip Hone—a prominent Whig and leader of New York society—declared he had not heard a speech "delivered with greater grace and eloquence" than was Hoffman's address to the alumni of Columbia in 1832. Generally regarded as "one of the great orators of his generation," Hoffman had a dignified bearing and possessed "a voice of magic eloquence and a court manner, polished, suave and courteous." Such traits served him well both on the political stump and in the courtroom.[9]

Hoffman's oratorical skills were extremely important to his fellow Whigs because such speechmakers were expected not only to defend the principles of Whiggery but also to inculcate these values among the people. Whereas today these nineteenth-century rhetorical productions may seem didactic, moralizing, and verbose, they were meant to appeal to both head and heart. In large measure a lost art form whose meaning and value have faded, the speeches that Webster and Hoffman delivered helped define the dominant American political imagery of the nineteenth century.[10]

In addition to his oratorical skills, Hoffman had exceptional social credentials. Beyond his immediate ancestors, Hoffman traced a relationship back to Alexander Hamilton. Murray Hoffman, a New York judge and a prolific treatise writer, was a closer relation whose reputation added luster to the family name. By marriage the Hoffmans were also related to the socially prominent Hone family of New York City. The combination of Hoffman's social credentials, professional talent, and political role brought his family within New York's most elite social circles.[11]

Despite his reputation, Hoffman repeatedly missed opportunities to consolidate a fortune. He had all the instincts of a well-born member of New York society, but he lacked both an inheritance to indulge his style of living and the drive to convert his professionalism into a sufficient source of income. One friend described Hoffman as having a "slip-shod laziness—a way of basking in the sun all summer at Rockaway and lounging at the Union Club and strolling through the [law] courts all the rest of the year, save when some special matter stirred up his faculties." Another friend described Hoffman as "an extravagantly high liver." Indeed, the cost of actively participating in New York City's finest clubs proved ruinous. Hoffman's financial difficulties, combined with his determination to live as a society gentleman, led to predictable results. Spending beyond his means and neglecting his business matters, he repeatedly brought his family into dire financial straits. In these crises, the Wickham money helped, but Hoffman invariably failed to reduce his spending.[12]

Whig President William Henry Harrison's election in 1840 brought Hoffman's reward: an appointment as the U.S. attorney for the Southern District of New York. To a friend, the appointment seemed "hardly . . . worth accepting to a lawyer of his distinction." But Hoffman readily accepted the post with its $6,000 annual salary. Nonetheless, he made almost desperate attempts to earn additional fees over and above his set compensation by characterizing lawsuits as outside his official duties. Yet in the midst of his financial difficulties, Hoffman spent money he did not have to fix up what he called the family's *"County Seat"* in Goshen. In any event, his federal salary came to an end when President James K. Polk, a Democrat, removed him from his post in 1845. Hoffman returned to private practice, but two years later his wife, Virginia, alluded to his "trouble" and struggle to "discharge his heavy duties." However, the election in 1848 of a Whig president, Zachary Taylor, held out the promise of additional federal patronage—especially given Hoffman's many services to the party as a stump speaker during the campaign.[13]

Unfortunately, his pride and his self-perception that he was not a politician interfered with his desired reappointment as the U.S. attorney. As much as he needed the job, he merely wrote to the secretary of state saying that the office "would be acceptable" to him and alluding to his prior record as federal prosecutor. Too late, Hoffman sent a note inquiring about the status of his application. "I have the vanity to believe that my appointment would be popular with a large majority of the Whigs of this city: But if my professional, political, or personal character . . . is not now strong enough, my pride will not suffer me to bolster it up by certificates." Hoffman did not get the appointment.[14]

Hoffman's behavior can best be understood in terms of an old-fashioned

Whiggery that marked the outlook he transmitted to his son. Essentially, such men were uncomfortable with the new form of mass-movement and organized politics emerging during the Jacksonian period. Despite their own political ambitions and goals, they continued to see themselves as antiparty, opposed to the demagoguery they saw around them, and committed to a personalized leadership that rose above parties. Such men had difficulty admitting their own ambitions and politicking; they preferred to believe, in the words of David Walker Howe, that high office "was a moral reward rather than an object of competitive striving." This distaste for political partisanship clearly hampered them in the competition for office, as Hoffman's experience in New York demonstrated. Likewise, this aversion to party politics would later frustrate the plans of Hoffman's son Ogden for judicial advancement in California.[15]

Hoffman had better luck capitalizing on his Whig connections within New York State. In 1853 he won election as the Whig candidate for state attorney general. But financial troubles still plagued him, and the "constitutional fetters" around what he called his "miserable compensation" of $2,000 a year did not improve matters. By April 1855 he was desperate. Many of the suits that he had filed as attorney general had not yet become judgments, and thus costs he was entitled to remained uncollectable. Moreover, he had spent most of his quarterly salary repaying loans from friends. Hoffman wrote a confidential letter to Thurlow Weed, a leading New York Whig, asking help to meet "a debt of sacred honor"—some $500 for a loan imminently due. He lamented being "cut off *from business, and all honors, without one dollar*" to meet his present emergency and hoped that after Weed helped him out, they could have "a frank conversation" so that Hoffman could "explain . . . the disease and consult [Weed] as to the remedy."[16]

Yet, Hoffman's financial health did not improve, and his physical health soon failed him. When he died at the age of sixty-three on May 1, 1856, he left his wife, their three children, and his two sons by his first marriage, Ogden and Charles, "absolutely penniless" and in debt. Hoffman's close friends discreetly took up a collection to stave off the disgrace of destitution that faced his family and to place them "above the fear of want." Even so, his widow opened a "school for young ladies" to support the family that Hoffman had left behind.[17]

Ogden Hoffman, Jr., nicknamed Og as a youth, grew up with an acute awareness of the need to maintain one's honor and pride as a gentleman. If he recognized that his father's sort of pride and honor had contributed to his indebtedness, it was a lesson Ogden chose to ignore. Indeed, the elder Hoffman succeeded very well in giving his son a heightened sense of the importance of living like a gentleman, even at the risk of exceeding one's financial limits.

In addition to leaving Ogden with a strong sense of pride and honor, Hoffman also encouraged his son's wide-ranging interests and intellectual curiosity. Ogden's inquiring mind and his interest in many subjects other than law owed much to his father's model and the salon atmosphere of the household. Hoffman's oratory drew on history and literature as well as a knowledge of law. As one biographer put it, Hoffman was never "a mere case lawyer." Moreover, a bent toward literature came naturally in a family where the writer Washington Irving bounced young Ogden on his knee and where one uncle, Charles Fenno Hoffman, attained contemporary distinction as a novelist and as the editor of the *Knickerbocker Magazine*. Ogden's father's house had been a common ground for great statesmen, lawyers, writers, and intellectuals of the day.[18]

Ogden's youth also bore the marks of his father's two marriages. Perhaps inevitably, the two surviving children of Hoffman's first marriage felt somewhat estranged from their stepmother, Virginia, with whom their father started a second family. Ogden apparently had few memories of his own mother. Rather, his childless aunt, Bridget Wickham, became a surrogate mother to him, as she had with his brother, Charles.[19]

Overindulged, Ogden grew up without developing habits of fiscal responsibility. His father hardly provided an appropriate model. The son, like his father, had a flair for living, and he managed from a rather young age to overspend—in part, perhaps, responding to social pressure to maintain the standards of a gentleman. Even as a minor, Ogden disposed of his independent income—made possible by bequests from his mother's family—too quickly. His letters to his Aunt Bridget were filled with requests for more money or with calculations of money due him under a family trust.[20]

Ogden's father, perhaps in part because of his frequent absences after their mother died, also indulged and spoiled the two boys. Not surprisingly, the effects of this behavior showed. Hoffman described Ogden at seventeen as "upon the whole . . . a good boy," who nonetheless needed to "correct the faults of his disposition." Warning Bridget Wickham, at whose home the Hoffman family was about to arrive, Ogden's stepmother noted, "[Ogden] is more unruly and ungovernable than ever—so I hope you will provide your-self with a large stock of fortitude and patience." Virginia also referred to "his ceaseless tongue," a trait that continued to characterize Ogden in later years, long after he mastered his temper.[21]

Indulgence as a child stemmed in part from his health. Frail from birth, Ogden grew up particularly susceptible to respiratory illnesses. During the long periods spent with the Wickhams in Goshen as a child, Ogden was cautioned by his father not to "overexercise" and thereby lose the "health advantages" of his stay. Persistent coughs continually threatened to become more serious, and even as he grew older the state of his health remained a concern.[22]

Still, Ogden managed to live the high life that the social elite enjoyed in New York. The Hoffmans, as a family, frequented the upper-class resorts, such as Saratoga Springs. Evenings of playing whist with prominent politi-cians or of attending fancy-dress balls with socialites left a taste for New York society that no amount of club life in San Francisco would erase.[23]

As did his father, Ogden attended Columbia College, and in 1840 he received his B.A. During this time Ogden studied the classics and read widely in history and literature—considered the correct foundation for a young gentleman of his background. Indeed, Columbia was only the first step in acquiring an elite education. Soon after graduation he began to study law under Justice Joseph Story and Professor Simon Greenleaf of the Har-vard Law School.

In 1840 Harvard offered the only national legal education in the country. It earned this reputation both from the geographical diversity of its students and the scope of its curriculum. The ninety-nine students entering with Hoffman, for example, came from twenty-one states, from Quebec, and from Ireland. More important, the school continued to embody Story's vision of a training ground for the country's future leaders, who would emerge knowledgeable about an American common law and imbued with a nationalistic constitutionalism. The goal of the law school, in Story's view, was "to teach law not as a body of fixed principles to be memorized but as a system and method of adjusting old rules to changing circumstances or, if necessary, of making new rules from old materials." Despite different teach-ing styles, Story and Greenleaf shared this educational mission. Hoffman's judgeship demonstrates that he grasped their message and took it to heart.[24]

The study of law at Harvard when Ogden entered consisted of a combination of lectures, recitations, and moot court experiences. Treatise literature formed the core of a reading course that encompassed commercial and
maritime law, real property, equity, crown law, civil law, the law of nations,
and constitutional law. In addition, both Blackstone's and Kent's commentaries served as standard texts. Despite the emphasis on treatises, case law
was not neglected, especially in the moot courts held two or three times a
week. Moreover, Greenleaf's students were assigned cases from law reports
"such as would likely come before one in an office." [25]

Both professors gave lectures and conducted the moots and recitations,
but Greenleaf took the main teaching and administrative burdens upon himself. Nonetheless, it was Justice Story that former students remembered with
greater affection. Beyond his fame as a judge and scholar, Story endeared
himself by taking a personal interest in his students and their advancement.
One of them recalled Story as a "father in the law" to his students and "the
patriarch of a common family." For his part, Story confessed that his "pride
was connected to them, and their fame." Story died before he could take
pride in Ogden Hoffman's judgeship, but the former student would later use
his famous teacher as the standard against which to measure himself as a
judge and legal scholar.[26]

After receiving his law degree in 1842, Ogden pursued the more traditional means of training for a would-be lawyer: reading law in the office of a
practitioner. His father arranged for him to work in the law office of Mark
Sibley in Canandaigua, New York. A fellow Whig who had served with Hoffman in Congress, Sibley put Ogden to work from morning until night. Ogden's father encouraged this regimen. "*Now* is the time, my dear Son, to
make yourself a Lawyer, and every hour's study *now*, will not only advance
you in your Profession, but save you so much time hereafter." Hoffman's
own experience inclined him to emphasize the importance of the apprenticeship period. Ogden's father had not gone to a law school. Rather, his
knowledge of law, rhetorical skills, and courtroom demeanor had been
gained through his own legal apprenticeship.[27]

Hoffman wanted his son to observe "the Eloquent Sibley" because he felt
Sibley could provide a model of successful oratorical skills. Sibley was a
shrewd choice for the father to make for another reason. Apart from being
a sound exemplar for his son, Sibley practiced in a town far removed from

the people and places that Hoffman knew would distract his son. Located in Ontario County in the western portion of the state, Canandaigua was remote, making it difficult for Ogden to neglect his studies by visiting friends, family, or the attractions of New York City. Although Ogden grew exceedingly homesick, he maintained an impressive work schedule during his year with Sibley.[28]

Turning twenty-one in 1843 entitled Ogden to the principal of the trust that had been paying him an annual income. He celebrated the occasion by ending his temporary exile and returning to New York City. There Ogden began his second legal clerkship, with friends and family and the social amenities he craved close at hand. After his admission to the bar in 1845, he took a two-year European tour during which he learned to speak French and Italian. More important, his exposure to European culture and history stimulated his cosmopolitan nature and interests.

If his travels broadened his perspective on life, they also delayed his start as a lawyer. With reason, Hoffman complained that his son seemed too lackadaisical about his legal career. Even after returning to New York, Ogden showed few signs of diligence. In 1847, when he should have been working in his father's law practice, he took extended vacations with his brother and friends.[29]

Ogden's lack of aggressiveness and zeal in practicing law did not prevent him from making a favorable impression at the bar. While in his father's office, Ogden learned the practice of the federal courts and worked with several prominent New York lawyers, including Daniel Lord, who later supported his candidacy for the federal judgeship. Lord described Ogden as "intelligent, well read for his years," and "of good judgment," an assessment that other lawyers who knew him during this period shared.[30]

Why Ogden Hoffman left New York for San Francisco in 1850 is a mystery. The opportunity for adventure and fortune might have played a role in the decision, as might have his unsuccessful courtship of a young woman in New York. Moreover, the perceived health advantages of the change in climate might have been another contributing factor. Whatever the reasons, Hoffman's future lay on the West Coast, and except for visits to New York, he lived in San Francisco until he died.[31]

When Hoffman passed through the Golden Gate on May 7, 1850, San

Francisco probably did not present an auspicious sight to the New Yorker. Cold winds buffeted the thousands of crude canvas and wooden structures that crowded the beach and sandy hills along the natural harbor of Yerba Buena. When he arrived, the city was still recovering from one of its many disastrous fires; a few days earlier, one had swept away three blocks of the downtown area. Hoffman would probably have agreed with a contemporary who disappointedly noted, "[San Francisco] does not look like a city that has recently attracted the notice of the whole world."[32]

What early San Francisco lacked in terms of comfort and sophistication, it more than made up for in excitement. Indeed, the extraordinary sights and sounds of the city fill the accounts of early travelers to San Francisco. The many hundreds of vessels anchored or abandoned in the bay created "a perfect forest of masts," and the "piles of silver and gold" in the gambling houses made other unforgettable impressions. The heterogeneous population produced "a confusion of men and tongues" and a cultural mixing that few had previously experienced. Inflation proved a common subject of discussion in letters to "the States," and correspondents dazzled themselves and their readers with news of the unheard-of prices for goods and services. For most, what they were experiencing was unique and bore little or no relation to the life they had left.[33]

In addition to their reaction to the physical and economic conditions of San Francisco, observers widely shared an initial optimism and sense of opportunity. Joseph B. Crockett, who later became a justice of the California Supreme Court, went to San Francisco to rid himself of debt, planning to return to Missouri with better health and a fortune in hand. Another future justice of the California Supreme Court, Oscar L. Shafter, did not seek "great wealth" but just "enough" to return to his family in Vermont and spend, as he put it, "the residue" of his days "under the vine and fig tree" that he had planted. Yet another San Francisco lawyer suffered a setback from a fire in 1851 but asserted that if wealth eluded him in his law practice, he would cheerfully go into other fields. "The whole drift here is money and to make a fortune in the shortest possible time." Many came armed with specific goals, like those formulated by the New York lawyer Henry Eno on the eve of his departure for California. "If there is to be a State Constitution framed I want a hand in it. If a Territorial Government, I should like the office of Judge. If there is any gold there I want that and intend to have it (i.e., some of it)."[34]

All of those who reached San Francisco brought their own expectations or hopes. Some succeeded but most failed in having their California experience match their initial expectations. Individual and collective disillusionment came later; for the moment, the new arrivals shared the sense that they were part of something special and had taken the first step toward their objectives in coming to California. John McCrackan, a lawyer from Connecticut who went to San Francisco in December 1849, enthused, "The excitement incident to a California life is of the most fascinating kind." Stephen J. Field, who arrived in San Francisco four months before Hoffman and who ultimately became a justice both of the California and the United States Supreme Courts, epitomized the enthusiasm of the new arrivals. Remembering his first day in San Francisco, he wrote: "I had not been out many hours that morning before I caught the infection; and though I had but a single dollar in my pocket and no business whatever, and did not know where I was to get the next meal, I found myself saying to everybody I met, 'It is a glorious country.' "[35]

Hoffman as well gave an indication of his confident expectations. Three weeks after he arrived in the city, he told a New York client and friend, "I am beginning to get into business and have little doubt that before long I shall be realizing a handsome sum by my practice." His prospects looked good to others, including R. L. Watson, who had also come to California. Writing to Hoffman's cousin Wickham Hoffman, Watson concluded, "[If Hoffman] is determined to establish a legal reputation here as he seems to be, he is sure to do very well every way both in reputation and in purse." But both Watson and Hoffman failed to anticipate the nature of legal practice in gold-rush San Francisco. Hoffman certainly had the talent and education to practice law well—he had proved that in New York. Rather, the question remained whether he had the temperament and character to succeed at the San Francisco bar of the 1850s.[36]

The frenetic pace of practicing law in San Francisco differed dramatically from the more leisurely routine Hoffman had known in New York. According to one early San Francisco lawyer, "the town was in a hum and bustle from morning until night, and from night until morning again: men rushed through the streets as to a fire—trading was done in a minute; there was no time for pause or reflection." In November 1850, the lawyer McCrackan declared that "an idle or inactive man would be out of his element here unless his object be to reform." The hectic nature of legal practice in San

Francisco—"this fast country" McCrackan called it—provided a contrast from lawyering on the East Coast. In San Francisco, McCrackan noted, "dispatch is the word" and every client "is impatient for his business to be acted upon first, his case brooks no delay, his interests must not suffer."[37]

San Francisco's heady atmosphere also put pressure on lawyers to develop more rigorous work routines. Many adopted the local custom of eating only two meals a day and working through lunch. Oscar Shafter detailed his daily schedule for his wife in 1854, noting that since his arrival in San Francisco, he had spent at least fifteen hours a day at the office. Three years later Shafter remained committed to the same punishing routine. Other lawyers, like Joseph Crockett and Henry Haight, also reported working thirteen or more hours per day, sometimes six or seven days a week. Not all lawyers, of course, worked so hard. McCrackan, for example, adhered to a six-to-eight hour workday with ample time for excursions, horse riding, and the "pleasures of the evening." But whereas Shafter, Crockett, and Haight grew wealthy by their law practices, McCrackan experienced only marginal success. Even after taking into account the natural tendency to exaggerate to friends and family about one's toils away from home, succeeding as a lawyer in San Francisco required considerable energy and clearly demanded more hard work from Hoffman than he had given to the practice of law in New York.[38]

The pressure, if not compulsion, for lawyers to work so hard in San Francisco during the 1850s derived from several sources. High inflation drove up one's expenses not only for everyday living but also for practicing law. More than one lawyer and gentleman of standing was forced into menial labor to make ends meet. Necessity aside, it seemed to many that fortunes could be made in law. With the many commercial enterprises and speculations, lawyers were in demand and their rewards quite good. In addition, much admiralty, land, and criminal litigation was generated by the frenetic pace and rapidly expanding population of gold-rush San Francisco. So many lawsuits, however, soon bred a fierce competition among lawyers and added another stimulus for long hours. Beyond necessity and competing for one's fortune, lawyers had an incentive to work hard to establish their social rank and worth. In the San Francisco of the 1850s, money made the man, and a lawyer's success at his practice was the only sure means of gaining the standing and respect he might naturally have commanded "back home." Finally, gold-rush San Francisco tempted men to spend money in many ways. The expensive habits that some lawyers developed provided yet another source for the pressure to succeed.[39]

Lawyers arriving in San Francisco simultaneously predicted great profits and registered dismay at the expenses they were incurring. Even while enthusing over his glowing prospects, McCrackan lamented that office rental obligations prevented him from sending home even "a few dollars." The great sums spent for office space resulted from more than the inflated value of rental property. Joseph Crockett explained that fancy offices were needed because "a great many people" were "influenced by such displays of folly"— because they thought "a lawyer must be something extra, who lives in that grand style." He remained convinced that "no lawyer could be respectable here in a shabby office and hence there is a struggle to see who can have the finest." Moreover, rental terms were invariably for cash in advance, placing lawyers under considerable pressure to produce substantial income on a regular basis.[40]

The professional expenses of a lawyer in San Francisco hardly stopped at office space. Many lawyers brought some law books with them, but the relative scarcity of books increased their value, and the series of early fires in the city took its toll on the private law libraries then in existence. By one account, a crate of law books in April 1850 would bring "almost any price." Lawyers also paid exorbitant prices to advertise their practice and even buy copies of statutes. Another lawyer prepared his father, who was contemplating coming to San Francisco to practice law, by noting that he and his law partner had debts approaching $40,000, with cash resources of only half that amount.[41]

There were, of course, ways one could reduce costs. Joseph Crockett slept on a cot in his office for the first six months after he arrived, and other lawyers slept "wrapped in blankets on the floor." And instead of employing clerks to draft pleadings, make copies, and do other scribal work, an attorney could elect to do the writing himself, usually at night. Only the busiest law practice could justify the cost of copying clerks. Perhaps most important, attorneys could try to curb their own spending impulses and the effect that California had on many men: that of making one "more liberal in . . . the use of his purse."[42]

Probably even more disturbing to Hoffman than the hard work and costly expenses was the relative lack of observance of social distinctions by those who flooded into the city. As McCrackan put it in 1850, "We all have a fair and equal start." Being placed on an equal footing with the mass of other lawyers arriving in San Francisco was troubling, if not a liability, to someone with Hoffman's background. Indeed, a British observer suggested, "Polished education was of little service, unless accompanied by an unwonted amount of democratic feeling; for the extreme sensitiveness which it is otherwise apt to produce, unfitted a man for taking part in such a hand-to-hand struggle with his fellow-men." Hoffman clearly lacked such "democratic feeling"; indeed, he regarded universal suffrage as "the pernicious fallacy that the pauper, the vagrant or the criminal" had as much a voice as "the respectable and intelligent citizen" who had "some stake in the concern." In addition, Hoffman probably felt increasingly out of place where "perfect freedom and independence" governed personal relationships and where society was "freed from the multitude of prejudices and embarrassments and exactions" that controlled the eastern cities.[43]

In this setting Hoffman was ill-equipped to practice not only law but also that "art and mystery of getting business." Initially, Hoffman handled admiralty matters in San Francisco for the Delano family of New York, business that came to him principally because of his childhood friendship with F. H. Delano. Late in May 1850, Hoffman wrote to Delano about his mixed optimism for success. "From what you know of California prices you will be prepared to believe that I am consoled by the reflection that I have *made* something." [44]

Hoffman could not count on business from his New York friends alone to keep him financially afloat. He needed to compete with other San Francisco lawyers for the wide range of local business, including admiralty and criminal litigation and divorce, contract, and land cases. This need was pressing because on the eve of his departure, Hoffman's father had failed in getting his son appointed as New York's resident commissioner in California. By supplying New York lawyers with needed depositions from people in California, Hoffman would have earned some regular income from the post. While Hoffman struggled to build a reputation and acquire clients, he encountered the success—and dreams of success—of other newcomers to the California bar.[45]

One recently arrived lawyer from upstate New York offered a prediction of his success in 1850, after four months of practice. "I think in two or three months more I may have a fair business, a business that will pay for coming to California, a business that will bring me as much clear profit each month as a year's practice would in Elizabethtown." Another lawyer also marked the happy contrast in practice. "Oh, how different it is from the little pinching, picayune business done by lawyers at St. Louis and other Western towns and how much I enjoy the big fat fees we so often get here!" Two months before Hoffman arrived in San Francisco, a lawyer interrupted a letter to his family in Connecticut to earn twenty-five dollars for "five minutes work." Even as late as 1854, San Francisco lawyers spoke, with reason, of the "perfectly fabulous" fees, judged by "Atlantic standards."[46]

Three months after he arrived in San Francisco, Hoffman gave vent to his frustrations by speculating about the future of California and, indirectly, about his own prospects. In a letter to a friend, he anticipated further emigration from the "U.S." because of a recent shipment of gold to the East Coast. "That the greater part of those whose minds are thus dazzled and who are induced to forsake regular employment at home will be disappointed and that grievously I do not doubt. A system of deception is practiced here by various persons connected with the press of which the effect if not the design is to beget the most exaggerated ideas of the chances and fortunes that await the immigrant." Ostensibly talking of gold seekers, Hoffman may have had in mind his own lack of success at the bar—quite different from the prospects and expectations he had had before leaving New York. Hoffman launched into a detailed analysis of an economy geared to gold extraction, and he concluded that all the exported gold barely exceeded the cost of maintaining the laboring miners. Virtually "all business" in San Francisco he considered "more or less gambling" and akin to "a lottery with many blanks."[47]

Hoffman's sobering appraisal displayed considerable insight as well as his personal disappointment. After initial enthusiasm, many other lawyers began to appreciate the constraints put upon the instant fortunes that had at first seemed possible. The burgeoning city offered great fees and equally great expenses; tremendous losses as well as profits could be realized. After Oscar Shafter made his fortune through his law practice, he reflected that of the group of lawyers who came to California in 1854 when he did, none had met with any "marked success," except for him and his brother. San Francisco's early bar could extract a high price for success: Shafter had lived frugally and "worked like a dog" for six years. But hard work alone did not guarantee success. Inflation and economic fluctuations affected lawyers as well as gold seekers and merchants. In analogizing business to a lottery, Hoffman accurately characterized commerce in the San Francisco of the 1850s.[48]

After ten months in San Francisco, Hoffman reported himself "gradually advancing" in his profession and "engaged pretty actively in trying causes." Still, it seems the New York connections that brought him most of his business were not enough to overcome the high expenses he incurred. Indeed, after Hoffman's death in 1891, one of his closest friends, James T. Boyd, recalled that Hoffman had not been "fitted . . . for the rough and tumble life of a frontier bar." More direct evidence of Hoffman's desire to cut short his struggles at the bar is contained in a letter written to his father after Hoffman was appointed a federal judge but before news of the appointment reached him. In the letter, Hoffman lamented the failure in getting "a first class lawyer" to accept the northern district judgeship, a prospect that seemed "hopeless"as long as Congress refused to "make the salary equal to the income of a 3rd rate practitioner." Nonetheless, Hoffman readily accepted the appointment, and in May 1851 he opened the court he would preside over for the rest of his life.[49]

In many ways, who Hoffman was and how he became a judge epitomize the composition and the selection of federal district court judges during the antebellum period. Despite the promise of wider democratic participation following the election of Andrew Jackson in 1828, presidents from Jackson until Lincoln—whether Democrats or Whigs—selected nominees with similar backgrounds. Men whose social class could be considered elite or prominent were overwhelmingly chosen as judges. At least in terms of federal judicial appointments, the social democratization of American politics during the antebellum period was strictly limited. After studying the background of these judicial appointments, one scholar simply concluded, "Advantage begat advantage." As with most other appointments of federal judges of this period, Hoffman's selection maintained and preserved his social status rather than marked his upward social mobility.[50]

In addition, Hoffman's appointment exemplified the shifting role that politics played in the nomination of such judges. All administrations were naturally concerned with the political aspects of judicial appointments, but the newer trend toward institutionalizing judicial appointments made uneven progress before the Civil War. Despite the rise of parties and the political modernization during this period, judicial selections were often influenced by kinship ties and personal connections rather than by partisanship alone. Moreover, appointments to the lower federal judiciary often resulted from a complex process that involved far more than mere party politics. Indeed, a study of the selection of California's first federal judges, including Hoffman, reveals that the nominations entailed issues of "personal ambition, sectional controversy, the expansion of slavery, economic interests involving land, gold, and transoceanic commerce, and the administrative exigencies of low pay and burdensome workload."[51]

Hardly anyone chose Hoffman first to be the judge of the northern district. As one of over a hundred aspirants to the judgeship, Hoffman received the post only after numerous other lawyers had refused to accept the appointment, had been rejected by the Senate, or had declined informal offers of appointment made by Millard Fillmore's Whig administration. In Hoffman's case, his father's professional and political standing in New York, including a friendship with Fillmore's secretary of state, Daniel Webster, proved to be a significant factor.

The consideration of candidates for California's two federal judgeships began in 1848, but the greatest number of applications occurred with Fillmore's presidency and the improved prospects for California statehood in 1850. Both Fillmore and Webster sought to fill the positions quickly with qualified individuals, but they shared a concern that the low salaries would not attract able candidates. On September 28, 1850, when Congress created California's federal courts, Fillmore nominated Judah P. Benjamin for the northern district, and the Senate confirmed him that same day. Benjamin, an active Louisiana Whig and successful lawyer and entrepreneur, declined the low-paying northern district judgeship in favor of his political and business prospects. Soon thereafter, Fillmore offered the northern district judgeship to John Plummer Healy. Although nominated and confirmed, he had earlier declined to become the first judge for California's southern district federal court. Healy was an accomplished Boston lawyer who had managed Webster's law office during the time the secretary of state had served in Washington. Webster vouched for Healy's personal character and loyalty as a Whig; in addition, Healy spoke fluent Spanish—an asset of particular value, especially in Southern California. But Healy also refused the judgeship because the appointment would separate him from his family and because of the low salary. Fillmore then offered the northern district post to yet another Boston lawyer, Charles B. Goodrich, also on the recommendation of Webster. The low pay of the judgeship once again frustrated the Fillmore administration, and efforts began anew to find a suitable candidate.[52]

These successive choices and resultant delays made Californians impatient for the establishment of their federal courts. Politicians from the new state had urged Fillmore to choose only California lawyers, but they were interested, above all, in having the posts filled. In early October, shortly after Fillmore had nominated Benjamin for the northern district, California's congressional delegation urged the president to act quickly. They could not "sanction" the appointment of non-Californians, given the "able and distinguished members of the bar in that country." Nonetheless, the "great necessity" of having the northern district court operating "with the least practicable delay" led them to suggest an acceptable non-Californian in case the president continued to adhere to his "policy" of selecting men from outside the state. The presence of Senator William M. Gwin complicated the process of selecting a judge for the northern district. Gwin—the spokesman for the southern-oriented wing of California's Democratic party—had his candidates, the California Whigs theirs, and Fillmore and Webster yet others. The unsuccessful appointments induced Fillmore and Webster to narrow their choices to "lawyers in California . . . without families."[53]

At this juncture Ogden Hoffman entered the judicial race, one of a half dozen California lawyers suggested for the position. Although some local Whigs backed him, New Yorkers were Hoffman's primary source of support. In his bid for the judgeship, Hoffman got the endorsement of such leaders of the New York bar as Judge William Kent, Francis B. Cutting, Benjamin D. Silliman (in whose office Hoffman had read law), and Daniel Lord, as well as such prominent New York Whigs as William Henry Seward, a lifelong friend of the elder Hoffman's. Support also came from an unexpected East Coast source: the president of the Pacific Mail Steamship Company, William H. Aspinwall. Aspinwall and others who owned steamships operating on the Pacific Coast had a special reason for urging Fillmore to fill the federal judgeship in San Francisco rapidly. State authorities had imposed taxes on steamship companies operated in California but owned in New York. Alleging the illegality of such taxation, Aspinwall and other owners considered a federal court in San Francisco "an indispensable tri-

bunal for the protection of citizens engaged in commerce and transportation
between this state [New York] and California." To expedite the operation of
the northern district—and presumably because he hoped the new judge
would side with the steamship companies—Aspinwall supported Hoffman's
candidacy.[54]

Although Aspinwall favored Hoffman, he had not initiated the candidacy,
nor was he the principal organizer of Hoffman's campaign. Aspinwall knew
Hoffman's father—they moved in the same social circles—but remembered
Hoffman primarily as his son's youthful friend. Besides Hoffman's father,
the principal organizer of Hoffman's campaign in Washington, D.C., during
the critical period of Hoffman's candidacy was John V. Plume, of the San
Francisco banking firm of Burgoyne and Company. After Hoffman's friends
rounded up testimonials from respected leaders of New York's commercial
and legal communities, Aspinwall threw his weight behind the cause.[55]

Only the strong efforts behind the scenes by Hoffman's father explain why
so many eminent figures recommended the relatively young and inexperi-
enced Ogden, then on the other side of the continent. References to his
father figured prominently in several letters of recommendation for Hoffman. Indeed, when Webster finally offered Hoffman the San Francisco
judgeship, he urged acceptance "first, for the sake of the public interest,"
second, because of Hoffman's "own character and merit," and "last, not
least," because of Webster's regard for Hoffman's "excellent father."Given
Webster's influence over Fillmore's nominations, the secretary of state's
friendship with and respect for the elder Hoffman certainly helped Ogden's
chances.[56]

Despite his emergence as a serious candidate, Hoffman received the
nomination only after another nominee failed to receive confirmation. The
Senate rejected the California lawyer John Curry following accusations of
immorality, abolitionism, and theft. Even as Curry's nomination languished
in the Senate, the search for a new candidate was narrowed to a handful of
lawyers, including Hoffman, with support divided among them. Hoffman
lacked Senator Gwin's support, and other rivals accused him of being too
young for the federal judgeship. Even some San Francisco lawyers were
disquieted by Hoffman's age. John McCrackan, who favored his own law
partner for the judgeship, received the news of Fillmore's nomination of
"young Ogden Hoffman" with some reservation. "[H]e is a nice boy however (being but twenty-five or six) to fill so important a 'Judgeship' and many

hope it will not be confirmed by the Senate." In fact, Hoffman was twenty-nine years old at the time. Ultimately, however, Fillmore concluded (as the Senate would) that the arduous demands of the northern district made youth an asset, and Gwin accepted Hoffman's appointment in order to make the court operational. Hoffman received his nomination on February 1, 1851, and on the twenty-seventh of that month the Senate confirmed him, five months after Congress had created the court.[57]

Even as news of Hoffman's confirmation worked its way westward, a vigilante movement—or, as contemporaries called it, a vigilance movement—developed force in San Francisco and would shortly usurp established authority in the name of popular sovereignty. Indeed, two of the most powerful and best organized vigilance movements in American history severely challenged judicial and governmental authority in San Francisco as Hoffman began his judgeship. The Vigilance Committee of 1851 was not the first time San Franciscans took the law into their own hands, nor would it be the last. Two years earlier, the city's first extralegal movement had been organized and had satisfied itself with banishing a handful of malefactors. In 1851, however, vigilantism resulted in the lynching of four men. Moreover, a new Vigilance Committee would emerge on a much grander scale in 1856, seeking both banishment and blood. That committee too would execute four men found guilty of crimes against the community. Even though the two major vigilance movements differed significantly, both had participants who justified their conduct by using quasi-judicial proceedings and by claiming that the existing courts had ineffectively dealt with crime.[58]

Hoffman began his judgeship not only in a general climate of public suspicion directed at courts but also amid the popular knowledge that he had opposed the 1851 Vigilance Committee when he was still a practicing lawyer. He had earned this reputation by defending a state judge who had defied the committee and by joining with a few other lawyers to draft resolutions "to vindicate the Supremacy of the Constitution and the Laws of [the] country." It should not be assumed that such opposition naturally followed from being a lawyer—both vigilance movements in California received substantial support from the legal community. Hoffman's opposition stemmed in part from his dislike of violence and his commitment to maintaining order through institutions—values that he shared with other Whigs. In the same month that Hoffman opposed this widely popular local movement, San Franciscans learned of his appointment.[59]

When Hoffman opened his court on May 19, 1851, he had much to prove to himself, to his family, to his friends, and to San Francisco. He could expect considerable indulgence from his family and friends, but San Franciscans viewed him far more critically. Apart from his opposition to the Vigilance Committee, critics could point to his struggles at the gold-rush bar. Although Hoffman was a good Whig, a large number of San Francisco Whigs preferred other lawyers for the northern district judgeship. Hoffman's youth and relative inexperience seemed to underscore the circuitous route by which he became San Francisco's first federal judge. One lawyer's bitter reaction to Hoffman's appointment might have been shared by others. "His father Ogden Hoffman of N.Y. has fed from the political crib for the last forty years, and now he desires his son to follow in his footsteps." Far from friends and family in New York, Hoffman faced an uphill battle to vindicate himself. On the eve of his judgeship, he sought to prove his legal competence as a judge and establish a good reputation for his court.[60]

———

Throughout his long residence in California, Hoffman remained in part a New Yorker in exile, avidly reading New York newspapers and begging his old friends to send word of New York. Hoffman's periodic trips back East were pilgrimages to his father and grandfather's society, which he continued to miss. Indeed, those who knew him understood that New York City represented "the only place on the continent for a gentleman of leisure . . . to find engagement."[61]

If San Francisco never matched his memories of New York City's sophistication and high society, the instant city created by the gold rush soon provided Hoffman with a club life that characterized his lifestyle in California. By 1854, two of the city's most exclusive clubs—the Pacific Club and the Union Club—had been established. They provided a comfortable, if not luxurious, setting for men of means and position to gather for conversation, drinks, cards, and meals—and often elaborate banquets. Furthermore, as the clubs increased in size, they became the residences of a portion of the clubs' members, including Hoffman. From 1851 until at least the early 1860s, Hoffman lived in rooms that were adjacent to his courtroom and chambers. Although he had long been a member of the Pacific Club, located a few blocks from his court, he did not take up residence there until 1868. When, in 1883, the Pacific Club moved to even more elaborate quarters elsewhere in the city, Hoffman was one of ten lucky club members, all bachelors, entitled to "elegantly furnished" suites. The principal exception to Hoffman's club life came when his half brother Southard brought his family to California after Hoffman appointed him clerk of court in 1876. Thereafter, Hoffman enjoyed a vicarious family life through his brother's family.[62]

When Hoffman first made the club his home in 1868, he was forty-six years old, and the move was that of a confirmed bachelor. His attentions to women circulated occasional rumors of marriage well into the 1870s, but Hoffman's friends, who gossiped about such matters, seemed mainly titillated by the unlikelihood that the judge would take such a step. When Hoffman moved into the Pacific Club (later the Pacific-Union Club), he did so for good. From 1868 until his death more than twenty years later, he remained a permanent resident—if not fixture—of the club.[63]

The most important consequence of Hoffman's bachelorhood and club life was his preoccupation with his judgeship. Lacking a wife and family, Hoffman wholeheartedly dedicated himself to his career. As Hoffman said in 1869, he had given his "whole life" to his judgeship. His statement came after he had been a judge for nearly two decades, and he could hardly have imagined that more than twenty years of judicial service lay ahead. As the years passed and higher judicial office eluded him, Hoffman increasingly identified himself with his court. The judgeship had long focused his life, but as he gradually surpassed most other judges in length of service, Hoffman more clearly conceived of the northern district court as his only legacy.[64]

Hoffman's self-consciousness about his judgeship led him to assert a judicial independence that he regarded as central to his role as a federal judge. Throughout his career, Hoffman followed the course of his own conscience and judgment irrespective of practical expediency or political considerations. Indeed, adverse reaction to his decisions seemed, if anything, to strengthen his resolve. His tenacious insistence on his independence as the judge of the northern district repeatedly angered and frustrated government officials, including fellow federal judges such as Stephen J. Field.

Hoffman believed his role as a judge entailed not only providing an impartial forum for federal litigants but also playing a vital part in the system of federalism. Litigants who sought relief in the northern district were invoking not merely the right to a fair hearing, but the national judicial power. Initially the only and later the principal federal trial judge in California, Hoffman remained acutely aware that he represented the federal judiciary.

This national dimension affected Hoffman's relationship with the state courts and influenced decisions in which he had discretion to assume jurisdiction. Hoffman carefully distinguished the appropriateness of his assumption of jurisdiction. He did not seek to expand his jurisdiction. Still, when matters were properly before his court, Hoffman dismissed suggestions that he not hear the case or that he allow the state courts to assume control. Relinquishing jurisdiction over matters properly before his court constituted an abdication of his duty as a federal judge, particularly when he was under pressure not to grant jurisdiction.

His belief in the special role his court played because it was a national tribunal was also shaped by Hoffman's political perspective. Inheriting his father's politics, Hoffman regarded the preservation of the Union as the single most important objective of public life in the 1850s. His public eulogy in San Francisco following Henry Clay's death in 1852 sounded this theme, as did his decision to support the compromise position of Millard Fillmore in the presidential election of 1856. An even more dramatic expression of his desire to keep the North and the South together was Hoffman's support of the Tennessean John Bell and his running mate, Edward Everett of Massachusetts, in 1860. Bell's presidential bid as the candidate of the Constitutional Union party was essentially a conservative Whig effort to resurrect the Whig party, which had largely disintegrated by the mid-1850s, by making an attachment to the Union the common cause of North and South.[65]

Apart from what Hoffman's affiliation with the Constitutional Union party suggested about the value he placed on the concept of the Union and national government, he provided additional insights into his motivations and his perception of politics. In 1860, Hoffman wrote to the chairman of the national committee to elect Bell, reporting that supporters of the Constitutional Union party were, in California, "as elsewhere the most respectable men in the state." Hoffman had been asked by California's central committee to request several thousand dollars to support the local campaign. Informed that with such a sum the party might carry the state, Hoffman cautiously endorsed that assessment but said, "I never go out of San Francisco and am perpetually on the Bench so my opinion is of little value." After 1860 Hoffman joined the Republican party and stayed with that party for the rest

of his life. Nonetheless, the essence of his politics (or antipolitics) was typified by his 1860 letter in which he distanced himself from the pragmatic
aspects of politics and merged his political affiliation with men of respectability and quality. Further isolating Hoffman was the organizational nature
of politics in post–Civil War America, locally represented by San Francisco's
"Blind Boss" Chris Buckley in the 1870s and 1880s. In the long run, Hoffman's old-fashioned view of politics and how he perceived and valued personal character gave a distinct cast to his political understanding.[66]

To maintain the nation's honor, especially within the context of treaties,
became an important function for Hoffman as a federal judge. Although
state courts might succumb to local pressures, Hoffman believed a federal
judge had a broader duty to perform, one that regularly conflicted with his
own predilections. Before becoming a judge, Hoffman had opposed vigilantism in San Francisco on the grounds of vindicating the federal constitution
and "the Laws of [the] country." Those concerns would magnify and guide
many of his most important decisions as a federal judge, even as they
brought him harsh public criticism.

If judicial independence as a national court formed the core of Hoffman's
understanding of his role as a judge, his character and personality influenced
how he performed that role. Hoffman's pride and his self-conscious effort
to establish his independence and integrity soon after his appointment combined to make him acutely sensitive to any behavior that might call his reputation or that of his court into question. In 1853, he testily reacted to an
attorney who inquired if Hoffman planned to hear a case in which he
thought Hoffman had a conflict of interest. Hoffman responded, "No one is
better apprised than myself of the gross impropriety of sitting as a judge in
any case, or passing upon any questions in the determination of which I have
the slightest personal interest." He did not deign to answer the question: "It
should have seemed unnecessary to make any inquiries as to whether in this
instance I propose to violate the most obvious proprieties of my station."
Such reactions exemplified what one close friend called Hoffman's "sensitiveness of temperament," which "restricted his familiar intercourse to a
small circle of friends."[67]

Hoffman's sensitivity produced an elaborately formal demeanor that left
him constantly concerned lest he and his court not receive proper respect.
Indeed, Hoffman carried his public persona as San Francisco's federal judge
into his personal life. Once, at his club, a group of lawyers were discussing

possible justifications for perjury, and they asked Hoffman's opinion. Hoffman replied that he found the question impertinent, whereupon his questioner persisted and pointed out that the judge was not in court. "Court," replied Hoffman, "is never so much adjourned that a representative may say anything that will bring discredit on its rulings, or bring past decisions into disrepute."[68]

If Hoffman believed that such a private conversation by fellow clubmen showed disrespect for his court, the writer J. Ross Browne gravely wounded the judge's pride by publishing a story in 1861. Browne satirized a trip he had taken with the "Coast Rangers," an informal group of a dozen prominent men, including Hoffman, who made an annual hunting excursion north of San Francisco to Mendocino County. Browne's story begins with a thumbnail sketch of the members, most of whom were easily recognizable to San Franciscans by slight name changes and Browne's characterizations. One adventure finds "the Judge" (Hoffman) and "Tom Fry" (Major John Caperton) trailing behind the rest of the Coast Rangers, when Fry's mule suddenly pitches him into a bed of quicksand. Tom cries out for the Judge to help him and asks, "What's to be done?" To this obvious question "the Judge" proceeds to speak at length on Indian ethnology, the federal government's Indian policy, the physics involved in Tom's sinking, and analogies to Sir Walter Scott's *The Bride of Lammermoor* and *Kenilworth*, while Tom sinks deeper and deeper into the quicksand. Just as Tom is about to go under, "Captain Toby" (the Indian fighter James Tobin) dashes down a cliff on his horse and lassoes Tom and pulls him out. Although the story underscored Hoffman's wide intellectual interests while lampooning his talkativeness, the judge felt the caricature undermined his authority, and he was not amused.[69]

Hoffman took criticism of his judgeship and the northern district so personally because eventually he drew little or no distinction between himself and the institution he headed. This merger of identity owed much to the fact that Hoffman, like other federal district court judges in the nineteenth century, sat alone as the court. The natural tendency to associate with one's institution was accentuated by the length of his judicial service. Ironically, Hoffman's identification with his court and his demand for respect placed additional pressure on him to maintain high judicial standards. His pride and self-proclaimed independence and integrity seemed to spur Hoffman toward fulfilling those ideals.

Sometimes, however, his pride drove him to results that struck others as stubborn and literal-minded. One dramatic instance involved Hoffman's narrow interpretation of an amnesty proclamation during the Civil War, an interpretation contrary to the expressed intentions of President Lincoln.[70] Hoffman rendered his opinion with the certain knowledge that his decision would be highly unpopular and that it might—as it almost did—cost him his office. Still, Hoffman had the advantage of remaining consistent throughout his tenure in proclaiming and acting on his judicial independence. And if Hoffman, by following his own lights, decided some cases by a semantical point or interpretation that seemed—to laymen and even to some lawyers— to be a quibble, then that too added to a grudging respect for Hoffman.

Although Hoffman's judicial posture may have saved him from some types of abuse and criticism, he was in fact far from being otherworldly. Hoffman speculated both in land and in the mineral wealth of his adopted state. During the 1850s he dabbled briefly in San Francisco city lots, but to little financial advantage. Even with profitable investments, it seemed as though the money went too quickly, and he never attained the financial security that many of his friends enjoyed. His most successful investment involved the purchase of mining stock that resulted in a small windfall in 1871.[71]

Hoffman's response to a congratulatory letter from a federal judge in Oregon suggests the dimensions of his gain and the state of his finances. Hoffman acknowledged: "[The stock] has risen and looks well—but as for the 'rich man' I do not behold him when I look in the glass. My dividends for a long time will be required to pay my debts. If the mine should hold out for a year and then look as well as now, I may have 50 or $60,000—which for us Judges predestined to chronic impecuniousness would be very well." It seems likely that he enjoyed a profit close to what he predicted, but he also did not exaggerate his debts. Between 1875 and 1891, when San Francisco's minimal reporting limits for personal property assessment fluctuated between $1,000 and $5,000, Hoffman never made the assessment list.[72]

From the first year of his appointment until well into his judgeship, Hoffman waged a battle to increase his salary. Eventually he persuaded Congress to grant him retroactive compensation for the early years of his judgeship. To some extent, California's high prices and the underpayment of public service explain Hoffman's campaign. It is more likely, however, that his ongoing struggle to live within his financial means underlay the continued ef-

forts he made to raise his salary. Even with "a sufficient slice of the 'bonanza'" in the 1870s, Hoffman's expensive lifestyle and recurring trips to
the East Coast drained his resources. When he died in 1891, Hoffman left
a meager estate: relatively little personal property and no real property.[73]

In time, Hoffman became a respected San Francisco institution. Despite
his lingering ties to New York City, the West would claim him as one of its
own, and the judge eventually acceded. During his forty-year tenure, Hoffman witnessed and participated in dramatic changes in the life of both San
Francisco and California. His lengthy labor on the northern district bench
provided a source of pride that assuaged the defeats and disappointments he
suffered in California. Inevitably, Hoffman's judgeship reflected his character, personality, and political outlook. But how his background meshed
with his experiences in San Francisco forms the larger story of his development as a judge. Hoffman's judicial decisions and how he reached them,
no less than the way he acted and the way he thought about himself, reveal
both Ogden Hoffman's odyssey as a federal trial judge and the significance
of his court.

2

Ogden Hoffman's Judicial Aspirations

Hoffman's judicial ambitions and the interrelationship of Hoffman and the other federal judges of the Far West's ninth circuit established the context of his judicial labors. The personal dynamics of the circuit—particularly Hoffman's relationship with the head of the circuit, Stephen J. Field—had an important effect on his judgeship. Indeed, for most of his time on the federal bench, Hoffman lived in Field's shadow and regarded him as his personal nemesis. Why this occurred had as much to do with fundamental differences in judicial style as it did with competition for judgeships.

In this context, *judicial style* refers to how the two perceived their roles as judges, what they regarded as acceptable behavior off the bench, and how they approached issues before their courts. With time the relationship between the two judges became characterized by suspicion, distrust, and dislike. Hoffman eventually blamed Field for impeding his judicial ambitions and reputation. What bothered Hoffman about Field also affected, to varying degrees, the relationships between Field and the other judges of the ninth circuit.

In the latter half of the nineteenth century the federal judiciary experienced considerable changes in its organization and jurisdiction. For most of that time the federal system consisted of three tiers: district courts (usually one or two per state) presided over by a single judge, circuit courts (consisting of a number of multistate regions equaling the number of Supreme Court justices during the period), and finally, the Supreme Court itself.

Both the district courts and the circuit courts were given original jurisdiction—that is, both functioned as trial courts—but in addition the circuit courts exercised some appellate jurisdiction over decisions of the district courts. Traditionally, the circuit courts were composed of one member of the Supreme Court and a district court judge. California formed a temporary exception to this practice when Congress authorized a separate circuit judge for the state between 1855 and 1863. Six years later all the federal circuits were allocated separate circuit judges. Even so, Supreme Court justices were each assigned to a circuit and presided over the circuit court on visits to the circuit, but, by statute, that court might be composed of different combinations of the circuit justice, the circuit judge, and the district court judge.[1]

During the course of Hoffman's tenure, over a dozen different judges served as members of the ninth circuit, but only four of them played central roles in the circuit between 1851 and 1891: Ogden Hoffman, Stephen Field, Lorenzo Sawyer, and Matthew Deady. In part their dominance was due to their longevity on the bench: Hoffman's northern district judgeship began in 1851; Field became the Far West's member on the U.S. Supreme Court in 1863; Sawyer was the resident circuit judge from 1869; and Deady served as Oregon's district judge from 1857. Matthew Hall McAllister played a slightly less important role as the incumbent of a short-lived special federal circuit court for California between 1855 and 1862.

Since Hoffman was San Francisco's earliest resident federal judge, his role and his expectations underwent considerable change with the successive appearances of McAllister, Deady, Field, and Sawyer on the federal bench. Collectively the ninth circuit consisted of the various district court judges, the circuit court judge, and the circuit's member on the Supreme Court. At the time of Field's appointment, members of the Supreme Court were expected to spend a portion of their time each year in the circuit to which they were appointed, presiding over the circuit courts for the various districts. Field took this assignment seriously, and his regular trips to California gave him considerable visibility within his circuit and frequent contact with the resident California federal judges.

Although a degree of collegiality and even friendliness existed among the principal members of the circuit, their interaction was often fraught with tensions, competing judicial ambitions, and conflicts. Some tension was in a sense institutionalized by the hierarchy: the district court beneath the circuit court, and both courts beneath the Supreme Court, represented by Field. Epitomizing this judicial hierarchy was the 1872 statute that permitted the circuit justice's opinion—that is, Field's—to prevail as the majority decision when the justice presided over the circuit court, even though the circuit judge and the district judges that might also have formed the court dissented. The clear understanding that certain courts were "inferior" to others not only instilled expectations of deference and different degrees of respect but also fueled judicial ambitions. During his forty years as a district court judge, Hoffman tried, but failed, to attain higher judicial office. His competitors subsequently became judges who outranked him, and their support (or lack of it) for his later bids for judgeships affected Hoffman's chances.[2]

Enhancing the normal sources of tensions inherent in the judicial hierarchy and in Hoffman's frustrated ambition were differences in approach, judicial philosophy, and personality. As the presiding judge of the circuit, Field might have inculcated a more harmonious atmosphere, but his domineering, even vindictive, personality antagonized his fellow West Coast judges and constituted a divisive element. Even Field's younger protégé and recipient of much support and favor, Judge Deady of Oregon, found himself aggravated at times by Field. Undoubtedly brilliant, Field was not able to suffer opposition, was certain of his convictions, and was often ruthless in promoting his objectives, bringing him into conflict with those around him. Field's colleagues on the U.S. Supreme Court tended to react similarly to him, whether they served with Field early or late in his judicial career. Justice David Davis called him a "damned rascal" in 1866, and Justice Horace Gray compared him to a "wild bull" three decades later. Indeed, Field was continually involved in controversies and feuds from his earliest days in California. Field acknowledged that in his visits to California as circuit justice, he had "generally succeeded in stirring up a great deal of feeling, mingled with much personal bitterness."[3]

Hoffman's relationship with Field was especially important because Hoffman, more than any other judge within the circuit, felt alienated from Field. The initial source of difficulty between the two was that Hoffman felt entitled to the Supreme Court judgeship that Field had received in 1863. A far more divisive element in their relationship was their strikingly different personalities and judicial behaviors. Field had a comprehensive judicial philosophy that he strove to implement, over time, through his decisions. Hoffman, however, lacked such a unified theory and tended to approach issues on a case-by-case basis. Moreover, Field aggressively and clearly sought to attain his jurisprudential objectives, actively involved himself in politics to that end, and exuded an air of infallibility. In contrast, Hoffman grappled with doubts about whether his decisions were correct, maintained a low political profile, was retiring by nature, and was often indirect in action. These differences estranged the two and led to behavior on Field's part that deeply wounded Hoffman and frustrated his judicial ambitions. The two judges never managed to maintain more than a formal civility.

Moreover, Field's inability to work harmoniously with the judges within the circuit found expression in the individualistic responses of ninth circuit judges when they were under attack or merely advancing their interests. Field's failure to inspire loyalty as the leader of the circuit encouraged the formation of groups that individual judges could count on for support. Public loyalty thus ran more toward individual judges than to the institutions they represented. The federal courts that composed the circuit were largely differentiated by the men who occupied the bench. In this way Hoffman, Sawyer, and Deady became synonymous with California's northern district court, the ninth circuit court, and Oregon's district court, respectively. Field, of course, had his own identity as California's voice on the Supreme Court. The institutional character of single-judge courts in the nineteenth century was largely responsible for the fragmentation within the circuit, but the degree of individuality reflects the strong influence Field had on the other judges in the circuit.

———

A degree of trepidation accompanied Hoffman's pleasure at his appointment as San Francisco's first federal judge in 1851. It seemed, as he expressed it in a letter to his father, that he was working in a vacuum, far from authoritative direction. As his confidence grew and the years passed, Hoffman could look back to those earliest years, from 1851 to 1855, as a time when he alone constituted California's federal bench. The delays in establishing the state's southern district and that district's lack of early business, except for land cases, made the northern district the only effective federal court in California. Indeed, until the establishment of the special circuit judgeship in 1855, Hoffman found himself exercising both district and circuit court jurisdiction. The prospect of Hoffman's hearing, in the circuit court, appeals from his own decisions in the district court partially motivated Congress to establish the special circuit judgeship. The primary reason for the legislation, however, was to provide additional help in hearing the very important private land-grant cases just then coming on appeal to the northern district from the board of land commissioners.[4]

Although California would get only a representative on the Supreme Court in 1863, rumors abounded in 1855 that the new judgeship for California either would be a justiceship or would be a circuit judgeship that would be converted to a place on the Supreme Court. This possibility helped explain the "considerable log-rolling and lobbying" for the position. During the time Congress debated the advisability of a circuit judgeship for California, Hoffman was on the East Coast visiting family and recuperating from the physically draining pace of his early years on the northern district. It seems likely that Hoffman expressed an interest in the new judgeship, since he returned to San Francisco on the same steamer that carried California's two senators.[5]

If Hoffman sought the circuit judgeship, it was more out of wishful thinking than out of any substantial claim to the office. After all, he was only thirty-three years old and had barely four years' experience as a federal judge. Furthermore, part of the objective of appointing another federal judge for California was to bring more experience, as well as help, to the task of adjudicating the land claims. Because of the objections to Hoffman's age at his initial appointment, he was hardly the ideal candidate, even though he seemed to be proving himself as a federal judge.

The choice of McAllister met with general satisfaction from a wide range of San Francisco newspapers, and Hoffman could hardly object to his credentials. Twenty years Hoffman's senior, McAllister had earned a substantial legal and political reputation in Georgia before coming to San Francisco in 1850. The onetime U.S. attorney for Georgia, state senator, and mayor of Savannah joined his son Hall—destined to become the leader of the California bar—in legal practice, and together they stood "high in the Profession" by 1851. Experience, achievement, and the right politics combined to make McAllister an appropriate candidate for the new judgeship. Hoffman's concession that McAllister was qualified for the circuit judgeship was eased even further by the fact that the two men were related by marriage and the fact that McAllister was a polished gentleman. Despite some initial misunderstandings, Hoffman and McAllister enjoyed an amicable relationship, with the district judge gracefully deferring to the senior and presiding judge even as Hoffman took the leading role in adjudicating the land grant cases.[6]

Although Hoffman may have resigned himself to McAllister's appointment in 1855, he was clearly thinking about becoming the older man's successor as ill health plagued McAllister early in 1862. By then Hoffman had more than a decade's experience on the district court and was the longest-serving federal judge on the West Coast. These circumstances seemed to indicate he had a fair chance for the position. Indeed, more than three months before McAllister resigned his post because of illness, Hoffman had secured the support of Senator Reverdy Johnson of Maryland—a prominent California land-grant lawyer and former attorney general under the Whig president Zachary Taylor. Johnson assured Hoffman of support when the circuit judgeship became vacant: "You will have no friend more anxious for your appointment to it, than myself." Though Hoffman may have blamed Johnson for not promoting his bid for the judgeship more aggressively, others had an edge in the crowded competition for the position. Unfortunately for Hoffman, his primary competition this time was Stephen Field, then the chief justice of the California Supreme Court and an imposing intellect.[7]

In thinking of McAllister's replacement, especially since the judgeship could evolve into a position on the Supreme Court, President Lincoln had special political criteria in mind beyond judicial ability and competence. In the context of important Civil War litigation then pending on the Supreme Court's docket, he sought to insure support from a court that had rendered *Dred Scott* v. *Sanford* (1857). One aspirant to the judgeship, Thompson Campbell, recognized this consideration by assuring Lincoln of his every effort to "crush the existing rebellion" and his willingness to support "every measure of the administration to that end." Yet another potential aspirant to the judgeship, the former California senator Milton S. Latham, was effectively out of serious contention because he had never been "sound on the Union question." Although a Buchanan Democrat as recently as 1860, Stephen Field had taken up the Union cause vigorously and publicly. Moreover, Field's brother, David Dudley Field, who had become a trusted advisor to Lincoln after playing an important part in Lincoln's nomination, could vouch for his brother's politics. In addition, California's Republican governor, Leland Stanford, after initially supporting another candidate, backed Field, who eventually received the unanimous support of California's congressional delegation.[8]

Along with all the other candidates who stood a realistic chance, Hoffman strongly supported the war effort, even though in 1860 he had voted the Constitutional Union ticket rather than for Lincoln and the Republican party. Hoffman, however, failed to make his political views known to the administration. Thus, even though he was ideologically closer to Lincoln than was Field, Hoffman's potential appointment was seen more in terms of a "promotion" or "advancement" than as the candidacy of a man whose credentials fit the expectations of Lincoln's administration. As the Far West's ranking federal judge, with more than a decade of experience on the bench, Hoffman might have seemed a logical choice but for the shadow cast by the figure of Field. In addition to his energetic self-promotion, obvious intelligence, and rehabilitated politics, Field also possessed considerable knowledge of the problems and circumstances of the circuit—particularly those involving land and mining claims.[9]

The California support for Field stemmed in part from his reputation and his inclination to settle troublesome disputes involving the state's natural resources. Hoffman actually had greater experience examining California's private land grants, but Field, unlike Hoffman, seemed determined to settle a crucial dispute over San Francisco's claim to land as a town under Mexican law—its so-called pueblo title, in the city's favor. Moreover, Field took a generally pragmatic approach toward land grant litigation, one that discounted the technicalities of Mexican law that concerned Hoffman. Field proved far more predictable than Hoffman in his approach to these issues, on which enormous fortunes depended. In challenging the widespread approval of Field's appointment, the *San Francisco Bulletin* alluded to the popular perception of how Field would resolve the dispute over the city's pueblo title. The *Bulletin* concluded, "It is an extraordinary state of things, when the politicians before a judicial election can pretend to say what specific decisions will follow the elevation of a certain candidate." The paper predicted, "[Field will] adhere to the doctrine of *stare decisis* so far as his own decisions are concerned." Since Field, as a member of the California Supreme Court, had already upheld the city's claim to land in the *Hart* v.

Burnett case in 1860, the *Bulletin* was confident that Field was a known quantity. Field's subsequent handling of the San Francisco pueblo case amply bore out the newspaper's contention.[10]

Field exhibited both self-confidence and the strength of his support by holding out for a place on the Supreme Court. McAllister's resignation left a vacancy in the circuit court, but it was unclear whether Congress would retain the special circuit judgeship or convert it into an additional seat on the U.S. Supreme Court—a seat whose incumbent would preside over the Far West's circuit courts during his circuit visits. California's senators telegraphed Field to tell him they had recommended him as McAllister's successor. By his own account Field rejected the offer, preferring "to remain Chief Justice of the Supreme Court of the State than to be a judge of an inferior federal court," but he said that he would accept an associate justiceship if an additional justice was created for the U.S. Supreme Court. In the face of more than a half dozen candidates—including Hoffman—applying for the position of circuit judge, Field must have been confident of his appointment. Indeed, that confidence would carry over to his service on the Supreme Court, for he regarded the creation of another seat on the Court and his appointment as a personal mandate "to bring order" out of the "confusion" of land titles and mining laws in California.[11]

However much a foregone conclusion, Hoffman's loss to Field placed an initial strain on the working relationship of the two judges. If Hoffman harbored a natural disappointment, his feeling toward Field deepened into resentment in the wake of disagreements soon after Field's appointment. In retrospect, it seems evident that Hoffman never forgave Field for supporting legislative measures directed at Hoffman, and for his part, Field, although he acknowledged Hoffman's ability, seemed to have little use for Hoffman.[12]

Field and Hoffman found themselves at odds from the very first case they heard together, the case of Ridgely Greathouse in September 1863—six months after Field's appointment by Lincoln. The case involved the prosecution and conviction of Confederate sympathizers on a statutory form of treason. Hoffman's later pardon of Greathouse after broadly interpreting a presidential proclamation earned him Field's contempt. In light of that decision and of concerns that Hoffman might present obstacles to the confirmation of San Francisco's pueblo title, Field lent his support to measures designed to strip Hoffman of judicial powers, if not abolish his judgeship. That Hoffman successfully fought off the most dangerous threats to his judgeship hardly meant he excused Field's behavior. On the other hand, Field continued to view Hoffman as an obstruction to the attainment of his judicial goals. Yet, the events triggered by Hoffman's release of Greathouse and the struggle over land in San Francisco were ultimately only manifestations of deep-seated differences between Field and Hoffman in personality, values, and judicial style.[13]

Both Hoffman and Field were proud men, but Hoffman lacked Field's tremendous ego. Field's self-perception showed when he lost to Morrison Waite in his bid to be the new chief justice of the United States in 1874. After Waite's appointment, Field objected, "It is an experiment whether a man of fair but not great abilities may make a fit Chief Justice." Field's self-confidence and determination to implement his ideas contrasted with Hoffman's painstaking appraisal of the various sides of a question. Moreover, Hoffman's reflectiveness was often seen as a sign of intellectual weakness and prevented him from making swift decisions in ways that recognized the pragmatic realities of a situation. If Field was result-oriented in a way that Hoffman was not, he also backed up his decisions with a clarity of analysis and conviction that Hoffman simply did not possess. Moreover, Hoffman never had Field's ability to declare insightfully what was right and wrong, good and bad, for a given judicial situation and feel comfortable about it.[14]

Part of their difference was that Hoffman lacked Field's certainty about constitutional theories and judicial philosophy, a certainty that offered Field clear solutions to legal problems for more than three decades on the U.S Supreme Court. According to his most recent biographer, "[Field] preached a radically new gospel of constitutional interpretation that fused natural law concepts, a theory of adjudication based on formally bounded categories of public power and private right, and a designing foresight about the court's unique capacity to shape American public life." His judicial philosophy drew on both laissez-faire constitutionalism and a version of Jacksonian democracy. Again in the words of Field's biographer:

> What made Field so formidable was his skill in translating the feature-less generalities of the Constitution into a coherent system of principled standards. He had an uncanny ability to diagnose recurrent problem-situations almost immediately and to frame rules derived from the common law or the structure of the federal system that accommodated his value-laden premises, anticipated future controversies, and sup-

plied mutually consistent solutions to all of them. For Field, these solutions were neither contingent nor variable; they were "true."[15]

Hoffman did not have his own legal or constitutional agenda to "preach,"
nor did he approach Field's conviction that his legal solutions were infallible.

Field's dynamism contrasted with Hoffman's caution, and, in comparison,
Hoffman was bound to cut a less noticeable figure, even discounting Field's
comprehensive constitutional theories. Field's impatience and unwillingness
to observe the niceties of a situation made him an effective if brusque character who consistently offended the more reserved and formal Hoffman.
Linked to Field's dynamism was his thoroughgoing political nature, interests, and ambitions. Once again, the contrast with Hoffman was striking—but more so in terms of how they each understood the nature of politics than in terms of their substantive political differences.

Hoffman—like Field—was ambitious, but his political heritage inhibited
aggressive and effective self-advancement. Instead, even though Hoffman
engaged in politicking to aid his judicial advancement or to protect his
judgeship or his court from attacks, he regarded those efforts as matters of
principle and not politics. Politics for its own sake he clearly and self-
consciously avoided as incompatible with his position as a judge. To the
extent he identified with the conservative wing of the Whig and later
the Republican parties, Hoffman's politics assumed a distinctively passive
character. Ironically, this stance gave him heightened individual influence
through the friendly connections he developed across party lines, based
on his identification with men of quality, education, and breeding. Moreover, throughout his tenure Hoffman strove to avoid the appearance of
impropriety or of being influenced by special groups or parties whose interests were at stake in his court.

On the other hand, Field had a deep and sustained political interest that
judicial office did little to curb. Soon after his arrival in California in 1850,
Field ran for and won election as the *alcalde* (a combination of mayor and
judge) of Marysville. He was subsequently elected to the state assembly,
made an unsuccessful bid for the state senate, and won election to the California Supreme Court in 1857. In 1868 Field was mentioned as a Democratic presidential candidate. During the 1880s, Field was an active leader
of the conservative wing of the Democratic party in California. He became
an active presidential candidate in 1880, but the Democrats instead chose

General Winfield Hancock to run against the Republican James A. Garfield. Four years later Field sought the presidency once again, a bid that faltered badly, in part because of the opposition from his own party in California. Field's overt involvement in the political process and his two campaigns for the presidency occurred during the time he served on the U.S. Supreme Court.[16]

If Field had no compunctions about running for political office while a judge, he had few when it came to using the political process to attain his objectives or simply to advance his political allies and friends. This attitude, as well, was bound to bring him into conflict with Hoffman and Sawyer. An example of their divergent views on what was judicially inappropriate occurred in 1885 when Field asked both Hoffman and Sawyer to endorse a particular candidate for U.S. marshal in the northern district. Both judges declined, citing their "invariable rule" not to "interfere with the appoint-ment of the officers of [the] courts." Hoffman explained to Field that the reasons for not making such an endorsement would "readily occur" to him. Hoffman said he wished "to keep unimpaired the authority of the Court over the marshal and deputies." He added, "Nor do I wish the incoming officer to feel he has succeeded in obtaining his appointment by defeating the Judge's candidate." Sawyer reasoned, "There ought to be no possible ground for favoritism or ill-will between the judges and their offi-cers." Nonetheless, both Hoffman and Sawyer were willing to express their agreement with Field that his candidate had the capacity and character for the job.[17]

Such a disparity in perception of acceptable judicial behavior not only widened the gulf between Hoffman and Field but also encouraged Field to gravitate toward judges he felt more comfortable with, especially Matthew Deady. Deady, for one, was willing to practice law while on the bench and accepted interest-free loans as well as monetary gifts from individuals who appeared before his court. Field apparently appreciated this relaxed attitude of Deady's far more than the moralizing he got from Hoffman. No historical evidence suggests that Field or Deady was a corrupt judge, but neither of them seemed troubled by Deady's behavior or by an active participation in politics. Likewise, neither was bothered by the free passes granted by the railroads, and they hardly viewed themselves as influenced by the acceptance of such favors. Indeed, Deady complained to a railroad magnate about not receiving railroad passes without asking for them. He later explained, "I had given my life to this country, . . . my brains and labor had shaped and made her laws and institutions which he was enjoying the benefit of, and . . . I was entitled to travel upon these roads [railroads] free of charge and . . . it was his duty to see that I did." [18]

Hoffman's rather straitlaced attitude about such matters was not the only thing that drew Field closer to Deady than Hoffman. As a man of action, Field placed a premium on physical courage. A former senator for California, Cornelius Cole, recalled that Field "seemed always concerned lest people should be unaware of his personal prowess" and that Field demanded "credit for personal bravery." Indeed, Field went to some lengths to contrast his perceived physical and moral courage with that of his judicial colleagues. One such incident occurred in the course of a bitter contempt hearing in which Field had taken part, along with Hoffman and Sawyer. After Field left for the East Coast, he received information that Hoffman and Sawyer had reservations about Field's proposed disposition of the case. In writing Deady, who was, in Field's words, the only ninth circuit judge "fit to sit on the trial of any case requiring courage," Field concluded, "It is not pleasant to find the moment one leaves the State, all spirit and courage ooze out from the Federal Judges in San Francisco." [19]

If Field preferred action to protracted deliberation, he also tended to view action as an attribute of manliness and physical courage. Some equation of this kind would appear to underlie the greater tolerance, respect, and affection he especially displayed toward Deady. Deady came from unprepossessing stock, and he had a hardiness and rough streak in him that apparently appealed to Field. Hoffman, the clubman and sophisticate, on the other hand, lacked this rugged quality. His participation in occasional hunting excursions in the Mendocino hills could not dispel the impression that Hoffman was really at home only in the rarefied atmosphere of elite social clubs. [20]

Field had an excellent opportunity to act on his different feelings for Deady and Hoffman in what one contemporary called "the celebrated fight" for California's circuit judgeship in 1869. In January of that year, as soon as it became evident that Congress would modify the federal judiciary to create judgeships for each circuit, Field sought the position for Deady, lining up support in Washington and offering Deady advice on how to promote his candidacy on the West Coast. The special circuit judgeship that McAllister had occupied had been a departure from the traditional operation of Supreme Court justices traveling to their assigned geographical circuits and forming circuit courts with the local district court judges. The innovation in 1855 had been prompted by the unique pressures of judicial business in California, but "circuit riding" had never been popular with the Supreme Court, and the increase in federal court business following the Civil War gave a compelling reason for appointing resident circuit judges throughout the country.[21]

Apart from being the beneficiary of Field's warm regard, Deady profited from the likelihood that Hoffman would seek the appointment. Even before the bill creating the judgeships had passed, Hoffman supporters were stressing his long-standing Republicanism in contrast to Field's political links to the Democratic party. "This is aimed," surmised a Deady supporter, "to break down Field's influence at Washington because F[ield] will move everything in his power to defeat Hoffman." The observer went on to remind Deady: "Ever since the appointment of Field to the Federal Bench there has been between F[ield] and H[offman] anything but kind feelings. H[offman] considered that he was treated badly in not being placed on the Supreme Court himself. That F[ield] will defeat H[offman] if he can there is no doubt whatever."[22]

Field's animus toward Hoffman did indeed date back to the 1863 *Greathouse* case, and the intervening years had placed Hoffman in a most uncomfortable position as the junior judge to the presiding justice who did not like him. Apart from their personal relations, Hoffman suffered from the indignity of having to accept Field's choice of a circuit clerk as the clerk of his own court. Hoffman's inability, dating from 1865, to appoint his own clerk was not a trivial matter. In a time before multijudge courts and the provision of law clerks for individual judges, clerks of court often provided the closest professional relationship judges enjoyed. As Hoffman put it, he was forced to be "on terms of daily and confidential intercourse" with his clerk. Being forced to deal with Field's clerk, who harbored contempt and ill will toward him, evidently made Hoffman very unhappy. As a result, Hoffman had been trying for some time before the reorganization of the federal courts to regain control over the appointment of his clerk.[23]

Even as Hoffman struggled to rid himself of a disagreeable presence in his court, Field was promoting the reputation and advancement of Deady. Field invited Deady on several occasions to hold terms of the circuit court in San Francisco in the justice's stead, and Deady himself disseminated, as broadly as possible, copies of his more important opinions. Such promotion evidently had an effect on Hoffman. In January 1869 Field informed Deady that Hoffman "could not bear the idea that another District Judge on the coast should be considered his equal" and was "in a bad temper that the bar of San Francisco expressed so strongly as they did their appreciation" of Deady. Hoffman's vanity, concluded Field, was "of great proportions" and was "easily offended." [24]

Field was undoubtedly correct about Hoffman's sensitivity; Hoffman's pride had suffered a good number of blows since Field had joined the federal bench, not the least of which was the lack of judicial advancement after eighteen years. Hoffman's resentment and frustration, however, were not and would not be directed at Deady, but rather at Field. Even before the Circuit Judge Act creating circuit judgeships for each circuit became effective in December 1869, the scene was set for a ten-month struggle whose primary feature was the feud between Hoffman and Field. For Hoffman, the stakes included personal vindication and recouping the loss of pride he felt he had suffered since his defeat by Field in 1863. [25]

If Hoffman and Field saw the struggle as a test of will between themselves, the eventual incumbent, Lorenzo Sawyer, aggressively pursued the judgeship as a desirable post. As a California Supreme Court member nearing the end of a term of service without having won reelection, Sawyer saw the circuit judgeship as a practical salvation rather than a prestigious advancement. Enjoying solid credentials as a lawyer, Sawyer had also been considered by incoming President Ulysses S. Grant for a cabinet appointment. Moreover, Sawyer, like Deady, had strong support from a member of the U.S. Supreme Court. In Sawyer's case, Justice Noah H. Swayne, in whose Ohio office Sawyer had read law in the 1840s, pushed for his candidacy. In addition, Sawyer received the endorsement of the California Supreme Court and General William Tecumseh Sherman. Although others were also interested in the position, it quickly became apparent that Hoffman, Deady, and Sawyer were the principal contenders for the ninth circuit judgeship. [26]

At the beginning of his campaign for the judgeship, Hoffman made his feelings clear to Deady about why he felt entitled to the position and why he objected to the idea of Deady as his judicial "superior." "I have been on the Bench since 1851—18 years—I have given my whole life to it and I think I have a right to expect that if promotion is to be made, I should be the person." Moreover, Hoffman regarded the prospect of Deady's appointment as "a public and emphatic declaration" of Hoffman's "unfitness." Were it not that he deserved the post and would "be written down as an ass" if he declined, he said that he would "very willingly jog on in the easier ways" in which he had "been going for so long." Despite his "priority of claim," Hoffman encouraged Deady to "sail in" if he could get the judgeship, and Hoffman proclaimed that he would have "the satisfaction of knowing" that he could not have been beaten "by a worthier man." Yet, Hoffman's claim that he would "not be particularly disappointed at not succeeding" came at a time when he seemed to have confidence that the position was safely his.[27]

Hoffman's reticence to explicitly and emphatically declare his desire for the position and his obsessive concern to avoid the humiliation he associated with the possibility of Deady's appointment ultimately contributed to his failure. Shortly after Hoffman communicated with Deady, a California lawyer wrote to Sherman in Washington, D.C., urging the general to support Sawyer for the judgeship. The lawyer suggested that Hoffman "would probably like the offer of the position as a compliment," but the lawyer added that from his conversations with the judge he had learned that Hoffman was "not trying for the appointment." It was perfectly in keeping with Hoffman's assumption that the job should seek the man that while he wrote letters to secure the endorsements for his candidacy, he also adopted an unconcerned posture, as if a bold declaration of his desires would be unseemly. Indeed, one month later an observer of the bid for the judgeship informed Deady that although Sawyer was "a candidate in earnest," Hoffman expected the appointment but was "doing but little to procure it." [28]

Hoffman's wishful hopes extended to declining, in the midst of the judgeship fight, an offer to lead the diplomatic mission to China, a post that paid $12,000 a year, more than twice his current salary. To be sure, his present lifetime tenure as a federal district judge may have seemed more attractive than the political uncertainty of ambassadorial duty, but Hoffman's interest in becoming the circuit judge probably also entered into his "private considerations of paramount obligation" that led him to decline President Grant's offer. In fact, Hoffman seemed to ignore the implication: if Grant was offering him the diplomatic post, Hoffman's appointment to the circuit court might not have been altogether secure.[29]

Part of Hoffman's confidence stemmed from the support he had garnered from New York connections. Both New York's Roscoe Conkling, a member of the Senate Judiciary Committee, and Hamilton Fish, Grant's secretary of state, were strong backers. Moreover, with California's Republican Central Committee behind him and with his own claims to a "priority" over the other candidates, Hoffman had reason to feel confident. Even the threat of Sawyer's candidacy—given his visibility with Grant—could have been diffused by Hoffman's elevation to the circuit court and Sawyer's appointment to the vacancy left by Hoffman. Although Field and his circuit clerk assured Deady that Hoffman's chances were nonexistent, to other observers it "seemed about certain" Hoffman would get the appointment—up until the last moment. Ultimately, what accounted for the widely differing perceptions of how the candidates were doing was Grant's handling of the matter. As he had done with the cabinet appointments earlier that spring, Grant insisted on keeping the final decisions a closely guarded secret.[30]

In some sense, Deady, Hoffman, and Field all contributed more to Sawyer's appointment than Sawyer did himself. With an otherwise distinguished judicial record, Deady suffered from the publicity surrounding his decision in *McCall* v. *McDowell* (1867). In that case Deady had ruled that a civilian illegally imprisoned by a military commander for exulting at the news of Lincoln's assassination could recover damages. Such a decision was hardly calculated to endear Deady to General Grant, and Deady's supporters plausibly claimed that the *McDowell* case had severely hurt Deady's chances. For his part, Hoffman had responded so indirectly to the California senator Cornelius Cole's inquiries about Hoffman's expectations that miscues were sent to Washington. Hoffman's concern that Deady's appointment would make him look ridiculous was eventually conveyed by a telegram to Grant stating that Hoffman would be satisfied as long as Deady was not put over his head. Although Hoffman vehemently denied that he had sent or authorized such a telegram and claimed that at the time of the "interview" he had been "perfectly convinced" that he had the appointment, it seems clear that such a telegram did reach Grant. Had Hoffman unequivocally stated his desire for the judgeship, it would have decreased the chances of his being misunderstood. Deady's friends assigned his loss to the telegram, which they felt Hoffman had sent or engineered, whereas Hoffman was equally convinced that the telegram had cost him the office.[31]

The final element that boosted Sawyer's chances was Field's hostility to Hoffman. On November 15, 1869, after hearing Attorney General Ebenezer Hoar's oral argument in a case before the Supreme Court, Field approached Hoar to discuss his concerns about the circuit judgeship. Field reputedly told Hoar that there was "one of the three candidates spoken of who he could never consent to the appointment of, their personal relations being such that they could never consult with each other," at which point Hoar agreed to oppose any such appointment. Field's objection to Hoffman obviously played a role in the process of appointment. Indeed, the *San Francisco Chronicle*'s Washington correspondent explained Hoffman's loss in terms of the mysterious telegram and Field's request "that it would be repulsive to him to be associated with Hoffman on the Circuit Bench for life, not being on speaking terms." The *Chronicle*'s reporter captured the sense in which the decision to appoint Sawyer seemed more a compromise than a positive first choice.[32]

Hoffman certainly did have a claim to the judgeship based on his length of service, a claim that seemed to appeal to the military man in the White House, and this, combined with Hoffman's powerful endorsements, probably would have gotten him the appointment—had all things been equal. Deady, on the other hand, suffered from his authorship of the *McDowell* case and from Hoffman's objections to his promotion. When the telegram arrived suggesting that Hoffman would be content as long as Deady was not appointed, Sawyer became an obvious compromise. Field's antipathy for Hoffman could be bypassed, and supposedly Hoffman himself would be satisfied. As it turned out, no one was really satisfied except Sawyer. Both Deady and Hoffman were naturally disappointed, and Field spoke ominously of Deady's "judicial enemies." Hoffman did have one consolation: the bill creating the circuit judgeships reinstated the power of the district court judges to appoint their own clerks.[33]

Ironically, despite the renewed animosity stirred up between Field and Hoffman, the aftermath of the judgeship struggle left Sawyer, Hoffman, and Deady on reasonably good terms. Deady eventually drew closer to Sawyer than to Hoffman, but Deady managed to put his disappointment behind him, even if he initially believed Hoffman had hurt his chances. Beyond Deady's forgiving nature, he and Hoffman were drawn together by their shared experiences and problems. For nearly twenty years they complained about their low salaries and lobbied together to improve the financial security of district judges. Moreover, they shared opinions and consulted with each other about issues before their respective courts. Hoffman's experience with admiralty and bankruptcy matters was a resource that Deady took advantage of time and time again.[34]

Sawyer shared the trial experiences of Deady and Hoffman, and the day-to-day work in hearing cases created a bond that united them during Field's frequent absences. By his elevation in 1863, Field had succeeded in becoming California's presiding federal judge, but during the 1869 judgeship fight, one of Oregon's senators offered a penetrating insight into Field's judicial ambitions. Much of Field's "opposition to Hoffman," he maintained, probably stemmed from the fact that Field wished "to be *the Judge* of California." Sawyer and Deady, as well as Hoffman, came to experience and in varying degrees to resent Field's domineering presence and his expectation that they would give allegiance to his views.[35]

If Deady readily overcame his disappointment at the events of 1869, Hoffman had a harder time accepting the loss and took it with far less grace. A San Francisco lawyer and Deady supporter reported that Hoffman was "raising the devil" and sending "a thousand telegrams" to correct his reputed statement that he would be satisfied to remain where he was as long as Deady was not put over his head. In fact, Hoffman not only hastened to explain the situation to Deady but also exhorted Secretary of State Hamilton Fish to expose the circumstances of "so gross a fraud upon the President." Hoffman also had friends making inquiries in Washington, and he kept up a barrage of letters to various senators in an effort to clear up the record. Hoffman's actions belied his philosophical advice to Deady: "What is without remedy should be without regard."[36]

Beyond his agitation over the telegram, Hoffman struck back at those he felt should have supported him. After the *Alta California* endorsed Deady for the judgeship, Hoffman punished the newspaper by naming a competing newspaper, the *San Francisco Bulletin* (which had been neutral), as the official publisher of the district court's legal notices. The decision hardly cast Hoffman in a favorable light, but his anger revealed his anxiety about his judicial advancement.[37]

Hoffman's reaction to the *Alta California* was only one example of the depth of his wounded pride. Four years after the fact, a Deady supporter complained, "Hoffman has never spoken a word to me since the celebrated fight for the Circuit judgeship." Hoffman also found it difficult, if not impossible, to agree with the *Bulletin*'s comment that his present position "in all but the name" was "equally honorable, permanent, and lucrative with the circuit judgeship." Although he retained lifetime tenure and, at $5,000 per year, was the highest-paid district judge in the country, Hoffman was acutely aware that he had been passed over. Indeed, his concerns on this point are reflected by the efforts by those, such as Senator Conkling, who sought to console Hoffman by arguing that "the honor and esteem" of his district judgeship was not less than he would have had with the circuit judgeship.[38]

Fortunately for Hoffman, Sawyer was no Field. The two federal judges based in San Francisco developed a good working relationship, buttressed, no doubt, by their similar political views as Republicans. Although Sawyer was technically Hoffman's superior, they both were essentially trial judges, and in that capacity Sawyer had more in common with Hoffman and Deady than he did with Field. Sawyer expressed this well in a letter to Deady, on the occasion of the three West Coast federal judges having each been reversed by their "superiors at Washington." "When we get to be Supreme Judges and consequently have *less* opportunities for acquiring a knowledge of the merits of a case, than we enjoy as *nisi prius* judges, we shall, doubtless, be wiser than we now are." Likewise, he later acknowledged a reversal by saying, "[Field] seems to have poured into me hot shot in a style that, if it should come from some of us smaller guns, would be apt to bring us a good drubbing from those overhead." This sense of being natural allies when Field sat in judgment of their decisions undoubtedly drew Hoffman closer to Sawyer. Indeed, they got along so well that Hoffman accepted in stride Sawyer's support of Deady for potential openings suggested in congressional discussions of federal judiciary reorganization in the 1870s and 1880s.[39]

With time, Hoffman overcame his sense of disappointment at not getting the circuit judgeship, but the tensions that marked his early relations with Field persisted. Indeed, Hoffman's last decade as a judge of the northern district found him involved in cases that pitted him and Sawyer against Field. The more than 10,000 Chinese habeas corpus cases heard by the two resident federal judges in San Francisco during the 1880s represented a final example of Field's aggressive judicial personality. Sawyer and Hoffman managed for a time to uphold their construction of the Exclusion Acts against Field's arguments for Chinese exclusion. Yet, in the end, it was Field who triumphed.

———————

As Ogden Hoffman lay dying in the spring of 1891, he had a chance to reflect on his judgeship. After he suffered a stroke in April, Hoffman's condition fluctuated for several months before it worsened and led to a slow decline. At first, in hopes that he might recover, Hoffman's friends wanted him to stay in his rooms at the Pacific-Union Club, but on June 15, the decision was made to move the judge to St. Luke's Hospital. There he remained, drugged with morphine and drifting in and out of consciousness, until he died on the morning of August 9.[40]

Toward the end, Hoffman confessed to a friend that his only regret was that he had not known "the love of a good wife and had not been blessed with children who could call him father." The lifelong bachelor conceded that the family of Southard, his half brother and clerk of court, had given him a vicarious experience of family life. The brothers had always been close; Southard's second son was the judge's namesake, and Southard left instructions that his body be interred near Hoffman rather than in his own family plot. During Hoffman's last few weeks at St. Luke's, Southard slept in the hospital to be near his brother.[41]

Given his condition, Hoffman's death had been anticipated for several months by his family and friends as well as by the San Francisco newspapers. To some extent his death was overshadowed by the discreet and not so discreet maneuvering of potential successors to the northern district judgeship. Ironically, Hoffman himself had rejected an expression of gratitude and respect for his long judicial service only a few months before his stroke. In February 1891 Hoffman had reached his fortieth year of service as the northern district's judge, and some of his closest friends had sought to celebrate that anniversary with a complimentary dinner in the judge's honor. Despite much urging, Hoffman had refused to participate on the grounds that "it would not be in good taste . . . while occupying a judicial position." Hoffman had relented only to the extent of considering such a dinner in his honor after his intended retirement in 1893.[42]

Hoffman never saw his retirement dinner, but he might well have been gratified by his funeral and the marks of respect attending his death. Both federal and state courts adjourned in his honor, and committees were appointed to draft appropriate memorials. His funeral, at the Trinity Episcopal Church, drew the leading members of San Francisco's bench and bar, as well as federal officials (including Justice Field, who acted as one of Hoffman's pallbearers) and members of the military.

Later that evening, the prominent San Francisco attorney E. J. Pillsbury gave a festive dinner party in honor of Justice Field at the Pacific-Union Club. The dozen guests included two other pallbearers at Hoffman's funeral, as well as the ex-congressman William W. Morrow, a leading candidate for the vacant judgeship. Beyond honoring Field, the apparent objective behind the dinner was to consolidate support for Morrow's candidacy. Also present were two important political kingmakers: M. H. de Young, prominent in local Republican politics and owner of the *San Francisco Chronicle*; and James G. Fair, a bonanza millionaire and former senator from Nevada. Whatever the intent of the dinner, it sparked "hostile comment" from Hoffman's friends, particularly from some of his fellow Pacific-Union clubmen. "Apart from the sentiment attaching in the institution to the personality of one who had been a faithful and eminently popular member for years, the bad taste of the festivity is aggravated by the position of the host and guest. The latter [Field], whatever his feeling towards the deceased jurist, should have had the keener sense of decorum than to have made the evening of his funeral an occasion for jubilance." Critics also took objection to the location of the festivities, for the clubhouse was "the late Judge's home."[43]

Several days after the dinner, Field left with his wife for the East Coast, having presided over the circuit courts in California and Oregon as well as the first session of the newly created U.S. Court of Appeals for the Ninth Circuit. Largely as expected, Morrow succeeded to Hoffman's judgeship, and the uproar over Pillsbury's dinner died down.

Only two years before his death, Hoffman had confided to Deady that he "felt how great is one's disadvantage in playing on the provincial instead of the metropolitan stage." Hoffman's remark reflected his unsuccessful efforts to gain higher judicial office and his sense that he had not achieved the professional reputation that he had aspired to when he was first appointed in 1851. Moreover, he could not escape the feeling that his prospects or at least his reputation would have been enhanced had he been a judge in New York rather than in San Francisco. In addition, a large part of Hoffman's professional disappointment stemmed from standing in the shadow of Stephen Field, who had clearly wrested away from Hoffman any claim he might have made to being California's most prominent federal judge.[44]

Despite his disappointments, Hoffman could and did take pride in his craft as a judge and in his court. He took special pleasure in the fact that he was the longest-serving federal judge in the Far West. No other judge could top him in this regard. Beyond his sheer longevity, he was proud that for nearly forty years he had done his duty, providing a useful forum in which litigants would get a full and fair hearing. Despite his failings as a man and as a judge, Hoffman emerges as a sympathetic character worth attention in his own right. Ultimately, Hoffman's judicial contribution and monument rested, as he knew it would, on his forty years of painstaking and conscientious labor preserved in the case files of his court.

3

San Francisco's Court
of Admiralty

Nearly two years before Ogden Hoffman opened his court in 1851, an observer counted one hundred ships in San Francisco Bay but noted them "daily increasing." Ten months later, "vessels of every description" were anchored at San Francisco "as closely together as convenient for a mile or two along the shore and half a mile back." By 1852 San Francisco was second only to New York City in terms of tonnage entering an American port. Since federal district courts had jurisdiction over maritime and admiralty cases, a harbor choked with ships foretold the nature of much of Hoffman's judicial business. Many who came to California during the gold rush arrived in San Francisco by sea, and the city quickly became the West Coast's foremost port and commercial center, remaining so throughout Hoffman's tenure. From the start, admiralty was Hoffman's largest docket, with cases ranging from seamen seeking their wages and passengers complaining of the conditions they had endured to disputes over shipments damaged and services or supplies provided to vessels. Indeed, the 1850s saw the greatest use of the northern district as a court of admiralty, with nearly half of all Hoffman's admiralty cases being filed during the first decade of his court.[1]

Hoffman's admiralty cases reveal much about him as a judge as well as about how a federal district court functioned in the latter half of the nineteenth century. His early decisions allowed San Francisco to appraise him while Hoffman sought to win the respect of the community. Three major groups of litigants appeared before Hoffman's admiralty court: passengers, businessmen, and sailors.

Well over a year before Hoffman opened court, the San Francisco lawyer John McCrackan complained about the "wretched" state of affairs created by the absence of any "marine or District court, before which . . . cases in admiralty come." Since the U.S. Constitution gave the federal courts exclusive jurisdiction over admiralty, the lawyer was technically correct. But his complaint stemmed mainly from frustration over California's delayed statehood rather than from the absence of an indispensable legal forum. Even before the creation of Hoffman's court—and long after—state courts in California heard a wide variety of admiralty and maritime cases. Indeed, when news of California's statehood reached San Francisco, McCrackan's practice included "a very important suit" in admiralty.[2]

McCrackan rightly stressed the importance of admiralty jurisdiction, for being limited to common-law courts posed significant practical obstacles to the interests of his and other lawyers' clients. Historically, the English court of admiralty (following the European civil-law tradition) had developed separately from the common-law courts. Despite some modifications, the distinctive practices of admiralty courts were preserved in the "reception" of English law in America. By Hoffman's time, admiralty cases before the federal courts were heard on a separate "side" of the district court, where special terminology and procedures prevailed. For instance, admiralty called the *plaintiff* the *libellant*, the *complaint* the *libel*, and the *defendant* the *respondent*. Substantively, admiralty—responding to the needs of commerce linked to the seas—developed free of many common-law technicalities and featured swift action, through expedited means of introducing evidence and through trial without a jury.

Admiralty's greatest attraction, however, was the availability of the maritime lien, a form of security that underlay a proceeding unique to admiralty. Admiralty libels could be filed either *in personam* or *in rem*. The libel *in personam* was familiar to the common law; it usually consisted of a suit against an individual and asserted personal liability. The libel *in rem*, however, allowed a libellant, in whose favor a maritime lien arose, to proceed directly against the tangible thing involved—usually a ship. During the course of the nineteenth century, American admiralty law gave a right to this special lien to many maritime claims: seamen's claims for wages; libels for supplies, services, or repairs; collision and personal-injury claims; and libels for breaches of contracts to ship goods.[3]

Although the common law also provided liens as a basis for litigation, maritime liens were significantly different in ways that made admiralty courts far more attractive to the litigant and his lawyer. At common law, the litigant could attach the ship as the property of the defendant, but did so subject to all existing liens and mortgages. The maritime lien, on the other hand, gave the libellant a right conceived of as a property interest in the tangible thing involved to the amount of the accrued liability. In practice, then, the efficaciousness of the remedy of the maritime lien, combined with relatively swift admiralty procedures, usually made admiralty the most popular court for any litigant with a maritime claim.[4]

The maritime lien became especially important for business because a great deal of American commerce in the nineteenth century involved water transportation. In addition to the eastern seaboard, the internal waterways of the United States were essential arteries of commerce before the railroads assumed increasing importance during the latter half of the nineteenth century. The opening of western lands was accompanied—and indeed accelerated—by an increase in commerce on inland waters. With the completion of the Erie Canal and an expanded use of steamboats, commerce dramatically increased on the Great Lakes and on the Mississippi and other rivers. By the time of Hoffman's appointment, water-based commerce played an integral part in the American economy, not to mention an indispensable one for isolated California.[5]

Only Hoffman's as yet unorganized district court had constitutional authority as a court of admiralty, but the maritime business of San Francisco and California did not abide by such technicalities. The exigencies of the Mexican War had introduced Californians in 1847 to admiralty in the form of prize jurisdiction. Prize cases involved the condemnation and sale of vessels and their cargoes captured from an enemy in time of war. As early as 1794, the Supreme Court had ruled that prize jurisdiction belonged to federal district courts sitting in admiralty. Nonetheless, when several Mexican vessels captured by the Pacific squadron in the 1840s were in no shape "to be sent round the cape for adjudication in the United States," the American military governor in California, Stephen W. Kearny, established a temporary court of admiralty at Monterey to deal with these cases.[6]

San Francisco also experienced admiralty jurisdiction prior to the opening of Hoffman's court, both before and after statehood. Before statehood, a Court of First Instance, modeled after a Mexican judicial institution but staffed by an American judge, heard a wide range of admiralty cases *in rem*. After statehood, but before Hoffman's court opened, maritime cases were also heard by the state courts operating in San Francisco. Occasionally, the exercise of admiralty jurisdiction by common-law courts produced anomalies, such as the *in rem* proceeding in San Francisco's superior court against the steamer *New World* for collision. Although admiralty did not provide a jury, the suit against the *New World* was heard by a jury.[7]

The adjudication of admiralty cases in California before the opening of Hoffman's court underscored the ongoing process by which admiralty jurisdiction adjusted to American federalism. From the moment Congress created federal trial courts, admiralty posed two central questions whose answers were still being worked out by the time Hoffman became a judge: what did American admiralty jurisdiction consist of and to what extent should such jurisdiction be shared between state and federal courts? The two questions were interrelated and were linked to the issue of how judicial power generally should be allocated between federal and state governments.

As a result, admiralty jurisdiction in the United States has had a tortuous history. Until well into the nineteenth century, opposition to the expansion of federal judicial power threatened to limit maritime jurisdiction. Largely through the efforts of Hoffman's teacher Justice Joseph Story, federal courts assumed jurisdiction over a wide range of maritime matters even though Story occasionally made significant concessions to advocates of states' rights. In *DeLovio* v. *Boit* (1815) Story examined at length the sources of American admiralty jurisdiction and concluded that it comprehended "all maritime contracts, torts, and injuries." By the time of Hoffman's tenure, the U.S. Supreme Court had asserted that all navigable waters—as opposed to only tidal waters—fell within the admiralty power. Nonetheless, the Supreme Court limited such jurisdiction to interstate commerce under the authority of the Commerce Clause. In 1858, for example, the Supreme Court declared that contracts to ship goods between ports within a given state were beyond the jurisdiction of federal district courts and were properly the province of state courts. Only after the Civil War did federal judicial power in admiralty break free of the restrictions of the Commerce Clause and pave the way for virtually exclusive legislative control over maritime law by Congress. Even as the limits of admiralty jurisdiction were being resolved, another issue arose: the role of the state courts in hearing maritime matters.[8]

The Constitution authorized the federal courts to hear "all cases of admiralty and maritime jurisdiction." Under the Judiciary Act of 1789, however, Congress gave federal courts "exclusive original cognizance of all civil causes of admiralty and maritime jurisdiction . . . saving to suitors, in all cases, the right of a common law remedy, where the common law is competent to give it." As one scholar has put it, the Judiciary Act seemed to grant exclusive federal jurisdiction "with one hand, and to take it away, in some yet to be defined part, with the other." In working out the meaning of the "savings clause" by determining the extent of concurrent state court jurisdiction over admiralty, the Supreme Court tried to distinguish admiralty from common-law remedies. On the eve of Hoffman's appointment, two cases—*New Jersey Steam Navigation Company* v. *Merchants Bank* (1849) and *Waring* v. *Clarke* (1848)—settled the issue that whatever the extent and nature of common-law jurisdiction left to state courts, federal district courts sitting in admiralty continued to enjoy concurrent jurisdiction. On the other hand, well into Hoffman's tenure, state courts exercised jurisdiction that ultimately came to be considered exclusive to the federal admiralty courts.[9]

As noted, admiralty's most important remedy was the maritime lien in a proceeding *in rem*. Only in 1867—sixteen years into Hoffman's judgeship—did the U.S. Supreme Court directly address the issue of exclusive federal jurisdiction over admiralty and hold that federal courts alone could hear libels *in rem* on the grounds that such proceedings were not a common-law remedy.[10] Until that time, state courts could and did hear similar maritime cases as federal district courts without violating the Supreme Court's understanding of federal judicial authority. Even champions of exclusive admiralty jurisdiction for the federal courts were forced to admit that the Supreme Court had allowed state courts to exercise "a *quasi* admiralty jurisdiction" before 1867.[11] Indeed, Justice Samuel Miller, the author of one of the opinions that withdrew *in rem* jurisdiction from the state courts in 1867, went even further. He acknowledged that virtually all states with inland waters had "statutes authorizing their courts, by proceedings *in rem*, to enforce contracts or redress torts, which, if they had the same relation to the sea that they [had] to the waters of those rivers, would be conceded to be the subjects of admiralty jurisdiction" and that such statutes had been acted on for "many years." [12]

Thus, the fact that *in rem* proceedings became the hallmark of exclusive federal jurisdiction should not obscure the widespread use of the state courts for admiralty and maritime cases in the nineteenth century. In 1869 a commentator noted that inquiries into "the exact effect of the savings clause in the Judiciary Acts," and into "how far the jurisdiction of admiralty" was exclusive of state courts were questions "never well understood, nor clearly laid down by the Supreme Court of the United States, until within a short time." When the Supreme Court finally did withdraw *in rem* proceedings from state courts in 1867, it not only precipitated jurisdictional conflicts but also imposed serious hardships on nineteenth-century businessmen involved in maritime commerce. The California Supreme Court, for one, did not easily acquiesce to exclusive federal jurisdiction. Indeed, California businessmen and courts could point to Theophilus Parsons, the Dane Professor of Law at Harvard and staunch supporter of federal admiralty jurisdiction, who concluded in 1869, "State courts might exercise jurisdiction *in rem* in the case of domestic vessels, where this jurisdiction is given by state statutes." [13]

In the context of the struggles that ultimately defined American admiralty jurisdiction and decided which courts would exercise it, Hoffman decided a series of cases that expanded admiralty jurisdiction significantly beyond that traditionally exercised by federal courts. Indeed, Hoffman developed law in areas in which few precedents existed, and he established remedies and procedures well ahead of the time when they would become commonplace. How and why Hoffman made this new law reveals him as a judge and gives insight into the role he envisioned for his court. This series of cases involved suits by passengers arriving in California by sea. The types of complaints—ill treatment, bad food and accommodation—as well as the circumstances in which litigants sought relief, explain Hoffman's judicial creativity.

Fully appreciating the significance of Hoffman's passenger suits requires placing them within the doctrinal context in which they arose. Justice Joseph Story, in his 1815 circuit court decision broadly defining admiralty jurisdiction, suggested a locality test for maritime torts and a subject-matter test for maritime contracts. In other words, where torts took place would determine admiralty's jurisdiction. For instance, tortious acts committed by a captain on the high seas established admiralty jurisdiction, whereas the same acts committed on shore did not. On the other hand, all contracts, no matter where executed, that related "to the navigation, business or commerce of the sea" were, according to Story, within the jurisdiction of admiralty.[14]

Ultimately, American courts accepted Story's definition and test for admiralty jurisdiction, but considerable uncertainty marked the process by which the Supreme Court recognized new actions as legitimate subjects for admiralty courts. For example, only in 1848 did the Supreme Court hold that contracts for the carriage of goods by sea were within admiralty jurisdiction. Even then, one justice dissented on the issue of jurisdiction, and two of the concurring justices construed the action for the loss of cargo as a "maritime tort" rather than a contract. Moreover, whether passenger suits were legitimate subjects of admiralty was not explicitly answered in the affirmative by the Supreme Court until 1867. Thus, even though lower federal courts had discussed the extent of admiralty jurisdiction, the Supreme Court had not ruled in many areas—particularly with respect to passenger contracts—by the time Hoffman took office. That many causes of action eventually became staples of admiralty jurisdiction should not obscure the contemporary doubts about their nature.[15]

In addition to the general state of flux in admiralty law, Hoffman began to hear passenger cases at a time when other legal doctrines undercut the practical relief he could give passengers. The most effective means of securing a potential judgment in admiralty was to bring suit *in rem*, in effect suing the owners of the ship on the basis of a maritime lien. Unfortunately for some passengers who had suffered injuries during their voyage, a general principal of the common law limited the liability of an employer for the torts of his employees to those acts committed within the scope of their employment. If, in the course of that employment, the employee caused harm to members of the public, the owner assumed responsibility. On the other hand, if the employee caused injury outside of the activity for which he was employed, the injured party was left to seek recompense from the employee. Invariably the employee had far less means to satisfy a judgment than his employer—leaving the injured party with an empty cause of action.

Common carriers, including shipowners, increasingly found themselves under a special duty of care toward their passengers. This new legal understanding, however, developed gradually and received its greatest impetus with the rise of passenger traffic on railroads later in the nineteenth century. On the eve of Hoffman's judgeship in 1851, shipowners could still avoid liability for torts of their employees committed outside the scope of employment. Leading admiralty courts in the country drew a distinction between the ship's liability for "any ill-treatment of the passengers by the master, in his capacity as such" and the captain's liability for acts of "personal malice or ill-will . . . not arising out of or connected with the exercise of his duties as master." Only when a captain misbehaved in his role as the master of a ship could passengers sue *in rem* and thus hold the shipowners responsible. In addition, the common law drew a distinction between intentional harm inflicted by employees (for which the employer was not liable) and negligence of employees acting within the scope of their employment (for which the employer was liable). But the special duty imposed on carriers that blurred the distinctions between acts committed within or without the scope of employment or done intentionally or negligently remained a theoretical base for holding shipowners accountable for passenger injuries. Until Hoffman's decisions in the 1850s, virtually all the reported breach-of-passenger-contract cases were brought *in personam*, against the individual causing the injury. Suits against the invariably solvent shipowner awaited Hoffman's development of *in rem* recovery and his enlarged concept of the passenger contract.[16]

Hoffman's passenger cases were unusual because he broadly construed breaches of passenger contracts to include behavior that was essentially tortious in nature. Moreover, he allowed passengers to sue the ship itself for damages that were normally limited to *in personam* suits. By allowing *in rem* suits, Hoffman provided an effective means of redressing passenger grievances. Even more important, such suits had the effect of forcing shipowners to settle. Not only did most passenger cases that were filed settle before trial, but also the availability of the maritime lien in Hoffman's court prompted the settlement of passenger complaints before they ripened into lawsuits. The exact dimensions of such capitulation by the passenger carriers is unknowable, but the inability to quantify it does not alter the fact that it occurred and stemmed from Hoffman's decisions. Hoffman's passenger cases are also interesting because they reveal how he viewed his obligation to the New York commercial interests—deeply involved in maritime transportation to California—that had helped secure his appointment as a federal judge.[17]

In the wake of the gold rush, fierce competition arose in the business of carrying goods and passengers to California. William H. Aspinwall, the New York financier who had supported Hoffman's judgeship, became heavily involved in this traffic. Aspinwall's Pacific Mail Steamship Company offered transportation from New York City or New Orleans to San Francisco via the isthmus of Panama. Passengers bound for California via Panama were taken to Chagres, on the Atlantic side, and then across the isthmus to Panama, to connect with Aspinwall's Pacific Coast steamers. Until 1855, when a railroad crossed the isthmus, travelers during the rainy season faced the prospect of going up the Chagres River in canoes with native boatmen and then over muddy trails to Panama. Torrential rains, poor supplies and accommodations, and tropical diseases such as yellow fever, malaria, amoebic dysentery, and blackwater fever made travel across the isthmus a risky proposition, particularly with delays that stranded passengers either at Chagres or Panama. Travelers crossing the isthmus in the early years found conditions uncomfortable at best and deadly at worst. The lure of California, however, bred an impatience to reach the Pacific Coast, and thousands—including Ogden Hoffman—traveled the Panama route rather than brook the delay of going overland or sailing around Cape Horn to San Francisco.[18]

If Aspinwall expected preferential treatment before Hoffman's court, he was disappointed at the result of lawsuits brought by passengers against his company. Five of the first suits before Hoffman's court involved libels against Aspinwall's steamships, and in each case the libellant prevailed and received damages. At an early date, Aspinwall's attorney challenged Hoffman's jurisdiction over passenger suits on the grounds that Aspinwall and the government had a mail contract that provided for the use of Aspinwall's steamers by the U.S. Navy in times of war and that therefore the company should be exempt from lawsuits. Hoffman dismissed the motion challenging his jurisdiction and embarked on a path that involved his court in monitoring the passenger routes to San Francisco.[19]

Hoffman further frustrated Aspinwall by imposing substantial penalties and even forfeitures against Pacific Mail steamships that violated federal laws regulating the ratio of passengers to the size of the vessel. The U.S. attorney for the northern district, Calhoun Benham, had been filing suits,

from the inception of Hoffman's court, against steamships for carrying excessive numbers of passengers. Benham warned the solicitor of the treasury
that the defendants, particularly Aspinwall's company, were making "strong
efforts to defeat the prosecutions." He reported that Hoffman had ruled
against the steamship company on several critical issues and urged the solicitor not to exercise his power of remitting the fines and penalties on too
liberal terms. "The parties . . . have been guilty of gross and flagrant
transgressions of the plain law, under circumstances which here, are not
thought to afford any excuse and which create no sympathy for them. They
are rich, very rich . . . and can well afford to defray the expenses to which
by their rapacity they have subjected the Government in prosecuting them."
Aspinwall's company did indeed exert considerable legal efforts and succeeded in having most of the decrees rendered against it reduced to the
nominal amount of $250 and the costs of litigation.[20]

Hoffman's adverse decisions were not limited to the Pacific Mail Steamship Company: libels filed by the U.S. attorney equally affected the other
steamship companies and ships engaged in passenger traffic.[21] Moreover,
aggrieved steamship passengers tended to prevail in Hoffman's court,
whether their suits were against the Pacific Mail Steamship Company or its
competitors.[22] In addition, Hoffman used his discretion to assume jurisdiction over foreign vessels and provided their passengers with a forum for their
grievances.[23] Although not all of these passengers who filed suits before the
northern district prevailed, the court—during the period of heaviest passenger traffic to California in the 1850s and 1860s—was decidedly a plaintiff's
court, where relief was likely to be had either in a decree or in a settlement.[24]

Underlying these passenger cases was Hoffman's effort to monitor the
behavior of captains and their crews who mistreated passengers. Whether
travelers came to California via the Panama route, by a competing Nicara-
guan route, or around Cape Horn, all of them were trapped, for a time, in
their mode of transportation. The captive environment of sea travel, combined with a sea captain's extraordinary power over all on board, prompted
Hoffman to respond to the experiences of passengers arriving in San Francisco. In deciding these cases, Hoffman could draw on his personal experience and observation as a passenger on vessels of the steamship companies
that transported people to and from the Pacific Coast.

The bulk of the cases before Hoffman alleged a breach of passenger contract consisting of the ship's failure to provide agreed-upon provisions, ac-

commodation, or transportation. The demand for passage to California tempted the steamship companies to overcrowd their ships. Evidence supported the U.S. attorney's charge of "rapacity" on the part of the steamship companies. In the first passenger suit against the Pacific Mail Steamship Company, a traveler in steerage class alleged that he had been given a fictitious berth number on the *Tennessee*'s voyage from Panama to San Francisco, forcing him to sleep on the deck. The company dismissed the incident as an honest mix-up, but another passenger testified that shortly before the steamer arrived in San Francisco, he saw the purser chalk the berths "so as to correspond with his tickets." [25]

Once Hoffman recognized passenger contracts as within the jurisdiction of an admiralty court, certain types of passenger suits were easily resolved under principles of contract. This followed because frequently the parties had explicitly agreed on the type of food or accommodation to be provided or the route to be traveled. Failure to transport travelers to the destination they had booked for, whether because the vessel was unseaworthy or had an accident or because the master stranded passengers or deliberately changed course, presented straightforward issues of fact establishing a breach of the contract.[26] Likewise, if a passenger had paid for a specific level of accommodation and food and had failed to receive it, steamship companies and other passenger vessels were held accountable in Hoffman's court.[27] But Hoffman went beyond the specific contractual nature of passenger travel (or what had been explicitly promised) to what could be implied in all passenger contracts. In the absence of explicit promises of food or accommodation, Hoffman eventually developed minimal standards to which he held shipowners.

At first, Hoffman determined breaches of contract based on egregious circumstances of travel. Conditions that forced 252 steerage passengers to share berths designed for 82, forced passengers to sleep on open decks or in passageways, forced 290 people to share two washbasins, or failed to provide minimal privacy and segregation of male and female passengers would simply "not be countenanced by the Court." Moreover, steerage passengers on Pacific steamers could recover for having to eat meals near where cattle had been slaughtered and with animal blood and dung underfoot.[28]

Unwholesome food, particularly during long sailing voyages, produced even more gruesome violations of what Hoffman regarded as minimally acceptable standards. One traveler from Australia in 1865 kept a daily journal of the food served to passengers during a ninety-two-day voyage to California. The ever-present salted beef or pork, whether for breakfast or dinner, constituted a monotonous diet that often bordered on the atrocious. A ship's carpenter on one voyage testified that as soon as he opened up a barrel of salt beef, it could be smelled "up on the deck" and that such meat, as well as rank, soft, and oily pork, was served to the passengers. Moreover, he noted that the biscuits "became full of weevils. He had to "take [them] into the galley to kill the insects. . . . The rice was at first filled with rat and mice dirt. It was . . . boiled altogether and unfit to be eaten." Yet, the captain, with five years' experience in carrying passengers, favorably compared the fare furnished on his vessel with that on other ships. The steward agreed with the captain's assessment and offered an explanation for the passengers' displeasure. "There was general complaint, nothing seemed to please. I attributed it to their never having been to sea and not knowing what ships provisions are." Still, their arguments fell on deaf ears when directed at Hoffman, who regarded such experiences as gross violations of the passenger contract.[29]

Extremely bad food or accommodations prompted Hoffman to decide for libellants, but he also developed standards of care that carriers owed to their passengers. In 1859 Hoffman sought to define the legitimate expectations of steamship passengers traveling first class. While conceding the inevitability of some discomfort and inconvenience, Hoffman held carriers to an objective standard of reasonable comfort. Distinguishing between reasonable comforts and unreasonable expectations, Hoffman dismissed the libel of two actresses, who had sailed to San Francisco from Australia, when the evidence established that they had kept unusual hours and made unreasonable demands of the stewards and waiters. On the other hand, pervasive overcrowding and hardships afforded "no justification for a continuance of the abuse." Hoffman held that the passenger's contract should "be construed to embrace a stipulation for such accommodations as . . . necessary to a reasonable degree of comfort, and to physical health and safety." Hoffman later extended his objective standard to all passengers, stating that even though those traveling first, second, or steerage class could not expect the same comforts, they were entitled to "such accommodations and conveniences as the exercise of reasonable care, and the adoption of reasonable means for securing them by the owners" could afford.[30]

Hoffman's development of implied standards for ship passengers would have been of little practical value to litigants if it had not been accompanied by certain procedural innovations. Early in his judgeship Hoffman permitted fellow passengers to consolidate their claims when suing carriers on a breach of the passenger contract. Allowing multiple joinder effectively provided a cause of action that would have been too expensive or troublesome for individual passengers to pursue, particularly given the high court costs in the early 1850s. Most of these early suits of numerous passengers suing under one libel were settled before they went to trial. A challenge to this practice first arose in 1858 in the case of *Downing* v. *The Schooner "Golden State."* Downing and thirty-eight other passengers alleged that because of overcrowding, the ship had turned back on a voyage from San Francisco to Victoria. The "great inconvenience and multiplication of costs" of separate lawsuits, Hoffman explained, "led the Court to sanction if not compel the practice of joining in one libel such suits when prosecuted by the same proctor [lawyer] and when the right of recovery" depended on the "same state of facts."[31]

Hoffman's procedural concession to aggrieved passengers, though novel, was not without analogical precedent. Hoffman correctly pointed out that admiralty law permitted seamen to consolidate their claims for wages in a single libel, but then sailors had always received special attention from the courts of admiralty. Admiralty treatise writers spoke approvingly of joinder when individual interests rested on a common cause of action, but only a few cases did not entail sailors as libellants. In 1857 one authority in the field confessed, "The extent to which different actions may be united in a single suit, and prosecuted together in the admiralty, is not very clearly defined by any settled rule of jurisprudence." In the final analysis, Hoffman drew on the equitable nature of admiralty and specifically justified his action by noting that unless passengers were allowed to join in one suit, their legal costs would exceed their recovery.[32]

In January 1859, Hoffman defended his approach in a libel joining over two hundred passengers against the steamship *Sonora* and vowed to continue his practice until reversed by a higher authority. Nonetheless, four months later, Hoffman abolished a rule of his court that routinely allowed multiple joinder in passenger suits and required separate filing unless libellants showed cause to the court. The rule change hardly deterred multiple joinder in passenger suits; Hoffman simply wanted to insure proper notice to defendants and agreement among the passengers. Indeed, soon after the rule change, Hoffman allowed the libel of a large number of passengers, some of whom had left San Francisco and were unavailable. A few of the passengers had been given power of attorney by the remainder to prosecute the suit, and Hoffman determined that sufficient evidence common to all the libellants had been presented to establish a breach of contract. As a result of Hoffman's allowing the procedure of multiple joinder, thousands instead of a handful of passengers were able to bring their grievances before the northern district court.[33]

Hoffman's assumption of jurisdiction over foreign ships also reveals the depth of his commitment to providing an effective national tribunal. American admiralty judges had discretion to assume such jurisdiction, but one authority in 1850 stated as a general proposition that courts of admiralty rarely, "except under very particular circumstances," entertained libels from foreign litigants. Foreign sailors suing for wages were the most frequent beneficiaries of this discretionary jurisdiction, though it extended, in theory, to situations where the "demands of justice" required it. In 1859 an admiralty treatise writer analyzed the assumption of jurisdiction over foreign ships as resting on one of two reasons, "either to protect . . . citizens, as where foreigners are discharged upon [U.S.] shores, or on account of the comity of nations."[34]

Normally Hoffman was reluctant to exercise jurisdiction over foreign ships, but he did so whenever it appeared that libellants had no other effective remedy. If the resolution of a grievance might await the return to the home port, Hoffman declined to accept jurisdiction. But when, for instance, Indian seamen who shipped from Calcutta were apparently treated with "singular cruelty" by being fed unwholesome rice and rotten fish, Hoffman had little hesitation in hearing their claims for damages. Passenger cases, in particular, prompted Hoffman to exercise jurisdiction over foreign ships, for reasons he made clear early in his tenure.[35]

In 1851, French immigrants who had arrived in San Francisco from Le Havre on board the ship *Henri* filed a libel for breach of passenger contract. The French consul in San Francisco vigorously protested that Hoffman should not accept *in rem* jurisdiction. The assent of the French consul would not have affected the issue of jurisdiction—that was a matter within Hoffman's discretion as an admiralty judge. But the consul's protest constituted

the declaration of the French government that it had no interest in Hoffman's assuming jurisdiction in the present case, precluding Hoffman from
basing jurisdiction on principles of comity. Neither could Hoffman justify
taking jurisdiction on the grounds of protecting American citizens.[36]

Nonetheless, Hoffman did assume jurisdiction. Hoffman said he preferred not to hear the case at all, since he was neither "hungry after jurisdiction" nor "anxious to increase the already severe labors" of his office. But
in explaining why he would hear the case, Hoffman touched on concerns
that guided his adjudication of passenger cases.

> The court cannot be insensible to the particular circumstances which
> are directing a constant stream of immigration to this country. The
> eagerness felt by large classes in foreign countries to reap the golden
> reward that is supposed to await their labors here is well calculated to
> stimulate cupidity and produce abuses in passenger ships. Bound to a
> remote and perhaps in his opinion lawless country the master of such a
> vessel may permit infractions of his contract, or be guilty of abuses
> which he would hardly venture upon were he less secure of impunity.
> To say to all who have thus been injured that being foreigners justice is
> not for them and it must be sought in the country they have left perhaps
> forever, and at a distance of thousands of miles is practically to deny it
> altogether and to establish a rule injurious to Commerce and inconsis-
> tent with sound policy.

Ultimately Hoffman proclaimed, "It is my duty sitting in a national tribunal
to administer justice to all who seek it except where controlling considerations call upon me to forbear." In the case of foreign ships, "controlling
considerations" essentially meant the existence of an alternative forum. On
the strength of his decision and reasoning in the *Fayet* v. *Henri* case, Hoffman proceeded to entertain a substantial number of passenger cases against
foreign ships for the next three decades.[37]

The same desire to "administer justice to all who seek it" also underlay
Hoffman's extraordinarily broad construction of the passenger contract.
Hoffman drew guidance from Justice Story for the basis of breaches of passenger contracts, even as he went considerably beyond his teacher in providing procedural remedies. In 1823 Story had delivered a circuit court opinion
that became the principal statement of rights for seaborne passengers under
contracts of passage until Hoffman began rendering his decisions in the

1850s. In *Chamberlain* v. *Chandler* (1823), a family sought damages from a ship captain for "continued wanton cruelty, and ill treatment." Although the captain had apparently struck the libellants, Story went out of his way to hold that even conduct that did not amount to assault and battery came within admiralty jurisdiction. Story declared that a passenger contract was "not for mere ship room, and personal existence, on board; but for reasonable food, comforts, necessaries, and kindness." Moreover, Story addressed the issue of proper conduct around women. "[The contract] includes an implied stipulation against obscenity, that immodesty of approach, which borders on lasciviousness, and against that wanton disregard of the feelings, which aggravates every evil, and endeavors by the excitement of terror, and cool malignancy of conduct, to inflict torture upon susceptible minds." Yet, recovery for such conduct, according to Story, would be permitted only if "the whole course of conduct" was "oppressive and malicious," and if "habitual immodesty" was accompanied by "habitual cruelty." Most important, Story's decision suggested that damages for assaults, emotional upsets, or other torts constituting a breach of passenger contract would be limited to *in personam* suits.[38]

Hoffman drew from the language of Story's opinion to supplement his own conception of what actions by the captain and crew constituted a breach of the passenger contract. But Hoffman significantly departed from Story in giving emotionally or physically injured passengers an effective means of recovering damages. From the start of his tenure Hoffman entertained *in rem* passenger suits alleging negligence as a reason for the libellants' physical injuries. In 1851, a passenger on the steamer *North America* badly broke his leg when he fell through a hatchway left open in an unlit area of the ship. Hoffman allowed the libellant to sue the ship over the objections of the ship's lawyers, who argued that the libellant should not be allowed to sue *in rem* on a cause of action that constituted a tort rather than a contract action. As an admiralty court, Hoffman felt free to reject "the nice and technical distinctions prevailing at common law between *case* against a carrier for his breach of duty under the custom of the realm and *assumpsit* for his breach of contract." In the present case, justice, in Hoffman's view, would be obstructed by "a rigid adherence to technical rules." Declaring it irrelevant whether the action arose in tort or in contract, Hoffman did take pains to characterize the suit as a "breach of the contract to carry safely—a promise implied by the law on the part of the carrier of passengers." At the time of this decision, admiralty treatises acknowledged the potential tort liability faced by a master who disregarded his high duty as a carrier of passengers, but no precedents existed for an *in rem* as opposed to an *in personam* suit.[39]

Hoffman explicitly linked his decision to permit an *in rem* suit with his commitment to offer effective relief to passengers arriving at the isolated West Coast.

> Under the circumstances of this state it is of peculiar importance that passengers should have a prompt and effective remedy for the breaches of contract entered into with them. The length of the voyage, the eagerness to reach California and the large profits derived from the transportation of passengers are well calculated to beget recklessness as the mode of fulfilling passenger contracts; and were the passenger left to seek his remedy against a master without pecuniary responsibility it might open the door to grave if not dangerous abuses.

By looking through form to substance, Hoffman managed to provide "a prompt and effective remedy." Hoffman held the owners of the *North America* liable for over $4,000 in damages to the injured passenger, compensating him for medical expenses, loss of work, and pain and suffering.[40]

Another type of negligence for which Hoffman permitted *in rem* suits were boiler accidents on steamships. An explosion on the steamer *New World* in 1851, during a trip from Sacramento to San Francisco, killed two passengers, injured more than a dozen others, and generated two libels by passengers who suffered severe injuries. The owners of the steamboat asserted that the accident was unavoidable and could not have been anticipated even by "the most consummate skill and carefulness." By the time of Hoffman's tenure, the gruesome death toll caused by boiler explosions had undermined congressional and judicial support for such arguments. Hoffman rejected the defendant's answer, being "persuaded that the progress of science and mechanical skill" had made it "possible to provide against either the occurrence, or the fatal effect of such accidents." Hoffman referred to the high standard of care that passenger carriers were held to and noted that, in any event, a federal statute made injury due to boiler explosions *prima facie* evidence of negligence. Not only did the defendant fail to disprove negligence, but the evidence suggested that a race between the *New World* and another steamer had preceded the explosion.[41]

The existence of a federal statute governing the consequences of boiler explosions made it easier for Hoffman to decide as he did in the *Reynolds* v. *New World* case. Nonetheless, the Supreme Court's affirmation of his decision marked the first time it had heard an appeal based on a passenger contract. Doctrinally more difficult were the passenger cases involving intentional harm inflicted by the captain or his crew. Ironically, in Hoffman's court, passenger cases involving negligence were far fewer than those involving intentional harm. In offering relief for intentionally inflicted injuries, Hoffman once again expanded the passenger contract.[42]

Hoffman's reaction to the insults and obscenities often suffered by passengers encouraged him to develop his own version of an implied agreement of proper treatment, which he made actionable by libels *in rem*. Late in 1852, Hoffman dealt squarely with the liability of shipowners to passengers for the rude and discourteous behavior of the captain and his crew. A dozen passengers libelled the ship *John Baring* after an eight-month voyage from New York to San Francisco. In addition to deficient food and accommodations, they alleged emotional distress due to the master's conduct. William Barber, the attorney for the *John Baring*, stated the issue simply: "How far is a ship responsible for the willful torts of the master?" Barber sought to limit the owner's contract with passengers to a swift and safe passage with adequate provisions. "If the master abuses the passengers it is his own act." The shipowners therefore argued that the passenger contract did not guarantee that passengers should "receive courteous treatment and be secured an immunity from outrages upon their feelings."[43]

Hoffman acknowledged the common-law principle that the employer was liable only for the negligence and not the intentional harm committed by employees in the course of the employer's business. Yet Hoffman questioned whether such a distinction was "satisfactory." He reasoned, "If a master is responsible for the character of his servant as respects skill and attention, it would seem no greater hardship upon him to hold him responsible for the character of the servant as respects malice and intentional wrong." Hoffman found the distinction a particularly weak one in the maritime context, given the captain's supreme authority aboard a ship. From the perspective of passengers, it mattered little whether the injury had "arisen from the negligence and unskillfulness of the master" rendering "him incapable of discharging his duties or from his violence and brutality" betraying "a moral incompetence equally unfitting him for his station." For these reasons, Hoffman believed that the libel could be sustained on the ground of tort alone, but he cited Story's opinion in *Chamberlain* v. *Chandler* for the proposition that a captain had implied duties under passenger contracts.[44]

Hoffman also felt sustained in his position by "every consideration of reason and policy" and declared that passenger contracts implicitly provided for the passengers' "moral requirements." "These are with respect to females, civility, decency and exemption from brutal, cruel or obscene conduct." Since shipowners were moving people, not cattle, they had to take into account "moral injuries." Thus, in the *John Baring* case, Hoffman held that if the allegations of the libellants were sustained, they constituted breaches of contract for which the ship's owners were responsible.[45] Likewise, when a captain used language and acted in ways "grossly indecorous towards any female" or even behaved in a manner "calculated to shock the modesty and wound the susceptibilities of a virtuous woman," he and the owners of the ship were liable in the northern district for the mental distress suffered by women passengers.[46]

In addition to emotional distress, Hoffman also allowed *in rem* passenger suits for physical assaults by the captain or his crew by construing the passenger contract even more broadly than he had already. In achieving this result, Hoffman had two chief obstacles to overcome. The first entailed the legal principle that employers should not be held liable for harm intentionally inflicted by their employees. The second involved a clear prohibition in the rules promulgated by the U.S. Supreme Court to govern procedure in admiralty courts. One rule provided that actions for assault and battery in admiralty could be brought only *in personam*.[47]

Despite these formidable obstacles, Hoffman heard *in rem* suits for assaults on passengers as early as 1853, but did not articulate his reasons justifying this practice until three years later. In 1856, two common seamen traveling as passengers on the Pacific Mail Steamship Company's *Golden Gate* had gotten into an argument with several of the ship's officers. During the dispute, one of the seamen was hit over the head with a capstan bar, pummeled by the captain, and then thrown down a hatchway. Even though the libellant may have been drunk and disorderly, Hoffman found the treatment inexcusable and clearly beyond the captain's authority to maintain good order and discipline on board ship.[48]

Hoffman justified entertaining an *in rem* suit for the assault and battery by characterizing the physical assault as merely the "gravamen," or gist, of the breach of contract. As with the cases concerning food and accommodation, Hoffman found an implied stipulation in passenger contracts. If denial of facilities, food, and the liberty of the deck constituted a breach, Hoffman asked, "Is it less of a breach if the master deprives him of them by driving him from the table or deck by violence or *insults*, or wantonly and maliciously places him in confinement?" The implied stipulation in passenger contracts simply meant "that the authority given to the master and officers" should not "be abused."[49]

The same reason that justified the implied stipulation in passenger contracts—the absolute power a captain wielded over his passengers—justified holding the owners liable for the captain's and his officers' actions. In *Place v. Steamship "Golden Gate"* (1856), Hoffman reasoned that by investing wide powers in their agents, the owners were obligated "to *treat passengers properly*" and were liable *in rem* for breaches of that duty. "To the passenger it affords the *only substantial* remedy—for a suit *in personam* against the master or the mates is in most cases fruitless." Given the nature and volume of travel to California, Hoffman considered it

> of the utmost importance when their safety, their health, and their comfort depend so entirely upon the manner in which the carrier performs his contract, to hold any acts of his agent in the course of his duties, by which passengers are injured, substantial breaches of the contract and this whether the passenger be deprived of suitable food and accommodation or be subjected to ill usage by blows and false imprisonment or by habitual *obscenity*, insult and opposition.[50]

Although Hoffman felt justified in entertaining an *in rem* suit, not everyone was persuaded by his reasoning, including the circuit judge, Matthew Hall McAllister, who heard the case on appeal. McAllister's principal concern was the lack of any judicial precedent for Hoffman's willingness to hold shipowners liable for clearly malicious and personally motivated attacks on passengers by a captain. Even though not happy with Hoffman's circumvention of the admiralty rule against *in rem* suits for assault and battery cases, McAllister reluctantly acquiesced to Hoffman's assertion of jurisdiction. McAllister conceded that the admiralty treatise writer Erastus C. Benedict supported Hoffman's position through his interpretation of the Supreme Court admiralty rule in question. McAllister did not find Benedict's interpretation "very satisfying." But he added, "As it has been published for some time, and has received no contradiction from any court or textwriter, I shall act upon it for the present to the extent this case goes." Although affirming the decision, McAllister rejected Hoffman's imposition of punitive damages on the shipowners as a means of inducing them to monitor more closely the behavior of their employees. Uncertain about the decision, McAllister tried, without success, to get the parties to appeal the case to the Supreme Court. Consequently, as late as the 1880s, Hoffman continued to provide a forum for passengers who experienced physical interference by members of the crew.[51]

Hoffman's passenger cases reflect his understanding of what constituted the proper treatment of ship passengers. Hoffman was a gentleman, and his sensibilities were offended by the crude conditions and practices that prevailed during voyages to California. Indeed, he had firsthand experience with such travel; his own passage to San Francisco had been accompanied with discomfort and illness. Though women invoked Hoffman's Victorian protectiveness, in the end all passengers, whether men or women or whether traveling first class or steerage, became objects of Hoffman's concern. The lack of acceptable food and accommodations, the deprivation of minimal privacy, and the infliction of emotional and physical brutality created an intolerable situation that prompted Hoffman to act. What had begun as a disagreeable experience—his voyage to San Francisco—became, with his judgeship and the task of hearing passenger grievances, a systematic effort to police an entire industry.[52]

Faced with the urgency to act, Hoffman developed remedies that made his court an effective forum for passengers who had suffered or had been injured during their voyages to California. The development of such remedies was directly linked to Hoffman's understanding of his role as a federal judge. In essence, that role, in his words, was "to administer justice to all who seek it." Confronted with litigants who could find relief only at his hands, Hoffman creatively expanded the grounds for bringing an *in rem* suit on a breach of passenger contract. He fully realized that if passengers could not sue *in rem* and join their claims in one suit, they were essentially denied relief. Likewise, passengers on foreign vessels who experienced behavior that breached their contract of passage were without help unless Hoffman exercised his discretion in assuming jurisdiction over such suits.

In assuming jurisdiction in a way that provided effective relief for citizens as well as foreigners, Hoffman took it on himself to prevent "the repetition of abuses" against "the rights of passengers." His goal was not merely to redress damages suffered by those passengers who brought suit in his court, but also to send shipowners a message that would improve the conditions of travel for all passengers. Punitive damages as well as ordinary damages helped send a message to shipowners. So did upholding the validity of a loan secured against the ship and taken out by a captain to buy passage to San Francisco on another vessel for some of his overcrowded passengers. Hoffman recognized "the novelty and difficulty" of the issue, since the so-called bottomery bonds were normally authorized for emergencies to save the ship. But Hoffman's court would not "shut its eyes to the moral compulsion under which the master acted." Moreover, taking the loan avoided "the infliction of great suffering upon the passengers, or else of a grievous injury to them by a flagrant violation of their contract," and that justified imposing the heavy loss on "those who ought in justice" to have borne it. Thus, the shipowners were financially obligated by a captain who sought, on his own initiative, to avoid breaching the passenger contract.[53]

The practicing bar also responded to Hoffman's attempt to improve the treatment of passengers. In 1870, an attorney who sought damages for the unseemly behavior of a captain in the presence of a woman passenger and her fourteen-year-old daughter conceded that the captain might not have known better but argued that he "should be taught better." "He was a low, vulgar, coarse man—the case doesn't call for vindictive [punitive] damages but passengers should be protected against arrogance and indecency." Hoffman agreed and awarded the libellant $150 plus costs.[54]

The boldness of Hoffman's decisions was the result of having to settle many of the passenger complaints—in effect insuring that his message about passenger treatment came through unequivocally. Whether Hoffman's judicial monitoring of the conditions of travel on the high seas really improved matters is not clear. Of greater interest here is why Hoffman took it on himself to play such a role. It seems probable that Hoffman's status as the only federal judicial authority on the scene made a difference. Hoffman was acutely aware that if he could not find some means to give relief to litigants, then for all intents and purposes they would get no relief. Hoffman could not defer to his judicial superiors for judgment in difficult or unprecedented situations until later, in 1855, with Circuit Judge McAllister's appointment, and really not until 1863, when Stephen J. Field became the circuit justice and representative of the Supreme Court in California. In the most critical period of resolving passenger cases, Hoffman acted as a judge without a realistic option of passing such difficult decisions on to those above him. In the early 1850s, waiting for guidance from higher judicial authority essentially constituted an abdication of judicial responsibility—at least in Hoffman's mind. This attitude and the plight of passengers overcame Hoffman's later tendency to defer to higher judicial authority. In the passenger cases, Hoffman exhibited a degree of judicial innovation and boldness that he would rarely match in subsequent years.

As a district court judge, Hoffman limited his scrutiny of the transportation industry to shipping. He heard virtually no cases directly involving the primary transportation industry in nineteenth-century California: the railroads. Admiralty jurisdiction clearly fell within his purview, but cases dealing with railroads did not, unless federal statutes formed the basis of a federal claim and the amounts in controversy did not send the matter jurisdictionally to the circuit court. Thus, given the jurisdiction of the district court, Hoffman's cases reflect only a segment of cases representing California's politics and economic growth. Nonetheless, an analysis of Hoffman's adjudication of commercial interests is valuable for creating another, different perspective on the role of a nineteenth-century court concerning business interests.[55]

Hoffman's admiralty court gave substantial relief to passengers, but businessmen and merchants made most frequent use of the court as an important commercial tribunal. Despite aggressively using his judicial discretion to hold shipowners liable for maltreatment of passengers, Hoffman received his strongest support from San Francisco's shipping interests and business community. Moreover, his reaction to the vigilance committees of the 1850s widely offended the strong commercial supporters of the extralegal movements. Nonetheless, from the start of Hoffman's tenure until his death, through times of crisis that threatened his judgeship and subjected him to public criticism, the business community repeatedly came to his assistance. Likewise, when Hoffman sought support for legislation to increase his salary or enhance the operation of his court, he invariably received help from San Francisco's business leaders. The secret of Hoffman's success with the business community lay in the predictability of his decisions, his judicial creativity in responding to the tumultuous conditions of commerce in California, and his conscientiousness as a trier of fact. Especially in the unusual commercial climate of San Francisco in the 1850s, local businessmen approved of Hoffman's combination of judicial orthodoxy and innovation.[56]

High risk and uncertainty characterized business activity in San Francisco during the 1850s. Hoffman did not exaggerate when he compared doing business in the city to playing a lottery. Cycles of oversupply of goods, the lack of commercial information, recurring fires, and a shortage of money and capital all contributed to the contemporary sense that the local economy was out of control. To most businessmen, San Francisco seemed a place where "luck alone ruled [one's] destiny, the requirements to success elsewhere . . . had little to do with it." These impressions were substantiated by the high rate of business failures. Indeed, in the decade of 1850–60, from one-half to two-thirds of all San Francisco merchants went bankrupt.[57]

The uncertainty of the local marketplace merely heightened a natural desire for predictability in business litigation. The historian Tony Freyer has shown that the federal circuit courts during the nineteenth century offered American business a preferred alternative to "the uncertainties of the tangled process of the states." Indeed, Hoffman's judgeship and the commercial nature of his admiralty docket suggest that the federal judiciary may have had an even greater effect on nineteenth-century American economic development. Frustrated by their inability to plan with any certainty, merchants found Hoffman's predictability especially welcome. Hoffman believed in precedent and sought to resolve disputes in accordance with traditional legal rules and principles. Some nineteenth-century judges, like Charles Doe of the New Hampshire Supreme Court, rejected the value of precedent and subsequently incurred the wrath of litigants dismayed at his unpredictability. But Hoffman was no Doe. Hoffman took precedent seriously even as he showed his capacity for judicial creativity when orthodox case law left legitimate claims without effective means of relief.[58]

Hoffman invariably began his legal analysis with the status quo: the existing case law and doctrine. He demonstrated his conscientiousness as well as his legal ability by marshaling a wide range of relevant legal authorities. His research typically ranged from American and English case law to admiralty treatises, commentaries, and compilations of European as well as American origin. Hoffman consulted this breadth of sources from the start of his judgeship. Apart from showing that Hoffman could and did draw on legal sources similar to those used by district court judges on the East Coast, the legal citations demonstrated that Hoffman sought to reach decisions resting on earlier decisions. Even without his access to law books, Hoffman would still have retained and relied on the legal culture he had brought with him from New York. The books, however, allowed him to craft opinions crammed with research and learning, opinions that sent a message to the business community: Hoffman would resolve disputes like a well-trained lawyer within the common-law tradition. Thus, to the extent that Hoffman blazed new paths in the law, he could be trusted to do so with respect for past practices.[59]

Hoffman's first passenger case illustrated how he could exercise judicial discretion to act innovatively and yet assuage the business community's fears that he was departing from a traditional calculation of damages. In 1851 Hoffman held the Pacific Mail Steamship Company liable because its captain had stranded passengers at Mazatlán during a voyage from Panama to San Francisco. The passengers sought their expenses at Mazatlán and the cost of transportation to San Francisco, as well as damages for their time lost. In addition, one libellant claimed the loss of money left in his luggage on board the steamer. Hoffman easily decided that the libellants were entitled to passage money to San Francisco and expenses in Mazatlán, since such costs were "natural and proximate consequences of the breach of contract." Profits lost because of being set ashore, however, involved "too many contingencies." Hoffman also rejected the claim for money lost in baggage, based on the established principle that the liability of a common carrier did not extend beyond the normal baggage of travelers. "To hold the Steamship Companies liable for all the treasure which passengers may choose to place in their trunks without paying freight upon it or even disclosing its existence would subject them to a dangerous and uncertain responsibility." Thus, while Hoffman assumed *in rem* jurisdiction over breach of passenger contracts, he took an orthodox approach in assessing damages in such suits.[60]

Shipowners, of course, were hardly pleased with their liability under the passenger contract as developed by Hoffman. The damage awards and the publicity they generated were not good for business, but Hoffman's consistency was appreciated. Although Hoffman imposed new liability on shipowners, his innovations were logical extensions—if not decisions at the forefront—of the law dealing with the duties that carriers owed their passengers. As a result, shipowners could plan to avoid or ameliorate anticipated losses. They could instruct captains about the importance of maintaining standards of treatment of passengers, and they could raise ticket prices to offset losses resulting from lawsuits.

Hoffman's development of guidelines for the allocation of commercial losses also enhanced his reputation with the business community. In dealing with unique problems presented by doing business in San Francisco, Hoffman showed common sense and commercial understanding. Particularly in the context of fluctuating prices and the risks involved in shipping goods to California, Hoffman's early commercial decisions provided a much-needed measure of stability. Though less dramatic than his passenger cases, the commercial litigation in Hoffman's admiralty docket also reveals his judicial creativity.

During the 1850s, Hoffman rendered several key decisions that allocated loss and developed measures of damage between consignees (receivers) of goods and shippers (those who transported goods). These suits, based on a breach of contract of affreightment, were common to other admiralty courts at the time, but Hoffman's resolution of them showed regional concessions prompted by circumstances in California. The traditional rule held common carriers strictly liable for all damage to goods except that caused by "the act of God, or by the public enemy." In the case of carriers by water, the liability of the shipper usually excluded those losses resulting from the "perils of the sea"—"those natural perils and operations of the elements" that occurred "without the intervention of human agency" and that "the prudence of man" could not foresee, "nor his strength resist." Still, the routes of transportation to San Francisco raised novel questions about whether certain forms of damage fell within "perils of the sea." Furthermore, even if the shippers' liability could be established, the issue remained of how to measure the consignees' damage, given San Francisco's fluctuating market.[61]

In measuring damages, Hoffman demonstrated a flexibility that took into account the economic climate of San Francisco. In 1851 Hoffman dealt with a case in which a shipper had failed to make a timely delivery from Boston to Sacramento because of the ship's unseaworthiness. Given rapid shifts in prices, Hoffman held that the consignee deserved damages measured by the value the goods would have had at Sacramento at the time they were supposed to have arrived. Hoffman imposed an even more accommodating measure of damages one year later in a case involving the loss of a steamship boiler during shipment. Hoffman toyed with the idea of giving the traditional measure of damages—the value of goods at the point of delivery minus freight charges. But expert testimony suggested that the price of a boiler depended on whether a steamship in San Francisco needed one at the time. Given this contingency, Hoffman decided that the best estimate of damages was the cost of building such a boiler in San Francisco. Both these decisions, then, took some of the risk out of the "lottery" of importing goods to the state, a fact San Francisco merchants could hardly fail to appreciate.[62]

Hoffman was not, however, one-sided in recognizing the concerns and problems faced by those involved in the shipping business. Shippers, as well as consignees, received Hoffman's attention. One recurring problem in shipping goods around Cape Horn was damage caused by "sweating." Humidity, brought on by swings in temperatures in the cargo hold on a long voyage, often caused damage. Thus, it became critical to know whether such damage was considered a natural "peril of the sea." In 1852 Hoffman found sweating to be incident to all ships traveling around Cape Horn. Since extraordinary care could not have prevented the condition, Hoffman placed the risks of such damage on the consignee. Three years later the general principle came into question when clipper ships began experimenting with ventilation to reduce cargo sweat. Testimony on the system of ventilation failed to convince Hoffman that it effectively reduced sweating, and therefore the consignee still bore the loss. Nonetheless, Hoffman noted that if a "generally recognized and adopted" means of preventing moisture came to light in the future, failure to use it would constitute negligence and would shift the risk of loss onto the shipper.[63]

In addition to establishing guidelines for the adjustment of losses suffered in the transport of goods to San Francisco, Hoffman also dealt with common problems in the delivery of goods. In 1851 an importing firm had chartered a vessel to bring a cargo of coal from Liverpool to San Francisco. On arrival the ship began unloading the cargo, but its agents suspended delivery after hearing a rumor that the firm was about to fail, resuming delivery only when the rumor proved unfounded. In the interim the price of coal declined, and Hoffman held the shipowners responsible for the difference in the market value of the cargo. Hoffman acknowledged that the decision had been "a hard one" for the shipowners. Nonetheless, in relying on rumor, they had assumed the risk if they guessed incorrectly. With little accurate information and with merchants at the mercy of speculative talk, Hoffman's decision made much commercial sense.[64]

In general, Hoffman's business decisions reflected his desire to understand the context of commercial litigation. In resolving commercial disputes, he sought, in his words, "to learn from merchants . . . the course of business and the general usage" so that he might judicially validate "established customs" or "the tacit understanding" of the business community. Taking this interest did not entail abdicating his responsibility to decide issues based on applicable law. Rather, he simply recognized that it was essential to consider San Francisco's unique circumstances in reaching reasonable solutions to recurring business conflicts. For example, when a consignee libelled a ship for an overpayment of freight, Hoffman rejected the argument that the consignee could bring only a common-law action against the individuals who had accepted payment. Hoffman permitted the libellant to sue *in rem* because if he had been "left to enforce his rights against distant owners, or perhaps an irresponsible [impecunious] master," the "practical effect" would have been to "break up a convenient usage of trade" then readily acquiesced in.[65]

Hoffman also understood that, above all, merchants sought to avoid litigation and to pursue business. Adverse rulings were palatable if they were consistent and predictable. More important was the fact that recurring conflicts were guided by commercial practices that had legal sanction. Hoffman recognized that out-of-court settlements in accordance with general business practices were of "the utmost importance to commerce." In the business uncertainty of the 1850s, Hoffman provided a welcome stability in the legal consequences of commercial transactions that fell within the jurisdiction of his court. The city's businessmen were not apt to forget that fact.[66]

On one occasion Hoffman even exceeded his court's jurisdiction in a claim of general average contribution to accommodate the needs of local commerce. The principle of general average, under which the owner of property that is sacrificed to save a ship or its cargo is compensated by a contribution from the property saved, had ancient roots in general maritime law. Despite the undoubted maritime nature of the general average principle, the English court of admiralty did not take jurisdiction over such cases. In 1849 the U.S. Supreme Court declined to assume *in personam* jurisdiction over a general average claim in *Cutler* v. *Rae* (1849) and in passing suggested that *in rem* suits would likewise be beyond American admiralty jurisdiction.[67]

In 1851 Hoffman followed *Cutler* v. *Rae* and dismissed a libel *in personam* for general average. Nonetheless, Hoffman prefaced his opinion by declaring, "If this Court were at liberty to disregard any decision of the Supreme Court on a point directly before it, I should be tempted to do so in this case." Hoffman found it "difficult to conceive of a subject more peculiarly maritime" and noted that general average had been considered a part of the maritime law—"from the time of the Rhodian laws"—virtually everywhere except England. Hoffman felt that if the Supreme Court declined jurisdiction over such cases, it "would almost satisfy the bigotry of Lord Coke." He wished to see his admiralty court meet the needs of seaborne commerce without the fetters with which the English common law had sought to bind admiralty. In Hoffman's view, "the interests of commerce" required a maritime tribunal to hear general average cases. Indeed, Hoffman's convictions led him to hear an *in rem* suit for general average in 1855, in the face of the Supreme Court's 1849 decision and two years before the Supreme Court reversed itself and accepted jurisdiction over general average cases.[68]

The support, respect, and appreciation Hoffman received from the business community stemmed as much from his manner of handling admiralty cases as it did from the decisions he rendered. From his earliest cases, Hoffman sought to establish his legal reputation by writing erudite opinions. Most of Hoffman's citations to Roman and civil law were, as they apparently were for Hoffman's teacher Joseph Story, "superfluous to his argument" and "merely pleasant excursions into esoteric learning." Nonetheless, citations left the impression that opinions were the product of deep learning, especially when coupled with exhaustive analysis. In an 1856 opinion, for example, Hoffman used twenty-four pages to elaborately analyze issues and case law before dismissing the libel for lack of jurisdiction. Hoffman also hoped to establish his reputation as a learned judge by trying (initially unsuccessfully) to have his opinions published.[69]

Although Hoffman's erudition may have impressed some lawyers and businessmen, he undoubtedly won their support by insisting that his court be true to the traditional de-emphasis of procedure in admiralty, by hearing the testimony of witnesses and the arguments of counsel with patience, by sifting and weighing evidence and arguments with extraordinary care, and by exhibiting a staunch judicial independence. Hoffman emphasized that admiralty courts should be "governed by equitable principles" and called them "the courts of chancery for the sea."[70]

Hoffman repeatedly admonished lawyers who objected to the inelegant pleading of their adversaries that the "nice and technical rules" of common law did not hold sway in his admiralty court. Hoffman's response to one lawyer and close friend, James T. Boyd, is instructive. Boyd had filed extensive exceptions to a libel on the grounds that it failed to provide the full Christian names of the libellants. Hoffman admitted that under the "somewhat antiquated rules of the common law," a mistake in the Christian names, as opposed to surnames, constituted a fatal defect to a legal instrument. Nonetheless, Hoffman argued that Boyd's exceptions lost "sight of the practical object intended to be obtained—viz the determination and identification of the party in the most certain manner." Reflecting his position that admiralty should be free of common-law constraints, Hoffman rejected the dead hand of "antiquated" procedure.[71]

Despite the large amount of business before his court, notably in the first decade of its existence, Hoffman took the time to insure that litigants had their day in court. On those occasions when the volume of business forced him to rush, he apologized for summarizing his conclusions and not writing more elaborate opinions. When cases came to trial, however, Hoffman diligently took notes of the testimony of witnesses and the arguments of lawyers. Hoffman's admiralty case files show that he routinely took notes of testimony in the first person, in effect creating a transcript of the evidence presented in court. In commercial cases, these notes ranged in length from just a few pages to several hundred pages. The thousands upon thousands of pages of such notes that Hoffman took during his tenure show his attention to detail. Even after the mid-1870s, when stenographers were increasingly used to record court testimony, Hoffman still took notes.[72]

Not only did Hoffman scrupulously record the testimony taken in his court, but he also conscientiously sifted through his notes and the often voluminous depositions before arriving at a determination of the facts. Perhaps in no other type of case was this process of sifting and weighing evidence as pronounced as in ship collision cases. Even though litigation before Hoffman's court inevitably entailed a conflict of evidence, normally one side or the other exhibited a preponderance of credible testimony—in Hoffman's eyes—to establish the facts. Collision cases, however, tended to present evenly balanced testimony, with two diametrically opposite accounts of events. In sorting out the evidence in these cases, Hoffman displayed his diligence as a finder of fact.[73]

Hoffman's opinions show his invariably detailed appraisal of evidence, but they also demonstrate his careful consideration of the assertions and arguments advanced by the lawyers appearing before him. Initially, at least, the extended factual discussions in his opinions stemmed from a desire not to slight the practicing bar. Out of deference and politeness to attorneys—many older and more accomplished than he—Hoffman addressed their points in depth. In time, this exhaustive response became his custom. His conscientious response to the claims of merchants and their lawyers accorded with the treatment that a proud, sensitive gentleman like Hoffman would himself have expected at the bar.[74]

Hoffman's early efforts and conduct paid off; the perception emerged that although the northern district's judge had shortcomings, he was at least hardworking and honest. These traits contributed to the support Hoffman received from the business community, even when he rendered decisions they strongly disliked. Before his appointment, Hoffman had shown his disapproval of the Vigilance Committee of 1851—a popularly supported extralegal movement that took law into its own hands in protest against a perceived laxness in the prosecution of criminal activity in the city. Moreover, he opposed the similarly motivated but even more powerful Vigilance Committee of 1856 in a series of admiralty actions brought by victims of the committee.

During and especially after the extralegal activities in 1856, supporters of the vigilance movement made strenuous efforts to portray the movement as a necessary and justified expression of popular sovereignty. A libel directed at the activities of the 1856 committee struck at the most vulnerable aspect of the history of the movement that its defenders were busily creating: the extralegal nature of the proceedings. Indeed, the success of this validation was what prompted a victim of the committee to sue in Hoffman's court after it became clear that the state courts would not entertain such a suit, much less would a jury convict a defendant for working with the committee. In fact, Hoffman not only accepted jurisdiction but imposed substantial damages that irritated and embarrassed those who sought to justify the committee's activities.

In March 1858, *Martin Gallagher* v. *James Smith, Master of the Barque "Yankee"* was filed in Hoffman's court. Gallagher, a night watchman at the customshouse, had been seized by the committee and found guilty, according to the testimony of one of the "judges" who had tried him, of ballot stuffing, of riotous behavior, and of being a "disorderly character—a pest to society, and a nuisance." Sentenced to banishment and threatened with

death if he ever returned to San Francisco, Gallagher found himself, at
midnight on June 5, 1856, in irons. He was placed aboard a small steam tug,
which headed out to sea. Outside the Golden Gate and still under guard,
Gallagher was transferred, by prearrangement, to the barque *Yankee* and
shipped to Hawaii. In Honolulu, with nothing but the clothes on his back,
he was put ashore, "a stranger in a strange foreign place." Six months later,
Gallagher made his way back to California, but the stigma attached to him
and fear of reprisals drove him out of San Francisco, and he returned to the
city only early in 1858. Gallagher's lawyer sought $25,000 from the master
of the barque *Yankee* for conspiring with the vigilance committee in effecting
the banishment. The *Alta California* warned, "One by one these miscreants
are returning to the city." The paper advised Gallagher and other victims of
the committee "to let lawing alone, eschew political matters and attend to
some regular work to earn an honest living."[75]

Hoffman rejected the defendant's argument that under California law
Gallagher had lost his cause of action by failing to file within one year. Given
the circumstances of the banishment and the hostility of state courts, Gallagher could not be assumed to have abandoned his claim. Hoffman also
rejected a challenge to his jurisdiction. He conceded that as a court of admiralty, he had no cognizance over Gallagher's seizure and confinement on
land. Nonetheless, he asserted jurisdiction over Gallagher's transportation
to and abandonment in Hawaii. Indeed, Hoffman linked his assumption of
jurisdiction in the case with his duty as a federal judge.

> So long as our country remains under the dominion of law, and so long
> as the great constitutional provisions which secure the citizen his life,
> liberty, and his property until deprived of them by due process of law,
> are prized by the American people, and are enforced by the courts, the
> deportation of a citizen to a foreign country in an American ship, com-
> manded by an American master, in pursuance or execution of a sen-
> tence of an illegal and self-constituted body of men, must remain a
> marine tort of a most flagrant character.[76]

Hoffman acknowledged that he could not redress the greatest injuries that
Gallagher had sustained, namely his seizure, disgrace, and damaged reputation. Nonetheless, of those acts within his jurisdiction, Hoffman intended
to make an example by imposing punitive damages of $3,000 in addition to
Gallagher's expenses. "It is of the first importance that masters and agents

of ships should learn, that whatever be the power that in moments of popular excitement, illegal bodies of men may usurp . . . yet on American vessels on the high seas the laws of the United States are still supreme." [77]

Hoffman's decision provoked a storm of criticism. San Francisco newspapers called the opinion "absurd and prejudicial," "a piece of arrant injustice," and "a mischievous precedent." Both the *Alta California* and the *San Francisco Bulletin* accused Hoffman of going "out of his way to strain law and facts in favor of the worthless individual [Gallagher]," and both expected the Supreme Court to teach the judge "a judicial lesson" by reversing him. In the midst of the reaction to Hoffman's decision, at least the *Bulletin* conceded that Gallagher's character offered no legal excuse for his banishment. "Nobody knows this better than Judge Hoffman. He, and his law-and-order friends have been hammering this point into our ears for nearly three years past." Of course, what all the supporters of the vigilance committee—including the two newspapers—had long argued was the movement's extralegal justifications, which stood little chance of acceptance in a court of law. Thus, the worst thing about the *Gallagher* case was that it would "encourage certain infamous people to institute proceedings against the good citizens of San Francisco," which would "necessarily cause annoyance and irritation." Hoffman bore a particular responsibility. "Just as the bitterness of the past was fading out, this Federal Judge transcends his duty to stir up the embers, and again fan the fire into a consuming blaze." [78]

The extent of the "blaze" of litigation coming before Hoffman's court was a series of suits filed in 1860 by Charles P. Duane, who, like Gallagher, had been banished from San Francisco by the 1856 committee. Duane's lawyer asserted the importance of the litigation to the community. "There have been two Vigilance Committees. There may be a third. Masters and Companies should know what liabilities they meet by kidnapping citizens." Duane succeeded in using the *Gallagher* case as a precedent. Ultimately, he settled for $2,000 in one case, and Hoffman awarded him $4,000 in another claim. Once again Hoffman provoked the ire of vigilance committee sympathizers, and the fact that the Supreme Court reduced Hoffman's award to fifty dollars did not erase the memory of Hoffman's decision. [79]

All things considered, Hoffman's popularity with and support from the business community might have seemed at low ebb. Yet within a year of Hoffman's decree of $4,000 to Duane, when the judge faced a major attack on his judgeship, the business community of San Francisco came to his aid once again. Many businessmen who supported Hoffman after the *Gallagher* and *Duane* cases apparently came to accept the *Alta California*'s view that it was more important that Hoffman be righteous than right. Even during the bitter aftermath of the *Gallagher* decision, the *Alta California* went out of its way to explain that it bore Hoffman no personal hostility. "The purity of his motives [we are] not now calling in question; but we maintain that personal prejudice has overruled better judgment." Hoffman's careful, patient appraisals and his reputation for integrity and independence made his decisions tolerable. In a strange way, Hoffman's most controversial decisions even generated a measure of support for him, especially since he took pains on such occasions to link his holdings with his judicial duty.[80]

The nature of the commercial litigation in Hoffman's admiralty docket and how he responded to the needs and desires of the business community are also suggestive of what role the lower federal courts played in the American economy during the nineteenth century. A number of scholars have argued that law—including case law and legislation—played an important part in promoting economic activity and in protecting the interests of entrepreneurs and commercial development during the nineteenth century. To the extent that these arguments are advanced to include federal district courts during the latter half of the nineteenth century, the experience of Hoffman's court would suggest a refinement in the interpretations. Whatever the situation before the state courts, the private law cases in admiralty in Hoffman's district court do not suggest that the court was protective of all business interests or that resulting case law promoted entrepreneurial activity.[81]

The majority of commercial litigation in Hoffman's admiralty court, for one thing, did not pit businessmen against individuals not involved in commerce. Rather, such litigation pitted merchants, mechanics, or businessmen against shipowners, with shipowners usually losing. Indeed, roughly one-fourth of all Hoffman's admiralty cases fit within the category of libels for supplies, repairs, or other services supplied to ships. Not only were such lawsuits a major portion of the commercial litigation of Hoffman's court, but their resolution also overwhelmingly resulted in decrees for the libellants or in the settlement of the cases. Moreover, libellants who sought damages on breaches of shipping contracts were usually substantial merchants or owners of large importing firms, and over 75 percent of the time, they succeeded in getting a favorable decree or settlement from the libelled ship. The resolution of most of Hoffman's commercial litigation thus consisted of adjustments between parties, each engaged in some aspect of the shipping industry. Hoffman's court performed a useful commercial function beyond what it provided to litigants suing under maritime liens. His court also helped an unknowable number of potential litigants whose resort to law proved unnecessary because shipowners and their agents, knowing the legal rules governing commercial practice that Hoffman would enforce, capitulated, avoiding litigation altogether.[82]

In one sense, Hoffman's admiralty court might well have been renamed "Jack-tar's tribunal" because of the large number of sailors who used his court. Nearly 40 percent of all libels filed in Hoffman's admiralty docket came from men employed aboard ships, men who were suing mainly for their wages, and the actual number of seamen who used Hoffman's court was even higher. For instance, when merchants or businessmen libelled a ship for breach of shipping contract or for supplies advanced, sailors often joined in the proceeding and submitted their claims for wages. Occasionally, sailors also sued for injuries they had suffered during the course of the voyage. Indeed, suits brought by sailors fell into two broad categories: those that dealt with the employment and compensation of seamen, and those that stemmed from conditions or occurrences at sea.[83]

In both types of cases, how sailors fared before Hoffman's court indicates not only the efficacy of his court in resolving their grievances but also the judge's response to the circumstances presented by the gold rush. In a series of cases interpreting the contractual basis of sailors' maritime service, Hoffman displayed a development in thought and a sensitivity to disparities in bargaining position. His reactions suggest that judicial thought and the role of contract in the legal history of nineteenth-century America were varied and complex. Moreover, Hoffman's response to sailors injured during the course of a voyage sheds light on tort law and economic growth in the nineteenth century and on how Hoffman struck a balance between judicial activism and the constraints of precedent.

Of all the litigants before Hoffman's admiralty court, perhaps no other suitors had stronger claims against ships under maritime law than sailors. Wages owed sailors created a maritime lien that took priority over all other claims. Indeed, in one of Hoffman's earliest opinions, he cited the considerable authority that supported the position taken in *The Consulate of the Sea*—the classic admiralty treatise compiled during the late Middle Ages. "Mariners shall be paid before all mankind and . . . if only a single nail of the ship is left they are entitled to it." An equally ancient right of sailors recognized by maritime law was their claim for so-called maintenance and cure. Such claims involved the right of sailors to be supported and cared for by their ship after injuries or illness occurring while in the service of the ship, irrespective of fault. Thus, sailors held favored liens that enabled them to seek recompense for a wide variety of accidents and potential tort actions as well as for the most common breach of contract to their disadvantage—failure to receive wages.[84]

In addition to specific doctrinal advantages and statutory enactments, sailors also had the benefit of a long-standing tradition of paternalism on the part of the courts. Seamen, called "the wards of admiralty," were often characterized as ignorant and incapable of looking out for themselves. By Hoffman's time, many decisions justified solicitous and indulgent attitudes toward sailors. In 1850, one admiralty treatise explained that seamen were "the favorites of the law on account of their imbecility" and were "placed particularly under the protection of the Admiralty," for they were "proverbially reckless and improvident, and on all accounts requiring protection."[85]

Nonetheless, several practical obstacles prevented sailors, particularly those seeking their wages, from receiving complete satisfaction in litigation brought during the gold rush. The experience of one sailor who sought his wages demonstrates some of the potential frustrations in such a lawsuit. The German sailor Adolphus Windeler arrived in San Francisco in December 1849 on board the ship *Probus*. After disagreements with his captain, he and several other sailors left the ship and sought legal advice to get their wages. The captain soon succeeded in having Windeler arrested on a charge of desertion and confined for two weeks while the sailor's lawyer sought his release and wages. The litigation produced mixed feelings on Windeler's part.

> Now in the first going to law we were led to expect that we would get all our wages, but o crackey, paying lawyers, court expenses, sheriff fees etc. took so much from it, that instead of receiving $113 we got only $14. So I think that it is best after all never to meddle with law and lawyers at all for we had some headache once in a while about our case,

before we knew how it had turned out and were also kept from regular employ[ment] although we had the satisfaction that our captain had to fork over.[86]

The state court's decision that Windeler and his fellow sailors were to bear their own legal expenses effectively negated their award. The amount in litigation—the sailors' wages—was quickly offset by the inflated cost of the legal process in gold-rush San Francisco.

Even when sailors were awarded their costs in suits for wages, as they usually were, the circumstances of early San Francisco could mitigate the practical benefit of their decrees. With hundreds of ships abandoned in the mud flats and often deserted by masters and crews alike, the thing sued—the ship—sometimes lost its value through dereliction and the absence of a market when it came to be sold. In Hoffman's court in 1851, for instance, the costs of litigation occasionally exceeded the amount realized by the sale of the ship, which was to have funded both the decree and the cost of litigation. In following state practice, Hoffman's court paid the northern district's clerk, commissioner, and marshal first, the litigant's lawyer second, and only then the award to the litigant. Occasionally, the costs were so high that sailors received little or nothing from the decree. More often, seamen received *pro rata* amounts of money but less than the entire judgment.[87]

This situation, however, did not last long, and by 1852 decrees in cases for sailors' wages were routinely satisfied. As the rush to California subsided, the conditions of shipping to and from San Francisco stabilized, resulting in fewer ships being abandoned on arrival in the state. In 1851 half of all lawsuits for sea wages resulted in default judgments against the ship because no one appeared to answer the allegations of the sailors. That figure rapidly declined after the first year. By 1852 most of this litigation by sailors reflected the greater stability of the shipping industry. In any event, many more suits for wages were settled before trial, and those that ended in decrees for the libellants were satisfied by the ships' agents without selling the vessel. Indeed, from the standpoint of libellants, Hoffman's court was very much a plaintiff's court, with sailors prevailing (either by decree or settlement) in over three-fourths of the cases. In the overwhelming majority of cases after the early 1850s, the decree for the sailors produced a cash payment of the full award and not the frustration experienced by Windeler and other sailors who filed the earliest libels for wages.[88]

The litigation over wages formed only a part of a wider struggle in which sailors were often victimized. Long before Hoffman's judgeship, notorious practices had emerged in the shipping of sailors and others aboard vessels. Shipmasters used liquor, deceit, and outright abduction to sign on common sailors for long voyages. Not all shipping masters were "crimps," who regularly engaged in a system of supplying crews by force and deception. But San Francisco in the latter half of the nineteenth century had more than its share of crimps. Indeed, practices along its waterfront coined the term *shanghaiing* to describe a particularly western brand of crimping.[89]

Shipping masters and their efforts to sign up sailors for voyages were only part of what a contemporary called the "shanghaiing fraternity." Since most of the crimping activities occurred on shore, few cases involving the practice found their way into Hoffman's admiralty court. Indeed, in 1859 Hoffman held that contracts to supply crewmen, as opposed to the contracts under which sailors were bound to voyages, were not maritime in nature and hence were outside of his jurisdiction in admiralty. Crimping thus lurked largely out of reach in many of the suits for seamen's wages. Only peripherally did Hoffman touch on the system in his efforts to deal with wage lawsuit issues that derived from the unique setting and circumstances of San Francisco.[90]

One troublesome problem in the gold-rush California maritime trade was the difficulty of keeping a crew together after arrival in San Francisco. The problem arose not only because of the lure of gold but also because inflation had dramatically increased the wages of seamen who shipped from San Francisco. Why should a sailor, working for relatively low East Coast wages, continue on the voyage when he might do substantially better by shipping out from the West Coast? Indeed, between the higher West Coast wages and gold fever, desertion from vessels in San Francisco became a chronic problem. According to one observer, by the winter of 1850 desertion by officers and crew alike had become "the general rule" as soon as ships dropped anchor in the bay. Some captains sought to restrain the practice by anchoring off Alcatraz Island, "although inconveniently distant from the town— with a view to render desertion on the part of the men more difficult." There is little evidence that such measures stemmed desertions.[91]

Because seamen tended to jump ship after passing through the Golden Gate, East Coast shipping masters were sometimes accused of chicanery in signing up sailors for voyages to, but not ending in, San Francisco. Sailors were required to sign a contract called the ship's articles, which itemized the voyage and the conditions of their employment—including wages. Maritime law prescribed clear consequences in the execution of the articles. Normally if a sailor abandoned a voyage before its conclusion, he forfeited his wages, but if the voyage had been misrepresented to him, he could receive his wages and leave the ship. Invariably the issue came down to this factual question, with contradictory testimony from the captain and the sailors.

Initially Hoffman took a narrowly contractual view and refused to establish "the precedent" that a seaman could "at any time, release himself from the obligation of his contract, by procuring a messmate to swear that the voyage" had been "misrepresented to him." In 1851 Hoffman felt "compelled by every consideration of justice and policy, to disregard the unsupported allegation of a mariner testifying to such a fact," since the means of disproving it were "necessarily beyond the reach of those representing the ship." Hoffman continued to take a hard line and enforced forfeitures of sailors' wages in the absence of proof of misrepresentation, until experience suggested that the practice of shipping masters and the circumstances of San Francisco warranted a different approach.[92]

At the same time, however, Hoffman sought to avoid forfeitures of seamen's wages if clear breaches of the contract did not exist or if ship captains had failed to follow exact procedure in seeking forfeitures. Hoffman followed the admiralty tradition of looking with a "vigilant eye" at contracts made by sailors. Ambiguities in the ship's articles were to be resolved in favor of the sailors. Nonetheless, the ship's articles—even though signed by sailors—was a contract and as such was entitled to strict enforcement. During the first decade of Hoffman's admiralty court, the tension between strictly enforcing the contracts and indulging the seamen was generally resolved in favor of the sanctity of contracts.[93]

In 1860, in *Thomas Dooley* v. *Ship "Neptune's Car,"* Hoffman reexamined the entire question of enforcing ship's articles. He characterized the inflation of seamen's wages in California as an almost "irresistible" temptation for sailors to desert and noted the "general custom" of the preceding years "not to insist upon the forfeiture of the whole wages, but merely on a deduction of a small sum to defray the expense of shipping other men, if the old crew" was not willing "to remain on board at port wages." In the present case, however, the master defended a libel for seaman's wages by claiming a forfeiture. No happier about the veracity of sailors—given "the recklessness of this class of men"—than he had been in 1851, Hoffman now acknowledged serious defects in the shipping master system.[94]

Hoffman lamented that Congress had not regulated the shipping of sailors more closely; ideally he wanted every crew to have its articles explained by a federal officer. In the absence of such a procedure, Hoffman undertook to devise a means of separating fraudulent from valid articles. His answer placed the burden on the master to show that the articles were fully explained to the men before a forfeiture of wages could be ordered. Essentially, Hoffman now embraced an idea that he had rejected nine years earlier under "every consideration of justice and policy."

Hoffman reasoned that clarifying the ship's articles could be more easily accomplished if the master explained the terms in front of the sailors as well as other reliable witnesses. Moreover, the equities demanded such a burden. "Aware, as the master is, of the strong temptation to impose on the men to which the shipping master, interested in filling up the crew list is subjected, and of the facility with which such impositions may be produced, especially on illiterate men; conscious too, of the rigor of the penalties he intends to enforce in case the contract be violated, such a precaution would seem to be the dictate not merely of policy but of justice."[95]

The effect of shifting the burden of proof from the sailors (to show misrepresentation) to the master (to show accurate representation) resulted in a decree for the sailors. The complaint of a shipowner that "the convenience of commerce" made shipping masters indispensable and that the requirement of proof thus normally remained outside the direct knowledge of the master did not sway Hoffman. If shipping masters were employed, it simply behooved masters to make sure that in the future they or other reliable witnesses were present at the signing of the articles.[96]

The decision to shift the burden of proof in disputes over ships' articles had the direct result of reducing the number of forfeitures of wages enforced in Hoffman's court. Moreover, after 1860 Hoffman took a more aggressive posture in defending sailors from shipowners' ploys to delay the payment of wages. He expressed serious doubts about whether the circuit court should entertain an appeal from a decree of wages when the shipowners had deliberately refused to make any defense at the district court level and had thus subjected a seaman to the "long delay" that had occurred while waiting for the suit to be heard in the appellate court. Hoffman cited the policy of maritime law to enforce seamen's liens for wages "in an expeditious and even summary manner" and expressed his agreement with pending legislation that would remove the power of masters and shipowners to withhold wages by virtue of "the unrestricted right of appeal." Likewise, in the case of a fishing voyage, Hoffman held that the owners were unjustified in waiting for a higher market price for the catch before paying off the crew.[97]

Hoffman still held sailors to their contracts, but how he enforced ship's articles showed a subtle shift from his earliest decisions. "Extravagant demands" by sailors "out of all proportion" to equity received little support. Indeed, Hoffman discouraged such suits, which he regarded as "vexatious," by refusing to give the libellants their court costs after awarding them their rightful wages. On the other hand, Hoffman tried to insure that within the contracting process, captains did not take undue advantage of crew members.[98]

In *Frederick Somerville* v. *Brig "Francisco"* (1870), for instance, Somerville had joined a fishing voyage as a cook, earning forty dollars per month. When Somerville injured his hand during the voyage, the captain replaced him as cook and pressured him to accept a new contract as a common sailor. In the new position, Somerville's wages equalled two-fifths of the value of any fish he caught. Even if the fishing had been good (which it was not), Somerville's injury impeded his ability to fish. As a result he stood to receive almost no compensation instead of his guaranteed monthly pay as a cook. Hoffman upheld Somerville's right to recover his original wages unless he voluntarily accepted a fair agreement for different wages. The disparity in bargaining power between the libellant and the captain weighed heavily in Hoffman's mind. The libellant, an old man, was "evidently not fitted to offer a determined resistance to oppression, or to make a vigorous assertion of his rights." Hoffman noted, "Few cases can be imagined short of actual or threatened violence where the parties to an agreement would stand upon more unequal grounds." Accordingly, Hoffman voided the second agreement and awarded Somerville his wages as a cook.[99]

Hoffman's new approach to forfeiture of wages resulted in compromises that were less strictly contractual and imposed fewer forfeitures. A test case dealing with desertion in 1870 provides a good example of Hoffman's development in thought and his mature approach to the issue. The libellant, an assistant steward on the mail steamship *Great Republic*, went ashore when the ship reached Yokohama, got drunk, and failed to return in time for the ship's departure. One month later, after stopping at several other ports, the *Great Republic* returned to Yokohama, where the libellant presented himself to the captain and sought to resume the voyage. The captain, however, considered the steward a deserter who had forfeited his wages as well as any right to be reinstated. Hoffman acknowledged the interest of masters and owners of steamships in "cases like the present, . . . said to be not infrequent."[100]

Hoffman first disposed of the steamship company's argument that the libellant had forfeited his wages. Although the steward had neglected his duty to return punctually to the ship, no evidence established his intention to desert. The steward had left his clothes on board, and at most, in Hoffman's view, he had behaved irresponsibly in getting drunk and missing the ship's departure. Still, Hoffman recognized the policy reasons for not forcing captains to accept wayward members of the crew who belatedly returned to duty. "If in such cases his [the libellant's] right to be reinstated at any subsequent period be recognized whenever the master is unable to show a voluntary desertion, or that he has employed another person in his place, an encouragement would be held out to the mariner to avoid the performance of his duty for perhaps the most important or the most arduous part of the voyage." Hoffman compromised: he did not consider the libellant a deserter, but he gave the steward only those wages earned up until he left the ship.[101]

In all of the civil admiralty litigation that came before the district court, Hoffman assessed the evidence without the help of a jury. Thus, Hoffman's personal evaluation of witnesses' testimony played an essential role in the practical outcome of cases. Hoffman's social origins and outlook influenced his assessment of the credibility of witnesses in that he developed an almost hierarchical structure for the credibility of oral testimony. At the apex of this structure were men like himself, gentlemen whose honor placed their word beyond question. Daniel T. Sullivan, a San Francisco lawyer and friend of Hoffman's, provided one example of what Hoffman considered an unimpeachable witness. With conflicting testimony that pitted the word of Sullivan against that of another witness, Hoffman observed, "The character of Mr. Sullivan forbids me to entertain the slightest suspicion of his veracity." In Sullivan's case, as with "two very respectable gentlemen" whose testimony conflicted, the only possible explanations were their own faulty memories or false statements by others. To such men Hoffman simply could not impute "intentional misstatements." The people Hoffman vouched for not only were unimpeachable witnesses but also were beyond reproach for other transgressions besides perjury. Hoffman found the suggestion that two such men had engaged in fraudulent schemes and bribery "too preposterous to be entertained by anybody acquainted with those gentlemen." In assuming that his peers and other gentlemen of standing observed a code of honor as scrupulously as he did himself, Hoffman created a category of witnesses whose word was given automatic credibility in his court. Even with a witness he did not know personally, it took a great deal of contrary evidence to prevent Hoffman from giving the gentleman's testimony "the weight which would otherwise be due to any statement of a person possessing . . . evidently high attainments and literary culture." [102]

Respectability could also help increase the probity of witnesses whose character and honor Hoffman could not personally vouch for or who were not gentlemen. Obviously swayed by the testimony of one sailor who claimed he had unjustifiably been placed in irons by the captain, Hoffman commented that the feelings of the seaman, who seemed to be "a very respectable young man," had been "deeply wounded." Lawyers, then or now, hardly advised clients to appear in court unkempt, in their scruffiest clothes, and with an insulting attitude. Given Hoffman's well-known views about honor and gentlemanly behavior, it behooved witnesses who came before him to act accordingly. The demeanor, manners, sensitivity, and appearance of witnesses played an especially important part in being accorded respectability by the northern district's judge. [103]

The greater the respectability, however, the greater the censure merited by transgressors. The obligation not to abuse social rank, particularly when accompanied with physical power, went hand in hand with the presumption of credibility. Hoffman's rejection of a captain's argument that he had been justified in striking a member of his crew revealed some of the underlying concerns of the judge. "If the Captains of our steamers who occupy so high and responsible a position not only in their calling, but socially and in the estimation of their fellow citizens, see fit to maintain their authority by the exercise of the prowess of a prize fighter, they should at least be held to a careful measure of the force they exert, and to a responsibility for its abuse." [104]

Inevitably, common sailors helped form the bottom of Hoffman's hierarchy of credible witnesses. The "well known characteristics of seamen," according to Hoffman, were "ignorance and recklessness." Hoffman believed that "little reliance" could be placed on the testimony of common seamen, "especially when testifying for each other," since sailors were unlike men "in a higher condition in life." As a consequence, the word of the ship's captain, owner, and officers tended to outweigh the testimony of common sailors. The exception occurred when the conduct of the seamen's superiors showed them to be taking cruel advantage of their rank.[105]

Compounding sailors' inherent lack of credibility was their tendency to exaggerate and overstate the facts supporting their case. Their lack of discretion on the stand further discredited their general probity because Hoffman regarded exaggeration as tantamount to perjury. Witnesses who appeared to be coloring the facts ran the risk of having their entire testimony impeached. Hoffman displayed his aversion to all forms of exaggeration by witnesses in his court—notably in his adjudication of land cases—but sailors singled themselves out because they more often fell afoul of Hoffman in this way.[106]

Hoffman's suspicion of the credibility of sailors worked to their disadvantage in suits to collect damages for the brutal behavior or conditions that sailors were forced to endure on board ship. Only in the most egregious situations and with strong evidence were seamen apt to collect damages. This stemmed in part from the wide latitude that ship captains enjoyed in enforcing discipline. As Hoffman put it, a sailor's general duty was to "submit even to injustice and wrong." But an additional difficulty in winning such cases arose when the evidence seemed at all balanced, for Hoffman tended to side with the captain rather than with the sailors. It was no accident that when Hoffman did decide against a captain's use of punishment, the libellant had seemed a sensitive, respectable man of "sober habits."[107]

Still, there were limits to the scope of a captain's authority to discipline his crew. Placing men in irons or on restricted rations and even corporal punishment were acceptable means of maintaining discipline, but arbitrary brutality or excessively cruel treatment were not. A captain who struck a sailor who came aboard drunk while the vessel was in port found himself liable for $500 in damages and costs. The fact that the captain's blow had come from behind and had badly broken the sailor's jaw influenced the amount of damages, but the captain's liability stemmed from his "unnecessary and unwarrantable" reaction to "a seaman demented by liquors." Moreover, when a captain had allowed a sailor to be severely beaten by the second mate (the captain's brother) after a fight had erupted between them, Hoffman held the captain liable even though he was not guilty of any willful wrong. Hoffman stated, "I consider it of much importance that masters should feel it to be as much their duty to restrain the violence of the officers, as it is to repress the insubordination of the men, and that they will be held responsible if they fail to do their utmost to protect the men from the outrages on the part of the inferior officers, which have so often brought disgrace upon our mercantile marine." [108]

The brutality of shipboard life was indeed notorious, and despite the occasional lawsuits by sailors and criminal prosecutions brought against captains, it is doubtful if general conditions changed very much. Nonetheless, Hoffman's court heard the first "hellship trials" in 1851—criminal prosecutions against a notoriously brutal captain. According to one historian, these trials "made possible, many years later, the freedom of the American merchant sailor from the brutality and tyranny of masters and mates." Captains at sea may have been a law unto themselves, but Hoffman insisted on reminding them that his court would be the final arbiter of their actions. [109]

Sailors before Hoffman's court also had success when they asserted they had been unjustifiably discharged or abandoned by captains. A long line both of maritime cases and of federal statutes underscored the policy of making the sailor's welfare the responsibility of the ship. Even though the captain exercised wide powers over his crew, he could not normally dispose of troublesome sailors by leaving them behind, and the captain and the ship's owners remained responsible for caring for any injuries or sickness that befell members of the crew during the voyage. Unruly sailors, or those who got drunk and even those who took a swing at the captain, could not simply be abandoned. [110]

Sick or injured sailors were also protected from being abandoned. Hoffman underscored this point with a $2,500 decree against a captain for what he considered a very strong case of "utter disregard, by a master, of his duty to a sick seaman . . . and of the dictates of common humanity." The libellant, a seaman on the steamer *Pacific*, came down with smallpox en route from San Francisco to Oregon. The captain had the sick man taken off the steamer near a small town, which had no doctor, and departed. The sailor wandered in his ill condition for two days seeking help and finally collapsed on a beach, where he recuperated for three weeks. As Hoffman stated the issue, if a sailor's disease was "malignant, loathsome and infectious," and if "his continuance on board" exposed "the remainder of the ship's company to the danger of contracting it," did that "justify the master in setting him ashore without any provision whatever for his care, his subsistence, or his proper medication or nursing?" Given that the steamer was only one day out of a port with proper medical facilities, Hoffman concluded that the captain had a duty to keep the seaman on board and isolate him rather than send him ashore "to propagate the disease among unsuspecting inhabitants, and at a place twenty miles distance from all possibility of assistance or relief." Although the circuit court later reduced Hoffman's decree to $750, the decision and opinion remained an accurate statement of the duty that ship captains owed to their sick or injured crew.[111]

Seamen's grievances that could form the basis of suits for damages were not limited to torts committed by the captain of the ship. Sailors also suffered at the hands of other members of the crew. Yet sailors' efforts to gain recompense from the ship beyond the nominal sums allowed for "cure and maintenance" were frustrated by two allied legal doctrines: the fellow servant rule and the concept of contributory negligence. The fellow servant rule prevented one employee from suing his employer for injuries caused by the negligence of a fellow employee. Even if the injured party was not in the relationship of a "fellow servant," the doctrine of contributory negligence could prevent recovery if the plaintiff's own negligence had contributed to the accident. The operation of both doctrines during the nineteenth century effectively narrowed the limits of employers' liability. Despite the hard results of these legal rules, they were well entrenched by the time Hoffman became a judge.[112]

Although Hoffman may have overestimated the credibility of gentlemen to the disadvantage of sailors, this social bias did not blind him to the condition and treatment of the common man. He clearly saw the precarious position of workers under the fellow servant rule and took issue with a public policy that promoted economic development at their expense. His personal conservatism, though influencing his thought and behavior, did not overcome his tendency to openminded intellectual inquiry that could lead him to challenge orthodox positions he felt were unsound as a matter of reason, logic, or policy. Hoffman's first encounter with the fellow servant rule proved to be one such occasion.

In 1864 Hoffman heard the case of a messboy who had suffered severe injuries from a falling bale of hay while on board the Pacific Mail Steamship

Company's *Sierra Nevada*. The boy claimed his injuries had resulted because the ship's officer overseeing the unloading of the hay had failed to warn him that a bale was about to be dropped. The steamship company, however, claimed not only that a warning had been given but also that the injuries were the messboy's own fault. Hoffman summarily disposed of the case by declaring the issue of contributory negligence irrelevant because the fellow servant rule barred the suit. Hoffman appended an opinion he had recently written dealing with the applicability of the fellow servant rule. The libellant in the earlier case had conceded the existence of the general rule but had argued against its "reason and policy." Hoffman wrote, "[If the question] could be regarded as an open one and I were at liberty to consult my own judgment, I confess that I should be disposed to assent to much that was urged against the justice and reasonableness of the rule." But the doctrine appeared "to be too well established, . . . to be shaken."[113]

Despite reaching the conclusion that the fellow servant rule governed the lawsuit, Hoffman analyzed the rule's justification and urged the Supreme Court "to revisit the foundations" on which the doctrine was based, to see if it rested on "any solid grounds of reason or policy." Hoffman considered the two central reasons assigned for the rule—that employees knowingly assumed the risks of their employment and that, knowing they had no legal recourse based on co-workers' negligence, employees would work more carefully—and found them bereft of reason or policy. He raised the example of a railroad bookkeeper whose office employment could hardly imply an assumption of the risk of injury caused by being run over by a train. He added, "No amount of care on the part of the bookkeeper in keeping his books, can add to or diminish the care of the conductor or driver of the car."

Hoffman proposed that the fellow servant rule be abolished and replaced by a rule that would make employers liable for all accidents except when the injured party himself was negligent. Such an approach would be more logical. In addition, Hoffman stated,

> The policy of holding the great Railroad and Steamboat Companies who virtually possess monopolies of the principal routes of travel, to the exactest diligence and utmost care, by making them responsible to everyone, whether servant or stranger who is injured by the negligence of their agents without fault of his own, appears to me far less questionable

than the supposed advantage of stimulating the servants to greater care
by denying them all indemnity for the carelessness of their fellows
which they are powerless to prevent.

Even while he suggested this wider scope for relief, Hoffman concluded that
as a "subordinate tribunal," he was faced with "a course of decisions too
numerous and respectable to be disregarded."[114]

Hoffman's opposition to the fellow servant rule was extraordinary because, at the time, "almost all American courts" accepted the rule with
"marked deference." Indeed, only much later in the nineteenth century and
in the early twentieth century would considerable judicial resistance to the
fellow servant rule develop. Hoffman's opinion of the rule clearly put him at
odds with business interests. The practical effect of the fellow servant rule
was to shift the burden of industrial accidents onto workers rather than their
employers, and thus the rule proved a critical boon to business in the latter
half of the nineteenth century.[115]

The legal historian Morton Horwitz has argued that, by the 1840s,
American judges and treatise writers had justified this shift away from the
traditional agency doctrine of *respondeat superior*—under which the principal (the employer) had responsibility for injuries caused by his agent
(the employee) within the scope of employment. According to Horwitz, this
shift away from traditional liability not only accommodated the business interests of the time but also was accomplished by the ascendancy of a "con-
tractarian ideology" that "above all expressed a market conception of legal
relations." Hoffman remained immune from the "market conception" that
underlay the fellow servant rule because he believed that the responsibilities
of the employer were broader than the doctrine allowed.[116]

The tort cases in Hoffman's admiralty court provide further evidence to
reassess the argument that nineteenth-century tort law incorporated a sub-
sidy theory that favored business and enterprise at the expense of personal
injuries.[117] In the passenger cases and the tort claims brought by sailors,
Hoffman displayed a great deal of sensitivity to libellants and rendered many
decisions contrary to the interests of business. To the extent that Hoffman
upheld the well-entrenched fellow servant rule, he took pains to question its
correctness and suggested the adoption of an approach more favorable to
those injured by the operation of corporate enterprises. Hoffman's decision
upholding the fellow servant rule was hardly the only case in which he

abided by precedent and thus ruled contrary to what he believed were the equities of the case.[118] In areas where Hoffman did not face strong precedents that he felt compelled to obey, he proved amenable and even zealous in providing remedies and amelioration for aggrieved libellants. In this process Hoffman was acting in a fashion quite in accord with what one would expect of a conscientious common-law judge. He certainly had his share of bias and prejudices, including a healthy respect for business and for gentlemen of economic standing, but his cases do not reveal a consistent or strong posture that could be described as probusiness. Indeed, in the passenger cases, he took positions that were distinctly critical of and contrary to the wishes of the New York commercial interests that had helped make him a judge.

If Hoffman toyed with the idea of breaking away from the conventional law that governed the tort liability of employers, he dramatically departed from nineteenth-century law in the passenger contract cases. He tempered his judicial boldness with the assertion that his actions followed naturally from his duty, as a federal judge, to offer justice to all who legitimately came before his court. Yet, confronted with harms arising in the captive society presented by the on-board world of passenger vessels, Hoffman creatively evolved standards, implied terms, and provided effective remedies for those who unfairly suffered during voyages to California.

4

Criminal Prosecution in the
Northern District

In Hoffman's adjudication of the most important criminal litigation before his court—crimes committed at sea—as well as in the politically charged atmosphere of prosecutions against military adventurers, he showed a distinct awareness of his role in maintaining national honor. As he did in the admiralty tort suits generated by the activities of the Vigilance Committee of 1856, Hoffman believed his court had the duty, as a tribunal representing the national government, to preserve and protect the nation's reputation. Yet, this belief conflicted, at times, with Hoffman's other convictions and created tensions that can be traced in his decisions in criminal cases. For instance, Hoffman's efforts to eradicate the national disgrace of wanton brutality in America's merchant marine were frequently frustrated by his own skepticism of the testimony of common sailors. Similarly, his personal admiration for the leaders of an illegal military expedition to Mexico worked against his need to secure a conviction that would uphold the nation's commitment to respect Mexico's sovereignty.

Hoffman's criminal docket also demonstrates the wide independence enjoyed by nineteenth-century federal prosecutors—U.S. attorneys. The Judiciary Act of 1789 gave the attorney general no authority to supervise or direct U.S. attorneys; such authority came only with the creation of the Department of Justice in 1870. Prior to 1870, and even thereafter, numerous federal departments sought to maintain control over the conduct of their litigation through communications to local federal prosecutors. And yet before 1870, only the Treasury Department was officially granted supervisory power over U.S. attorneys. Such sporadic guidance left much discretion in the hands of local U.S. attorneys. This lack of centralized administrative supervision, and Hoffman's understanding of his limited role in controlling the work of U.S. attorneys, largely explain the dynamics of federal prosecution in the northern district. As a result, criminal prosecution varied greatly among the fourteen U.S. attorneys who served during Hoffman's tenure, and their actions were influenced as much by their private predilections as by public pressure.[1]

The source of part of Hoffman's criminal docket—dealing with the commonplace crimes of assault, battery, and manslaughter—arose at sea. Typical cases were the prosecutions against captains and their officers for beating or cruelly punishing sailors. In addition, Hoffman heard prosecutions for mutiny, attacks on officers, and refusals to sail. Indeed, most of the criminal cases arising out of a maritime context involved either conduct that exceeded the limits of maintaining shipboard discipline or resistance to a captain's rightful authority. The tension between Hoffman's desire to reduce shipboard cruelty and brutality and his predisposition to side with captains and officers emerged in the first of the so-called hellship cases over which he presided in 1851. The issues of these first criminal cases influenced Hoffman in later cases—to weigh the rights of sailors to just treatment by officers against the necessity of obedience to shipboard authority.[2]

The hellship cases arose after a voyage captained by Robert H. Waterman, long notorious for running excessively tough ships. The condition and stories of Waterman's crew when they arrived in San Francisco on the clipper ship *Challenge* outraged even the most hardened observers. A mob of two thousand threatened to lynch Waterman and his first officer, James Douglass, but the two men slipped away while the municipal authorities, aided by members of the Vigilance Committee of 1851, succeeded in disbanding the mob.[3]

The removal of the threat of extrajudicial action gave federal authorities their first opportunity to show what kind of justice they offered. While the U.S. marshal invited aggrieved sailors to lodge their complaints formally, the

U.S. commissioner examined the charges, and the U.S. attorney assembled the district court's first grand jury. The public interest in what had happened during the voyage brought Hoffman's court under close scrutiny. In his first criminal trial, Hoffman sought both to distinguish himself and to establish respect for the power and the authority of his court.[4]

The evidence established both that sailors aboard the *Challenge* had been brutally treated and that their maltreatment had prompted some of them to attack the first officer. This circumstance undercut the public support for the sailors and the success of the prosecutions against the captain and his officers. Ultimately the grand jury brought in over a dozen indictments against Captain Waterman and First Officer Douglass, and eight jury trials were held between December 1851 and January 1852. The indictments included assault, malicious beating, cruel punishment, and murder, but in the end Captain Waterman stood convicted of one count of cruel punishment, his first officer, Douglass, of two counts of beating sailors, and his second officer of one count of beating a sailor. Waterman received a $400 fine, Douglass a $250 fine, and the second officer thirty days' imprisonment.[5]

Both the *Waterman* case and the other brutality prosecutions Hoffman heard arose under a federal act of 1835. That act provided that if captains or their officers "from malice, hatred or revenge, and without justifiable cause," beat, wounded, or imprisoned any crewmen or withheld from them "suitable food and nourishment," or inflicted "upon them any cruel and unusual punishment," they could be subject to a fine of up to $1,000 or a five-year imprisonment or both, "according to the nature and aggravation of the offence." Thus, the key question in every alleged brutality case became the motives behind the actions of the captain or his officers. Given the wide power of the captain to maintain discipline on board ship, the statute inevitably placed a heavy burden on the prosecution to establish unjustified conduct coupled with personal malice.[6]

Ironically, the origins of the 1835 act lay not in a growing humanitarianism toward seamen but in a desire to more effectively punish revolts and mutinies by sailors. Before 1835, and since an act of 1790, revolts by seamen had been defined as acts of piracy, punishable by death. The objective of the 1835 act, explained its sponsor, Senator John M. Clayton of Delaware, was "to define and punish the revolt of crews of American ships." According to Clayton: "Criminals of this description often escape punishment altogether, owing to the excessive severity now imposed upon the offence. It was therefore thought best . . . to define it and attach such severe punishment to it as would effectively suppress it." The final version of the 1835 act gave federal judges a considerable range of fines and imprisonment to gauge the serious-ness of the offence and to punish the criminal behavior of both sailors and their officers.[7]

Twelve years before Hoffman began hearing admiralty cases, Richard Henry Dana, Jr., strongly criticized how the federal courts were interpreting the 1835 act. Dana, shortly to publish his classic *Two Years Before the Mast*, was practicing law in Massachusetts when he wrote an article, entitled "Cruelty to Seamen," for the *American Jurist and Law Magazine* in 1839.[8] Dana's criticism was prompted by the excessively lenient sentence that he believed his former law professor, Justice Joseph Story, had imposed on a captain and his first mate after their conviction under the act of 1835. Story had agreed that the evidence in *United States* v. *Nichols* established that the defendants had ruthlessly beaten a sailor and had tortured him by repeatedly stabbing him with a sail needle attached to a piece of bamboo, contributing to the sailor's death. Notwithstanding these circumstances, Story had sen-tenced the captain to three months' imprisonment and a $100 fine and his first officer to thirty days' imprisonment and a $10 fine.

Dana argued that if under these circumstances, which Story himself had characterized as an extremely aggravated offense, defendants received much less than their potential sentences, then the 1835 act would become a dead letter. Dana worried that failure to invoke the substantial penalties provided by law in appropriate cases undermined the potential of the statute to re-strain abused sailors from taking the law into their own hands. In his words, "The silent operation of this statute has sheathed many a knife, and quelled many a mutiny." Dana thus broached a concern that later preoccupied Judge Hoffman in his efforts to balance the rights of sailors to be free from unjus-tified physical punishment with the wide, lawful authority of the captain to maintain shipboard discipline. Dana anticipated Hoffman in suggesting, "Every day upon the high seas the crews of vessels, in whose hands the physical force is, are kept from resistance by the consciousness that there is a law which will call the captain to account when the voyage is up." Dana's and Hoffman's belief in the efficacy of the 1835 statute to alter shipboard behavior may seem overly optimistic, but it was sincerely founded.[9]

Dana speculated that "a want of confidence in the testimony of seamen" ultimately accounted for Story's lenient sentences. Dana urged that the testimony of sailors be assessed like any other testimony. He conceded that the "danger of crews combining against their officers" imposed the necessity of "making allowances for exaggeration," but he argued against disbelieving sailors as a class. Dana had good reason to fear that sailors suffered from the tendency of admiralty judges to view their testimony skeptically, but in Hoffman's case that skepticism did not prevent him from imposing significantly heavier sentences on offending captains and officers than Story had done in comparable circumstances. Still, the testimony of sailors in Hoffman's court came under special scrutiny, and sailors had to overcome the impression—rightly or wrongly—that they tended to be unreliable witnesses.[10]

Hoffman's criminal docket suggests that in the northern district, at least, the 1835 act did function to punish wayward officers and monitor the conditions on the high seas. In cases from the 1860s to the end of his tenure, Hoffman's sentences for brutal treatment of sailors ranged from six months' imprisonment to six years' hard labor. Such sentences were substantially heavier than the one- and three-month sentences Story had imposed in the *Nichols* case. The relatively longer sentences, although less than some observers wanted, served to send the message that Dana had urged, namely that captains and their officers were not free to act with impunity on the high seas. Indeed, even as early as 1854, a captain of a vessel, on reaching San Francisco, swore out an affidavit of complaint against one of his officers for biting off the ear of a member of the crew. Convicted of mayhem, the officer received three months' imprisonment.[11]

However, an examination of the northern district's cases alone would not support Dana's critique of the probable weakness in enforcing the 1835 act. Many of the most serious violations under the 1835 act were tried before the federal circuit court and not before Hoffman's court. Moreover, in many cases the circumstances were far from clear that captains or others had exceeded the wide scope of their authority to command obedience and maintain discipline. In close cases or in those, such as the the *Waterman* prosecution, in which the evidence showed defiance, if not physical resistance, to the captain's authority, such circumstances tended to mitigate the imposition of prison terms.

Lastly, because the 1835 act placed great emphasis on the motives of the officers, their credibility did affect both juries and judges, particularly when the circumstances of authority and obedience were unclear. Yet, the traditionally poor reputation seamen had as credible witnesses increased the difficulty of attaining convictions under the act. This reputation was well established by Hoffman's time and was linked to the paternalistic attitude that courts had taken toward sailors. The historic protectiveness of admiralty courts, which described sailors as "wards of the admiralty," recognized the sailors' supposed childlike limitations and their reckless and imprudent ways. Although sailors did receive a measure of legal protection as a result of these attitudes, they also suffered from the perception that they were inherently not credible. Ironically, San Francisco juries, more often than Judge Hoffman, tended to discount the credibility of sailors.[12]

Before 1864, when Congress passed a law allowing federal district judges to hear minor criminal offenses of physical violence by officers or sailors without a jury, Hoffman was limited to the role of sentencing captains and their officers once a jury returned a verdict of guilt. After 1864, Congress gave federal prosecutors discretion to bring all but "capital or otherwise infamous" offenses before federal district judges without a jury. Under the act, trial by jury might occur if the defendant requested one, but if such a request was not made, the judge alone would hear the case and was limited to imposing a sentence of one year's imprisonment or a $500 fine or both. Judicial efficiency, more than anything else, seems to have accounted for the act. The time and cost of getting an indictment from a grand jury followed by a jury trial seemed excessive, given such minor shipboard crimes. Indeed, that lengthier process could subject defendants to confinement while awaiting trial that was longer than the actual sentences imposed after conviction. Although some federal courts apparently had doubts about such non-jury criminal trials, the Senate Judiciary Committee, Congress, and Hoffman did not seem troubled by the absence of juries in these criminal prosecutions.[13]

In the northern district, before and after 1864, either juries found captains and their officers not guilty or they split in their deliberations and so prompted federal prosecutors to enter a *nolle prosequi* (a dismissal). This circumstance probably prompted a local newspaper to complain: "San Francisco juries are in evident sympathy with brutal shipmasters and their officers. No wonder that the American merchant service has gone to the dogs."[14]

Even though Hoffman could not control the outcome of jury trials, his discretion in imposing sentences allowed him to indicate his view of the defendant's culpability and the heinousness of the crime. In 1859, for example, Hoffman disagreed with a jury verdict rendered by the circuit court in a prosecution against a ship's captain for manslaughter and for inflicting cruel and unusual punishment on three members of his crew, one of whom had died. Hoffman believed that the evidence established that the captain had ordered saltwater be poured over the back of a sailor who had just received thirty-five lashes. The sailor, wearing a few rags, had then been put in irons and confined for eight days in a cargo hold containing coal. He had been given two biscuits a day and some water. After similar treatment, other seamen of the voyage were, in Hoffman's words, "in a state of extreme emaciation" and bore the marks of "severe flogging." The jury, however, limited its verdict to finding the captain guilty only of beating his seamen, a lesser charge.[15]

In sentencing the captain, Hoffman explained that he had tried to be entirely governed by the jury's verdict rather than by his "own convictions of what that evidence showed [the captain] to have been guilty of." "But," continued Hoffman, "I also feel that it is among the most important sacred duties of the Court to protect, so far as it may, seamen from injustice, tyranny and oppression, and to restrain within the limits of humanity and justice the . . . irresponsible authority of the master." Humanitarian considerations aside, it was important that seamen be encouraged to take voyages and that mutinies be averted by the knowledge that law afforded sailors "a real and practical protection." For both humanitarian and policy reasons, Hoffman imposed the unusually stiff sentence of both one year in county jail and a $175 fine.[16]

The one-year sentence was an unusually stiff punishment because in most brutality cases before Hoffman, captains and their officers convicted under the 1835 act frequently received only fines, ranging from $20 up to $400. That such sentences were typical seems to bear out Dana's concern that the 1835 act might not operate to send sufficiently strong messages to the maritime community.[17]

One way to test the strength of the 1835 and 1864 laws is to examine the cases Hoffman heard. During Hoffman's tenure, he would hear more than 300 cases dealing with the maltreatment of sailors or with sailors who turned on or disobeyed their captains and officers. The outcomes of these cases, many of which were heard without a jury, reveal Hoffman's predisposition to believe men of higher social rank and his antipathy toward perjury or exaggeration. Hoffman held not only captains and sailors, but also captains and their officers, to differing standards of acceptable conduct. The verdicts and sentences bear out these distinctions and offer a rough guide on how specific defendants fared in Hoffman's criminal docket.[18]

To Hoffman, shipboard violence was unjustified and repugnant. His court—and not mistreated or brutalized sailors—had the task of punishing vicious captains and officers. Hoffman acknowledged his obligation to convince sailors "that wrongs done to them" would be "punished by the justice of the country as surely as by the wild justice of revenge." Thus, Hoffman showed little sympathy for sailors who physically resisted their officers. In civil cases involving marine torts, he made it clear the sailors owed obedience to their captains even when faced with tyranny and oppressive behavior. In criminal cases, he underscored that point by his sentences of seamen convicted of disobeying orders of the captain or resisting his authority. Refusing to go to sea, deserting, or otherwise refusing to do one's duty on board ship was routinely punished by several days' to several months' imprisonment in the county jail.[19]

Riotous behavior by drunken sailors could result in longer sentences of three to four months' imprisonment, since Hoffman sought to prevent mutinies and validate the captain's authority to keep sailors in line. In fact, Hoffman urged one jury to find "at least a technical violation." Hoffman wanted sailors to "understand that the first duty of seamen, as of the soldier in the army" was "obedience to a superior officer." He feared that disobedience over simple orders might grow into wholesale rebellion.[20]

How Hoffman perceived the relative seriousness of crimes of violence by seamen can be assessed by other sentences he imposed. A sailor who threw hot grease into the face of his messmate could expect a six-month imprisonment in county jail, and a knife attack among the crew might earn the guilty party one year of hard labor. When sailors attacked their officers or captain, however, the penalties were usually heavier, ranging from several months' to five years' imprisonment. Moreover, the longer sentences were often accompanied by the stipulation that the incarceration be at hard labor in the state prison as opposed to confinement in the preferable county jail. One seaman, for instance, received a $500 fine and a three-year prison term at hard labor at San Quentin state prison after his conviction for having attacked the second officer of his ship with a two-foot-long iron pipe. Yet, fines for such crimes were more the exception than the rule because most sailors were in no position to pay them.[21]

The relative severity of the sentences for violence inflicted by sailors among themselves and directed toward their officers must be placed within the context of what sentences were statutorily possible. A comparison of this type indicates that Hoffman showed leniency to seamen as well as their officers. During Hoffman's tenure, statutes provided that anyone (for example, a sailor) who assaulted someone with a dangerous weapon might, on conviction, be sentenced to three years' hard punishment or a $3,000 fine or both, depending on the circumstances. Likewise, sailors who attacked their superiors with an intent to subvert lawful command might, on conviction, face ten years at hard labor or a $2,000 fine or both, depending on circumstances. Although such sentences were technically possible, they—like the maximum penalties for officers who abused their men—were rarely if ever imposed by Hoffman. A failure to invoke the harshest penalty allowed by statute did not mean, however, that Hoffman found the violence of either sailors or officers unimportant.[22]

Rather, Hoffman balanced his concern that sailors obey their captains and officers with his desire to inculcate conditions at sea that gave sailors some hope that brutality for its own sake would not be tolerated. The most dramatic instance in which Hoffman demonstrated this dual commitment occurred when he instructed jurors in an 1866 mutiny trial that the jury could consider whether, given all the circumstances, the sailors were justified in taking command away from their officers and confining the captain. When the jury entered a verdict of not guilty, in the face of an obvious mutiny, the verdict and Hoffman's charge made maritime history.[23]

The historic nature of the case lay more in its factual circumstances than in the legal principle that underlay Hoffman's charge. In no other reported case, prior to 1866, that involved legitimate resistance to a captain's authority had a federal court justified a full-scale mutiny. Nine years earlier, in 1857, Peleg Sprague, the federal district court judge for the district of Massachusetts, had noted in a criminal charge to a jury that some circumstances might justify "the crew to prevent the master in the free exercise of his authority, or even to deprive him of it altogether." Judge Sprague pointed out that the crime of revolt or mutiny under the 1835 act required "unlawful" acts of the crew. If because of a captain's "improper conduct" the sailors had "good reason" to believe that they would be "subjected to unlawful and cruel or aggressive treatment" or "that a great wrong was about to be inflicted upon one of the crew," they were entitled to take "reasonable measures" to protect themselves. In the case before Judge Sprague, the sailors were charged with refusing to continue a whaling voyage.[24]

What influenced Hoffman to give the charge he did clearly hinged on the moderation the sailors showed in the face of the first mate's brutality. During the clipper ship *White Swallow*'s voyage from New York to San Francisco in 1865, the men were beaten and put to dangerous tasks that cost the life of at least one sailor. When their complaints were met with even more beatings, the crew met in secret and decided to take over the ship, but without hurting any of the officers. After confining their officers without incident, the mutineers, in conjunction with the captain, drew up a remarkable document that both he and the leaders of the mutiny signed. Written in the first person, the document admitted the existence of the mutiny and its reputed source (the first mate's brutality) and spelled out that control would be returned to the captain, who in turn promised to prevent his officers from abusing the crew. Hoffman, in his charge to the jury, warned that acquitting the mutineers might establish a dangerous precedent, but he summed up his instructions by saying that if the jury believed the mutiny was justified, its duty was "to acquit without regard to consequences."[25]

The practice, if not the success, of Hoffman's district court in bringing unjustifiably harsh captains and officers to justice is suggested by the sheer number of prosecutions. More than thirteen times as many prosecutions were brought against captains and their officers for physically abusing their crew as were brought against sailors for attacking their officers. Given the fact that captains had little reticence in filing complaints while sailors might have feared reprisals, the disparity is telling. Yet, the number of prosecutions forms only part of the story. The number of convictions and the type of sentences meted out to convicted captains and officers offer an important measure of the practical effect that Hoffman's court had in punishing shipboard brutality.[26]

The prosecutions of ships' officers were based on serious assaults on members of the crew (especially beatings of sailors) or cruel and unusual punishment. Although captains and first and second officers were all charged with such crimes, the degree of success in obtaining convictions and the resulting criminal sanctions tended to follow the hierarchy of command. For similar offenses, captains usually received more lenient sentences than did first officers, who in turn fared better than second officers. Moreover, captains stood a far better chance of being acquitted or having their case dismissed than did their subordinates.

Prosecutions for cruel and unusual punishment illustrate this hierarchical pattern. Captains, to the extent they were convicted, received fines ranging from $1 to $75 (although in one instance a captain was fined $200 and costs). First officers got moderate fines as well as imprisonment for from three to six months (although in one instance a first mate received a sentence of two years' hard labor). Second officers, however, not only were fined but also received longer prison sentences than first officers, ranging from six months in county jails to three years' hard labor in state prisons. The chances of conviction also followed a similar pattern: 43 percent, 60 percent, and 75 percent for captains, first officers, and second officers, respectively.[27]

Ships' officers dealt harshly with sailors who physically resisted shipboard authority. The most common form of brutality sailors suffered—beatings— was consistently disapproved of and dealt with in Hoffman's court, even if captains once again received greater leniency than their first and second officers. Although no captains were fined as heavily as Waterman in 1851, their fines ranged from $5 to $200. At least three captains were sent to the county jail. Indeed, one captain received a six-month sentence. First officers suffered a lower range of fines (between $5 and $100) but were jailed more regularly and for longer terms than captains convicted of beating sailors. The heaviest sentence imposed on a first officer consisted of a $100 fine and one year in the county jail. Second officers, on the other hand, typically encountered lower fines than first officers for such convictions (between $10 and $50) but tended to receive stiffer jail sentences. In one case a second mate received one year at hard labor in the state prison for beatings he administered to two sailors. And unlike captains and first officers, second officers were far less likely to be acquitted either by Hoffman or by a jury.[28]

The graduated conviction rates stemmed, in large part, from the key role the captain played in maintaining shipboard discipline and the greater credence given to his testimony. In many ways, he epitomized authority at sea. Frequently a target of lawsuits, captains were variously protected from criminal prosecution. The greatest shield to captains as well as their officers was, ironically, sailors' lack of credible testimony. Consequently, captains and their officers benefited from any doubtful testimony, despite the trust that was imposed by law on the captain. Hoffman explained: "It is as much his duty to protect seamen from the violence of his officers as it is to enforce obedience and maintain discipline. It is a double trust, therefore, and the Captain who allows his men to be ill-treated is as much guilty of a violation of his duty as if, having the power, he failed to suppress a mutiny and maintain discipline on board ship." [29]

Rebellious or even rambunctious sailors hurt themselves because they often made poor witnesses. In a criminal charge to a jury in 1882, Hoffman reflected on his "very long experience" as a trial judge, during which he had found sailors to be "addicted to exaggeration." He had "often seen justice defeated" because juries were put off by overdrawn testimony of sailors, "when if a candid and unembellished statement of the facts had been made," convictions "without hesitation" would have followed. Hoffman believed that his aversion to exaggerated testimony was shared by jurors. Just why so many juries could not agree on the guilt of captains and officers prosecuted for brutality or why they acquitted such defendants is uncertain, but Hoffman may have been right that jurors shared his suspicion of sailors' testimony.[30]

The results of prosecutions provide evidence that maintaining shipboard discipline often won out over disciplining wayward officers. In a summary trial in 1867, Hoffman found the captain of the ship *Shatemuc* not guilty of attacking a crew member with a belaying pin. However, when another member of that same crew attacked the captain with a knife, Hoffman imposed an eighteen-month prison sentence, even though both cases were considered assaults with a dangerous weapon. Likewise, Hoffman found Henry Rock, the first officer of the ship *Western Empire*, not guilty of six counts of beating and wounding members of the crew, but the lone sailor indicted for stabbing Rock received a six-month prison sentence. Yet, both of the sentences meted out to the sailors fell short of the possible legal sanction—ten years at hard labor.[31]

Despite the number of prosecutions that did not result in convictions, Hoffman's criminal docket reveals that the *Waterman* case did set the tone for the district court's attempts to evaluate criminal cases brought before it. Hoffman intended to curb brutalities against seamen "by men," as he put it, who seemed "to think that a sailor" had no "rights that an officer" was "bound to respect." Hoffman also believed that he had the duty to preserve American honor at sea. In one criminal charge he commented, "Our flag has been more dishonored, and the mercantile marine of America incurred more reproach by cruelties and abuses of this description than perhaps any other flag or mercantile marine in the world." Although Hoffman's court may not have ended the abuses, Hoffman's judicial actions helped monitor the criminal brutality and maltreatment suffered by common sailors whose vessels touched port in San Francisco.[32]

Hoffman's concern for maintaining the nation's honor extended from maritime practices aboard American vessels to activities of self-declared patriots who invaded sovereign nations. In 1854, a series of prosecutions in the northern district resulted in the first convictions in the nation under the Neutrality Act of 1818 and sought to restrain quasi-military incursions into Mexico by both Americans and foreigners. Why these convictions occurred in Hoffman's court, despite the predisposition of the local U.S. attorney not to prosecute, provides an example of political and other pressures affecting the course of criminal justice. During these prosecutions, Hoffman found himself embroiled in a controversy largely brought on by his own misjudgment, a controversy that not only antagonized San Francisco's sizable French community but also created an international incident requiring political adjustment at the highest levels of government.[33]

More important, the prosecutions occurred in a context that favored the notion of America's Manifest Destiny and raised the issue of what sources of law should govern a federal judge. Associated with an aggressive, aggrandizing foreign policy and program of territorial acquisitions, Manifest Destiny also embodied an assumption of the regenerative moral effect of American values on what were perceived as "backward" nations, such as Mexico. Hoffman struggled between his sympathy with American violators of the Neutrality Act and his obligation to enforce that law. Moreover, the prosecutions presented another conflict that Hoffman had to resolve: the constitutional right of a criminal defendant to compel witnesses to testify versus exemptions from court appearances granted to consuls under a treaty with France.[34]

The expeditions that California federal officials attempted to prevent in 1854 were largely composed of adventurers who sought glory and wealth by seizing the reputedly mineral-rich Mexican state of Sonora. A variety of purposes cloaked the motives of these filibusters, or freebooters. Some, like the American William Walker, portrayed themselves as harbingers of civilization with a noble purpose: bringing order to a Mexican population unable to exploit its natural resources and protect itself from the Apache Indians. That Walker and his band were justified in assuming control over parts of Mexico struck many as part of America's Manifest Destiny of continued geographical expansion, notwithstanding the fact that Walker intended to make himself president of an independent state. He and his supporters deliberately ignored the nation's obligation to respect the sovereignty of another country with which it was at peace and its duty to enforce neutrality laws to prevent such hostile military expeditions from being launched from the United States.[35]

Other filibustering efforts organized in San Francisco during this time included Frenchmen enlisted by Count Gaston de Raousset-Boulbon ostensibly as beneficent colonists of Sonora whose presence would protect the Mexican population from Indian attacks. Indeed, the Mexican government had encouraged the count, through its San Francisco consul Luis Maria del Valle, with the expectation that the Frenchmen might make an effective buffer against American expeditions. The hope of pitting filibuster against filibuster to Mexico's advantage faded when Raousset, like Walker, displayed his own plans for Sonora. Indeed, del Valle's conduct as well as the plans of Raousset and Walker became the target of American military scrutiny that resulted in prosecutions under the Neutrality Act of 1818.[36]

The act of 1818 provided punishment by a fine of up to $3,000 and imprisonment of up to three years if "any person" within the jurisdiction of the United States began or "set on foot" or provided for "any military expedition or enterprise to be carried on from thence against" a nation at peace with the United States. The act also made it a crime to enlist persons for a filibustering expedition (punishable by a maximum fine of $1,000 and three years' imprisonment) or to outfit vessels for such a purpose (maximum fine of $10,000 and three years' imprisonment). Between 1845 and 1853 the numerous national attempts to enforce the act against incursions into Mexico had proved futile. To some extent this resulted from the act's vague wording, which made it difficult to ascertain just what conduct was proscribed. Most important, however, the act lacked public support. Lackluster federal prosecutions, weak charges by judges, and sympathetic juries insured that the act of 1818 remained unenforced in federal courts. Ironically, the first successful prosecution for illegal incursions into Mexico occurred

before a sympathetic federal judge (Hoffman) in California, where senti-
ments ran high in favor of American filibustering expeditions to Sonora.[37]

The impetus for the enforcement of the Neutrality Act in California came
not from the federal prosecutor but from the president, through the military.
Acting under the instructions of President Millard Fillmore, the commander
of the U.S. Army's Department of the Pacific, General Ethan Allen Hitchcock, seized the brig *Arrow* in San Francisco in October 1853. The *Arrow*
had been chartered to carry Walker's men and supplies to Mexico. During
the summer of 1853, Walker and his confederates had been planning an
expedition to capture Baja and Sonora. Their efforts to gather recruits to
their cause were openly conducted in San Francisco and met with widespread approval. Thus when Hitchcock moved to frustrate Walker's expedition, his actions were branded as hasty and unjustified. The *Alta California*
advised the general to consult his "lawful advisor," U.S. Attorney Samuel W.
Inge, before making such moves. The same newspaper suggested that San
Francisco federal authorities were "in a fog as to their rights and duties
under the neutrality act."[38]

In fact Hitchcock got little help from Inge, a former Democratic congressman from Alabama, who advised the general that public pressure and
opinion dictated the return of the vessel to Walker. Hitchcock allegedly replied, "Damn public opinion." He persisted and bullied Inge into filing a
libel in Hoffman's court against the *Arrow*. Walker responded by initiating
proceedings in San Francisco's superior court to regain possession of the
ship. During the legal struggle over the *Arrow*'s seizure, Hitchcock inter-
cepted ammunition for Walker's party about to be loaded aboard the brig
Caroline. Walker and some of his party nonetheless slipped out of San Francisco for Mexico in the *Caroline*. After proclaiming himself "president" of
an independent republic consisting of Baja California and Sonora, Walker
and his men ultimately encountered such local resistance that in May 1854,
the remaining members of the original expedition were forced out of Mexico
near San Diego, where they surrendered to American troops and were arrested for violating the neutrality laws.[39]

Why Judge Hoffman sympathized with a man like Walker is worth pon-
dering. Hoffman would seem to be an unlikely supporter of the filibuster.
Hoffman's strict legalism, of course, presented a major obstacle to his support of such blatant violation of the Neutrality Act. Moreover, Walker, in his
brief newspaper career in San Francisco, had attacked a San Francisco

judge for criticizing the Vigilance Committee of 1851. Articles written by Walker had prompted Hoffman to come to the judge's defense. The regret Hoffman expressed three years later at the conviction of men who had followed Walker was partly linked to Hoffman's sympathy for Manifest Destiny.

However morally bankrupt the concept of Manifest Destiny appears to modern eyes, the doctrine "still had much luster" in 1854. Even though the Whig party, to which Hoffman belonged, had opposed the blatant expansionism of the Mexican War, many Whigs were reconciled to the acquisition of new territory, provided it could be redeemed through Christianity and commerce. To some Whigs, acquiring California seemed "destined" to make the country "the world's historical centre." What disturbed Whigs, including Hoffman, was the price to be paid in terms of social disruption and national honor. Hoffman's later charges to the juries in the neutrality prosecutions reveal these concerns as well as his belief in the moral superiority of the American nation. That belief alone implicitly offered support for filibustering impulses.[40]

More significantly, however, Hoffman's sympathy seemed less a result of attitudes linked to Manifest Destiny than of his perceptions about the character and motives of the filibuster himself. Walker's evident education, his proud and aloof bearing, were bound to strike chords of recognition if not approval on the part of the judge. Walker's experiences gave him a brooding presence that some people, including Hoffman, found charismatic.

Hoffman's sympathies also ran counter to public opinion that ultimately turned against Walker. The *Alta California*, along with most other newspapers, gave much attention and initial support to Walker's preparations during the summer of 1853. The *Alta California* hailed Walker's expedition as "another advance toward that 'manifest destiny' of the Anglo-Saxon race," but by late February 1854, the paper spoke of "misguided men" who had undertaken "a lawless and criminal foray on a neighboring state." Only after public sentiment turned against Walker and after the once glorious adventure seemed defeated did the *Alta California* withdraw its praise, denounce the expedition, and call for Walker's prosecution under the act.[41]

Even at the height of popular support for Walker's filibustering efforts, General John E. Wool, the commander of the Pacific Department, energetically sought the enforcement of the neutrality law and pressured the federal prosecutor to act. Wool, who arrived in San Francisco in early 1854 to replace General Hitchcock, had spoken with President Franklin Pierce and

Secretary of War Jefferson Davis about suppressing filibustering expeditions from California. The Walker expedition, already launched from San Francisco before Wool arrived, was complicating the diplomatic negotiations, then under way, that later resulted in the Gadsden Treaty of 1854 between Mexico and the United States. Before leaving Washington, D.C., for his new post, Wool received from Davis written instructions that seemed explicit on the subject of filibusterism. "Confidence is felt," wrote Davis, "that you will to the utmost of your ability, use all proper means to detect the fitting out of armed expeditions against countries with which the United States are at peace, and will zealously co-operate with civil authorities in maintaining the neutrality laws." [42]

Some of Wool's zeal in carrying out his orders probably stemmed from a career officer's contempt for young amateurs playing at soldiering. But though his instructions seemed clear, Wool never understood that filibustering activities were politically charged affairs, perhaps best illustrated when President Pierce recognized Walker's self-proclaimed republic in Nicaragua in 1856. Wool's single-minded pursuit of filibusters ultimately won him an official reprimand for slighting his other duties and underlay his transfer back to the East Coast. [43]

As with General Hitchcock, U.S. Attorney Inge proved a reluctant ally to Wool in initiating prosecutions against members of Walker's filibustering expedition even after the U.S. attorney general instructed him to strictly enforce the neutrality law. As the *Alta California* put it, federal authorities had "winked" at the violation of the neutrality law when Walker had first left San Francisco. Moreover, Wool did not find "the civil officers . . . very anxious to check these expeditions." Indeed, even after Wool conducted an extensive investigation into violations of the Neutrality Act, Inge insisted on Wool's written request for the arrest of violators even though a federal grand jury had already brought in an indictment. Nonetheless, by mid-March 1854, Wool reported to Secretary of War Davis that he had caused the arrest of Henry P. Watkins and Frederick Emory, associates of Walker's who were in California to secure supplies for Walker's expedition in Sonora. Wool also suspected Count Raousset-Boulbon of cooperating with Walker and believed that both the Mexican consul, del Valle, and the French consul, Patrice Dillon, were involved in helping mount illegal expeditions to Mexico. [44]

Watkins's five-day jury trial, which began before Hoffman on March 20,

1854, presented a classic instance of a federal court doing its legal duty despite obvious judicial sympathy for the defendant. Watkins also had the benefit of distinguished counsel, including the Virginian Edmund Randolph. Randolph's argument to the jury embodied the essence of the defense: that the trial was a "persecution" of a man of good character who was held in high public esteem, that the jury should sympathize with the noble purpose and ambition of the adventurers even if their intentions were "nominally criminal," and that by openly organizing its expedition in San Francisco with impunity, Watkins and Walker's party had been indirectly encouraged by the authorities. For the government, Inge took the position that Watkins's actions had violated an international agreement that the United States had to acknowledge. Inge thus stressed the contractual obligation of the nation to adhere to the Neutrality Act rather than implied any inherent wrongfulness on the part of the defendant.[45]

Hoffman's charge to the jury shared much of Inge's approach toward the prosecution and skillfully encouraged the jury to find a verdict of guilty, against its own inclination. From the start Hoffman had indicated his personal sympathies "with the accused in their motives." He noted, "I may appreciate the gallant ambition of the man who attempted to build up a flourishing colony on a territory now devastated by the savage, but my duty and my oath remains the same." Here Hoffman made it plain that the jury members too would have to suppress their sympathies. Though both he and the jury might want to "unite with the counsel for the defense in eulogium upon the character and motives of the expeditionists," Hoffman could not have them ignore the evidence or permit them "to be influenced by such appeals" as had been made "on points not connected with the evidence."[46]

As a matter of law, Hoffman continued, the defendant was guilty if the evidence established his participation in the expedition. Hoffman stressed the independence of this issue from any consideration of the merits of the expedition or the Neutrality Act itself. Knowing where his sympathies lay, the jury might reluctantly accept Hoffman's assertion that "for the honor and credit of the nation and the Government," it was of "great importance" that the verdict be rendered according to the evidence, or in other words that Watkins be found guilty. Hoffman conceded that the neutrality law might be "opposed to the spirit of the age and unfavorable to the progress of civilization and of . . . our free institutions," but he cautioned the jury not to be swayed by such considerations. Despite Hoffman's charge, the jury took over five hours to reach a verdict of guilty. The *Alta California* exulted that this first conviction of filibustering would show the East Coast that San Francisco was not "lawless."[47]

If Hoffman felt he had vindicated the neutrality law and the nation's international obligations to Mexico by giving a strong charge to the jury suggesting Watkins's legal guilt, the judge was hardly prepared to go much further. After the jury reached its verdict, Hoffman responded to a request to show mercy to the defendant by indicating that he "would not be severe in his sentence." Indeed, in passing sentence on both Watkins and Frederick Emory—who pleaded guilty after Watkins's conviction—Hoffman even more clearly revealed his attitude toward the filibusters and his understanding of their motives. Hoffman fined each defendant only $1,500, feeling that "the great moral effect" of the prosecution had been "attained by the conviction." He asserted, "[Many men] of high character and otherwise unblemished reputations have embarked in these expeditions, to whom no merely sordid or selfish motives can with justice be attributed, and who, thinking perhaps they were but responding to the call of humanity or the dictates of patriotism, however mistaken, have joined expeditions which appealed irresistibly to their courage and spirit of adventure." Such were the motives Hoffman admired in and attributed to Watkins and Emory. Despite his obligation to acknowledge their violation of law, the judge did not wish to "subject" their "character to degradation by imprisonment."[48]

In the two weeks between Watkins's trial and his sentencing, General Wool had succeeded in having the British ship *Challenge* detained and the Mexican consul, del Valle, arrested on grounds that the consul had gathered the Frenchmen, then on the ship, for deployment as soldiers in Mexico. On April 5, 1854, the federal grand jury indicted del Valle after Hoffman told the jury that the objective of the Neutrality Act was to protect the United States as well as the countries with whom the nation was at peace. Hoffman also observed that the case assumed greater significance because the government had already enforced the act against Americans. The *Alta California* predicted that the U.S. attorney would seek only nominal punishment, rather than maximum penalties, for both del Valle and Watkins, so that both sides would "be satisfied, and the vulgar be gratified with two farces instead of one."[49]

The real excitement, however, began during del Valle's trial only after his attorney sought the testimony of the French consul, Dillon. On April 18,

1854, Dillon declined the court's invitation to appear as a witness, citing a treaty that the United States and France had concluded the previous year. Article two of that treaty exempted consuls of either government from being forced to give testimony but permitted courts to invite them to do so. Hoffman initially agreed that the clear language of the treaty justified Dillon's refusal. However, U.S. Attorney Inge, rather than del Valle's lawyer, reacted most strongly to Dillon's refusal, calling it an "outrageous contempt" of Hoffman's court. Inge maintained that if the treaty's consular exemption was extended to criminal cases, then a defendant's constitutional right, under the sixth amendment, to have compulsory process for obtaining witnesses in his favor would be violated.[50]

Under Wool's influence, Inge had grown deeply suspicious of Dillon and resented the consul's forceful attitude in representing France and the French community in San Francisco. Among the later charges leveled against Dillon was his "studied insolence of manner" toward American representatives. Thus, the frustration Inge experienced at Dillon's recalcitrance led him to pressure Hoffman into agreeing to subpoena the consul and his secretary five days later. The degree to which Hoffman lost control at this critical juncture of the proceedings can be measured by the fact that Inge apparently drafted a subpoena—contrary to Hoffman's intentions—requiring Dillon to bring documents with him to court.[51]

On April 25, 1854, del Valle's lawyer asked for an attachment, or arrest, of Dillon after the consul failed to respond to the subpoena. Hoffman regretted that the issue had arisen and said it put his court "in a delicate position." Nonetheless, Hoffman felt the treaty implied broader exemptions from testimony in criminal cases than it should have. In Hoffman's view: "The Constitution gives the right; the Treaty denies it. I must follow the Constitution." As word spread that Hoffman had granted the attachment requested, several thousand Frenchmen and their supporters gathered outside the French consulate to protest Dillon's arrest by the U.S. marshal. The seizure of the *Challenge* had upset the French community in San Francisco, and Dillon's arrest aroused the local Frenchmen even further. Although Dillon calmed the crowd, they marched behind and filled the federal courtroom to see what Ogden Hoffman would do.[52]

Dillon's lawyer, Edward D. Baker, entered Dillon's formal diplomatic protest. Dillon then observed that he meant no disrespect to Hoffman or his court in refusing to attend but that under the terms of the treaty he would not answer any questions in the current trial. Hoffman reiterated his regret over the confrontation, noting that he hoped Dillon would abandon his standing "on the mere letter of the treaty" and asserting that he was bound to grant del Valle's rights under the sixth amendment. Baker argued that Dillon's rights as consul of France had been violated by the summons and arrest. The protest entered by Dillon and Baker's suggestion of impropriety caused Hoffman to waver, and he announced his intention to hear full arguments the next day on the issue of whether or not Dillon was in contempt of court. Dillon, however, considered himself arrested and the dignity of France violated and immediately hauled down the French flag over his consulate after the court proceedings.[53]

After declaring the issue of Dillon's contempt "entirely open," Hoffman heard two days of argument. He regretted that the issue had not come before him as an order to Dillon to show why compulsory process should not issue against him to appear as a witness. And despite the fact that Hoffman had already authorized the subpoena and arrest of Dillon, the court and the attorneys for Dillon and del Valle agreed to present arguments as though the issue had just arisen.[54]

After hearing the arguments, Hoffman reversed himself and delivered an opinion sustaining Dillon. Hoffman addressed the apparent conflict between the treaty and the Constitution, a conflict that seemed to force him either to deny a right secured by "the fundamental law of the land" or to declare the treaty unconstitutional—"a duty at all times the most delicate and important an American court of justice is called upon to perform." Hoffman finessed the conflict by arguing that Dillon's status as a consul put him outside the reach of the court and that del Valle's rights under the sixth amendment were no more violated than if he were unable to compel a witness to testify because of that witness's physical unavailability. Moreover, Hoffman held that any subpoena requiring Dillon to bring documents with him to court, in the absence of a showing that such documents were not official papers protected from seizure under the treaty, should not be granted.[55]

In his opinion, Hoffman stated that he had granted the attachment for Dillon because the consul had not given his reasons for not appearing. In fact Hoffman knew full well the reasons for Dillon's refusal to obey the subpoena: before the issuance of the subpoena, Dillon had refused Hoffman's invitation to testify, explicitly relying on his consular exemption. Indeed the muddled chronology and the pretended state of the proceedings in Hoffman's opinion could not undo the damage already done. Dillon had been subpoenaed and brought into court under arrest. Dillon's protest reached Washington and prompted the secretary of state to demand from Hoffman an explanation of his conduct. After extensive discussion between the State Department, the American ambassador to France, and the French government, normal diplomatic relations were restored between the two countries.[56]

If Hoffman's opinion sought to suggest that he had not intended to have Dillon subpoenaed and arrested, it failed to convince San Franciscans who had followed the events of del Valle's trial. The *Alta California* congratulated Hoffman for "acknowledging his own error." The paper noted, "The ablest judges will differ and change their opinions." Other newspapers were not so kind. The *New York Times* referred to Hoffman's "awkward blunder," and the *San Francisco Herald* impugned his motives. William Tecumseh Sherman, along with the *Alta California*, disputed the *Herald*'s implications and asserted that Hoffman had simply changed his mind after more reflection. Sherman summed up the affair by saying that the judge was "a young man, but . . . above suspicion as to integrity and ability." Nonetheless, Hoffman's conduct in the Dillon matter showed him to disadvantage; Hoffman appeared vacillating and capable of being bullied into precipitate action. The lesson was not lost on Hoffman: in the years ahead he would act more deliberately and carefully, and he would develop more confidence in his own counsel.[57]

After the excitement of the Dillon controversy, the conclusion of the del Valle trial proved an anticlimax. Although the jury found the Mexican consul guilty, U.S. Attorney Inge subsequently dismissed any further proceedings, effectively releasing del Valle. The decision to release del Valle came after Inge's attempt to convict Dillon under the Neutrality Act ended in a hung jury and a motion for a *nolle prosequi*. Indeed the conviction and sentencing of Watkins constituted the highest point of the filibuster prosecutions. The results of the del Valle and Dillon trials reflected the changed mood of the community. The Watkins case and to some extent the del Valle case found public vindication for the neutrality law. However, the efforts against Dillon seemed personally motivated by Inge, and consequently when Walker finally came on trial in San Francisco in October 1854, before a visiting district court judge—Hoffman having left for a visit to the East Coast—San Franciscans were fed up with the whole business. Walker argued on his own behalf, and after eight minutes of deliberation, the jury brought in a verdict of not guilty. Applause broke out in the courtroom, and many came forward to shake Walker's hand.[58]

A nineteenth-century perception of the hierarchy of sources of law accounted for Hoffman's charge to Watkins's jury and why he upheld Dillon's refusal to testify. Hoffman's references to upholding national honor by enforcing the neutrality laws despite sympathizing with American defendants were not rhetorical or offhand remarks. The importance placed on national honor as an element in assessing the authority of treaties in federal litigation was apparently part of a wider consensus among federal judges of his day. For Hoffman, treaties and agreements with foreign nations embodied more than constitutional authority: they were the nation's version of a gentleman's word of honor. For that reason especially, treaties (though equally binding as congressional legislation) placed federal judges, particularly someone like Hoffman, under greater imperatives than did federal statutes. Almost thirty years after the filibuster prosecutions, Hoffman and the other federal judges in the ninth circuit would reluctantly make similar choices that pitted Chinese immigration—which they disfavored—against the nation's obligations under the Burlingame Treaty with China.

Although the Dillon affair and the criminal cases arising in admiralty reveal how Hoffman dealt with some criminal matters before his court, they only partially illuminate the institutional dynamics of a criminal docket of a nineteenth-century federal district court. Celebrated cases such as those involving filibustering expeditions or the more common instances of criminal behavior on ships or crimes such as counterfeiting, false voting registration, or selling liquor to Indians ultimately accounted for little more than 20 percent of all the government's prosecutions in the northern district. More than half of Hoffman's criminal cases dealt with failure to pay applicable taxes or import duties. In the maritime context, most prosecutions by the government consisted of libels for the forfeiture of ships and cargo for violation of federal statutes—usually revenue laws. Another substantial series of government cases involved the bonds posted by importers of goods to San Francisco; if the importer failed to establish the domestic port of shipment, the government sued on the bonds to secure foreign import duties.[59]

When and how the government used Hoffman's court to prosecute even these numerous revenue cases was not a straightforward matter. All the cases filed by the U.S. attorney, of course, involved violations of federal law, but not all such crimes were prosecuted or, if prosecuted, were pursued with equal vigor. Unlike the admiralty cases brought by private parties, Hoffman's criminal docket experienced cycles of rapid expansion and contraction in the number and type of crimes prosecuted. Whereas admiralty cases overwhelmed Hoffman during his first decade as a judge and then tapered off to a modest level for the rest of his tenure, the criminal docket followed an opposite pattern. That is, over 75 percent of Hoffman's criminal cases were filed between 1877 and 1891. Consequently, it is important to examine the principal causes for the timing of criminal prosecutions.

The fourteen U.S. attorneys for the northern district during Hoffman's tenure enjoyed wide freedom of action in their ability to initiate and conduct prosecutions. Although routinely removed from office with changes in the administration, U.S. attorneys, once appointed by the president and confirmed by the Senate, experienced little systematic superintendency from Washington. Circulars directed toward uniform practices and procedures were sent to government attorneys from U.S. attorneys general starting in the late 1860s. However, the limited resources of the attorney general's office underscored the fact that his primary responsibility was to provide legal advice to the president and to represent the government in cases before the Supreme Court. Apart from the inherent practical difficulties of overseeing the work of U.S. attorneys, the attorney general's office in the nineteenth century merely shared such supervision with a wide variety of other officials and departments. Depending on the subject matter at issue, the solicitor of the treasury, the secretaries of war, treasury, and interior, and postmasters general were among the Washington officials who might legitimately claim a say in the conduct of cases brought by the U.S. attorney. The diffusion of authority led not only to confusion but also ultimately to greater freedom of decision for federal prosecutors.[60]

The adjudication of California's private land grants formed the principal exception to the free rein federal prosecutors in the northern district usually enjoyed in substantive matters. The extraordinary importance of the land cases and the fact that so many of them would be appealed to the U.S. Supreme Court account for the extensive communication from U.S. attorneys general and other Washington officials to the local U.S. attorneys. Still, the degree of involvement in this special area only emphasizes the independence that federal prosecutors such as those in California enjoyed in most matters.[61]

Occasionally, complaints that government attorneys were not doing their job or were acting improperly resulted in direct action by Washington. The accusations that the northern district's U.S. attorney, William Blanding, had failed to aggressively prosecute members of the Vigilance Committee of 1856 led to his removal in 1857. Moreover, after U.S. Attorney Samuel G. Hilborn allowed the statute of limitations to run on members of the "Humboldt Ring"—who successfully defrauded the United States of huge quantities of timber lands along California's north coast—investigations were launched by the office of the solicitor general, the Department of the Interior, and the attorney general's office. The reports resulted in Hilborn's removal from office in 1886.[62]

California's geographical remoteness accentuated the independence of its U.S. attorneys. Even in areas where direction was sought or given from Washington, as in land adjudication, the slowness of communication delayed the process and frustrated the parties. In situations like those involving the Vigilance Committee of 1856, the criminal episode had passed before directives were received from the attorney general. As late as 1879, the year Circuit Judge Lorenzo Sawyer relinquished his criminal docket to Hoffman, geography had a way of frustrating justice. Sawyer explained the "practical inconvenience" in waiting so long for copies of federal statutes. He noted, "In some instances parties have been tried before me, and convicted for offences committed *after the repeal of the act creating them*, and before notice to the courts of such repeal."[63]

Not only did California's U.S. attorneys experience little regular control from Washington, but they were also largely free of institutional constraints within the northern district. This was reflected by Hoffman's response in 1886 to a motion asking the court to force the northern district's U.S. attorney to bring certain criminal cases to trial. Hoffman called the motion "wholly inadmissible" and declared he had "no power to compel the District Attorney to try the cases." Hoffman then outlined his official relationship with the United States attorney. "He conducts the public business according to his sense of duty. The Court has power to call upon the District Attorney, to say when he will be ready to try the case, and if not [ready, to set trial] within a reasonable time, and if other circumstances make it proper the Court may discharge the Defendants upon their own recognizances." Although Hoffman conceded that he had not done extensive research on the point, it is significant that after thirty-five years as a judge, Hoffman believed his statement reflected "the only authority" his court exercised over the U.S. attorney.[64]

The operation of the office of the U.S. attorney thus rested largely on the incumbent. Although U.S. attorneys succeeded in justifying the appointment of assistants to help them during the course of the nineteenth century, that office remained quite small and was ultimately dominated by the political appointee. If he wanted, the U.S. attorney could frustrate prosecutions. An agent investigating the possible wrongdoing in the U.S. attorney's office for the northern district noted one such possible means. "It is to be presumed that when a man is indicted for a criminal offense, the prosecuting officer believes there is to be sufficient evidence upon which to base a conviction. But how easy it is to fail in a prosecution, no matter how strong may be the evidence, if the prosecutor has not his whole soul in the matter."[65]

In addition to having no power to force the U.S. attorney to bring criminal charges or aggressively pursue cases, Hoffman had no say in the U.S. attorney's decision to abandon a prosecution or enter a *nolle prosequi*. That decision ostensibly rested on a determination that insufficient evidence existed for a conviction or that in the case of a hung jury, for example, the time and expense of a retrial would outweigh the probabilities of a conviction. But here again only the U.S. attorney's "sense of duty" guided him, and the docket books during Hoffman's tenure show wide variation in how these attorneys interpreted that duty. One example of such discretion by prosecutors is the relative number of *nolle prosequis* entered in cases against sea captains as opposed to other seamen and officers, but the most dramatic instances of different treatment among defendants occurred in prosecutions against the Chinese.[66]

The fluctuations in some categories of government prosecution, such as revenue matters in Hoffman's criminal docket, are also partially linked to the wide discretion of U.S. attorneys. Although filings and prosecutions by the U.S. attorney for revenue violations occurred in that docket in spurts, the statutes that formed the basis for such prosecutions were substantially unenforced for significant periods of Hoffman's judgeship. Whether because of the press of business in other dockets, such as land or U.S. admiralty, or because of a disinclination or inclination to punish certain offenders, governmental prosecution varied from attorney to attorney. Thus, the individuality and discretion available to the office of the U.S. attorney influenced how the federal government's business was conducted.[67]

To say that U.S. attorneys were free from judicial control over the conduct of their office is not to say that they were immune from other significant pressures. The zeal of Generals Hitchcock and Wool, for instance, succeeded in forcing the reluctant U.S. attorney, Samuel Inge, into prosecuting American filibusters. Likewise, lower-ranking members of the federal service, including customs officials, land agents, and treasury agents, could also force prosecutions by making charges and arrests or writing letters.

In some respects public opinion proved to be an even more effective influence on U.S. attorneys. Calhoun Benham, the northern district's first U.S. attorney, could hardly have ignored the public outcry over the perceived brutality of Captain Waterman and his officers when the ship *Challenge* arrived in San Francisco in 1851. Even without mobs gathering in the streets threatening to take matters into their own hands if the federal authorities failed to act, U.S. attorneys were hard pressed to ignore crimes or violations that attracted substantial public notice. Occasionally, public opinion opposing popular mobs resulted in dictating the course of governmental action. Indeed, according to U.S. Attorney William Blanding, the prosecution against several members of the Vigilance Committee of 1856—for piracy in seizing military arms being shipped across San Francisco Bay—had been instituted by "some of the 'Law and Order party.' "[68]

Moreover, certain periods, such as during the Civil War and during the height of the anti-Chinese feeling in the 1880s, were marked by public concerns, occasionally bordering on hysteria, to which U.S. attorneys responded. Similarly, the aggressive prosecution of would-be privateers and the proceedings to confiscate southern property were fueled and validated by public concerns over secessionist plots and the danger of Confederate sympathizers in California.[69]

A more difficult influence to trace involved federal attorneys' remuneration, which also affected how they exercised their discretion. From the earliest organization of the federal courts through the nineteenth century, U.S. attorneys, marshals, and court clerks were paid on a fee system rather than by salary. That is, for specific official functions and acts, they received set fees that were primarily paid by the parties who used the courts. Although fees were the ostensible means of compensating U.S. attorneys, in practice they especially relied on payment for legal services that fell outside their official duties. As U.S. Attorney General Felix Grundy observed in 1839, it had "long been the settled opinion" of his office that U.S. attorneys who defended federal officials before state courts or federal interests not within their official duties were "employed and paid as other members of the profession for such services." In such cases the U.S. attorney was entitled to "reasonable" compensation. What the federal officials in Washington, who essentially contracted the services of the U.S. attorney, regarded as "reasonable" invariably differed from what the U.S. attorney deemed fair.[70]

In the early 1870s, for example, U.S. Attorney Lorenzo D. Latimer defended the collector of the port of San Francisco and some of his revenue agents in numerous suits in state courts charging them with extracting excessive duties. After his legal services in one suit, Latimer submitted a bill of $1,142 to the secretary of the interior, who called the charge "exorbitant" and suggested that a fee of $500 and expenses was reasonable. Ultimately they compromised on $600 and expenses, but Latimer continued to grumble that the government should be "liberal" in its compensation in those "occasional cases" permitted by law. As a result of such haggling, Latimer eventually collected some $3,500 as payment for his special services between 1871 and 1872. Such lump-sum payments were bound to be far more attractive to U.S. attorneys than were the ordinary fees set by statute.[71]

As Latimer put it, the fees for cases within his official duties were often "absurdly disproportionate to the services required." He noted, "I have tried cases for the Government for the legal docket fee of $10.00 only, in which the attorneys opposed have received one hundred times that amount in gold, and that but a reasonable fee." This disproportionate compensation affected U.S. attorneys in terms of what types of cases they preferred to spend their time prosecuting, particularly since they were allowed to pursue a private practice to supplement their income when not occupied with their official duties. More than one U.S. attorney complained that the press of underpaid government business excluded more lucrative practice. In 1876 the northern district's U.S. attorney resigned with a pithy telegram to the attorney general: "The office don't pay for the abuse and annoyances."[72]

Even though government attorneys complained about the fee system, it

still had the potential to make them substantial money. Early critics of
the system noted its possible abuse by officials who might unscrupulously
"make" fees to enhance their income. Until the mid–nineteenth century,
however, the fees collected by court officials varied from district to district
because they usually followed the differing fee schedules of the states. On
occasion, federal fees were established with reference to another district
court. California's fees, for instance, were incorporated by Congress by reference to those of the southern district of New York.[73]

The pattern in California, however, reflected the success of arguments
that inflation caused by the gold rush justified higher-than-average fees and
compensation for federal officials. As a result, federal clerks, attorneys, and
marshals were accorded the right to charge double the fees of their counterparts in New York for four years after the passage of the act organizing
California's federal courts in 1850. Thereafter, California officials had to
content themselves with the amounts paid in the southern district of New
York. In addition to higher-than-average fees, California's federal attorneys
and marshals were permitted an annual salary of $500—more than the
salary paid in most other districts.[74]

Before federal officials in California could take full advantage of the 1850
act, Congress passed the first uniform fee bill in 1853. The act itemized
what federal court officials could charge as fees and, importantly, placed
upper limits on the amount of fees that U.S. attorneys, clerks, and marshals
could collect. U.S. attorneys and marshals were allowed up to $6,000; any
fees beyond that sum went into the U.S. Treasury. Clerks faced a lower
ceiling of $3,500. But clerks could, and in the northern district frequently
did, simultaneously serve as U.S. commissioners and earn as many additional fees as they were able.[75]

A special proviso of the 1853 act allowed all California court officials to
receive twice the specified fees and salary until 1855, after which they were
entitled to 50 percent more than the specified fees until 1857, when California fees would be decreased to equal all other district courts. The incentive to "make" fees had always been present in the fee system, and even with
an imposed ceiling, the motive remained to collect the maximum amounts.
The special salary concessions that U.S. attorneys in California enjoyed in
the 1850s had the clear potential to influence governmental prosecutions.

The act of 1853 regulated the costs of what both U.S. attorneys and private attorneys could charge in federal courts. The act made it clear, however, that beyond the specified costs, private lawyers could charge clients—other than the government—"such reasonable compensation for their services" as was "in accordance with general usage in their respective States" or as was "agreed upon between the parties." Thus, the private fee arrangements of most lawyers remained largely hidden, but the fees that U.S. attorneys might charge were strictly itemized. For civil or criminal jury trials or for final hearings in equity or admiralty the U.S. attorney received a docket fee of $20. In "cases at law" where Hoffman sat as trier of fact, the U.S. attorney could claim $10 if judgment was rendered or $5 if the case was discontinued. Thus, since the decision to discontinue a case rested with the U.S. attorney, the multiple filing of cases with their subsequent discontinuance was one obvious way to "make" fees.[76]

In addition to docket fees, the U.S. attorney received $5 per day for his courtroom attendance and a similar amount for examining witnesses. Taking depositions and proceedings on recognizance yielded $2.50 and $5.00, respectively. Moreover, the act built in an incentive for criminal convictions. In criminal jury trials resulting in convictions, federal attorneys could claim, in addition to their other fees, "a counsel fee in proportion to the importance and difficulty of the cause, not exceeding thirty dollars." Thus, despite its efforts to reform the fee system, the act of 1853 left intact significant incentives to generate a higher volume of governmental prosecutions.[77]

The operation of that incentive can be traced in the series of early bond cases filed in the northern district. Between August and October 1851, U.S. Attorney Calhoun Benham filed over five hundred cases against importers of goods to San Francisco, alleging a failure to comply with revenue regulations by not demonstrating that the goods were exempt from import duties. His successor, Samuel Inge, complained in 1853 about the many cases that Benham had filed in which nothing had "been done beyond the initiation of a suit." Inge eventually discontinued all the libels in question. Still, at a fee of $4 per libel, Benham received over $2,000 in fees for what amounted to a perfunctory process. Indeed, between 1851 and 1867 over 1,100 bond cases were filed by various U.S. attorneys. To some extent it can be argued that the filings were justified as a means of making the commercial community of San Francisco aware of the revenue regulations and the determination of federal authorities to enforce them. Even so, revenue prosecutions, such as the bond cases, provided a significant source of revenue for the U.S. attorney as long as other dockets (such as criminal and land) had little business.[78]

An even more fruitful area for fees for U.S. attorneys throughout Hoffman's tenure was libels for forfeiture of cargo or vessels for violations of federal statutes, usually revenue laws. These cases, arising in Hoffman's U.S. admiralty docket, were sometimes related to prosecutions in the criminal docket against individuals whose alleged violations subjected themselves to punishment and their goods to seizure. Although public safety sometimes underlay the law, more often the objective was to collect revenue. During the last six months of 1851 alone, the U.S. attorney received at least $1,500 in fees in cases of forced sales of cargo based on attempts to avoid duties.[79]

A seizure of goods like opium could be especially profitable to U.S. attorneys. Because of the 100 percent tax on the drug, opium was an obvious target for attempted smuggling. Enforcement of the duty on opium became popular both with the collector of the port's revenue officers, who sought to detect smuggling, and with the federal U.S. attorneys, who filed libels for forfeiture. Because both sets of federal officers received a percentage of the value of the seized opium, not only did each have an economic incentive for such prosecutions, but also the operation of this system inevitably brought them into conflict. The U.S. attorney received a percentage only if the amount of opium seized was worth more than $500, but the collector benefited from a share of even smaller seizures. In 1881 U.S. Attorney Philip Teare accused the collector and his men of breaking up seized opium into separate lots and hence cheating him out of his rightful percentage. Despite such squabbles, it is clear that both the government attorneys and the revenue officers made sizable amounts of money in the seizure of opium and other goods for violation of the revenue laws.[80]

Like the fluctuations in the number of bond cases, the frequency of government filings before the U.S. admiralty docket reflected the judicial business (and hence fees) competing for the U.S. attorney's attention. In the first three and a half years of the northern district's operation, over ninety cases were filed in that docket, but in the next six years, 1855 through 1860, merely eleven cases were filed.[81] Thereafter, however, filings in that docket picked up substantially. This pattern conformed very closely to the advent of the largest number of land cases coming on appeal from the Board of Land Commissioners and the most intense period of land adjudication before the district court. The preoccupation of the U.S. attorney with the land cases and his necessary appearance in court apparently left little time for him to bring libels in the admiralty docket. Only in the early 1860s, when the land-grant adjudication began to subside, did the government's prosecutions in admiralty begin to increase once more.[82]

The criminal law docket also witnessed similar signs of temporary dormancy. After 1854 the number of criminal cases dropped dramatically; indeed, no cases were filed between 1861 and 1863. In fact fewer cases were filed between 1855 and 1864 than in the single year of 1854. By the late 1860s, the number of criminal cases showed a dramatic rise, followed by yet another, even more substantial increase after 1879 when Hoffman inherited the circuit court criminal docket. Part of the reason for the decline of criminal cases in the period from 1855 to 1879 may have been due to the establishment of California's special circuit court in 1855. U.S. Supreme Court Justice Field continued this trend after he presided over the circuit court beginning in 1863. However, Lorenzo Sawyer, as the resident circuit judge, voluntarily surrendered much of his criminal docket's work load to Hoffman after 1879. Thus, the availability of a circuit court obviously drew some of the weightier criminal cases away from the district court, but this can only partially account for the degree to which Hoffman's criminal docket slowed, virtually ceasing from the mid-1850s to the mid-1860s and again throughout most of the 1870s. Crime and criminal violations did not disappear during these years; rather, the U.S. attorneys for the northern district simply lacked the time or interest to prosecute offenders.[83]

The resurgence of the criminal docket in the mid-1860s also brought with it an example of the discriminatory potential of the discretion possessed by U.S. attorneys. In 1868 the U.S. attorney for the northern district, Delos Lake, initiated a series of prosecutions against individuals for conducting their businesses or practicing their professions without paying a requisite license fee. Chinese defendants accused of selling or making cigars without a license were brought into court and convicted. Non-Chinese defendants charged with the same crime faced a rather different experience. Prosecutions against non-Chinese stockbrokers, real estate agents, lawyers, civil engineers, building contractors, doctors, and dentists were often abandoned when the government's attorney entered a *nolle prosequi*. When the U.S. attorney did pursue such prosecutions, non-Chinese defendants essentially plea-bargained by pleading guilty and receiving a $1 fine and court costs.

Chinese defendants, however, whether they pleaded guilty or were found so, received fines of $300 and costs or sentences of twenty days' (and in one case four months') imprisonment. The disparity in sentences, of course, reflects on Hoffman rather than Delos Lake and forms part of the complex story of how the Chinese fared before the northern district. Of relevance here is the discretionary power of the U.S. attorney, who dismissed many of the cases with non-Chinese defendants but none at all with Chinese defendants.[84]

Hoffman's criminal docket reveals his assumption of and practice at a judicial role in which he sought to arbitrate between competing values while trying to rise above personal predilections. In the adjudication of criminal activity on the high seas, for instance, the value of maintaining shipboard discipline was counterpoised by the need to prevent the maltreatment of sailors. Likewise, the filibuster prosecutions placed the nation's obligation of neutrality toward Mexico in opposition to the American spirit of Manifest Destiny. Finally, in the controversy over the French consul, Dillon, Hoffman felt bound to choose between the federal constitution and a treaty with France.

In each instance, Hoffman struggled mightily to strike a correct balance between competing values. Invariably what swayed him in difficult cases was the importance of upholding the nation's honor through his role as a federal judge. In maritime cases this took the form of rehabilitating what Hoffman viewed as the country's bad international reputation for brutality in its merchant marine. In the aftermath of the filibuster expeditions, Hoffman's concern to sustain the nation's solemn obligations guided his ultimate decisions, whether those obligations were contained in a neutrality law affecting Mexico or in a treaty with France.

Such decisions were frequently difficult ones for Hoffman because he self-consciously overcame his personal proclivities in adhering to his judicial duty. What is most significant about Hoffman's articulation of his doubts and uncertainties in reaching decisions was not his indecisiveness but rather the deliberation and weighing process that characterized him as a judge. Occasionally, as in the sentencing disparities between officers and sailors who were criminal defendants, Hoffman succumbed to bias. But more often than not his understanding of, and the pride he took in, his role as a federal judge found him wrestling with and often overcoming his personal instincts.

His decisions in the seamen's brutality cases reveal his struggles to draw a line between legitimate discipline and illegitimate brutality even while he entertained deep misgivings about the veracity of sailors' testimony. Similarly, his sympathies with the motives of the filibusters made it more difficult to do his judicial duty as he saw it; but in that case he not only overcame his personal inclinations but also persuaded a jury to overcome its emotional sympathies with the filibusters.

Hoffman's understanding of his role as a federal judge entailed forbearance as well as action, and this also affected the criminal docket of the northern district. How the U.S. attorney conducted his office (what cases he prosecuted and how he prosecuted them, for example) was, in Hoffman's view, essentially beyond his judicial control. This understanding, combined with the institutional autonomy all U.S. attorneys then possessed, left Hoffman with marginal influence over what kinds of criminal cases were filed or, in many cases, over their ultimate disposition.

The wide discretion of prosecutors, influenced by many different factors, characterized Hoffman's criminal docket. Financial incentives inherent in how federal officials, including U.S. attorneys, were compensated provided only one possible reason that certain types of cases were filed in Hoffman's court. A variety of other pressures, some public and some private, helped account for what cases were prosecuted, as did the demands placed on U.S. attorneys to deal with noncriminal matters. The most striking aspects of the statistics of Hoffman's criminal docket during his forty years on the bench are the fluctuations, cycles, and gaps in criminal prosecution. Crime and criminal violations probably did not remain constant during the forty-year period, but by the same token crime hardly disappeared for years at a time or suddenly reappeared, as the statistics might suggest. Instead, that data graphically illustrates the dynamic and discretionary nature of federal criminal prosecution in the nineteenth century. In the final analysis, the quality of criminal justice in the northern district rested as much on the conscientiousness and integrity of its various U.S. attorneys as it did on Judge Hoffman.

CHAPTER

5

California Land

The Struggle over Titles

More than with any other docket, the adjudication of California's land grants brought Hoffman dramatically and consistently under public scrutiny. Besides the state, regional, and national attention Hoffman received for these cases—of vital importance to westerners—his land-grant opinions generated the closest and most sustained review by the U.S. Supreme Court. This process of review—largely resulting in reversals of his decisions—reveals a tension between trial and appellate court law-making and involved extrajudicial influences on the rule of law.

After the cession of vast lands to the United States by Mexico in 1848, Hoffman found himself charged with the awesome task of assimilating property rights based on Mexican law into the American common-law system. Guided by precedents of the Supreme Court, Hoffman began his land adjudication in 1853 by requiring strict observance of the Mexican law before he confirmed such grants. Hoffman particularly relied on the Supreme Court's decisions of *United States* v. *Kingsley* (1838) and *United States* v. *Boisdore* (1851). When the Supreme Court later decided not to follow these earlier land-grant precedents that Hoffman had relied on and announced a very liberal and flexible approach to the California grants, the trial judge found himself reversed. In *United States* v. *Fremont* (1855) and *United States* v. *Cruz Cervantes* (1856), the court rejected its earlier position that compli-

ance with the requirements imposed in Spanish land grants was strictly necessary, holding instead that in the case of Mexican land grants in California,
subsequent performance of the conditions imposed in those grants would be
sufficient for confirmation. Although disagreeing with the Supreme Court,
Hoffman dutifully and carefully followed the Court's direction, even as he
entertained grave doubts about it.[1]

After the *Fremont* decision, Hoffman adhered to a policy of liberal confirmation of land claims. However, by the time large numbers of appeals from
his decisions reached the Supreme Court, starting in the late 1850s, a considerable shift had taken place in the minds of the Court, the federal prosecutors (including the attorney general), and the public. An atmosphere
of suspicion and caution had emerged that undercut the foundation on
which Hoffman, reluctantly, had confirmed many land claims. The Supreme
Court's new direction, epitomized by *United States* v. *Teschmaker* (1860),
owed much to a growing perception—largely stimulated by a new attorney
general—that fraud underlay many land grants.[2]

At stake in the land-grant litigation was whether claims would be confirmed to individuals or would be rejected and become part of the public
domain. In this process of quieting titles in California, Hoffman played an
important role that extended from the 1850s through the 1870s. Mexican
land-grant litigation could involve three adjudicative levels: an appointed
board of land commissioners, the federal district courts in California, and
the U.S. Supreme Court. Hoffman not only heard appeals from the board
that arose in the northern district but also, between 1853 and 1856, served
as the only judge hearing such cases. After 1856, Hoffman frequently
joined Matthew Hall McAllister—the specially appointed circuit judge for
California—who by statute presided over the district court when hearing
land cases. As this litigation continued for decades, it ultimately involved
fifteen different U.S. attorneys general, with Caleb Cushing (1853–57) and
Jeremiah S. Black (1857–60) having the greatest influence.

Resolving the conflicts over California's grants also necessarily entailed
interactions between the three institutions delegated to quiet title. The final
confirmation of titles rested with the Supreme Court, but because of the
length of appeals, the district court inevitably found itself responding to the
high court's shifting positions on California land claims. As a result, Judge
Hoffman, as the principal figure in the intermediary stage between the board
and the Supreme Court, frequently found himself in a strange position that

resulted from his adherence to the Court's early decisions on California grants. Impelled by his understanding of precedent and his sense of judicial duty, Hoffman confirmed titles that he did not believe in and that the Supreme Court subsequently rejected. The growing suspicion of fraud and conspiracy that emerged toward the end of the first decade of litigation over Mexican titles accounted for Hoffman's unenviable position.

Different understandings of land holding and conflicting interests inevitably produced disputes. The settlement of those disputes was invariably delayed because the claimants (whether Hispanic or non-Hispanic) asserted title to large portions of some of the most desirable land in the state. Such claims predictably produced resentment and opposition from many immigrants to California who expected cheap and readily available land. Resolving these titles involved more than simply balancing the claims of grantees against those of settlers. Rather, the conflict over land in California entailed a multiplicity of conflicting interests: grantees, settlers, land speculators, municipal authorities, and the federal government. Ultimately that struggle pitted those who philosophically objected to the monopolization of land against those who believed in the sanctity of vested interests; those with an antipathy toward Hispanics against those with a recognition of the letter and spirit of treaty obligations to Mexico; those involved in real estate speculation against those concerned with protecting the public's welfare; and the common-law tradition against the civil law.

Settlers seeking California land after the gold rush realized that Mexican private land grants were their greatest obstacle. The Treaty of Guadalupe Hidalgo established the terms of the Mexican cession of lands to the United States following the Mexican War of 1846. That treaty guaranteed that Mexican ownership of "property of every kind" within the territory ceded would "be inviolably respected." The treaty thus committed the United States to recognize the legitimate ownership of substantial tracts of land held largely under Mexican grants in the new state.[3]

Congress passed the California Land Act of 1851 to implement the treaty and confirm legitimate land claims. Most commentators have blamed the act for delays in settling titles in California, needlessly involving the courts and creating litigation that stripped Hispanic native Californians (or Californios) of their land. There were indeed long delays and unfortunate consequences, but the delays resulted from the clash of the strong competing interests at stake rather than the act of 1851. Nonetheless, a lawyer accurately and prophetically observed in 1852, "[The act] is very hard on the land-owners and it is utter nonsense . . . to say that all a man has to do is *present* his claim."[4]

The act reflected its checkered background. By 1851, the battle lines were fairly well drawn. California settlers and those averse to individuals owning large tracts of land made Democrat William M. Gwin, one of California's U.S. senators, their champion. Senator Thomas Hart Benton, a Democrat from Missouri, became the principal spokesman for the interests of land claimants. Their diametric viewpoints were grounded in both ideology and self-interest. Gwin sought to consolidate the political support of the settlers in California; Benton defended the interests of land-grant owners, including his sons-in-law, John C. Frémont and William Carey Jones. In fact, Frémont owned the claim to Las Mariposas, situated in the heart of the southern gold region and then estimated to be worth $10 million.[5]

By the time Congress debated what policy would govern California's land grants, two influential—and conflicting—reports had appeared. These reports established the context within which Gwin and Benton debated. Captain Henry W. Halleck, California's military secretary of state, had written one report in 1849. The attorney William Carey Jones, while an agent for the Department of the Interior, had compiled the other report in 1850. Halleck's report concluded that most of California's land titles were "at least very doubtful, if not entirely fraudulent," and that land had "been divided up and sold to speculators," who would endeavor "to dispose of it to the new settlers at exorbitant profits." Halleck emphasized the inchoate nature of titles, the sketchy boundaries, and the failure of grants to conform to requirements of Mexican law. He urged a critical examination of Mexican land grants, preferably within the context of a trial that would test titles in strict accord with Mexican law.[6]

Jones, on the other hand, concluded that the grants were "mostly *perfect titles*," meaning that under Mexican law the holders had either the equivalent of a patent or the equity of a perfected title. He conceded that many grants failed to comply strictly with Mexican procedures for perfecting title. But, Jones countered, in the "rude and uncultivated" state of California before the American conquest, "these formalities were to a great extent disregarded," and "the law of custom, with the acquiescence of the highest authorities, overcame, in these respects, the written law." Jones urged that titles be confirmed swiftly after their survey, reserving government opposition only to those cases for which "there may be reason to suppose a grant invalid." Whatever their merits, Jones's recommendations were hardly those of a disinterested observer. While investigating California land titles, Jones had bought the twelve-square-league (over 53,000 acres) San Luis Rey and Pala tract in San Diego. Before he submitted his report, he had acquired interests in at least two additional land grants. Although Jones said he had bought the San Diego property only after making a "full examination" of its title, he obviously had personal reasons to favor the swift confirmation of Mexican land grants.[7]

Halleck may not have owned any California land grants at the time, but his report also involved an important conflict of interest. Despite his suspicion of many California titles, Halleck recommended that the government summarily confirm American *alcalde* grants in San Francisco. As the owner of a dozen very valuable city lots that had been *alcalde* grants, he had much to gain. In addition, Halleck's chauvinistic insistence that Mexican law conform to "the spirit of [U.S.] laws" colored his conclusions. Insistence on written documentation accorded with traditional land settlement practices and common-law principles; had all things been equal, it might have been the best way of settling the Mexican land grants. Nonetheless, Jones had a telling point: the isolation of California and the ease of obtaining land there prior to the American conquest had diminished the practical importance of compliance with the formalities entailed in granting land. Before the gold rush, land did not generate heated disputes. Under those conditions, equity did not demand formal compliance with strict written law as the basis for determining all titles in land. Fraudulent titles would have been a problem whatever approach was adopted, but insistence on formalities probably stimulated the "manufacturing" of needed but missing documents.[8]

Halleck and Jones agreed on one point: the urgency of settling private land claims and thus segregating public from private property. Even in 1849 Halleck described land-title disputes as "exceedingly numerous," and he stressed the vital importance "to the peace and prosperity of the country that measures be taken without delay for the speedy and final settlement of these titles upon principles of equity and justice." The sectional conflicts that beset the country accounted for Congress's delay in enacting such legislation, which hinged on the issue of whether California should be admitted as a free or slave state. When Congress finally focused on the Mexican land grants, it relied on the two land reports. Gwin carried the day, and the bill that emerged in early 1851 reflected the skepticism of Halleck's report and the legislative authorship of Gwin.⁹

The California Land Act of 1851 departed from earlier congressional methods of resolving land titles held under foreign governments in areas that subsequently became part of the United States, such as Louisiana and Florida. By giving the federal courts, rather than Congress, the final authority, legislators hoped that titles might be settled more quickly. This result might have been achieved had Congress not interfered with the process at the behest of interested parties. Instead, Congress permitted claimants to file late, ordered the district courts to hear claims not filed before the board, and conducted independent hearings on the validity of grants and the correctness of their surveys.¹⁰

The Land Act established a board of three land commissioners before whom "each and every person claiming lands in California by virtue of any right or title derived from the Spanish or Mexican government" was required to present "such documentary evidence and testimony of witnesses as the said claimant" relied on "in support of such claims." The act thus placed the burden on the grantee to establish title, in the absence of which the land claimed would become public property and open to settlers. Since many settlers had taken up residence on claimed land by the time the board met, any decision was bound to be unpopular. Although most of the land claimed under the act consisted of Mexican ranchos (usually very large tracts of land), many other types of land, including mission lands, pueblo lands, and smaller tracts, were involved in the decisions of the board.¹¹

Both the claimant and the United States could appeal from the board to the appropriate northern or southern federal district court, and then to the U.S. Supreme Court. Appeals to the district court essentially provided a new trial, since both sides could introduce additional evidence. Faced with the prospect of litigation at all three levels, claimants discounted the importance of the board's decisions. In 1855 John Sutter dubbed the board a "great humbug" and "farce." Some lawyers told their clients not to worry about the outcome of their claims before the "board of Examiners," since any decision would "in no way prejudice" claimants.¹²

Although its decisions were final in only three claims, the board was not simply a screening committee. The inevitable appeals taken from the board obscured the importance of its decisions. In most cases the district court adopted the exact decree of the board, including the grant's boundary description, which dictated the amount and location of the land eventually patented. Even more significant were the many cases, particularly in the southern district, in which the United States dismissed appeals and allowed claimants to proceed with the board's decision as a final decree. Although seemingly a technical point, substantial interests depended on whether or not the decree of the board included a limitation on the amount of land to be surveyed as confirmed land under the boundaries given in the decree. Such decrees meant a difference of many thousands of acres and often gave claimants greater control over the more easily manipulated survey process.[13]

Under the act, the president appointed the members of the board and a Spanish-speaking lawyer to represent the interests of the government. Most important, the act listed, but did not prioritize, the sources of law that were to govern the board and the federal courts, namely "the treaty of Guadalupe Hidalgo, the law of nations, the laws, usages, and customs of the government from which the claim . . . derived, the principles of equity, and the decisions of the Supreme Court of the United States, so far as . . . applicable." The differing weights and interpretations these sources received at the hands of the board and the federal courts account for much of the convoluted legal history of the California land cases.[14]

The land unsuccessfully claimed under the act or not presented to the board by 1853 automatically became part of the public domain of the United States. Successful grantees, however, received a federal patent after presenting the General Land Office with certification of confirmation and a survey duly approved by the U.S. surveyor general of California. The Land Act of 1851 dealt with the issue of title only between the United States and the claimants, reserving by its terms the interests and rights of third parties. Inserted by Senator Gwin, ostensibly to protect settlers, this reservation generated considerable litigation over conflicting surveys between claimants and sometimes between claimants and settlers. The clause also produced state lawsuits, often simultaneous with actions before the federal board and courts. Almost every claim spawned some—and often an enormous amount of—state court litigation.[15]

Reviewing the Mexican law on which title to most of the ranchos rested became a critical task for both the land board and Hoffman. The Colonization Act of 1824 and the Supplemental Regulations of 1828 embodied Mexico's land policy. Although a handful of grants had been made under these laws, beginning in 1833 the secularization of the missions stimulated a dramatic increase in the number of large ranchos granted to individuals. Between 1822 and 1832 less than 5 percent of the total number of ranchos were issued, yet by the end of 1836 the number of ranchos granted exceeded 100, or about 25 percent of the total. An even greater distribution of land occurred during the last decade of Mexican rule: 112 grants of ranchos in 1843 and 1844 alone. By 1846 the total number of ranchos approached 500. When the United States took California in 1846, half of the ranchos were held under grants less than six years old.[16]

A simple procedure for granting land emerged under the Colonization Act and its Supplemental Regulations. First, the prospective grantee submitted a petition to the governor, describing the land requested and stating that it stood vacant. The petition had to include the *diseño*, a rough sketch map that showed the location and proposed boundaries of the grant and often included topographical features. Second, after receiving the petition, the governor normally forwarded the request to a local official, the *alcalde*, for verification. Third, the *alcalde* had to confirm that the petitioner was a person of good standing in the community and that the land requested stood vacant. If the *alcalde* made a favorable report—or *informe*—the governor issued a concession, a *concedo*, which usually contained special conditions to be fulfilled by the grantee. Fourth, grants commonly stipulated that the grantee was to take possession of the land by building a house and occupying it—usually within one year—and that if the grantee failed to comply with the conditions, the land could be "denounced," or claimed by another person, and regranted if circumstances warranted. Fifth, a survey was witnessed by neighboring rancheros and an act of possession was ceremoniously performed by the *alcalde* and the grantee, completing the formalities of granting land. Finally, the petition, *informe, concedo*, and survey notes were supposed to be sent to the territorial legislature for its approval.[17]

Just how the Mexican law on granting land would initially be interpreted depended on the various members of the land board. Between 1852 and 1856, during the actual operation of the board, seven different commissioners took part in its deliberations. President Millard Fillmore, a Whig, appointed the first board's commissioners, who were promptly removed with the election of Democrat Franklin Pierce in 1853. Despite their political differences, the commissioners who heard the California land claims had much in common. Nearly all of them were former congressmen. Indeed,

President Pierce's appointees in 1853 were all Democratic congressmen denied reelection. It is difficult to escape the conclusion that these posts functioned as a political consolation prize for faithful members of the Whig or Democratic party, with relatively little consideration given to an appointee's substantive knowledge of Mexican land grants. Although the commissioners had varying degrees of familiarity with land adjudication, probably none of them read Spanish fluently or knew very much about the Mexican law governing land grants. Nonetheless, both boards were composed of experienced lawyer-politicians facing as much a political as a legal question.

Better command of Mexican law and Spanish would certainly have helped the board's deliberations. The necessity of translators delayed the process of adjudication. Moreover, occasionally poor translations resulted in mistakes that critics of the board gleefully pointed out as evidence of its incompetency. One grantee, Pablo de la Guerra, ridiculed a commissioner for translating *cultivo* [cultivation] as the raising of a patch of corn. He asked: "Why not the serving of a plate of hot cakes?" Both boards committed errors of language and law. Their mistakes, however, were not widespread, and most commissioners worked conscientiously to understand the law governing land grants. In any event, the mistakes they did make were mitigated by the nature of their task.[18]

The fate of titles held under Mexican land grants rested on the guiding principles adopted by the commissioners rather than on the resolution of specific legal issues. How two broad issues were handled was of particular importance to claimants. First, would titles depend on strict compliance with written Mexican law, or would the board agree that in pre-1846 California such legal formalities had rarely been observed? The issue was whether customary law existed in California with reference to land grants. If so, how far could such custom alter the written Mexican law on the subject. The Land Act of 1851 offered little guidance; it merely referred the commissioners to Mexican "laws, usages, and customs."

The commissioners also had to decide what form of documentation would suffice to establish Mexican titles. Were documents issued under Mexican authority essential, or could oral testimony prove the existence of missing documents as well as compliance with Mexican land law? The answer to this question depended, in part, on how the commissioners decided the written law versus custom issue. To an even greater extent, however, the commissioners were influenced by their perception of Hispanic witnesses. During the first decade of land litigation, the reputations for honesty of Hispanic claimants and witnesses suffered a sharp decline. As the non-Hispanic legal community increasingly perceived Hispanic testimony as suspect, the scope for oral evidence narrowed sharply. The second board, appointed by President Pierce, and the federal courts began insisting on documentation. By the 1860s, claims relying primarily on oral testimony, be it non-Hispanic or Hispanic, had to overcome the unwritten presumption of invalid if not fraudulent title.

Claimants were naturally interested in the attitudes of the first board's commissioners appointed by President Fillmore in 1851. Even before he left New York for San Francisco, one commissioner, Harry I. Thornton, a former U.S. senator and judge of the Alabama Supreme Court, found himself questioned about his views. His responses found their way back to an anxious claimant in California, with the secondhand assurance that titles would "be decided on equitable principles, and the strict letter of the law not enforced, nor claimants held to a strict compliance with the conditions of the grant."[19] Thornton's characterized views boded well for claimants, but he was only one of three board members. Hiland Hall of Vermont, the chairman of the first board, was a former Whig congressman and judge of his state's supreme court. The third member of the board, James Wilson of New Hampshire, had been in his second term in the House of Representatives in 1850 when he resigned and left to practice law in California.

Lawyers in San Francisco quickly made their own appraisals of the board. By 1852 Henry W. Halleck's land speculation and law practice had built his fortune. His firm—Halleck, Peachy, and Billings—represented many land claimants, and Halleck's concern now shifted to the dangers of an overly strict scrutiny of land titles. Soon after the commissioners arrived in San Francisco, Halleck spent the better part of a day with them discussing their "course of proceedings." Halleck thought the commissioners were thorough and industrious, "good men" from whom he expected "honest and just decisions."[20]

Despite personal observations and private assurances from individual commissioners, the claimants and their lawyers waited nearly a year, until December 1852, before the board began rendering its decisions. Some delay stemmed from disagreements among the commissioners over their authority and role in the adjudication process and the lack of specific instructions from the Department of the Interior. The department urged a speedy disposition of cases but provided only a recapitulation of the act of 1851. Notwithstanding the universal desire for speed, the commissioners sought an understanding of Mexican legal issues, as well as an approach concerning which sources of law would control their decisions and to what effect. Confronted with hundreds of claims, the first board deliberately took its time.[21]

In order "not to injure one claimant by anything" decided in another case, "the commissioners tried to familiarize themselves with as many of the titles and hear as many witnesses as possible before tendering any decisions." Although contemporaries would later describe the first board as liberal in its adjudication of titles—especially when compared with the second board—this judgment should not be confused with a sloppiness or virtually automatic approval of titles. Henry Halleck warned his clients, "The commissioners [of the first board] are scrutinizing the titles very closely, requiring us to prove the *genuineness* of every paper presented and that it was signed and issued at the time it purports to be." A southern Californian in San Francisco during the operation of the first board, before it rendered any decisions, grew concerned for grant holders because the government's lawyer seemed "determined to catch at every little quibble and technicality."[22]

Yet, contemporaries correctly described the first board as liberal, since it did not insist on strict compliance with the written Mexican law concerning land titles. In addition, it gave wide scope for oral testimony to buttress or even substitute for a lack of documentation on the part of the claimants. In its earliest decisions, the board acknowledged the efficacy of custom and usage in two aspects of Mexican land granting that had widespread significance for claimants. The first board declared its guiding principles and philosophy in its opinions on the claim of Cruz Cervantes for rancho San Joaquin and especially Frémont's claim for rancho Las Mariposas.[23]

First, the board decided that a grant did not need Mexican departmental assembly approval and that, under Mexican practice, claimants with a *concedo* from the governor established good title. In reaching this decision, the board overcame the apparent obstacle of the fifth article of the Mexican Supplemental Regulations of 1828, which provided that all grants would "not be held to be definitely valid without the previous consent of the Territorial Deputation." William Carey Jones, for the claimant Cruz Cervantes, argued that a *concedo* from the Mexican governors passed perfect title or estate in fee to the claimant, subject only to the condition that the territorial or supreme government might annul the grant. Jones argued that

1. Judge Ogden Hoffman, around 1887.
Courtesy of the Oregon Historical Society, neg. #68025.

2. San Francisco Bay, early 1850s.
Courtesy of the Bancroft Library.

3. U.S. courthouse, San Francisco, around 1856.
Courtesy of the Bancroft Library.

4. Ogden Hoffman, Sr.
Courtesy of the New York Historical Society.

5. Josiah Ogden Hoffman.
Courtesy of the New York Historical Society.

6. *Stephen J. Field, U.S. Supreme Court justice.*
Courtesy of the Library of Congress.

7. Lorenzo Sawyer, U.S. circuit court judge.
Courtesy of the Northern District Archives.

8. *Matthew Hall McAllister, special circuit judge.*
Courtesy of the Northern District Archives.

9. *Matthew P. Deady, U.S. district court judge for Oregon.*
Courtesy of the Oregon Historical Society.

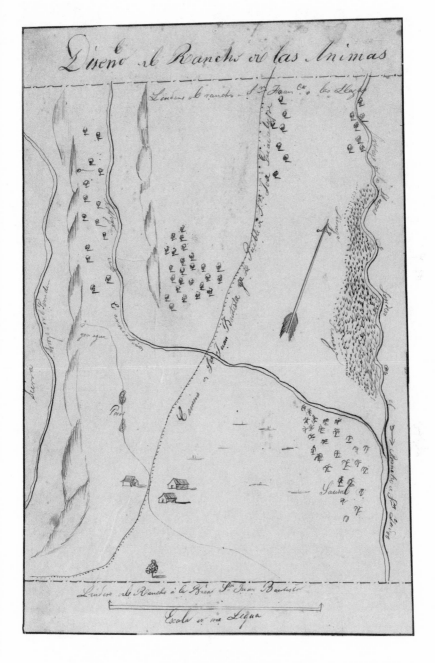

10. Diseño, *Rancho de las Animas private land grant, Santa Clara County.*
Courtesy of the Bancroft Library.

11. Chae Chan Ping, who despite a return certificate issued in 1887, was denied entry into the country under the Chinese Exclusion Act of 1888. Courtesy of the National Archives.

No. 849.

DEPARTMENT OF HIS IMPERIAL CHINESE MAJESTY'S
SUPERINTENDENT OF CUSTOMS.

Canton, 15th October 1883.

I, the undersigned, His Imperial Chinese Majesty's Superintendent of Customs in the Kwang-tung Province, hereby certify that *Fung Yeong*, a subject of the Empire of China, to whom this certificate is issued, is entitled under the provisions of the Treaty of the sixth year of the Emperor Kwang-Sü, i.e. 1880 between China and the United States, to go and come of his free will and accord to the United States on the presentation of the same to the Collector of Customs of the American port at which he shall arrive.

The required description of his person follows :—

NAME.	AGE.	OCCUPATION.
Fung Yeong.	Thirty four.	Trader.

RESIDENCE.	HEIGHT.	COMPLEXION.
Nam hoi District	Five ft. 2 3/4 in.	Dark.

COLOUR OF EYES.	PHYSICAL PECULIARITIES.	OFFICIAL TITLE.
Black		None.

崇 (Chung.)

SUPERINTENDENT OF CUSTOMS.

Per Deputy 庸 寳 書 (Ah Pan Shü.)

*12. Canton certificate, issued by the Chinese government under the
Chinese Exclusion Act of 1882.
Courtesy of the National Archives.*

13. Return certificate for Chae Chan Ping, issued by the San Francisco collector of customs on June 2, 1887.
Courtesy of the National Archives.

Mexican authorities had ignored article five and that therefore article five did not apply. Thus, Jones concluded, denying the validity of grants that lacked Territorial Deputation approval contravened the Treaty of Guadalupe Hidalgo.[24]

Second, the board concluded that the one-year habitation and occupancy condition commonly annexed to *concedos* was often not met. The board decided that these conditions were not essential for good title. Unless another person petitioned for the same land, the original claimant could fulfill the conditions after the time period specified in the *concedo* had passed. Moreover, oral testimony could prove possession and improvement of land as well as the validity of documents. Unlike the second board, the first commissioners allowed claimants "to make up, with [oral] testimony, any gaps and flaws in the written testimony, and to prove away and account for anything in the archives" that may have appeared "against the title." The board's wide scope for oral testimony slowed down its progress. In one case alone, the Las Pulgas grant in San Mateo County, the commissioners spent over six weeks hearing the testimony of witnesses in place of missing documents.[25]

This easier confirmation of land titles found its natural enemy in settlers—be they legitimate settlers or squatters. To them, confirmed grants represented land removed from the public domain. In many cases, settlers and squatters already on the land gambled that they would prevail against claimants. To such settlers, the first board was anathema. According to Henry Halleck, squatters had threatened the commissioners. Settlers on the confirmed grant to the Milpitas rancho in Santa Clara County did not resist the claim "because it was generally understood that nearly *all alleged titles* would be confirmed, whether worthy or not."[26]

With President Pierce's inauguration in 1853, Democrats replaced the first Whig board. The second board consisted of Alpheus Felch, recently defeated for reelection to the Senate from Michigan, and Thompson Campbell and Robert A. Thomas, unreelected representatives from Illinois and Virginia. After one year, Campbell's resignation saw his replacement by Seth B. Farwell of Illinois.

As with the first board, claimants and their lawyers anxiously sought indications of the new commissioners' views. Henry Halleck attributed the removal of the first commissioners to the "squatter influence" of California's senators, William M. Gwin and John B. Weller. By July 1853, the second board had resumed the hearing of cases. Elisha O. Crosby, representing many land-grant claimants, informed his clients that he did not know if the new board would follow the approach taken by the old. Still, based on his "acquaintance with the men," Crosby predicted that they would "give very liberal constructions to grants." Nonetheless, Crosby thought that the commissioners might be influenced by "squatterism," and he later became convinced that "the political influence, by pampering to the squatter vote . . . had more or less to do with the enacting of the law creating this Land Commission and the continuance of the cases by appeals through the different courts." [27]

In assessing the second board for the attorney general, the U.S. attorney for the northern district of California concluded that Hoffman and the first board had conflicted over "all the substantial points" involved in land-title litigation but that the second board generally accepted Hoffman's position of stricter interpretation of claims. Thus, the new commissioners appointed by President Pierce dramatically changed the complexion of land litigation in California. The posture of the new board took both lawyers and claimants by surprise. Henry Halleck wrote a disgruntled client that the new board required "strict legal proof" of the claim of title from the original grantee to the present claimant, whereas the first board had been satisfied with "mere *prima facie* evidence." One of Halleck's law partners, Archibald C. Peachy, described the new commissioners as having "entered upon their duties in quite a different spirit" from that of their predecessors. After a series of decisions in November 1853, Halleck bluntly declared, "I have no further confidence in this board and I am fully satisfied that they are—or at least two of them are—*squatters* and were appointed as squatters." Thomas Larkin, an American, old-time Californian and owner of numerous claims to large ranchos, saw the second board as "very severe on titles." The necessity of numerous witnesses to establish one's claims under the second board led him to predict, "Many fine estates will be lost to the owners for want of evidence that they can command with proper care and trouble." [28]

Between December 1852, when the first board confirmed John C. Frémont's claim to Las Mariposas, and March 1855, when the Supreme Court rendered its opinion on that claim, claimants and Hoffman could only speculate if the ultimate disposition of land grants would be governed by the first board's liberal approach or by the stricter one of the second board. The 1855 *Fremont* decision did reveal the Supreme Court's response to California land claims. However, both the *Cervantes* and the *Fremont* cases first came before

Hoffman before being appealed to the Supreme Court. In both cases, he reversed the first board before he in turn was reversed by the Supreme Court. Hoffman's reasoning in the two cases illustrates his approach to the land titles as well as his attitude toward precedent. Ironically, his restrictive approach, though initially rejected by the Supreme Court, was later accepted by that court.

The board that had considered the *Cervantes* case did not regard the fifth article of the Supplemental Regulations of 1828 as an explicit requirement of Mexican law, but Hoffman did. Without both a concession from the governor and approval by the territorial government, the grantee still had an interest, but it was an imperfect or inchoate title to land. In Cervantes's case, he could show only a concession from the governor. In such cases, the question for Hoffman was whether the United States, succeeding to the rights and duties of the Mexican government, should perfect title to the grant. He concluded that claims should be confirmed if the grantee had performed the conditions of the grant. Hoffman also disagreed with the land board on how to establish compliance with conditions in a grant.

Hoffman concluded that the decision of whether the title of grants held merely under a concession should be perfected had to be "tested by the principles laid down in similar cases by the Supreme Court." In the *Cervantes* case, Hoffman saw a "total neglect" on the claimant's part to comply with any of the conditions (including habitation on the land within one year) for at least five and possibly eight years after the concession in 1836. After reviewing Supreme Court cases dealing with land concessions by the Spanish government in its former dominions in Louisiana and Florida, he concluded that in the absence of any excuse for the claimant's failure to comply with the conditions of his grant, the title could not be perfected. Hoffman's "stringent rule" about conditions, complained the U.S. attorney, induced claimants to introduce additional evidence in "nearly every case" on appeal from the board and thereby further taxed the federal prosecutor's overburdened staff.[29]

Hoffman explicitly rejected the argument (accepted by the board) of William Carey Jones that the conditions annexed to concessions were conditions subsequent and not precedent. Nonperformance of the conditions, according to Jones, implied only that the land could be "denounced" by another and, if vacant, regranted by the government. Jones further argued that if denouncement had not occurred and the claimant eventually complied with the conditions, the title should be confirmed in equity. Hoffman rejected Jones's position because the grant clearly stipulated that if the claimant failed to comply with conditions, the claimant should "lose his right to the land" and the land should "be denounceable by others." Had Hoffman been "at liberty to follow blindly the dictates" of his own judgment, he might have confirmed the claim, but the principles established by the Supreme Court concerning land in Florida and Louisiana—requiring the adherence of conditions in Spanish land grants—bound Hoffman to "the spirit, if not the letter," of those rules. Hoffman anticipated the Supreme Court might reverse him by modifying or departing from these earlier decisions, but he emphasized that such a course was outside of his role as a federal trial judge. Unlike Hoffman, the Supreme Court at first did not examine the merits of the *Cervantes* claim. On appeal, the Supreme Court reversed and remanded the case to the southern district on the grounds that Hoffman lacked jurisdiction because the land lay outside of the northern district.[30]

The first difference of opinion between Hoffman and the Supreme Court over what principles should govern California land claims arose in the *Fremont* case in 1854, involving the extremely valuable claim to Las Mariposas. Both the *Cervantes* and *Fremont* claims were test cases, raising issues that affected the settlement of the remaining claims. However, unlike Cruz Cervantes, John C. Frémont had powerful backers, including Joe Palmer of Palmer, Cook and Company. This San Francisco financial house had early associated itself with Frémont's fortunes, not only investing heavily in schemes for extracting gold from Las Mariposas but also strongly supporting Frémont's presidential ambitions.[31]

Frémont's supporters pushed hard for the confirmation of his claim. After the first board ruled in his favor and before Hoffman heard the government's appeal, U.S. Attorney General Caleb Cushing came under pressure to dismiss the appeal. On Frémont's behalf, the lawyer Joseph Wilson wrote Cushing that Congress intended the attorney general "to guard against the vexation, the malice, the meanness incident to protracted litigation." Wilson raised the specter of automatic appeals from the board. "Every private land claim in California, hung up by the heels, beyond the earthly probation of the current generation!" He warned that appealing all decisions of the board would prompt the intervention of "Judge Lynch" and urged Cushing to dismiss the appeal in Frémont's case. The government's ostensible interest in Frémont's claim, as with private land grants generally, was to see the lands of invalid claims become part of the public domain. Cushing did not deny the appeal, and Hoffman reversed the board's decision and rejected Frémont's claim.[32]

Frémont's supporters took Hoffman's decision hard. Montgomery Blair, a friend of and legal advisor to Frémont, claimed the result had been a foregone conclusion, since "the Judge" was "a violent partisan and unfriendly to Frémont, Benton and that whole political connexion." Blair also found Hoffman "in the dark" about the claim and considered its rejection "the most absurd conclusion on the admitted facts of the case." Hoffman did differ politically from Frémont, but his decision did not rest on that ground. Even though Blair objected to Hoffman's reasoning as overly technical, the judge had rejected Frémont's claim in a short opinion for the same reason that he had rejected the *Cervantes* claim two months earlier: nonfulfillment of the conditions of the grant. Indeed, his decision in the *Cervantes* case gave special urgency to Frémont's efforts to have the appeal from the board dismissed.[33]

When the case came before the Supreme Court, William Carey Jones, once again, made the argument for the claimant, although he had much illustrious help. Jones fully understood that more than his brother-in-law's mining interests in the gold-bearing claim was at stake. Indeed, Chief Justice Roger B. Taney prefaced his opinion in *Fremont* by noting, "It is understood that many claims to land in California depend upon the same principles, and will, in effect, be decided by the judgment of the court in this case." Yet, the *Fremont* claim was an anomalous choice for a test case on California land grants, for at least two reasons. The claimant, John C. Frémont, largely epitomized the struggle that had wrested California away from the Californios and Mexico. This impulsive adventurer had achieved national renown for his daring and danger-filled topographical explorations of the Far West and for being the victim, as many thought, of a court-martial animated by professional jealousy. Although the Las Mariposas claim had been granted by Governor Manuel Micheltorena to Juan B. Alvarado in 1844, Alvarado had sold his interest to Frémont for $3,000 in 1847. Thus, the case did not entail protection of the property rights of the conquered Californios under the Treaty of Guadalupe Hidalgo. Rather, in question was whether one who had done so much to insure the American possession of California would share in the wealth of the new state and benefit as a purchaser of a Mexican land grant. Frémont's supporters thought the explorer deserved the prize of Las Mariposas for his troubles, but Montgomery Blair doubted whether "the sops of the Supreme bench" would confirm the claim because, like all men, the judges would resent bestowing "such unbounded wealth on one individual."[34]

Also anomalous was the "floating" nature of the grant. Unlike most grants, which specified an amount of land in terms of given boundaries, the Mariposas grant purported to give the grantee ten square leagues of land (44,380 acres) within an area of one hundred square leagues (443,800 acres). Frémont claimed the right to locate his grant within an area of the Sierra Nevada that contained some of the richest deposits of gold. Indeed, during the time the land board considered his claim, Frémont secured a survey of ten square leagues of land that included the rich gold mines near Mariposa and Agua Frio and took in nearly all of the watershed of the Mariposa River. The dispute over the shape of Frémont's grant and his claim to the mineral riches on it proved to be one of the great legal battles waged in the California Supreme Court and ultimately was laid to rest by that court.[35]

The U.S. Supreme Court's reversal of Hoffman in the *Fremont* case set the context for further adjudication of California land grants. Chief Justice Taney agreed with the board that Louisiana and Florida land grants were fundamentally different from those in California. Many of the southeastern grants, he contended, had been intended to encourage settlement and improvement and were not complete as grants until the conditions of occupation and cultivation were fulfilled. On the other hand, many of the California grants, Taney asserted, were rewards for the benefit of the grantees—like Alvarado, under whom Frémont based his claim. As such, the conditions attached to the California grants were merely conditions subsequent, and their nonfulfillment did not invalidate the grants. Taney thus held that the Mexican governor's *concedo* passed an immediate and present interest in land. In effect, Taney denied the applicability of previous land-grant decisions in which he had insisted on strict compliance with conditions and on which Hoffman had relied.[36]

Equally important, the Supreme Court accepted the first board's decision to ignore written law in preference to such departures as were established by custom and usage. The board had accepted the testimony of witnesses and the arguments by Jones that many practices contravening the strict letter of the Colonization Act and Supplemental Regulations had received the sanction of the Mexican authorities. Attorney General Cushing had argued in *Cervantes* that even if usage and custom could be established, that custom lacked the effect asserted by Jones. "No usage or custom can grow into such strength as to oppose, overcome, and put down the written law." The Supreme Court disagreed and upheld Jones's view that failure to submit a *diseño*, to survey the land, and to receive departmental assembly approval for the grant did not necessarily invalidate a claim. So too, nonperformance of other conditions might not undermine a claim unless circumstances indicated an unreasonable delay or an abandonment of the claim. The Supreme Court accepted the presence of hostile Indians on Las Mariposas and the general "confusion and disorder of the times" as legitimate excuses for nonperformance in *Fremont*. Since no other person had denounced the land in question, Frémont's interest in the grant remained intact and would be upheld.[37]

Both Justice John Catron of Tennessee and Justice John Campbell of Alabama dissented. Each considered the Court's previous decisions dealing with Spanish land concessions applicable, requiring the rejection of the Mariposas claim. Justice Catron, in particular, identified many precedents establishing the necessity of complying with the condition of habitation within one year under Spanish concessions and barring the citation of Indian hostility as an excuse for nonperformance. Justice Catron thus fully endorsed Hoffman's position. Moreover, Catron cited the vague description of Frémont's floating grant as an additional reason for rejecting the claim. Likewise, Justice Campbell assigned the unspecified description of the grant as an important reason for rejecting the claim and cited similar precedents dealing with Spanish concessions. Justice Catron, however, uttered a prophetic statement about the implications of the majority's position in *Fremont*. "If this claim is maintained, all others must likewise be, if the first step of making the concession is proved to have been performed by the acting governor; as no balder case than the one before us can exist in California where the grant is not infected with fraud or forgery."[38]

The strongest criticism of the ruling came from a member of the court who had not even participated in the *Fremont* case, Justice Peter Daniel. In later cases Justice Daniel took the majority to task for following and even expanding on the liberal approach taken toward the Mariposas claim. His most caustic dissent occurred in *Arguello* v. *United States* (1856) in which he decried what he saw as the departure from Mexican statutes in favor of practices in violation of them, resting on the testimony of interested persons. Daniel characterized the testimony of Hispanic Californians as worthless and "marked by the traits which tyranny and degradation, political and moral, naturally and usually engender." Daniel accused his brethren of having been duped into, if not actually having abetted, a system of land frauds.[39]

Unlike Justices Catron and Campbell, who rested their dissents principally on a different interpretation of Mexican law and on the applicability of earlier decisions of the Supreme Court, Justice Daniel displayed a violent opposition to the claimants themselves and to large land grants given to individuals. Daniel thought the *Fremont* decision and others following it were "inciting and pampering a corrupt and grasping spirit of speculation and monopoly" in California land, a situation that was excluding "the honest citizen of small means, by whose presence and industry the improvement and wealth, and social and moral health, and the advancement of the country" were "always sure to be promoted." In a choice between settlers and large claimants like Frémont, Justice Daniel had little difficulty in concluding that the equities did not favor the grantees.[40]

Since many members of the Supreme Court, including Chief Justice Taney, shared Justice Daniel's antimonopolistic attitudes and Jacksonian preference for the small settler against the large grantee, it may seem strange that the Supreme Court took such a liberal attitude toward the confirmation of Mexican grants. Protecting private property and adhering to the obligations assumed under the Treaty of Guadalupe Hidalgo offer obvious explanations. It would seem, however, that the types of cases first brought before the Court—at the insistence of Jones and other lawyers representing claimants—might also have influenced the outcome. In all of the first three California land-grant cases to be decided by the Supreme Court, the claimants were Americans.[41]

Treaty obligations and the sanctity of property aside, it might well have been easier to accept Americans who favored and fought for the American possession of California as beneficiaries under the act of 1851. Although title to land rested on circumstances under which a Mexican governor granted land to the original grantee—usually a Californio—the Court obviously knew that American claimants were benefiting from confirmation. The Court even validated the claim of an American who had become a naturalized Mexican citizen in order to qualify for a land grant in 1844 but who had quickly joined the American forces in overthrowing Mexico's hold on California in 1846. As Justice Daniel pointed out in his dissent, the majority had accepted the claimant's "inconsistency of urging a right founded on duties sustained to the Mexican Republic" while at the same time admitting his "hostility and faithlessness to that government."[42]

For two years after the decision in March 1855, the *Fremont* case established the terms by which land claims were confirmed in Hoffman's court. After the *Fremont* case, Hoffman announced that the principles laid down by the Supreme Court were applicable to all Mexican colonization grants. Judicial duty required him "not to seek to limit the operation of the decision of the Supreme Court by subtle and unsubstantial distinctions" but to apply the principles of *Fremont* to all similar cases. Indeed, even though he mentioned the *Fremont* case by name in relatively few instances, a close analysis of the facts and reasoning in Hoffman's opinions after the Supreme Court's ruling reveals that his decisions rested on the landmark case in most instances where he confirmed claims, whether the board had rejected or confirmed them.[43]

The impact of the *Fremont* case came close to Justice Catron's prediction that it would effectively mandate the confirmation of all Mexican land grants. Of the first ninety claims coming on appeal to Hoffman after the *Fremont* case, all but five were confirmed. Of those five claims, only three were rejected on their merits; one claim had been abandoned and the other had not been filed in time. Part of the early success of claimants stemmed from the inadequate advocacy of the U.S. attorneys. In retrospect, their losing streak before the courts compares quite unfavorably with the aggressive and successful advocacy for the government beginning in 1857. Hoffman frequently lamented the lack of argument from the government, especially when the circumstances of the grant seemed suspicious. Laying the blame for the confirmation of suspicious or fraudulent claims on the failings of the government's counsel, though, can be exaggerated. The early U.S. attorneys for the northern district were understaffed, underpaid, and overworked when compared with their successors under Attorney General Black's administration. The sweeping precedent set by *Fremont*, however, was of even greater significance because it undercut most objections that the early government attorneys might have advanced. Under this aura of defeatism, the government offered no argument or objection in nearly half of the cases appealed to Hoffman's court. With the "expectation being confidently entertained that the rules laid down" in *Fremont* would govern all claims, both the claimants and the government offered less and less argument on

the legal issues. Nonetheless, Hoffman carefully examined the often voluminous board transcripts, reviewed the evidence, and invariably confirmed
claims. Occasionally, this process found Hoffman advancing objections "that
could have been made" to confirmation, while in the same breath conceding
that the Supreme Court had "repeatedly" overruled them.[44]

How Hoffman wrote opinions when confirming claims after the *Fremont*
case reveals the tension underlying his decisions. His judicial opinions
clearly reflect his understanding that the *Fremont* case dictated results he
questioned. Eighteen months after the *Fremont* decision, the district judge
continued to speak in terms of the obligatory nature of his decisions. Although he disagreed with the analysis of land claims imposed on him by
Fremont, he held his tongue in judicial opinions for a considerable time.[45]

Hoffman's first judicial disagreement with the Supreme Court took place
in the case of *Andres Pico* v. *United States*, decided by the district court in
April 1856, one year after *Fremont*. The land board had rejected the claim
for eleven square leagues of the rancho Arroyo Seco in Amador County, but
Hoffman confirmed it, against his better judgment. Although authenticity
was not an issue, the grant had not been approved by the departmental assembly. Moreover, eight years had elapsed between the date of the grant and
the land's occupation, the delay being attributed to Indian hostilities. Under
Hoffman's "former views" he would have rejected the claim, but he now
acknowledged that the *Fremont* decision established "other rules for . . .
guidance." Under *Fremont*, the claimant, by virtue of being issued a grant,
had a vested interest that Hoffman had to respect in the absence of an unreasonable delay or circumstances giving rise to a presumption that the
claimant had abandoned the grant. Still, Hoffman questioned the logic of
the Supreme Court's conclusion that a grantee under Mexican law held a
vested interest.[46]

Nonetheless, since Hoffman's views had been branded "erroneous" by the
Supreme Court, it was his "duty to ascertain and obey the rule of decision
which that venerated authority had laid down." Though disassociating himself from the reasoning of the Supreme Court, Hoffman reaffirmed his judicial obedience to the Court. His criticism of the *Fremont* case stemmed
from "an anxious desire correctly to understand and apply the principles
laid down" by the Supreme Court. Having made his own views clear, he
confirmed the claim to Arroyo Seco only because it could not be rejected
under the *Fremont* case.[47]

The seemingly inevitable confirmation of claims before Hoffman's court rested as much on the philosophy as on the legal principles espoused by the Supreme Court in deciding the *Fremont* case. In May 1857, Hoffman echoed the opinions of most Californians when he suggested that land claims were being confirmed by the Supreme Court in a "generous and benignant" spirit. He then dutifully assumed this liberal attitude when examining land claims. Although he preferred documentary evidence, Hoffman acquiesced once again to the Supreme Court and confirmed claims in the absence of a grant or even basic documentary evidence. Given uncontradicted evidence—frequently oral testimony produced by claimants—the lesson of *Fremont* induced Hoffman to confirm land grants even if he entertained suspicions about the grant or doubted the veracity of witnesses. In April 1857, Hoffman in one opinion described "the facility and unscrupulousness" by which "frauds" had been "perpetuated and sustained by testimony apparently conclusive." But even in cases involving a grant unsupported by archival evidence, he deemed that his court was "not at liberty in the face of the uncontradicted testimony of unimpeached witnesses to substitute its own suspicions for proofs."[48]

Claimants might celebrate the Supreme Court's early decisions on California lands and Hoffman's adherence to them, but the saga of land litigation was far from over. The individuals who most influenced California's early land-grant litigation were the first two U.S. attorneys general who dealt with the issue: Caleb Cushing and Jeremiah S. Black. Their perception of the circumstances and condition of Mexican titles dictated the government's strategy and posture in opposing the land claims. Their decisions established an overwhelming case load for Hoffman, and Black's administration, in particular, made the issue of fraud central to Hoffman's adjudication of land titles.

Cushing, the first attorney general to deal with the Mexican land grants, proved singularly ineffective when opposing private land-grant claims. The liberal precedents established by the Supreme Court during Cushing's administration guided Hoffman during the critical early years of land litigation. Despite Cushing's conscientious efforts, the California adjudication moved slowly. Attorney General Black, Cushing's successor in 1857, ended the government's losing streak by defeating a notorious claim of José Y.

Limantour for much land in San Francisco, including valuable government property, by demonstrating the claim's fraudulent nature. Although it seems clear that Limantour had attempted a massive swindle of the government and San Francisco property owners, Black's charge of fraud became the opening gambit of the government in many subsequent cases and proved highly effective.

Assertions of fraud succeeded in tainting and ultimately defeating many claims. In time, Black's approach to land-grant claims won approval from the Supreme Court and altered the precedential value of *Fremont* in Hoffman's court. Indeed, Black even persuaded the Court to exceed its traditional scope of review of lower federal court decisions. On several occasions the Supreme Court, in rejecting land claims that Hoffman had affirmed, relied on issues of fraud based on evidence introduced for the first time on appeal.[49] The recurrent suspicion of fraud not only began to undermine the value of oral testimony but also led to a general reappraisal of land grants, ultimately resulting in widespread reversals of Hoffman's decisions.

The adjudication of California land claims also had the effect of introducing new and closer relationships between the attorney general and his regional subordinates. Before the Civil War, U.S. attorneys were largely independent of the attorney general, who normally lacked the official authority as well as the resources to supervise them. With California's land litigation, however, both Cushing and Black assumed direct control over the litigation in the northern district, expanded the work force of their office, and obtained the necessary resources for effective supervision and control. The California cases foreshadowed, if not accelerated, the increased control the attorney general would gradually assume over the local U.S. attorneys.[50]

Throughout Attorney General Cushing's administration, he encountered pressure from all sides for quick resolution of land claims. One claimant captured the spirit of many complaints when he stated, "That we should be kept back to be made the football for squatters and speculators and lawyers to kick at is something I never looked for when I invested my money in this property." In early December 1853, members of California's congressional delegation, including Senator Gwin, urged the quick disposition of land-grant cases. Gwin wanted Cushing to dismiss one of the first land cases appealed to the Supreme Court on the grounds that both the board and Hoffman had confirmed the claim.[51]

Cushing understood that delay caused hardship, and he emphasized his commitment to a swift resolution of claims. He rejected the idea of taking indiscriminate appeals. "On the contrary, I hope after some of the leading cases shall have been discussed and considered in the Supreme Court, to receive thereupon rules of construction, which may enable me to dispose summarily of many subsequent cases." Nonetheless, Cushing would not "forego the most complete investigation" of the earliest cases to come up for review. The stages of adjudication embodied in the 1851 act sponsored by Gwin ironically frustrated Gwin's efforts to speed up the settlement of titles.[52]

During the time it took for test cases to reach the Supreme Court, Cushing faced the decision of which cases to appeal from the board to the district courts. California's remoteness did not make this task easy. The act of 1851 allowed either the claimants or the government to appeal from decisions of the board, provided they did so within six months of a decision. By the time a transcript could be made and forwarded to Washington for study and instructions could be sent back to San Francisco, six months could easily elapse. Rather than giving blanket instructions to California's U.S. attorneys to appeal all adverse decisions of the board, Cushing sought a change in the law. The congressional act of August 31, 1852, required the board to make two certified transcripts of each case, one to be filed with the district court and the other to be sent to the attorney general. The filing of the transcript with the district court acted as an automatic appeal for the losing party. If, however, the claimant, as the losing party, failed to file with the district court an intent to prosecute the appeal within six months of the date of the filing or, in the case of the government, within six months of the date the attorney general received the transcript, the appeal was regarded as dismissed.[53]

Cushing's successful amendment, therefore, did not seek automatic appeals and further delays but sought the dismissal of appeals at an earlier stage of land-grant litigation and the avoidance of automatic appeals. By December 1854, Cushing reported that of 813 claims filed before the board, 320 cases had been certified to his office, from which 157 appeals had been taken to the district courts. At the time only four cases were pending before the Supreme Court. "The effect is to hold in suspense all the land titles in California greatly to the prejudice of the state, its inhabitants, and of the United States." Cushing and his small staff were unable to review hundreds of board decisions. Cushing therefore hired nongovernment lawyers to examine the transcripts in selected cases and give him their analyses and recommendations. From a staff of two clerical assistants in 1853, Cushing's office swelled to about twenty people in 1857. Cushing's employment of "accomplished and learned jurists" to give advice proved an expensive but effective means of processing the more complex cases. The reports of these consultants discussed the merits of the claims in terms of the issues of fact and law and were sent to the appropriate U.S. attorney. Cushing's technique thus reduced the work load of his West Coast subordinates as well as his own office.[54]

Conscientiousness and caution marked Cushing's handling of appeals in California land cases. From the start of his administration, local federal officials recognized that the attorney general in Washington intended to direct the land litigation. Although Cushing considered the views of his California subordinates, they did not control the decisions to appeal, particularly after Cushing established his system of delegating cases. Only rarely did the local U.S. attorney's discretion affect appeals and even then usually only in the direction of prosecuting an appeal the attorney general had dismissed. Cushing diligently responded to letters and lobbying efforts concerning specific cases. Using legal consultants did not mean an abdication of decision making. He carefully reviewed the reports and gave them substantial weight, but he did not automatically accept their conclusions.[55]

Cushing showed firmness in handling the land-grant titles. Anxious not to make mistakes, he refused to be bullied into decisions. Faced with dire predictions whether he did or did not immediately dismiss appeals, Cushing relied on his own counsel. He neither accepted the desperate urgings of lawyers and his own subordinates at face value nor yielded to the veiled bribery that he become a claimant's "friend at Washington." Cushing admitted the "desirability of disposing of the land claims" but responded that he was "doing it so fast that the only danger" was "going too fast." He further explained, "I have already had occasion to overrule two orders of dismissal, but in no case as yet any order to prosecute."[56]

The land claims pertaining to the enormously valuable mercury deposits of the New Almaden mine in Santa Clara County provide an example of Cushing's approach to California land claims. Cushing had been besieged by interested parties to resolve claims out of chronological order and dispose of them summarily and without notice to adverse parties. His commitment to hear all sides and not act swiftly in a complex case earned him a harsh letter from Senator James A. Bayard, Jr., of Delaware, accusing Cushing of unjust delays. In justifying his conduct, Cushing said, "If I had precipitately, and in the dark, disposed of this case to the prejudice of absent parties, then indeed I should feel I had done injustice." He summed up his experience with the California land cases. "I am discharging an irksome and painful task in these cases, with solicitude only to do justice to all the world. Not the least disagreeable part of my duty has been to be compelled to refuse to surrender my convictions of duty to the personal representations of gentlemen like you who have enjoyed my respect."[57]

Cushing's understanding of his duty and authority under the laws designed to settle titles in California typified his caution. In several opinions Cushing viewed appeals from the land board to the district court as an administrative act rather than a legal decision. Thus he thought his decisions to appeal or dismiss an appeal from the land board did not legally bind his successors, who might decide that Cushing had made a mistake. Moreover, he believed the secretary of the interior had the discretion to appeal from the district courts to the Supreme Court. Cushing perceived his role as limited to a written and oral advocacy of the government's position before the court.[58]

Even if he would not be rushed, Cushing did take other measures to expedite the settlement of titles. Hoffman's court proved to be one of the earliest bottlenecks in land-grant litigation. Lawyers handling claims before the board and the northern district said that in Hoffman's court, business proceeded "more leisurely." Actually, although lawyers experienced delay in Hoffman's court, that resulted not from a leisurely pace but rather from an excessive amount of judicial business.[59]

Impatient claimants failed to see that the land cases coming before Hoffman were considered—under the 1851 act—as new trials that often entailed much new testimony and evidence. The land cases competed for Hoffman's attention with cases on the court's other crowded dockets. Under the statutory organization of his court, Hoffman assumed both circuit and district court duties, and two years later the duties of the southern district judgeship were imposed on him as well. In 1853 Hoffman's father approached Senator Hamilton Fish of New York, seeking to relieve his son from the "incessant" business of the court that kept Hoffman "a Prisoner" and denied him "all chances of paying . . . a visit." Later that same year Hoffman himself sought relief in a letter to Cushing. He detailed the burden of his dockets, the physical impossibility of holding all his court sessions and those of the southern district as well, and urged the appointment of a southern district judge to hear cases in the event of his absence, illness, or conflict of interest. It was only fair or, in Hoffman's words, "simple justice." He added, "After two years and a half of almost uninterrupted toil at a compensation very less than the smallest professional income of respectable lawyers, I should at length have an opportunity for occasional leisure and relaxation, and should no longer be discouraged by the anticipation of unremitting and interminable labor." Hoffman's self-pity stemmed from the over 1,500 cases filed in the northern district from 1851 to 1853, when appeals from the land board started reaching his court.[60]

The punishing schedule of hearing cases and writing opinions took its toll on Hoffman and left him sick and near collapse by 1854. The U.S. attorney for the northern district, Samuel W. Inge, wrote Cushing in July 1854 that California's "present judicial arrangements" made it "impossible to make any progress in the disposition of appeals from the land commission." Inge described Hoffman as "so infirm" that he was "unable to dispose of the ordinary civil and criminal business of the court," and Inge related that Hoffman intended to return to New York as soon as his health permitted. Hoffman's illness and his subsequent convalescence on the East Coast did delay the judicial business of his court, but Inge's report implied a more serious disruption than what in fact occurred. After a visit to New York in August 1854, Hoffman returned to conduct most of the land cases in his district as well as to cope successfully with his other dockets. Nonetheless, the dire circumstances described by Inge prompted Cushing to act.[61]

In 1854 Cushing revived a proposal for national reform of the judiciary, tailoring it to the needs of California. As attorney general, Cushing had unsuccessfully proposed the appointment of circuit court judges to relieve Supreme Court justices from the onerous duties of "circuit riding" and to facilitate the judicial business before the Supreme Court, reviving an idea embodied in the short-lived Judiciary Act of 1801. The bill incorporating Cushing's proposal provided for an extension of the circuit court system to the Pacific Coast. When this measure failed, Senator John Weller of California, with Cushing's support, introduced a bill in 1855 calling for the creation of a separate circuit court for his state. Both Weller and California's other senator, William Gwin, justified the special judgeship in terms of the pressure of extremely numerous, burdensome land cases. Cushing lobbied congressmen by stressing the existing burdens of the district courts and the hardships caused by a delay in settling land titles. The new federal judge, he argued, would both help Hoffman hear land cases on appeal from the board and alleviate his circuit court duties.[62]

The bill sparked extended debate, the main controversy being the introduction of an anomaly into the traditional circuit system of the federal courts. Notwithstanding opposition, the bill became law on March 2, 1855. The bill's proponents were helped by referring to the growing backlog of land cases in San Francisco while Hoffman lay "prostrated" by illness in New York. The act allowed the circuit judge to "form part of, and preside over," the district courts when they were hearing appeals from the land commission.[63]

Matthew Hall McAllister became the first and only incumbent of the special California circuit, established in 1855 and abolished in 1863. President Pierce's selection not only bowed to the precedent of senatorial dictation of lower-court appointments but also placated the southern wing of the Democratic party. McAllister had come to California in 1850 from Georgia, where he had served as a U.S. attorney, a member of the state senate, and the mayor of Savannah. McAllister personally lobbied the California senators and received their recommendation.[64]

Unfortunately, McAllister's appointment failed to decrease Hoffman's work load and did not appreciably speed up the disposition of appeals from the land board. Seeking to increase the operation of the circuit court, in 1856 Congress defined California's circuit as McAllister and the district court judge in whose district McAllister might be sitting, "either of whom" should "constitute a quorum." In practice the amendment returned circuit court jurisdiction to the district judges in McAllister's absence. Between 1856 and 1863 Hoffman spent much time hearing criminal, civil, and admiralty matters with McAllister. Indeed, for over two months in 1859 and between April 4, 1862, and June 29, 1863, Hoffman held the circuit court for his district by himself, in addition to handling the work of his own court. Although McAllister often heard land cases with Hoffman in the northern district—the great number of appeals not reaching the district court until 1855—Hoffman assumed the leading role. Despite lacking precedence over McAllister when the two judges heard cases together, Hoffman and not the circuit judge rendered the controlling opinion in over one hundred of the most important land cases between McAllister's appointment, in 1855, and 1859. Ironically, McAllister—appointed to relieve the ailing Judge Hoffman—ultimately became ill and unable to deal with the press of land appeals. Toward the end of McAllister's judgeship he became "a confirmed invalid, incapable of attending to business."[65]

Even if the special circuit judgeship did not effectively expedite California land titles, it showed Cushing's efforts to settle the cases speedily. Cushing's critics, who proliferated during his administration, often assigned neglect or inefficiency as reasons why land titles were not settled promptly. Frequently overlooked, however, were Cushing's responsibilities as attorney general and his reliance on the Supreme Court for guidance. Responsible for protecting the government's interests, Cushing needed to concern himself not only with valuable federal property claimed under overlapping grants but also with the possibility of wrongful confirmation of public land to private parties. Until the Supreme Court clarified the principles by which Mexican land grants would be confirmed, Cushing had many unanswered questions affecting the dismissal of appeals. He pointed out that by 1855, only two cases had been decided on their merits by the Supreme Court. Insufficient guidance from the Supreme Court did not "make it safe or convenient . . . to proceed to re-examine cases in order to dismiss appeals." Nonetheless he expected that by June 1, 1856, enough Supreme Court cases would have been decided to provide the criteria for reexamining the many transcripts in his office "with a view to the discontinuance of appeals, in all cases where justice" required it and where it could be done "without manifest prejudice to the United States."[66]

Cushing's reputation also suffered from the perception that he deliberately obstructed and prolonged land litigation. The act of 1852 gave the attorney general discretion to dismiss appeals from the board to the district courts. When large numbers of transcripts began arriving at the attorney general's office in 1854, the Supreme Court had not yet rendered any decisions, and Cushing did what he had hoped the amendment to the 1851 act would avoid: he appealed every case. Cushing sought "only to suspend the cases" and preserve the government's appeal in the event that the principles eventually enunciated by the Supreme Court justified an appeal.[67]

Claimants and their lawyers who wanted summary confirmation of claims were furious with Cushing's stance. William Carey Jones denounced Cushing for "groundless litigation" that was "consuming the time and devouring the substance" of claimants. Automatic appeals were "the crowning aggravation" of the act of 1851, "a law, the most ill-advised, uncalled for, oppressive and unjust that was ever enacted by a constitutional Legislature." To vindicate his position, Cushing published a circular in 1856 that explained the causes of delay, defended the necessity of automatic appeals, and promised to begin dismissing appeals in appropriate cases in June of the same year. Seeking to improve the public image of his administration, Cushing sent an agent to California with specific instructions that every claimant receive a copy of the circular.[68]

When Cushing left office he had largely fulfilled his promise. In a letter to President Pierce on March 4, 1857, Cushing reported that of 793 claims filed before the board (and not abandoned), 278 had been rejected and 515 confirmed. Of the 515 cases in which Cushing initially exercised appeals, he ultimately dismissed appeals in 434 cases and pursued government appeals to the district courts and the Supreme Court in only 81 cases. The attorney general incorrectly assumed that his four-year administration had resolved the litigation over California titles. Cushing simply failed to foresee the actions of his successor and the Supreme Court, and he overlooked the extraordinary monetary value of claims that promised years of litigation.[69]

If pressure for swift decisions marked Cushing's term of office, exposing fraud in land titles characterized the tenure of his successor. Between 1857 and 1860, Jeremiah S. Black developed a reputation for stemming the tide of perceived fraud, forgery, and perjury in California land titles. Black's role in defeating fraudulent titles included exposing alleged conspiracies against the United States. Indeed, only during Black's administration did the assumption of widespread fraud in California land titles arise. The emergence of this threat became linked with a public perception that Black's administration single-handedly saved the nation and California settlers from a conspiracy of stupendous frauds.

Even as Black garnered praise for his efforts in defeating suspect claims, Cushing's reputation declined. Cushing naturally suffered in a comparison between the two men. Cushing's administration of land claims simply lacked Black's dramatic results and personality. Black's administration, however, also left a harmful legacy of suspicion and distrust of California land claims generally. Indeed, Black's attitude as attorney general contravened the spirit of the Treaty of Guadalupe Hidalgo. The atmosphere of distrust he created affected the Supreme Court and Judge Hoffman as well as many others involved in settling titles. How the issue of fraud emerged reveals much about the adjudication of California's land disputes and why the federal courts responded the way they did.

In one respect it was natural that fraud became a factor in resolving California land claims. Americans had plenty of experience with spectacular land frauds and swindles. Examples abounded, from the Yazoo land frauds in Georgia in the early national period to the chicanery that underlay the settlement of title to lands that were part of the Louisiana Purchase. Indeed, land disposition invited fraud. What made the California land claims different was the perception of fraud and its effect on the settlement of titles.[70]

Allegations of California land fraud were not new to Black's office. Cushing had heard similar accusations, but the issue of fraud underwent significant change during Black's administration. First, the number of accusations and the extent of alleged frauds greatly increased. Second, the sources of purported fraud expanded, as did the range of people who made such allegations. Finally, and most important, Black became convinced of pervasive fraud and channeled his efforts into defeating claims on this issue alone. By contrast, Cushing had not opposed any claims before the Supreme Court on this basis; rather he had sought rejection on the grounds that the claims lacked merit under Mexican law.

Cushing had apparently not worried very much about the indications of fraud that came to his notice. Of the half dozen letters he received warning of fraud, most came from California settlers who as a group harbored a natural antipathy toward the Mexican land-grant claimants. Those who moved onto lands claimed under Mexican grants were directly interested in seeing such claims defeated, since unconfirmed private land grants became public land open for preemption. Moreover, many settlers considered large grants of land to individuals intrinsically wrong and objectionable. The criticism of the board's confirmation of a thirty-three-square-league grant to John Sutter provides a case in point. A petition from hundreds of men on the land claimed by Sutter warned Cushing of "unconscionable land pirates" and "plundering schemes" to deprive the men of land made "desirable and valuable by the honest industry of those" who had established themselves as "tillers of the soil." The petitioners denied the general validity of Mexican land grants. "They are so numerous, and cover such a vast extent of country, that it is believed, if they were all sustained, there would not be an acre of the public domain left for the actual settler that is worth having."

They charged that many grants and claims were "spurious or fraudulent" but had been confirmed through corrupt means. The settlers urged Cushing to appeal every case decided against the government.[71]

Convinced that some fraud existed and warned of even more, Cushing proceeded carefully to separate good from bad claims without developing a fear of widespread fraud and conspiracy. In August 1856, toward the end of Cushing's administration, an open letter from the attorney William Carey Jones addressed the issue of fraud. Of the over eight hundred claims filed, Jones asserted that no more than thirty suffered from even the suspicion of fraud. "The great bulk of the claims in California," he concluded, "are known to be both genuine and legal." Although Jones was hardly a disinterested observer, his summary comported with the facts as Cushing perceived them.[72]

Unlike Cushing, Black became convinced of widespread fraud and brought an excessive zeal to attacking claims. Initially suspicious of a few claims widely believed to be fraudulent, Black soon developed an all-encompassing suspicion of Hispanics and of Mexican land grants. With help from two subordinates, Edwin M. Stanton and Peter Della Torre, Black convinced himself and many others that fraud was everywhere. By repudiating oral evidence—especially of Hispanics—and relying on supposedly infallible techniques of examining documentary evidence for genuineness, Black succeeded time and again in defeating claims before the Supreme Court. Jones's list of thirty "suspicious" claims received considerable attention and opposition from Black. The harm lay less in what claims Black's administration succeeded in having rejected than in how those claims met defeat. The legacy of suspicion created in the minds of judges, administrators, and the public affected claims indiscriminately and most certainly delayed the final settlement of claims by encouraging challenges to the title, survey, and patent of legitimate Mexican grants.

The claims of José Limantour provided a turning point for the issue of fraud in California and profoundly altered the context within which Hoffman adjudicated land cases. Although a native of France, Limantour had traded in Mexico and California for a decade before he filed eight claims with the land board just before the deadline in 1853, claims asserting title to over a half-million acres in and around San Francisco Bay. The immensity of the claims, their last-minute filing, and the fact that rights to valuable and improved land allegedly granted nearly a decade earlier were so belatedly asserted immediately cast suspicion on Limantour. His casual abandonment of six of his claims did nothing to enhance his credibility. The two remaining claims covered half of San Francisco, part of Marin County, the islands of Alcatraz and Yerba Buena in San Francisco Bay, and the Farallon Islands off the Pacific Coast. Frederick Billings, an attorney hired by the city of San Francisco, described Limantour's claim as "well gotten up," but he felt it posed no real threat. Although Limantour eventually lost in Hoffman's court, Billings's prediction proved slightly premature: early in 1856 the second board confirmed both claims.[73]

Despite all the documents Limantour produced in support of his claims, Cushing and his subordinates strongly suspected fraud. After the board's confirmation, Cushing specifically instructed the U.S. attorney in San Francisco on how to defeat the claim. He reported to President Pierce, "All known circumstances tend to show that the claim of Limantour is a fraudulent one." Cushing also proposed the employment of special counsel as well as an agent who could gather evidence against the claims in Mexico. The claims threatened the government with the loss of such valuable property as the Marine Hospital atop Rincon Hill and militarily strategic sites such as Fort Point near the Golden Gate and Alcatraz Island in the bay. Even though the city of San Francisco had early hired legal talent to protect its interests against Limantour's claims, individuals who owned much valuable land under dispute moved slowly in opposition to Limantour.[74]

Described as a "sharp, shrewd fellow," Limantour used a strategy that diffused resistance to his claims and prodded the United States into taking special measures. Limantour undercut local opposition by offering individual property owners quitclaims, or releases of his property interest at a fraction of the assessed value of their land, and by gratuitously releasing his claim on all church property. In addition to his liberal policy of compromises, Limantour gathered support by hiring the well-known writer for the *Alta California*, John S. Hittell, to propagandize his claims and to argue the benefits to property owners if the Frenchman succeeded. A confidential treasury agent pointed out the "anomalous" position of San Francisco property owners, who might have been natural allies of the government in defeating Limantour. "It is useless to look to the adversary claimants to assume the burden of the prosecution; they will make no further effort than will subserve their interests."[75]

For all the suspicion, Limantour's position seemed a strong one, particularly after the board's confirmation. The U.S. attorney accurately summed up the situation. "A great many persons prefer this compromise to the chances and expenses of litigation, and thus he [Limantour] neutralizes hostility and has secured a large fund with which he further prosecutes his claims against the United States." Indeed, those hedging their bets with Limantour included the leading businessmen and lawyers of the city. In all, Limantour collected over $100,000 for quitclaims.[76]

Limantour's policy of offering quitclaims convinced government officials of his intention to defraud the United States. With individuals out of the way, the government stood to be the primary loser. Limantour's "game" was to get a patent to lands "absolutely necessary for government defences, and obtain millions for his property or else clamor to the world that the United States" would be "faithless to its treaty stipulations and prompt to defraud an innocent foreigner." Limantour might have hoped for such a payoff, but his plan—had it been successful—would have fleeced both the government and the individual property owners. Limantour's sophisticated scheme, and the enormous threat it posed to the government, launched the most intensive examination of a Mexican land-grant claim up to that point. The result of this investigation, conducted almost entirely during Black's administration, dramatically changed the course of the California land-grant claims.[77]

Placing a high priority on Limantour's defeat, Attorney General Black soon assembled a staff of like-minded individuals. His new U.S. attorney for the northern district, Peter Della Torre, soon had a reputation for "readiness and zeal" in fighting Limantour's pretensions. In October 1857, Black sent Edwin M. Stanton to California as a special counsel entrusted with Limantour's case. Stanton, the future secretary of war under Lincoln, had a national legal reputation when the new attorney general gave him the appointment. Able and energetic, Stanton had demonstrated his appetite for winning cases. His ruthlessness and questionable means were noted by his peers, but none could deny his successful advocacy. To Black, Stanton seemed a good choice as the man to defeat what the attorney general later called "the most stupendous fraud ever perpetrated in the history of the world." Black ordered Stanton to win or "prove that success was utterly impossible." Black conceded to Stanton, "I can't float unless I ride on the wave of your reputation, and I want it to roll high." Directed to Stanton, such a mandate did produce results.[78]

Gathering evidence to rebut Limantour's claim became of prime importance. Even during Cushing's administration, rumors had circulated that informants might shed light on the Limantour fraud. A variety of individuals intimated direct knowledge. Auguste Jouan, for one, told Black that he had altered the dates on Limantour's island claim. Intrigued by such information, Black nevertheless harbored natural doubts about the probity of testimony requiring a $30,000 payment to a party to the fraud. Black explained that payments for testimony required congressional authorization but encouraged his subordinates to glean what they could from such informants. Both Black and Della Torre recognized the weakness of witnesses such as Jouan. A Virginian like Bernard Peyton, who rebuffed Limantour's offer of a percentage interest if Peyton would present the claims in his own name, made a far stronger witness than a confessed forger. Della Torre wrote Black that Peyton was "the very kind of witness" they wanted, "a gentleman of integrity and standing" whose word would carry "great weight" in Hoffman's court.[79]

Even before Stanton arrived in San Francisco, U.S. Attorney Della Torre identified the lack of oral testimony as a major source of difficulty in building the government's case. While Limantour had rounded up well-known witnesses, including the former governor and high-ranking officials of the Mexican government in California, Della Torre had had little comparable success. He thought that many knowledgeable Hispanics refused to help because it would bring them "into direct conflict with their old friends and associates of the same race and class" and because they stood "in fear of their lives from Limantour's agents." Sympathy for Limantour's associates, rather than fear of them, appears to have been the stronger influence at work. Thomas Larkin, who enjoyed the confidence of both Hispanics and non-Hispanics in California, observed, "Californians are apt to wish well to L[imantour] if it may injure Americans." Larkin touched on an important undercurrent in the private land-grant litigation in California: the deep-seated resentment and hostility that many Hispanics felt toward "Yankees." Although some non-Hispanics, like Larkin, were accepted by Californios, many others were not and openly expressed their sense of superiority over Hispanics and their culture.[80]

As many Hispanics saw their lands slip away from them during the first generation after American control, their antipathy increased toward Americans and the legal process established to confirm their land titles. Jaime de Puig, a claimant to the Noche Buena rancho in Monterey County, wrote of "those boas, designated by the name of Yankee," who were "more enormous than rattlesnakes" and who would "swallow" Hispanics "one by one in their enormous and disgusting gullet." Smarting from losses they attributed to Americans and the government, disaffected Hispanics were somewhat con-soled by the spectacle of the United States and Yankee businessmen running scared at the prospect of losing valuable property. Thus, the difficulty of finding cooperative Hispanic witnesses should not have been so surprising.[81]

Della Torre's concern about the weakness of the government's case prompted his recommendation to Black that a criminal suit against Liman-tour, instituted under Cushing's administration, be delayed. Della Torre worried that if Limantour was acquitted of forgery and perjury, the civil case would be "seriously compromised." The criminal case, observed Della Torre, "shifted the burden of proof and placed it on the United States," thereby giving Limantour "all the prisoner's advantages in the law and be-fore a jury." Given the difficulty of getting witnesses to testify, Attorney General Black agreed with Della Torre's strategy and dropped the criminal prosecution.[82]

Rejecting Limantour's claims as false, Black, Stanton, and Della Torre concluded that Limantour's Mexican witnesses had committed perjury. Since the government lacked oral testimony in support of its case, Stanton emphasized archival evidence. When archival evidence proved claims to be fraudulent, the general credibility of Mexican witnesses, in Black's mind, suffered an irretrievable blow. Black saw California land-grant claims as marred by the "most enormous frauds, forgeries and perjuries." Della Torre urged Black's opposition to a bill permitting claimants to use depositions gathered in Mexico. He explained, "There is nothing he [Limantour] could not prove, if his witnesses were to be examined in Mexico." Stanton too rejected Hispanic oral evidence and said, "I do not mean to spend a single dollar to buy up Mexican or Spanish witnesses—I would not spend a cent for a regiment of them." Stanton's short stay in California convinced him of the state's marvelous potential if it could be settled with "a new race of people," and if "all the thieves, forgers, perjurers, and murderers" that had "infested it beyond any spot on earth" could be driven off. Ultimately both Black and Stanton believed they had fulfilled such a mission by virtue of their efforts in fighting California land-grant claims.[83]

Stanton's appointment as a special counsel introduced a new methodology in opposing suspect claims. Stanton's contract gave him the huge fee of

$25,000 as well as liberal allowances for expenses and the employment of a staff. Shortly after his arrival in San Francisco in March 1858, Stanton paid the first of many visits to the archives office of the U.S. surveyor general. Although he met many San Francisco lawyers and undoubtedly discussed with them the *Limantour* and other land claims, Stanton spent most of his time examining documents in the archives. Directing the collection of official documents related to land claims scattered throughout the state, Stanton assembled a centralized archive in San Francisco. In connection with his archival research, Stanton drafted two bills, for which Black got immediate congressional approval. One required the return to the archives of all official Mexican documents wherever they might be found, and the other severely penalized making false claims to land or taking documents from the archives. Only rarely did Stanton bother with taking depositions; he consistently favored the documentary record as the means of defeating Limantour.[84]

Within two weeks of his arrival in San Francisco in 1858, Stanton devoted ten hours a day to "examining and arranging Spanish documents, letters, [and] records." Within a month Stanton proudly reported to Black that he had personally "examined every book and paper in the Archives" covering the years 1824 to 1846. His examination convinced him that records relating to the *Limantour* case showed signs of tampering and that other documents impeached various assertions made by Limantour and his witnesses. He assembled his proof of the documentary fraud in a bound volume of some 250 photographs. After comparing "genuine" documents and signatures with those submitted by Limantour, Stanton believed that one-third of the photographic exhibits were forgeries. "In the face of these," Stanton asserted, "all Mexico may perjure itself at leisure. A lie can't be made the truth as these photographs will prove."[85]

Although expensive, Stanton succeeded in convincing Black and others that photographic exhibits provided indisputable proof of fraudulent or altered documents.[86] The technique obviously impressed Hoffman, who rejected Limantour's two claims on November 19, 1858. After an extensive review of the testimony and documents introduced in the case, Hoffman acknowledged "no slight satisfaction to feel that the evidence" left "nothing to inference, suspicion or conjecture, but that the proofs of fraud" were "as conclusive and irresistible as the attempted fraud" was "flagrant and audacious."[87] When Limantour, who had gone to Mexico before Hoffman's decision, declined to appeal, the case ended. Nonetheless, Stanton and Black did not want their handiwork to go to waste. Black presented a book of the Limantour photo exhibits to Chief Justice Roger B. Taney and the Supreme Court. Stanton's photographic approach was crucial because it bred the belief that photographic comparisons could detect fraud not only in the *Limantour* claim but in many other private land grants as well. The scientific aura of the technique of photographic comparisons proved highly effective in convincing the Supreme Court of land fraud in California. Before he was done, Stanton had ordered over twenty other volumes of photographic exhibits in land cases appealed by the government.[88]

While he gathered documentary evidence pertaining to the *Limantour* case, Stanton also consolidated the archives dealing with California land-grant claims. After identifying all the relevant materials he could find and putting them in chronological order, Stanton had clerks assemble copies, translations, and photographs of documents and then bind them into over four hundred large volumes. Attorney General Black received one set of these bound archives, as well as a large volume of photographic copies of official correspondence and seals, with examples of supposedly genuine and fraudulent documents. The results of Stanton's three months of research furnished, in Black's view, "irresistible proof that there had been an organized system of fabricating land titles carried on for a long time in California by Mexican officials; that forgery and perjury had been reduced to a regular occupation; that the making of false grants, with the subornation of false witnesses to prove them, had become a trade and a business." Black's exaggerated sense of the comprehensiveness of the frenetically gathered archives supplied him with both a justification and a potent weapon for his crusade against Mexican grants.[89]

How Black used Stanton's documentation approached a science. From the records sent by Stanton, Black created lists of "professional witnesses" and other perjurers. Moreover, he compiled biographies "of nearly all the men . . . engaged in these schemes of imposture and fraud, from the governors down to the lowest of the suborned witnesses." Finally, Black routinely filed photographic copies (as opposed to handwritten transcripts) of the original papers before the land board in all cases that came to the Supreme Court on appeal. With his photographic comparisons, master lists, and biographies, Black said he could "determine, with almost absolute certainty, the truth or falsehood of any claim."[90]

Black's and Stanton's confidence that they could detect forgeries was exceeded only by their belief—nurtured by the *Limantour* case—that many conspiracies existed to cheat the United States and "the honest inhabitants of California." Limantour represented the tip of the iceberg. The Treaty of Guadalupe Hidalgo, charged Black, had "tempted many corrupt men, both American and foreigners, to regard California as a spot where forgery would win fortunes and where principalities could be purchased by perjury." Black resolved to teach would-be perpetrators a "wholesome fear of the law" and declared that he did not intend "to spare any of them."[91]

Starting with the active investigation of Limantour's claims and especially after Stanton arrived on the scene, a perception emerged that a growing conspiracy and fraud infected the California land claims. In July 1857, U.S. Attorney Della Torre warned Black of the "extent" of Limantour's organization, which had "grown by degrees" and wore "the aspect of a vast conspiracy." Limantour's many agents in San Francisco and Mexico, his successful strategy in offering quitclaims, and his ability to pay for effective propagandists, witnesses, and legal talent all indicated a well-orchestrated plan. Stanton's many reports to Black on his researches in the archives completed the picture of devious forgery and tampering with documents. In April 1858, Stanton wrote Black that his preoccupation with tracing the documentary evidence of Limantour's claims had left him "as yet unable to say much about the other cases pending in the District Court." But Stanton soon found the time to assess the other cases and saw evidence of similar fraud and perjury.[92]

Black found himself deluged by a steady stream of correspondence warning of fraud and perjury connected with Limantour's claims. Moreover, Black had ample testimony to the existence of "many immense frauds" to be "punished and checked." In explaining the ubiquity of fraudulent land grants, Della Torre suggested how Black perceived the California situation. "Perfect success so far has induced a boldness in such matters almost beyond belief." The number of allegations of fraud in specific land claims greatly exceeded those that Cushing had received, contributing to Black's perception of widespread evil doings. By December 1858, over fifty California land claims were docketed with the Supreme Court. By then, in less than two years of his administration, Black could report, "The most atrocious frauds ever perpetrated on any government have been detected and exposed to the great terror and just punishment of many evil doers." Not only had

Limantour's claims been defeated, but "many others of the same character" were "on their way to the same result." [93]

The path that led Judge Hoffman toward an acceptance of many of the assumptions of Attorney General Black distanced him even further from the Supreme Court. Hoffman's disagreement with the Supreme Court's legal philosophy expressed in *Fremont* and other early California land cases grew as he confirmed claims he felt were suspect. In deciding *Nunez* v. *United States* in May 1857, Hoffman found the oral testimony so unreliable that he regretted not being able to insist on proof of occupation and cultivation "as the best, if not the only check upon forgeries and frauds" in cases in which the archives contained "no evidence of the grant." Hoffman's complaints about the veracity of witnesses began to emerge with his judicial opinions in the *Andres Pico* and *Limantour* cases in 1857 and 1858. Increasingly throughout this period, Hoffman caught witnesses, including former high-ranking officials in the Mexican government, in inconsistencies and outright contradictions. Toward the end, he regarded unsubstantiated oral evidence as worthless unless it came from men whose character and reputation he trusted. Men like John Sutter, John Bidwell, and Henry Halleck formed "a class, unfortunately too small, upon whose veracity" Hoffman felt he could rely. As Hispanic witnesses began to lose their credibility in Hoffman's eyes, virtually the only oral testimony to sway the judge came from non-Hispanics like Halleck or from those Hispanics, like Pablo de la Guerra, with "unimpeachable character." [94]

Hoffman's sense of honor directly affected his manner of appraising oral testimony. In the land-grant cases, as with the voluminous admiralty docket, Hoffman sat as the finder of both fact and law. Thus his attitudes toward and expectations of witnesses appearing in his court assumed critical importance in his judicial decisions. As in the admiralty cases, Hoffman expected differing levels of probity based on the social background and education of the witnesses. He combed through the testimony looking for inconsistent or contradictory statements, which, if found, tended to impeach the credibility of witnesses. When he suspected perjury, Hoffman spared neither non-Hispanic nor Hispanic witnesses in showing his disgust and contempt for lying. [95]

Hispanic testimony developed its sorry reputation in Hoffman's court for several reasons. The resolution of titles in a strange legal setting undoubtedly affected some Hispanic claimants and witnesses. From their lawyers, claimants learned that the federal tribunals expected them to prove their title to land, though just what proof would be necessary not even the lawyers knew. Indeed, the standards of proof remained in flux as the opinions of the land board changed with its composition. With the fate of their lands in the hands of strangers, Hispanic claimants had an incentive to strengthen their cases any way they could, including by securing the strongest testimony. Often claimants testified for one another, and a mutuality of interests produced strong evidence, if not collusion.

Positive assertions of occupancy or the existence of documents, however, proved counterproductive when they were successfully rebutted. Hoffman could accept lapses in memory and inaccurate or imprecise recollections from Hispanic witnesses. He noted, "It is only when they undertake to speak positively on these points, and are found to be inaccurate, that a doubt as to their good faith is suggested." When Hispanic witnesses avoided unequivocal assertions, Hoffman received their testimony more favorably. In the *Limantour* case, Francisco Sanchez testified that he knew a part-time clerk of the Mexican governor Manuel Micheltorena and had seen him write. Hoffman commented approvingly, "With a scrupulousness that adds force to his testimony, he declines to say that he remembers his handwriting well enough to say that he knows it." Numerous Hispanic witnesses—some undoubtedly convinced of the genuineness of certain claims and determined to give unequivocal evidence to support them—were impeached on the stand, which ultimately undercut the probity of Hispanic witnesses in general.[96]

Part of the problem stemmed from a basic unfamiliarity with the process and procedures of a common-law trial. Early in his practice of bringing land claims before the board, Henry Halleck lamented, "Californians are the worst witnesses I ever saw, and when cross examined by the Government attorney, unless watched with the utmost care, they say something to completely destroy their testimony." Almost two years later, matters had not changed for the better. Halleck wrote that one of his "Californian" witnesses on the stand forgot places and dates that he had known while in Halleck's office, thereby gravely hurting his case. Any witness might have been rattled by the courtroom setting, but those unfamiliar with the language, law, and process that surrounded them were especially uncomfortable.[97]

The veracity of Hispanic witnesses also suffered because some of them knowingly supported a certain amount of perjury and forgery. At one level, land fraud depended on one's cultural perspective. Americans and Californios were apt to have quite different opinions about the Mexican governor Pio Pico's last-minute efforts to grant land on the eve of American control. Americans viewed such grants as blatant efforts to cheat settlers out of their rightful due, but Hispanics saw them as a means of diminishing the spoils of war to be enjoyed by their military conquerors. Certainly some claimants, sure that their titles were valid but leery of what the courts might decide, were tempted to doctor the record with some additional documentary or oral evidence. Indeed, even Henry Halleck—a man whose testimony Hoffman implicitly trusted—made excuses for such practices. Writing to Pablo de la Guerra, Halleck denied that all the blame rested with the United States for the difficulty and slow process of settling titles. He noted that de la Guerra's "own 'paysanos' " were largely responsible, "first in not proceeding according to [Mexican] laws in making their grants, and in the second place by making false and antedated papers, and then *swearing* to them." He had personal knowledge of "numerous false and forged papers" submitted to the board and "sworn to by some of the *Honorable* ex-officials of the Mexican government in California." "Nevertheless," he continued, "I must confess that our government has been culpably negligent in this matter, and that the commissioners have been unnecessarily dilatory." Halleck displayed much less understanding when it came to irregularities in the claims of nonpaying clients. In 1853 he complained that members of his law firm had "worked like dogs" for the claimants of the rancho Sespe in Santa Barbara County and had won confirmation before the board "by the skin of [their] teeth." He continued: "I know enough about that title to cause its rejection, and if they treat us so meanly as to refuse to pay our bill, I *will* defeat it. That they may rely on."[98]

Perhaps the most compelling influence on Hoffman's attitude toward Hispanic testimony and land-grant claims generally came from the new approach of the Black administration. Before Black became attorney general, Hoffman had confirmed several claims in which allegations of fraud were made or in which gaps had existed in the documentary record. Only after 1857 did Hoffman begin to reject claims regularly because of fraud or a lack of documentary evidence. In September 1857, Hoffman rejected a claim for the first time on the grounds that neither documentary evidence nor oral testimony established the existence of a grant. One month later, Hoffman first rejected a claim because of fraud. Thereafter, a spate of claims were rejected by Hoffman's court on the same grounds.[99]

Hoffman's departure from a liberal confirmation of land claims under the influence of the *Fremont* case began during the period when defeating the notorious *Limantour* claims was receiving increasing attention. With the Black administration's strong emphasis on fraud, forgery, and perjury, Hoffman became more sensitive to these issues. Moreover, despite his steadfast, if reluctant, allegiance to the precedent set by *Fremont*, Hoffman also detected a shift in the attitude of the Supreme Court. Indeed, the change that Hoffman noted dated from the first California land-grant case that Attorney General Black argued on its merits before the Supreme Court.

In *United States* v. *Cambuston*, decided in January 1858, Hoffman found himself again reversed in a major land-grant case. Attorney General Black urged the rejection of the claim because of fraud and because he regarded the circumstantial evidence of fabrication "irresistible—sufficient to convict the best citizen of the worst crime." Even though suspicious of the grant, the Supreme Court rested its decision on the meager documentary evidence produced by the claimant. Despite the absence of the original grant and other papers, both the land board and Hoffman had confirmed the claim on the basis of oral testimony. Hoffman had wanted fuller documentation, but since the U.S. attorney for the northern district had not disputed the genuineness of the grant, he had felt the claim must be confirmed.[100]

Justice Samuel Nelson, for the Court, remanded the case to the northern district for further hearing, saying that the Supreme Court would have readily rejected the claim had it not been for the lackadaisical preparation by the government's lawyers. Nelson emphasized the apparent nonobservance, by the claimant, of the preliminary steps requisite to receive land under Mexican law. Moreover, the absence of sufficient corroboration by the archives, particularly in cases involving purported grants made on the eve of American occupation, called for strict scrutiny "in order to prevent imposition and frauds." In characterizing the case as "too defective" and "unsupported by the evidence," the Supreme Court implicitly rejected the value of oral testimony and put a premium on archival documentation. The ultimate effect of the *Cambuston* case, as the lower courts worked out its implications, was an important shift in the burden of proof. Whereas earlier the government had had the burden of proving fraud, now the claimant—when the archival record was missing or imperfect—had to establish the genuineness of the grant. The *Cambuston* case initiated a series of victories for the new attorney general.[101]

Hoffman interpreted *Cambuston* as a retreat from the liberal guidelines of the *Fremont* case. He acknowledged that of the two principal means of testing the genuineness of alleged grants, one—establishing the claimant's occupation of the land—had been largely ineffective under *Fremont*. That decision gave claimants wide latitude for using oral testimony to excuse or explain their failure to occupy. Since the Supreme Court seemed to be applying, "with rigor," the other primary test of genuineness—substantiation by the archival record—Hoffman decided not to confirm claims in the absence of any documentary proof in the archives or evidence of widely known possession prior to the American occupation. Hoffman welcomed the new emphasis on archival documentation as a means of grounding his decisions on evidence better than "utterly unreliable" oral testimony. Despite his misgivings about such testimony, Hoffman continued to accept oral evidence long after the Supreme Court, under the prodding of Attorney General Black, had in effect made archival evidence the only successful basis for confirmation.[102]

When Hoffman reconsidered the *Cambuston* case, he rejected the claim, though not because of fraud but because of Cambuston's ineligibility, as a Frenchman, to receive a grant under Mexican law. To his opinion, rendered in June 1859, Hoffman attached an appendix unnecessary to the resolution of the case. Obviously responding to the reversal and concerned about being misunderstood, Hoffman offered a general analysis of the legal requirements of Mexican land grants, the Supreme Court's ruling in *Fremont*, and the adverse consequences that, in his view, had followed from that case. Hoffman acknowledged that he might have confirmed fraudulent grants because "it was always easy . . . to locate the land in districts where it could readily be shown that Indian hostilities presented an insuperable obstacle to a settlement" and because it was easy to manipulate oral testimony "to make the case precisely analogous to that of *Fremont*." Even more galling to Hoffman had been his inability to use the test of long-standing possession in the cases of Governor Pio Pico's "eleventh-hour grants." Hoffman noted, "Unapproved by the assembly, issued with evident signs of haste if not carelessness, never occupied or cultivated, they seemed to possess less equities than almost any other." "But," complained Hoffman, "these grants were precisely those with regard to which the court could not declare that they had been forfeited by abandonment," since under *Fremont* the "distracted condition of the country, and the impracticality of occupying the land, could always be alleged in excuse for the omission to do so." Whatever vindication Hoffman might have felt for his original position on the land titles, he had just experienced the first of many reversals stemming from his adherence to the precedent set by *Fremont*.[103]

Between the Supreme Court's opinion in the *Cambuston* case in January 1858 and the end of Black's administration in 1860, the Court rendered over thirty opinions dealing with California land grants.[104] In one way or the other, the cases continued to chip away at the *Fremont* precedent, although the Court did not explicitly overrule itself. Rather, Black's and Stanton's repeated assertions and warnings of fraud had succeeded in convincing the Supreme Court that California land-grant cases should be strictly scrutinized and rigorously tested. By March 1860, the Court was reversing land-grant cases decided by Hoffman in the mid-1850s, cases that had been squarely based on *Fremont*, while at the same time the Court cited the decision as good law.[105] Although the case name stayed the same, the principles of *Fremont* were now being applied in a quite different spirit. Thus, the lack of archival documentation created a presumption or implication of fraud.[106]

This shift in the approach taken by Black and the Supreme Court toward California land-grant claims was epitomized by *United States* v. *Teschmaker* (1860). In 1855 Hoffman had confirmed the grant claimed in that case, resting his decision on the *Fremont* case. The genuineness of this grant to Salvador and Juan A. Vallejo was not disputed. When the case reached the Supreme Court on appeal, Black and Stanton—who argued the case—made fraud and suspicion of Hispanic witnesses the central issue. Characterizing the grant as "false, forged, fabricated," they stressed the fact that no reference to the grant could be found in the archives assembled by Stanton. They added, "The bad character of the Vallejos, as well as their principle witnesses, renders it extremely probable that all the papers, including the petition for license to occupy, the license itself, and the pretended grant from the governor, are sheer fabrications, fraudulently got up long after the change of government." Citing the lack of documentary evidence, the Supreme Court reversed and remanded the case to Hoffman's court. After reexamining the grant under the stricter standards now established by the Supreme Court, Hoffman rejected the claim.[107]

By 1860 the Supreme Court had established a rule that impeached Mexican officials' oral testimony that was unsupported by archival documentation. Moreover, by that date the attorney general was urging the Supreme Court to imply a lack of genuineness in any grant in which the claimant failed to abide by the requirements of Mexican law. Hoffman had insisted on observing Mexican legal requirements from the very first—before the Supreme Court brushed his views aside with the liberal construction adopted in *Fremont*. But Hoffman had never suggested that a failure to meet legal requirements implied bad faith on the part of claimants. The fact that Black seriously urged such a stand in 1860 indicates how much the setting in which California land claims were decided had changed in the five years since *Fremont*.[108]

One could describe the course of California's land-grant cases simply as a shift from a liberal to a strict construction of land grants on the part of the U.S. Supreme Court. That description, though correct at one level, misses the most intriguing lesson those cases have to offer. Namely, they provide an example of how shifting perceptions about discrete litigation can subtly, but profoundly, influence the course of law. The key to the Supreme Court's shift lay not in doctrinal change but in newly emerging and critical attitudes about the general validity of California land grants. The emergence of these perceptions was a complex and pervasive process that eventually affected federal officials, the general public, and the courts. Although such patterns of thought and reaction are evident with the benefit of hindsight, it was much more difficult for contemporaries to understand what was happening. In part, this contributed to Hoffman's frustration at being reversed in cases in which (despite reservations) he had dutifully followed the *Fremont* case, before the Supreme Court undermined the precedential value of that case. These swings in opinion and prejudice not only confused Hoffman but also produced the most enduring legacy of California's land-grant litigation.

CHAPTER

6

The Litigious Pueblo

Largely created by the gold rush, San Francisco became a focal point for the struggle over land titles. Central to disputes over San Francisco land was whether the city had inherited the land rights thought to belong to a Mexican pueblo. Assuming an entitlement to four square leagues (approximately 28 square miles) of land under Mexican law, San Francisco had granted and sold valuable city lots, which, in turn, had been sold. In addition, most of the San Francisco peninsula was the object of a number of individual claims to Mexican land grants. If, however, the individual grants and the pueblo title were rejected, then enormously valuable land was available for the taking, and existing land ownership would be overturned. As a result, conflicting interests vied to establish clear title to San Francisco land, including the interests of the municipality, alleged Mexican grantees, lot holders who traced title to land granted or sold under Mexican and American authority, settlers who claimed under preemption laws, individuals who claimed land by virtue of execution sales against the city, and people who simply took what they could and held it as squatters.[1]

In many respects, San Francisco's experience mirrored the tensions that underlay land settlement in the state as a whole, and the resolution of San Francisco's pueblo title provides a good example of how federalism affected the struggle over California land. Determining the validity of claims, hence separating public from private land, was technically the exclusive province of the federal government in its examination of Mexican land grants. In practice, however, the state courts' early involvement with land issues influenced how the federal courts would exercise their "exclusive" jurisdiction. Therefore, the struggle over land in San Francisco offers a microcosm of the elements that determined the pace, nature, and ultimate outcome of California land litigation.

The final, judicial confirmation of the pueblo title by the federal circuit court in 1864 was hardly as inevitable and naturally beneficial as its proponents asserted. Few of those who struggled for land in San Francisco possessed clear-cut legal or moral equities. Opponents of San Francisco's pueblo title—in common with plaintiffs in any land struggle in California—were often branded "speculators" or "squatters," depending on the size of their investment. The final confirmation represented the political and legal success of certain groups of speculators over others more than it did a settlement of municipal claims that were advanced for the public welfare.

Principally, however, the struggle over the pueblo title offered a contrast between the judicial styles of Ogden Hoffman and Stephen Field, the two federal judges who played a central role in resolving the disputes over San Francisco land. Both held strong but divergent views about the litigation over San Francisco land. Each also had extensive judicial experience with this key issue. By the early 1860s, Hoffman had heard many appeals of land-grant cases from the land board to his district court, whereas Field, as a member of the California Supreme Court from 1857 until his elevation to the U.S. Supreme Court in 1863, had also had considerable experience in resolving land titles within the state. The relationship and approaches of Hoffman and Field during the litigation over San Francisco's pueblo illustrate important differences in their respective views about settling title to land in California and in how each perceived his judicial role in that process. Hoffman's pride, stubbornness, faithfulness to strict textual analysis, and judicial restraint collided with Field's aggressive, free-wheeling, and openly political behavior. This contrast prompted an attempt—supported by Field—to strip the district judge not only of judicial power but of his office itself. Moreover, aided by Senator John Conness of California, Field took steps to insure that his own resolution of the pueblo dispute would prevail. This record of acrimony and conflict between Hoffman and Field not only shaped the settlement but also affected the character of federal justice in the Far West until Hoffman's death in 1891.

———————

Years before the gold seekers reached San Francisco by the thousands, a smaller group of individuals began laying the foundations to their fortunes in San Francisco real estate. The four-year period between the outbreak of war with Mexico in 1846 and California's statehood in 1850 saw the sale or transfer of much San Francisco land that later became the extremely valuable prize over which so many would struggle. Mexican *alcaldes*—municipal officials akin to mayors—also granted San Francisco lands prior to 1846, the so-called Mexican *alcalde* grants. Most of the disposal of city lots, however, occurred after 1846 with the so-called American *alcalde* grants between 1846 and 1850 and with sales of municipal lands that continued into the 1850s. Between 1846 and 1848, some 1,200 lots in the heart of the future city were granted or sold. This disposition of land also included areas that were part of San Francisco Bay. For instance, "beach" and "waterfront" lots had the promise of great value after land became scarce and mud flats were converted into solid ground.[2]

The influx of population accompanying the gold rush greatly inflated the value of property that many early residents had purchased for speculative purposes. For example, one lot in the center of the developing city that had cost $17 in 1847 was sold in early 1849 for $6,000 and at the end of that same year for $45,000. The sale of public land provided an important source of city revenue and was popular with potential speculators. This early disposal of San Francisco's most valuable municipal lands was fraught with greedy speculation, irresponsibility, and fraud. Some of the earliest to profit from San Francisco land investments were members of the American military stationed in California in the mid-1840s. One soldier who did very well for himself was Army Captain Joseph L. Folsom, who served as the chief quartermaster at San Francisco beginning in 1847. At that time town lots were sold for as little as $16 each, but every person was limited to a single purchase. William Tecumseh Sherman, a West Point classmate of Folsom's and then also stationed in California, recalled that Folsom "had got his clerks, orderlies, etc., to buy lots and they, for a small consideration, conveyed them to him, so that he was nominally the owner of a good many lots."[3]

Indeed, Folsom's efforts were so successful that when he died in 1855, many believed him to be the wealthiest man in the state. One observer, however, described Folsom's property as "all held by titles more or less uncertain," and consequently Folsom spent his last years "engaged constantly in lawsuits and broils, worried, vexed, and harried to death." Few individuals were immune to the allure of land speculation, particularly with the occasional examples of astounding fortunes made on rapidly appreciating real estate. In some ways, land speculators shared a fate with the gold miners; most did not strike it rich, and fluctuating conditions beyond their control could easily frustrate even the most determined seeker of wealth. One San Franciscan in 1855 described the city's "mushroom" millionaires, whose wealth had been calculated by inflated real estate values while "their unimproved and unproductive lots" were "nothing but a curse, devouring themselves and their owners" with taxes. [4]

The principal vulnerability of these early land speculations was their uncertain title. Apart from such frauds as Folsom's use of "straw-men," many contemporaries expressed doubts about the legitimacy of land sales in the city. In 1850, Henry H. Haight, a San Francisco lawyer and future governor of California, detailed the different "tenure and titles" to land in San Francisco, determining that virtually all the land granted or sold after 1846 was "of dubious legality" if not tainted by "fraud and corruption." He regarded the sale of water lots as "not authorized by, or in conformity to law," but noted the "general expectation that they will be sanctioned" by Congress because of the valuable improvements made on them. Another San Francisco lawyer, John McCrackan, thought that the city had "no good right or title" to lands it had received from an American military governor before statehood. Rather, he believed, "The land held by our city, as her own, is held under the squatter title, [through] *possession* and *improvement*." Thus, McCrackan observed, "In one sense of the word we are all squatters." [5]

Even those like Haight and McCrackan, who were trained lawyers and aware of the suspect titles, could not resist the lure of San Francisco real estate: both subsequently invested in city lots. McCrackan, who had been retained to validate title to San Francisco's water lots, explained a circumstance that made his task easier. "One of the most favorable features of the case is in the fact of every lawyer in town, being a grantee, . . . consequently [is] interested in having them sustained." Lawyers were hardly the only group interested in such lands, but their heavy involvement strengthened the argument that ownership of city land deriving title from sales or grants between 1846 and 1850 involved legitimate investments and not irregular speculations.[6]

By 1852, another series of events had caused the city of San Francisco to lose more of its land and presented a challenge to the earlier lot speculation. A number of creditors of the city had sued for money owed them and had received judgments in their favor. To satisfy these judgments, the cash-poor city made a series of execution sales—sales to execute the judgments—of municipal land. As a result, many thousands of acres were auctioned off for ridiculously low prices. Collectively these sales became known as the Peter Smith deeds, named after a principal creditor of the city. The deeds became the subject of widespread resentment based on the suspicion that collusion among the buyers had kept low the bidding on the extremely valuable property. Ultimately, the municipality lost much of its principal tangible asset: land.[7]

Opponents of the Smith deeds accurately described them as a plunder of municipal lands, but objections also stemmed from the threat that the deeds posed to the holders of earlier sales of city lots. Joseph Folsom, who had previously acquired many San Francisco lots by dubious means while in the military, now, as a state legislator, opposed the Smith deeds because they meant "utter ruin" to the value of the older downtown lots. Along with Archibald Peachy, another state legislator and a partner in a major San Francisco law firm, Folsom plotted to abolish the superior court in San Francisco because it had sanctioned the execution sales. The pair's strategy also entailed securing judges on the California Supreme Court who would favor their position. The threat posed by the Smith deeds was eventually avoided, but through court action rather than through Folsom's crusade.[8]

The Smith deeds posed a threat to lot holders in part because powerful and prominent people had invested in them. Serranus Clinton Hastings, the first chief justice of the California Supreme Court, and Hall McAllister, the leading advocate of the California bar and son of Matthew Hall McAllister, represented only two of the "Peter Smith men." By July 1855, holders of Smith deeds had filed over 300 lawsuits to remove people on land they claimed. Both Hastings and McAllister were wealthy and highly respected, and their speculation in Smith deeds represented only part of a wider investment in real estate. Prominent politicians who were also holders of

Smith deeds included David C. Broderick, a leading Democrat in San Francisco and later a state senator, and John McDougal, California's second
governor.[9]

Squatterism posed a final source of difficulty for San Francisco lot holders. Robert F. Peckham, who had arrived in San Francisco in 1846 and later
served briefly as the district attorney and county judge of Santa Cruz, described the 1850s:

> Society was divided into three classes; land grabbers [i.e., Mexican
> grantees and lot holders], those that had grants for the lands and be-
> lieved they were the owners; the squatters [i.e., settlers], who knowing
> they had no title, would take possession of lots and hold them by
> making improvements; [and] the jumpers [i.e., squatters], who stood
> ready to ignore all law either of strict title or prior possession, and to
> intrude themselves, either by force, stealth or fraud, into another man's
> possessions and despoil him of his improvements.[10]

Lot holders and grantees faced a common enemy in the form of settlers
and squatters. The settlers were motivated by the prospect of gaining valuable city land by settling on it and then filing a preemption claim under
federal law. The logistics of this process required a rejection of the pueblo
title, with the implication that such land was part of the public domain.

Although some individuals showed a willingness to abide by the federal
preemption laws, squatters made little distinction between the lots held
under grants or sales and the land that the city claimed under its pueblo
title. If Peckham's categories of land "grabbers," "squatters," and "jump-
ers" tend to merge into one another, it is because he perceived the one
uncontested fact regarding the struggle for land in San Francisco: everyone
wanted a piece of valuable city property. To speak of preemption settlers in
the quickly urbanizing setting of San Francisco was an anomaly. Few, if any,
of the "settlers" who sought 160 acres from the federal government had any
intention of working the land by themselves or with their families. Such
"settlers," along with lot holders and squatters, sought mainly to acquire
land that was or might become valuable. The possibility of gaining valuable
city land by preemption spurred conflict and sporadic violence throughout
the 1850s, with squatter activity closely mirroring judicial and legislative
decisions. Initially, squatterism received considerable support from California's courts and legislature as well as the federal government. In addition to

early decisions of the California Supreme Court, California's legislature passed a preemption law in 1852 that gave settlers on public land who made $200 worth of improvements the right to sue those who interfered with their possession. Three years later the legislature passed a law (seemingly applicable to Mexican grants) that promised good title to a five-year adverse possessor. Moreover, two federal statutes in 1853 permitted preemption claims on Mexican land grants determined to be invalid, as well as on unreserved public land (surveyed or unsurveyed) to which there were no other claims.[11]

Confronted by the court decisions supporting squatterism, San Francisco's business community grew increasingly concerned in the early 1850s because much land rested solely on possession, and the unoccupied lands that had been purchased during the American period were open prey for squatters. The *Alta California* placed much of the blame for squatterism on San Francisco's "capitalists." It claimed that "an extensive and systematic organization" for squatterism was led by "foreigners" who were also "prominent citizens and . . . merchants." Purportedly, the organization existed to induce squatterism on vacant lands in the city, "the capitalists bearing a small proportion of the expense, and the squatters taking all the responsibility." The property, so seized, was later to be sold for the profit of the organizers, with "squatters getting but a nominal consideration, or none at all." The *Alta California* warned against further "public robbery."[12]

Historical evidence tends to bear out the *Alta California*'s assertion that squatterism in San Francisco was not simply a helter-skelter activity of disorganized and disgruntled "settlers." Substantial interests were involved, and although a systematic organization for squatting may not have existed, speculators sought legal advice and readily took advantage of the opportunities provided by the early decisions of the California Supreme Court. On June 9, 1853, property owners who held title to city land established the "People's Organization for the Protection of the Rights of Property and the Maintenance of Order" to oppose the "bands of armed men" who "have been organized in our midst." A "recipe" appearing in the *Alta California* on August 4, 1853, indicated the mounting tension: "HOW TO COOK A SQUAT ('A short and easy method of acquiring property, by which stealing is not [a] felony, and robbery becomes a rapid and legal cut to wealth')."[13]

The key issue regarding San Francisco land had always been whether the city had inherited the land rights of a Mexican pueblo. One way "pueblo lands" were thought to arise was from the establishment of Spanish missions in California. Missions were churches, but they also functioned as agricultural pueblos or towns, with cultivated lands to support an indigenous population. Each pueblo was thought to be entitled to four square leagues, a right San Francisco claimed as the successor to the Mexican town of Yerba Buena. In the course of resolving conflicting titles among San Francisco's lot holders, the California state courts preceded the federal courts in discussing the merits of the city's pueblo claim. Indeed, although the state courts lacked official jurisdiction to settle the pueblo's Mexican origins, a decision of the California Supreme Court in 1860 provided the blueprint for the final settlement of the issue by federal authorities.[14]

The California Supreme Court first considered the pueblo title in *Woodworth* v. *Fulton* (1850), a dispute over a San Francisco lot. Woodworth, who claimed title on the basis of an American *alcalde* land grant to him in 1847 while he was a naval officer in San Francisco, sought to recover possession of the lot from Fulton, who had purchased it from a third party whose title stemmed from a land grant given by a justice of the peace in 1849. Woodworth prevailed in the lower court, and Fulton appealed to the Supreme Court, where Justice Nathaniel Bennett, for the court, reversed the lower court and held for Fulton. Justice Bennett denied the existence of a San Francisco pueblo and hence the authority of American *alcaldes* to grant lands. Moreover, even if a pueblo did exist, Bennett concluded that "all laws of Mexico concerning the disposition of public lands must have ceased the moment California was effectually subdued and occupied by the American forces," and on that basis Woodworth's title would be invalid. *Woodworth* effectively placed a cloud over all titles depending on the pueblo claim. Chief Justice Serranus Hastings dissented principally on the grounds that under Mexican law—which he deemed applicable—the respondent had a better claim to possession.[15]

In *Cohas* v. *Raisin and Legris* (1853), however, the court, composed of entirely different justices, reversed itself and upheld the pueblo title. The seller of an American *alcalde* grant, for which the seller warranted title, sued on a note for the unpaid balance due from the purchaser. The purchaser denied that the seller could warrant title to the lot in question and sought a recision of the contract. The seller appealed to the California Supreme

Court, where the respondent, the purchaser of the lot, relied on the *Wood-worth* case. Declaring itself not bound by the *Woodworth* case, the court reexamined the Spanish and Mexican law relating to the disposition of land in San Francisco. In the opinion for the court, Justice Solomon Heydenfeldt concluded that a pueblo did exist and that all grants of land, whether by Mexican or American *alcaldes*, were presumed to be valid.[16]

By 1857, the supreme court, with yet another change in personnel, reluctantly concluded that it could not reject the Smith deeds unless it was also prepared to reject the pueblo and the post-1846 grants. *Welch* v. *Sullivan* (1857) involved a Smith deed holder who had brought an action of ejectment to recover possession of a San Francisco lot. The lower court had held for the plaintiff, and the defendant appealed on the grounds that the sale of the lot was invalid. Chief Justice Hugh Murray reaffirmed the *Cohas* case, stating that a return to the holding in *Woodworth* would be "to destroy every title in the city" except those pre-dating 1846. Both Murray and Associate Justice Peter Burnett held the execution sales to be valid because title to the land involved had previously passed to San Francisco by virtue of its status as a pueblo. Confirmation of the suspect Smith deeds seemed to be the necessary price for a pueblo and for a validation of title to highly developed commercial property.[17]

The California Supreme Court solved this legal quandary in 1860 in the case of *Hart* v. *Burnett*. *Hart* addressed the nature and source of San Francisco's pueblo in relation to the validity of the Smith deeds. Relying on a Smith deed, the plaintiff, Hart, sought to eject Burnett from a lot in downtown San Francisco. Burnett claimed the property under federal preemption statutes. After the lower court gave judgment for Hart, Burnett appealed to the California Supreme Court. In resolving the controversy, that court established a landmark in the history of the public trust doctrine. On the San Francisco land issue, however, *Hart*'s important contribution was its conclusion that the city could enjoy the benefits of a pueblo without validating the Smith deeds.[18]

Before advancing its new theory on the nature of San Francisco's tenure of pueblo lands, the *Hart* court dealt with the extent of the pueblo and the consequences of the American conquest of such lands. Rather perfunctorily, the court concluded that San Francisco was "beyond a doubt" a pueblo. It followed that the city was entitled to four square leagues of land. As to the nature of the city's pueblo title, the court reviewed various forms of land tenure and concluded that Mexican law gave "but one sensible answer": the city's pueblo lands were not given to the city and its officials "in absolute property, with full right of disposition and alienation, but to be held by them in trust, for the benefit of the entire community." The court determined that as trustees, the city officials could not allow the execution of city lands to pay debts that such officials created. On the other hand, procedures did exist for selling or granting such lands outright. Therefore, the Smith deeds, which originally stemmed from such executions, were void, whereas the post-1846 land grants and sales were valid.[19]

The *Hart* decision also revealed the justices' disagreement over the final solution to the pueblo dispute. Justice Warner Cope dissented in *Hart* simply on the grounds that the court's earlier decision validating the Smith deeds represented controlling precedent. More important, however, the case introduced into the controversy Stephen Field, whose forceful will would dictate the end of the dispute. Although Justice Joseph Baldwin wrote the majority opinion for the three-member court, Field, as the chief justice of the California Supreme Court, apparently contributed significantly to its reasoning and later wholeheartedly embraced it as a final solution. In the majority opinion, Baldwin exerted considerable effort trying to reconcile *Hart* with the court's prior decision that the Smith deeds were valid. At one point, Baldwin argued that California land law had been so chaotic in the previous decade that no precedents existed. Ultimately, however, the court defended its *Hart* decision as necessary to "settle and quiet the titles of the larger number [of people] now in possession." The court also postulated that a contrary decision would strip San Francisco of "her magnificent endowment" in favor of speculators who had invested "but a trifling proportion of the value of the property bought."[20]

Long before *Hart* was decided, and prior to Field's assumption of an active role in settling San Francisco's titles, he had demonstrated opposition to what he called "the spirit to invade other people's lands." In prior years, as an *alcalde* in Marysville, California, he had chased squatters off town lots, including lots that he owned. His election to the California Supreme Court in 1857 was widely viewed as a setback for the pro-squatter or settler movement in the state. On the court, he increased his unpopularity with squatters and would-be settlers with opinions strongly favoring the interests of Mexican grantees over other competitors for land. Field described the *Hart* case as a "just and most beneficent judgment" that insured peace "to thousands of homes." He attributed the "fierce howl of rage and hate" directed at Justice Baldwin and himself as stemming from self-interested speculators and a temporarily misguided public.[21]

Even though the state supreme court's decision in *Hart* encouraged the settlement of land-title disputes in San Francisco, the issue of the city's pueblo title ultimately rested with the federal authorities. By 1854, the city had secured a partial victory before the land board: a confirmation of the pueblo title, but for only three rather than four square leagues of land. The board's opinion thus reminded the city that it might lose the extra league of land if the pending claims covering much of the San Francisco peninsula (and in competition with the pueblo title) were confirmed. Given the land board's decision, it was inevitable that the city would appeal to Hoffman's court.

Soon after the land board's decision, however, the city of San Francisco moved to take advantage of the partial but favorable ruling and struck a compromise between the holders of post-1846 grants and the squatters and settlers. On June 20, 1855, the city council passed the Van Ness Ordinance, which was later ratified by the state legislature in 1858 and by Congress in 1864. By the ordinance, San Francisco's claim to all land within the city limits was relinquished "to the parties in the actual possession thereof, by themselves or tenants," who had lived there on or before January 1, 1855. Moreover, holders of post-1846 grants to lands lying east of Larkin Street and northeast of Johnston Street were "deemed to be the possessors of the land so granted" even though others were in actual possession. The practical effect of the Van Ness Ordinance was to protect landowners who held land under title in the older, commercial, and developed parts of the city. At the same time, the ordinance legitimized squatting in the vast area west and southwest of Larkin and Johnston streets—the area that included most of the land claimed under Smith deeds.[22]

Neither the Van Ness Ordinance nor the land board's 1854 decision settled the issue of the pueblo title. Other individual claims still conflicted with the city's pueblo claims. In addition to José Limantour's notorious claim to most of San Francisco, there were dozens of other claims that threatened the city's right to significant portions of city land. Although the *Limantour* case was certainly the most dramatic, two other claims figured even more importantly in directing the course of San Francisco's pueblo claim. The adjudication of the *Bolton* claim and the *Sherrebeck* claim resulted in a judicial confirmation of claims that were adverse to the city's pueblo title.[23]

The *Bolton* claim presented a classic confrontation pitting the interests of settlers and squatters against those of the land-grant claimants. James R. Bolton alleged that certain land had been granted to a Mexican priest in 1846. A conflict arose because the land claimed under this grant overlapped with much of the city land already claimed by Limantour and also overlapped with the desirable lands adjacent to the city's commercial areas. When the grant was filed with the land board in 1852, it was no longer owned by Hispanics, and by 1853 it was owned by the San Francisco Land Association, a land-speculation venture headquartered in Philadelphia.[24]

Before the *Bolton* claim could be filed with the board and in the wake of the gold rush, many individuals acting in good faith had settled on the land. In 1851, an English traveler described the area as "fully cropped with the preemption squatters." The number of people attracted to the area continued to increase even after Bolton filed the claim, in large part because many people believed the claim to be as fraudulent as Limantour's. Yet, the land board confirmed Bolton's claim in 1855, which "produced a perfect howl among the squatters."[25]

The board's confirmation of Bolton's interest also initiated a bitter five-year struggle that pitted local settlers and land speculators against large corporate speculation involving East Coast and European investors. The San Francisco Land Association refused to compromise on easy terms. Much capital had been invested in the association, and the land board's confirmation induced a new issuance of stock. The squatters and individuals on the land were faced with the prospect of either being forced to leave or repurchasing the land at inflated prices. The struggle reached its peak when the case went to the northern district court. Hoffman, with no more evidence than that introduced to the land board, in 1857 entered a summary confirmation designed to avoid the merits of the case and expedite review at the Supreme Court. U.S. Attorney General Black later remarked that Hoffman's decision resulted because the judge had lacked "those tests which the archives" had "since furnished."[26]

The adverse effect of the *Bolton* claim spurred settlers to organize a legal fund to resist that claim. They produced additional evidence demonstrating potential fraud in the grants on which Bolton's claim rested, and they agitated for a reconsideration of the claim before Hoffman's court. When it became evident that the case would be settled only by the U.S. Supreme Court, a petition with 10,000 signatures was sent to the Supreme Court and all members of Congress, urging the defeat of the claim on the grounds of fraud.[27]

Attorney General Black and his special counsel, Edwin Stanton, were accused of being influenced by the San Francisco Land Association and of accepting bribes to dismiss the appeal. Indeed, Black was pressured by his Philadelphia friends to make a quick decision favorable to their interests. Moreover, Stanton had once represented the association, and Black had secretly written to one of the settler's lawyers to arrange the attorney's services as special counsel for the *Bolton* case in Stanton's place. Black believed that the *Bolton* claim was fraudulent but described the accusations against himself and Stanton as "a sheer fabrication" and branded their accuser "a cold blooded and deliberate liar." Still, Black aggressively developed the evidence necessary to defeat the claim. On May 4, 1860, the Supreme Court reviewed the voluminous testimony in the case and rejected the *Bolton* claim on the grounds that insufficient evidence had been presented to establish the grant. Beyond this failure to demonstrate a legal basis for the claim, the Court felt that equity favored the "thousand settlers on the land" who, in the Court's opinion, had bought such land from American officials after the conquest, without notice of an adverse private claim.[28]

An even greater threat to San Francisco's pueblo title was posed by Peter Sherrebeck's claim. This claim involved the land known as El Rincon, which comprised part of the downtown section of the city, adjacent to the bay and slightly south of Market Street. In support of his claim, Sherrebeck introduced evidence showing that El Rincon was part of the common lands of the pueblo of Yerba Buena and an authorized Mexican grant. Although the government's lawyer did not challenge the claimant's testimony, the land board rejected the claim on November 6, 1855, ostensibly for lack of evidence to prove that the grant was within the pueblo's common lands. The board's decision revealed its reluctance to exclude such valuable commercial property from San Francisco's pueblo.

The case was appealed to the district court, where Hoffman seemed equally reluctant to validate the claim but felt bound to decide the case in accordance with the evidence presented. Hoffman regretted the dearth of government testimony and argument before the board, a lack that had not been supplemented on appeal. Thus, in December 1859, Hoffman felt he had no choice but to find for the claimant. Five months after the decision, Attorney General Black described Hoffman's opinion as an honest mistake. In Black's words, "The high character of Judge Hoffman for ability as well as integrity, entitles every opinion of his to profound respect." Within a year, Hoffman's decision was reversed by the Supreme Court.[29]

The Supreme Court's rejection of the *Bolton* and *Sherrebeck* claims left the city free to seek an expansion of its pueblo lands in the district court. Although the government had initially indicated its intention to appeal the land board's 1854 decision granting three of the four square leagues claimed by the city, Attorney General Black reversed his predecessor, Caleb Cushing, and dismissed the appeal in 1857. In March of that same year, Hoffman, on a motion of the U.S. attorney, gave the city permission to proceed under the land board's decree as if it were a final decree. The city, however, still wanted title to the extra land, and after the decision in *Hart* v. *Burnett*, which acknowledged the city's right to four square leagues, San Francisco's board of supervisors retained special counsel to prosecute the case before Hoffman's court. Between 1860 and 1863, the city filed extensive briefs supporting its claim to the four square leagues, but no decision was rendered. Proponents of the city's pueblo title could only wonder what Hoffman would decide; his decisions in the *Bolton* and *Sherrebeck* cases fostered the rumor that he would not confirm the pueblo claim.[30]

By the early 1860s, San Francisco's legal claim to pueblo lands was still a matter of considerable controversy. During this time, San Franciscans could perceive subtle but important differences in the attitudes of two of California's federal judges. Hoffman seemed to be dubious about the existence of the pueblo, and his approach to the land-grant adjudication emphasized the technical requirements of the pueblo under Mexican law. On the other hand, Field clearly indicated his support for the existence of a pueblo by joining the majority opinion in *Hart* v. *Burnett*. Moreover, Field's approach to the issue seemed much more pragmatic and attuned to the economic and political realities of the situation.[31]

The tension created by the two judges' different approaches to the vitally important pueblo issue heightened and assumed an increasingly personal dimension after Field's federal appointment in 1863. Having served as a federal judge for twelve years and thus longer than any other federal judge in California, Hoffman had hoped and expected that he, rather than Field, would be elevated to the U.S. Supreme Court. Under the circumstances, some degree of stiffness might have been expected between the judges, but in 1864 an exceptional treason trial arising out of the Civil War served to widen and greatly personalize the gulf between Hoffman and Field. Even more significantly, the aftermath of the treason case triggered an assault on Hoffman's judgeship, the objective of which was to insure that Field and not Hoffman decided the pueblo case. Thus, the ultimate settlement of San Francisco's land title disputes was directly connected to events originating in the Civil War.[32]

The Civil War presented many intriguing constitutional problems, including whether Confederates were guilty of treason and hence subject to the death penalty. Fear of reprisals, the impracticality of such a stance, and Lincoln's conciliatory approach to the South resulted in a statutory form of treason enacted in 1862 that imposed only imprisonment and fines. Even under this modified form of treason, indictments were typically delayed and invariably dismissed. The few convictions that resulted proved an embarrassment to the government. The aim of Lincoln's administration was legally to assert the disloyalty of the South rather than to exact punishment for secession. In this context, the zealousness of Justice Field, Senator John Conness of California, and the public over California's treason trial ran counter to the general approach of the administration. That fact, however, did not protect Hoffman from the vindictive reaction of those who sought vengeance against Confederate sympathizers.[33]

California's statutory treason case involved Ridgely Greathouse and two other Confederate sympathizers in San Francisco who had conspired to raid the gold shipments leaving San Francisco for the eastern states. Their trial, held in late September 1863, was Field's first case as the newly appointed U.S. Supreme Court justice presiding over the federal circuit court, although he was joined by Judge Hoffman. After a two-week trial and four minutes of jury deliberations, the prisoners were found guilty. On October 16, Field imposed on each conspirator the maximum sentence of ten years in prison and a $10,000 fine. Shortly thereafter, Field left for Washington, D.C., having only partially satisfied the public outcry for retribution against the "pirates."[34]

Less than two months after Greathouse's conviction, his lawyers sought his release on the basis of President Lincoln's amnesty proclamation of December 8, 1863. Yet, Lincoln had southerners primarily in mind when he offered a full pardon to "all persons" who had "directly or by implication, participated in the existing rebellion," except for certain classes, such as high-ranking Confederate civil and military officers, who were required to "take and subscribe an oath" to henceforth support the United States. Nonetheless, lawyers for Greathouse planned to move for his release. President Lincoln, Justice Field, and Senator Conness were quickly alerted to the situation. To head off Greathouse's potential release, Lincoln telegraphed Hoffman on December 15, explaining that his proclamation was "intended for those who ... *voluntarily*" took the oath and not for those who were "*constrained* to take it, in order to escape actual imprisonment or punishment." [35]

In his return telegraph Hoffman contended that nothing in the language of the proclamation excluded those who were already confined or convicted. He reasoned that the proclamation was "a public official document" that a court was "compelled to construe according to its terms," and he suggested that Lincoln "declare by an equally formal document the intention of the Executive in making it." With no clarifying proclamation forthcoming, Hoffman reluctantly released Greathouse on a writ of habeas corpus on February 15, 1864. Although Hoffman's decision did not come as a complete surprise, it was widely denounced. Even newspapers normally supportive of Hoffman called his decision "an absurdity" and declared, "Very queer things are done in the name of justice." Less sympathetic papers spoke of the perversion of Lincoln's proclamation "through a Copperhead judge." The *Sacramento Union* went so far as to call for the abolition of Hoffman's court. [36]

Although he freed Greathouse, Hoffman was no Copperhead. That label had been applied by the *Missouri Democrat*, but California newspapers knew better. Even the *San Francisco Bulletin*, which greeted the *Greathouse* decision with dismay, was forced to admit, "Politically ... Judge Hoffman and Mr. Conness agree, [and] both are earnest in the support of the Government and the prosecution of the war." Hoffman took an avid interest in the daily progress of the war and regularly sent his amateur military advice for more effective campaigns against the Confederacy to former clubmen and friends like Joseph Hooker and Henry Halleck, who were Union generals. For Hoffman, even the "most humble" participation in the "gigantic

contest" to preserve the nation was "worthy [of] every man's ambition."
Hoffman justified his decision in the *Greathouse* case on the grounds that
"no upright judge could have decided otherwise" than to interpret the language of the proclamation on its own terms, without regard for subsequent
explanations. This same literalism had strongly influenced Hoffman's earlier
decisions regarding fulfilling the statutory terms of Mexican land grants.[37]

Both Judge Field and Senator Conness showed little tolerance for what
had been a difficult decision for the Republican Hoffman. Field, like
Conness, was a strong Union Democrat, and both were incensed at the
result of Hoffman's decision. In addition, Field could not help but view the
decision as a legal hair-splitting repudiation of his very first action as California's circuit justice. The connection between that incident and the city's
land claim became evident in the wake of Hoffman's decision to release
Greathouse. If Hoffman could not be trusted to do the right thing in a case
involving secessionist privateers, how could he be trusted with San Francisco's pueblo title? Field and Conness took advantage of Hoffman's unpopular
and easily misunderstood decision by attempting to remove Hoffman as a
factor in resolving the pueblo issue. Indeed, Hoffman was to become the
target of punitive legislation designed by Conness and Field.[38]

An ally of Hoffman's accurately described the legislative "programme"
that Field and Conness aimed at Hoffman as "very comprehensive and
thorough." Together they worked to eliminate Hoffman's judgeship and to
insure that San Francisco's pueblo title was confirmed. Although Hoffman
retained his judgeship, they succeeded in their second aim. The initial effort
to guarantee confirmation of the pueblo title began even before Hoffman
released Greathouse, but at a time when the pending release was evident.
On January 12, 1864, Senator Conness introduced a bill that would transfer,
from the northern district court to Field's circuit court, all proceedings concerning claims "to land situated wholly or in part within the city and county
of San Francisco." The bill also made the clerk of the circuit court the *ex
officio* clerk of the district court. Hoffman was "somewhat indignant" at the
attempt to deprive him of "the right to select an officer with whom" he was
"necessarily on terms of daily confidential intercourse." Hearing that Field
had prepared the bill only aggravated Hoffman's displeasure. Ultimately,
however, the legislation that passed Congress dealt only with details of the
circuit court's operation. Even though Hoffman's and Field's relationship up

to that point had been reported by Hoffman as "friendly and cordial," it was destined to become increasingly strained.[39]

A more ambitious and successful effort to limit Hoffman's role in land-grant litigation arose through another collaboration between Conness and Field. On February 9, 1864, Conness introduced a bill ostensibly designed "to expedite the Settlement of Titles to Lands in the State of California." In effect, the bill functioned to repeal an 1860 act that had given California's federal district courts the authority to adjudicate surveys in the land cases. Conness's proposed bill shifted this authority from Hoffman in San Francisco to the General Land Office in Washington. According to a critic of the plan, that shift would result in "Conness's man, as Surveyor General, giving Conness and Field control of that department in a great measure." Conness inserted another section, eventually rejected, that would have had a direct effect on the pueblo issue in San Francisco. Conness proposed that in determining the validity of land claims under the 1851 act, both the district courts and the Supreme Court be limited to objections specifically stated by the U.S. attorney prior to the hearing. Although a technical rule, such legislation would have assumed great practical importance in limiting the issues surrounding the pueblo case because the northern district's U.S. attorney, like Field and Conness, wanted the pueblo title confirmed.[40]

Field's contribution to the proposed bill consisted primarily of sections designed to give him control over land cases, including the San Francisco pueblo case. Section 4 of the bill mandated the transfer of land cases to the circuit court whenever the district judge was "interested in any land" that was part of the claim before him. Moreover, the same section permitted district judges to transfer to the circuit court any claim that dealt with title to lands within towns or cities—an indirect reference to the San Francisco pueblo case. Another section drafted by Field ratified the Van Ness Ordinance and thereby relinquished most of the federal government's claims to land within the charter limits of San Francisco.[41]

The final and most sweeping congressional attempt to undercut Hoffman came on February 24, 1864, when Conness introduced a bill "to consolidate into one district for judicial purposes the northern and southern districts of California." Its title notwithstanding, the bill was quickly and accurately perceived as an attempt to oust Hoffman and his judgeship under the guise of reorganizing California's federal judiciary. The bill provided that as of

January 1, 1864, California would have one federal district court and that both existing courts would transfer all pending cases to the newly created court. Judicial economy supposedly rationalized the consolidation, but it remained clear that Hoffman's "extraordinary decision" in the *Greathouse* case lay behind the bill that would "legislate out of office both the present judges." Hoffman himself understood the significance of the "great clamor" over his release of Greathouse. He stated, "It has been said that that decision would cost me my office." [42]

Beyond its intended purpose of ousting Hoffman, Conness's consolidation bill played an integral role in strengthening Field's and Conness's control over the pueblo case. One of Hoffman's supporters in Washington noted that the consolidation bill permitted the replacement of Hoffman with a "devoted friend" of Field's. John B. Williams, a San Francisco lawyer, explained:

> The consolidation bill intended that the Pueblo title should be confirmed, for the new judge, knowing nothing about land cases, would, under the Act [1864] to repeal the Act of 1860, have transferred the case to the Circuit Court and *Field would have confirmed it.* Then, the appeal of [the] U.S. to [the] Supreme Court would have been *dismissed*, or failing in that, Field's position as Supreme [Court] Judge would have great weight in confirming it. [43]

Only one of the three bills Conness introduced met with success: the February 9 bill that stripped Hoffman of jurisdiction over surveys. In fact, the most dramatic attempted curtailment of Hoffman's court—the consolidation bill—never emerged from committee. This demonstrated the extent of Hoffman's support despite his extremely unpopular decision in the *Greathouse* case, as well as the strength of the American tradition of judicial independence.

After the initial shock of the *Greathouse* decision, San Francisco's legal and business communities rallied to defend Hoffman, especially with the news of the attempt to displace him. Hoffman's integrity and past services as a judge made it easier to accept the unpopular decision. The *Alta California*, which had at first joined others in castigating the district judge, later queried: "Is it not better that the Judge should be righteous than right? Should we feel ourselves, or our property or even our lives safe for a moment if we had known or even suspected that he decided against his conviction and in accordance with public clamor?" The newspapers focused on the danger posed to the independence of the judiciary if the senator's political maneuvering was permitted. The *Alta California* warned: "If Judge Hoffman has committed errors, let him be impeached. This thing of legislating him out of office . . . is a deadly blow aimed at the Federal Judiciary everywhere."[44]

During the month of March 1864, an active campaign sought to rehabilitate Hoffman in the eyes of the potentially hostile members of Congress. On March 17, the San Francisco Chamber of Commerce adopted a series of resolutions, signed by over fifty prominent California businessmen who asserted their "implicit confidence in the loyalty and patriotism of Judge Hoffman." They protested that "any legislation" pertaining "to the removal" of the judge was unconstitutional. Copies of the resolutions were sent to other chambers of commerce in New York and Boston, where they were published. They were also sent to members of the New York and California congressional delegations in Washington. In addition, letters of support and petitions from members of the California bar and the state supreme court were made available to Hoffman's defenders in Congress.[45]

Hoffman himself took a major role in his own defense and in securing congressional support. Shortly after learning of the consolidation bill, Hoffman wrote a letter of protest to Republican Senator William P. Fessenden of Maine, the powerful chairman of the Senate Finance Committee. Hoffman explained that he was "not tenacious" of his judgeship but added that he would not "submit to be the victim of a political intrigue." Hoffman noted that Conness, since his election to the Senate as a Union Democrat, had sought to punish those who had not favored his election; as a Republican, Hoffman presented a plausible target. Hoffman's lobbying efforts and those of his supporters were successful, and on April 14, 1864, the chairman of the Senate Judiciary Committee informed Hoffman that Conness's bill had been rendered harmless through amendments.[46]

Although Hoffman succeeded in defeating the consolidation bill, Conness had considerable success with his bill to strip Hoffman of jurisdiction over land surveys, portions of which had been drafted by Field. Before the Senate debate, Californians learned that the bill would repeal the 1860 act that gave Hoffman jurisdiction over land surveys. Those who opposed the repeal stressed the expense and inconvenience of moving the decision-making authority for resolving titles from San Francisco to Washington, intimating that Conness sought influence over the General Land Office for political reasons.[47]

When the Senate finally considered Conness's survey bill on March 28, 1864, it rejected the portion of the bill that permitted California's federal courts to consider only those defects in the title assigned by the U.S. attorney. Senator James Harlan of Iowa predicted, "[I]f the Government should unfortunately appoint a blundering lawyer to act as [United States] district attorney who would not file very perfect pleadings, the interests of the United States would be prejudiced by compelling the court to follow the pleadings." Besides, if other cases before the Supreme Court were not so limited, as Senator Thomas A. Hendricks of Indiana observed, why would Congress "establish a different rule for the cases coming up from California"? Conness, however, professed an inability to see "what possible injury" could have occurred "to any interest under this section." Responding to the suspicions entertained by some senators over his plan to confine the duty of the federal district courts, Conness denied the presence of "a covert purpose" in the section that was "to produce the confirmation of titles to land." Nonetheless, the Senate struck the section from the bill.[48]

The Senate then moved to consider the bill as it stood. Senator Reverdy Johnson of Maryland, who had enjoyed a lucrative law practice arguing appeals in California land-grant cases, questioned the necessity of repealing the act of 1860. The settlement of titles involved two steps: confirming or denying the claim, and locating the claim. The General Land Office, he declared, had neither the talent nor the independence to decide questions "involving thousands and millions of money." Since the location of surveys was so intimately connected with the validation of claims, Johnson felt that both issues should be undertaken by the courts, which were "free from all extraneous influences." He asked what particular aspect of the act of 1860 had made it necessary to "dispense with courts altogether and leave these questions to be decided by the executive officers."[49]

Conness, on the other hand, characterized the determination of surveys as a "ministerial or administrative question." He claimed that giving the courts authority over these matters had simply brought delay. He further expressed the belief that judicial incompetence to adjudicate surveys had produced grants that caused "wonder to any intelligent person." Conness also exaggerated Field's support by intimating that the entire Supreme

Court supported the bill. He claimed, "They ask, without doing it officially, that the provision of the existing law be repealed or changed." The bill drafted by Conness and Field became law on July 2, 1864; however, the portion confining the courts to considering defects in the title raised by the U.S. attorney was conspicuously absent.[50]

Under the terms of section 4 of the 1864 act, Hoffman was required to transfer a land case to the circuit court only if there existed a conflict of interest in adjudicating the case. Hoffman himself had suggested such a conflict provision earlier, and though it was a beneficial reform, its passage in 1864 served mainly as a means of effecting the transfer of the pueblo case to Field. Because he denied having a financial interest in the outcome of the case, Hoffman might have resisted a transfer of the pueblo case to the circuit court, but it was not in his nature to do so. Aware that Field had actively participated in an effort to obtain jurisdiction over the case and that Congress concurred in such action, Hoffman was swayed. On September 5, 1864, he transferred both the Sonoma and the San Francisco pueblo cases to the circuit court, after providing the following interpretation of section 4: "The language of this provision is evidently not mandatory. But it is advisory, and I consider it the duty of the court to follow a suggestion of this nature, emanating from the National Legislature."[51]

Transferring the pueblo case did not necessarily preclude Hoffman's participation, since Field could still invite Hoffman to sit with him on the circuit court. Under the circumstances, it was hardly likely that Field would seek Hoffman's participation. In fact, Conness later claimed that his sponsorship of the act of 1864 was, in effect, a summary confirmation of the city's claim in the circuit court, since he knew Field would confirm the pueblo claim. The *Alta California* saw no "good reason for authorizing the transfer [of courts]," although it mentioned the rumor that Hoffman probably would have rejected and Field probably confirmed the city's claim.[52]

Once he had jurisdiction over the pueblo case, Field fixed an early date for the final submission of briefs. The city's brief, a scholarly production that had taken years to assemble, was already on file; hence San Francisco was prepared to go to trial immediately. However, the government's case proved somewhat more difficult to prepare because attorneys ostensibly on the same side were working at cross-purposes. The lawyers appearing for the federal government fell into two major camps, one headed by Delos Lake, the U.S. attorney, and the other headed by John B. Williams, special counsel for the United States and an advocate for settlers' interests. In the internal conflict pending in California's federal judiciary, Lake proved as strong an ally to Justice Field as Williams did to Judge Hoffman.[53]

Field and Conness approved of Lake, who was a recess appointment made by President Lincoln in August 1864, even though, ironically, Lake had represented Ridgely Greathouse. Williams, a long-time clerk in the U.S. attorney's office before joining the bar, had been empowered since 1861 to act as a special agent of the United States, especially in cases dealing with disputes over surveys. In many such cases the United States was only a nominal party, with the real parties in interest, settlers who objected to the survey, paying Williams for his advocacy. His efforts as a government lawyer on behalf of settlers were extensive and brought him into frequent contact with Judge Hoffman's court. In fact, Williams had prepared the extensive appendix for Hoffman's *Land Cases* and had strongly supported the judge during the consolidation bill crisis.[54]

Lake, on the other hand, had been a state judge in San Francisco in the 1850s and had upheld the pueblo title. Lake regarded the existence of the city's pueblo as "the fixed law of this state under the repeated decisions" and declined to insult Field by asking him to reexamine the question of the pueblo claim that he had earlier considered as a member of the California Supreme Court. These prior decisions, of course, were decided in the state courts and did not bind the federal courts, which had final authority to resolve land titles arising under the California Land Act of 1851. Nonetheless, Lake insisted on the right of the government only to the federal reserves within the pueblo, which Field concluded had been acceptable to the city attorney. Given Lake's concessions, Field declared that the amount of, and not the actual title to, pueblo land presented the only legal issue before him.[55]

On October 31, 1864, Field confirmed the city's claim for four square leagues in *San Francisco* v. *United States*. He conceded that the appeal opened up the entire question of San Francisco's pueblo title, but he held that Attorney General Black's dismissal in 1857 of the government's appeal from the land board's decision constituted an acceptance of the city's claim. Field thus asserted that the U.S. attorney did not "controvert these positions" but "on the contrary" admitted them "as facts in the case."[56]

The land board, according to Field, had based its decision on a document, the "spuriousness" of which was "now admitted by all parties." Relying on

Hart v. *Burnett*, Field awarded the city four square leagues. In excusing the brevity of his three-page opinion, Field directed those desiring "to extend their inquiries" to read the opinion in *Hart*. However, the short opinion underscored the fact that the decision in the case was a foregone conclusion. In fact, after his decision, Field informally advised the city's lawyer to detail the manner in which San Francisco's pueblo title had been relied on and to publish the brief. Such a document, Field suggested, would probably result in the dismissal of any appeal to the U.S. Supreme Court.[57]

Soon after Field delivered his decision in the pueblo case, he departed for Washington to rejoin the Supreme Court. Meanwhile, Delos Lake appealed the case to the Supreme Court, evidently to attain a quick and final confirmation of the decision. Shortly thereafter, it became evident that Williams's brief disputing the existence of the pueblo had been either suppressed by the circuit court clerk, George C. Gorham, or ignored by Field on the grounds that Williams had no authority to represent the government. A flurry of charges, denials, and countercharges followed this news, and Williams sought a rehearing. He asserted that since his brief had been suppressed, Field had not considered his arguments. Williams also claimed that Hoffman criticized Gorham's action as unauthorized. Actually, Field had known of Williams's arguments but had given them no weight because he believed Williams lacked standing in court. Lake too questioned William's authority. Thus, neither Field nor U.S. Attorney Lake had included Williams in their "free conversations" over the "law and facts" of the pueblo title that had taken place in Field's chambers before he had rendered his decision.[58]

Field resisted considering the pueblo case on its merits, even with considerable evidence that Williams spoke for the attorney general. Field showed his determination to settle the pueblo title by ignoring Williams. To avoid a summary denial of the motion for rehearing, Williams urged U.S. Attorney General James Speed to insure that the motion be presented before both Hoffman and Field. Hoffman accepted the motion in the circuit court but refused to rule on it until Field returned. When Field reached San Francisco in May 1865, he assumed the circuit court bench alone (not inviting Hoffman to join him) and quickly entered an opinion rejecting Williams's motion for a rehearing. Field denied any wrongdoing on the part of the clerk or himself during the disposition of the case. While Field frustrated Williams's efforts in San Francisco, Conness pressured Attorney

General Speed to remove the special counsel from the case and to dismiss the appeal.[59]

The denial of the motion for rehearing prompted an appeal to the U.S. Supreme Court on May 18, 1865. Field then demonstrated just how anxious he was to confirm the city's title by denying the appeal on the grounds that the Supreme Court lacked jurisdiction. Field argued that since the act of 1864 did not expressly authorize an appeal to the Supreme Court, the Court had no appellate jurisdiction in the case. Field also reasoned that Congress intended the act of 1864 to expedite the settlement of land cases in California and that the finality of the circuit court was implicit in this objective. Field concluded that if the case had been "less clear," he might have allowed the appeal *pro forma*, but having "no doubt whatever" about the finality of his decision, his duty was "plain." [60]

Although the *Alta California*, and perhaps Field as well, thought that the pueblo issue had been "finally settled and confirmed" in 1864, the struggle soon renewed itself. Despite Conness's efforts, the attorney general insisted on the government's right to contest before the Supreme Court the existence of the San Francisco pueblo. The government sought a writ of mandamus from the Supreme Court, requesting an appeal. In *United States* v. *Circuit Judges* (1866), the Court, with Justices Field, Robert C. Grier, and Samuel Miller dissenting, overruled Field and granted the writ of mandamus.[61]

The Court rejected Field's position that proceedings under the California Land Act of 1851 merited procedural treatment different from that of other cases either in law or equity (i.e., final appeal only to the circuit court). Rather, the Court regarded such cases as proceedings in equity; thus an appropriate appeal brought "the case up to the appellate court for review," and such had been "the uniform practice under the act." Field's dissent reiterated his circuit court arguments and characterized the land cases as administrative matters that were not "converted into suits in equity" because judicial agency was "brought in to aid the administrative proceeding." [62]

Facing the prospect that the pueblo claim would come before the Supreme Court and the possibility that it would be rejected, Conness and Field formulated their final solution. While the pueblo case remained in the Supreme Court docket pending appeal, Conness introduced a bill that undercut any judicial review in the case. The proposed bill provided that "all the right and title of the United States" to the lands claimed under the pueblo title were to be "relinquished and granted to the City of San Francisco." When the bill passed on March 8, 1866, it effectively ended the long struggle.[63]

The dispute over San Francisco's pueblo and its eventual resolution clearly bore the marks of federalism. Although the adjudication of private land grants from the Mexican period was ostensibly the exclusive province of the federal courts, in practice the state courts played an integral role. California's state courts had considered questions related to San Francisco's pueblo before the federal land board and judiciary became involved in the issue. The nature of the pueblo case, involving as it did the validation or rejection of lots held under the post-1846 grants and the Peter Smith deeds, inevitably generated case law that contributed to, and in some sense dictated, the terms of the debate over the existence of a San Francisco pueblo. *Hart v. Burnett* (1860) marked the culmination of this process, offering a resolution that incorporated previous state and federal decisions and also contributing a new element by characterizing the city as trustee of pueblo lands. Thus, *Hart* removed the obstacle of the Smith deeds and provided a solution for the ultimate confirmation of the city's title. The city of San Francisco's promulgation and the state legislature's and Congress's approval of the Van Ness Ordinance provided another example of the joint character of the final resolution. Given the twenty-year struggle over land in San Francisco, it was perhaps inevitable that state court decisions and legislative efforts intruded into the final solution fashioned by the federal authorities.

The adjudication of the pueblo case also illustrated the complexities and multiple interests involved in California land controversies and the difficulties in obtaining a quick settlement. Most historians of California's early land adjudication have commented on the harmful effects of extended litigation and have assumed that a less legalistic procedure than that adopted under the act of 1851—such as congressional hearings—would have quieted title more quickly. San Francisco's land experience casts considerable doubt on this assumption, since it seems likely that the value of conflicting interests would have insured a rich harvest of litigation regardless of which procedure was involved.[64]

The legal issues—although complex—were hardly so insurmountable as to warrant the length of time spent in litigation. Yet, the San Francisco pueblo remained a live issue for two decades because of the practical consequences of the pueblo's confirmation or rejection. For those claiming land on the basis of possession only, federal preemption laws offered the opportunity to retain such holdings as long as the overlapping Mexican land-grant claims (including the city's) were rejected. On the other hand, the Van Ness Ordinance encouraged many squatters to support the pueblo claim because that compromise validated such possessory rights in areas outside of the older, commercial portions of the city. Lot holders faced a more precarious situation, since absentee ownership of land—always vulnerable to squatters—depended on the validation of San Francisco's pueblo. As the *Alta California* so graphically pointed out, the rejection of the pueblo claim could have affected the "richest man in the city" by stripping him "in a single day . . . of all else that he was worth." [65]

Adding to the conflict were the proponents and opponents of the Smith deeds. Whether such claims were valid depended, at least until the *Hart* v. *Burnett* decision in 1860, on the existence of the pueblo. Finally, Mexican land grants not only threatened many landed interests in San Francisco but also were often held by claimants who had substantial resources within and without the city and who pressed for confirmation. This constellation of competing interests for overlapping land claims in San Francisco was constantly shifting with each successive judicial decision, legislative measure, or revelation of the weakness or strength of a particular claim. The overlapping and often antagonistic interests in San Francisco land made a final resolution difficult to achieve. It took Stephen Field's strong will and determination to force a final settlement.

The affirmation of the pueblo title and how the courts characterized the solution obscured the nature of the San Francisco land dispute. In *Hart*, State Supreme Court Justice Baldwin justified affirming the pueblo title on the grounds that land speculators should not profit at the expense of the city. Describing the holders of the Smith deeds as speculators was accurate enough, but suggesting that they presented the only or primary example of such activity distorted the early history of San Francisco. From 1846 onward, the city had been prey to speculators, be they squatters, purchasers, or grantees of city lots. [66]

The essential issue in *Hart* was whether the land speculation would be validated to the detriment of the owners of the initially developed commercial and downtown city lots (and those with possessory interests outside that area) or whether the later Smith deeds would be upheld. By the time *Hart* was decided and Field became involved in the 1860s, many of the initial purchasers and grantees of the valuable downtown property had conveyed their interest to others. Moreover, even though the chain of title grew longer, the dubious legal and equitable circumstances of the initial acquisitions of such lots were commonly known to most San Franciscans. Thus, although the amount of time and money expended on improvements to the downtown property seemed to warrant a confirmation of such titles, the disposal of city lots in the 1840s represented a situation in which the local government had "laid aside conscience as a useless encumbrance, and plunged headlong into jobbing and speculation." The awareness of the pervasive speculation and a sense of the mixed equities in determining the land titles explain both the ambivalence in contemporary accounts of San Francisco's land disputes and the mixed reaction to the *Hart* case. Ambivalence to the pueblo solution also derived from those who claimed under the Smith deeds. Although many were audacious speculators, others were prominent businessmen, lawyers, and politicians. Thus, although their speculations threatened the interests of many San Franciscans, they were not casually or easily brushed aside.[67]

When Field later recalled his part in settling the pueblo title, he justified his aggressive behavior and his collaboration with Conness as necessary to expedite the action under adjudication. He pointed to the length of time the case had technically been before the district court. Field's motives, however, warrant closer investigation.[68]

The underlying issue in California's land disputes was not simply quieting title quickly, but resolving those disputes fairly. By the late 1850s, the federal government had become increasingly suspicious of quick confirmations of large land grants, and there were differing opinions on the existence or desirability of a San Francisco pueblo. Even as Field, Conness, and U.S. Attorney Lake anticipated an imminent confirmation of the pueblo title in 1864, doubts about that title mounted in the attorney general's office. This suspicion intensified with reports of the transfer of the case to Field and of Lake's governmental concessions.

Faced with the prospect of a renewed struggle over the city's title in the U.S. Supreme Court and the possibility of the title's rejection, Field and

Conness resorted to extrajudicial means to achieve a final settlement. Field and Conness displayed more concern about how Hoffman would decide the pueblo case than about the need to expedite the case. Hoffman's decisions in the *Bolton* and *Sherrebeck* cases hardly reassured Field and Conness. Also, Hoffman's highly developed sense of his judicial role, duty, and propriety made him less susceptible to pragmatic considerations of expediency. It made little sense to Field and Conness to risk the rejection of San Francisco's pueblo claim at the hands of the proud, stubborn, and at times literal-minded Hoffman when Field clearly supported the pueblo. Nevertheless, Field's conduct in the pueblo case—in getting jurisdiction and especially in circumventing the Supreme Court after it reversed his circuit court decision denying an appeal—was clearly a breach of judicial propriety. In fact, the federal government challenged the city's claim only after the U.S. attorney in San Francisco had abdicated his responsibility by making concessions that did not have the approval of the attorney general. Thus, Field's heavy-handed manipulation of the decision was not justified on the grounds that Hoffman had unduly delayed a decision in the case.

Throughout Field's judicial career, he apparently believed that "only the courts were capable of resolving allocation problems so as to simultaneously protect property rights, release entrepreneurial energies, and provide all men with an equal opportunity to share in the material fruits of a vigorously-expanding capitalistic society." In the pueblo case, however, Field displayed little aversion to abandoning the judicial process and actively engaging in and manipulating legislation when it suited his purpose. Indeed, even as late as 1893 Justice Field engaged in extrajudicial maneuvers to overturn Supreme Court decisions to which he objected.[69]

Field's and Hoffman's respective views of their judicial role had a direct effect on the degree of restraint or activism each employed in doing his job. Confident in his ability to perceive the problems inherent in the struggle over the pueblo title and solve them, Field proceeded with aggressive determination. Even if his means were questionable, there is no denying that he ended a troublesome dispute. To Field, Hoffman's careful, conscientious, and seemingly plodding approach to judicial questions probably seemed unnecessary, indecisive, and overly legalistic. On the other hand, Field's aggressive behavior in the pueblo dispute, and his legislative collaboration with Conness, insulted Hoffman and estranged the two judges. As a political, proactive problem solver, Field posed quite a contrast to the contemplative

Hoffman, who harbored a narrower vision of the role of the judiciary than did Field. These differences in judicial style between Field and Hoffman formed an important part of the fabric of federal justice in California as the resolution of land questions often wove back and forth between the judiciary and the legislature.[70]

CHAPTER

7

The Chinese before the Court

Chinese plaintiffs found Hoffman's court to be a useful forum in which to bring civil suits. In addition, whether as civil litigants or criminal defendants, the Chinese showed initiative and a keen awareness of how to beneficially use the legal system. Ultimately, however, Hoffman's commitment to legal equality and his understanding of his duty as a judge and especially of the role of his national court accounted for the considerable advantage and favorable decisions the Chinese obtained in the northern district.[1]

Chinese businessmen were effective in using bankruptcy law as a means both for debt relief and for recovery of debts. When these businessmen became the target of aggressive prosecution by various U.S. attorneys for revenue violations, instead of pleading guilty, they sought to meet the technical requirements of the law or they persisted in claiming their legal rights.

Chinese petitioners, in over ten thousand habeas corpus cases after 1882, sought entry into the United States and freedom from detention by federal authorities. Appearing before the federal courts of Hoffman and Circuit Judge Lorenzo Sawyer, each petitioner presented evidence, testimony, or arguments in favor of establishing the right to enter. In these forums, on a case-by-case basis, the Chinese crowded the federal court dockets and created a "habeas corpus mill" for nearly a decade. In the process, thousands of Chinese entered the United States through the port of San Francisco despite intense public opposition and racial prejudice. In interpreting a treaty that guaranteed the Chinese civil rights as immigrants to and resi-

dents of the United States, Hoffman clashed both with zealous federal officers attempting to exclude the Chinese and, again, with Supreme Court
Justice Stephen Field.[2]

Chinese civil litigants could effectively use Hoffman's court because he decided not to follow California's statutory and case law that banned Chinese
testimony. In the early 1850s, California's legislature excluded Indians and
blacks from testifying for or against whites in criminal and civil cases. By
the end of the decade, the California Supreme Court had construed those
statutes to exclude Chinese testimony in both civil and criminal cases, and
in 1863 the legislature codified these decisions. This statutory exclusion of
Chinese testimony remained in force until 1872. The testimony ban not only
limited the usefulness of courts for the Chinese in California but also permitted most criminal attacks on the Chinese by white perpetrators to go
unpunished.[3]

Despite Hoffman's adoption of California's Civil Practice Act (including
provisions excluding testimony) as the "rule of practice" in the northern
district, the case files establish that Hoffman did not exclude Chinese testimony in his court. In 1871 San Francisco's *Alta California* described the
filing of a breach of contract case by a Chinese plaintiff against a white
defendant in the federal circuit court as a test case to see if Chinese testimony would be accepted in California's federal courts. In fact, Hoffman's
district court had accepted such evidence since the 1850s and apparently
became the first court in California to admit Chinese testimony against a
white criminal defendant.[4]

Having access to Hoffman's court and using it were two different matters.
The hostility generally directed at the Chinese gave potential litigants pause
about what sort of reception they were apt to receive at the hands of the
American legal system, whether in state courts or Hoffman's court. Indeed,
one impetus behind the formation of the Chinese Six Companies—a coor-
dinating council for the various district associations that represented the
Chinese community—was the resolution of internal disputes. According to
a historian of the Chinese Six Companies, "since the courts and the majority
of the Americans were plainly prejudicial against the Chinese," it was only
natural that the Chinese sought to resolve their disputes outside the American courts. Yet, the Chinese did bring disputes—both those that were inter-

nal to the Chinese community and those that were not—into state and federal courts.[5]

Chinese willingness to file lawsuits was facilitated by the availability of legal talent. Whether in lawsuits of collective or individual concern to the Chinese, it is clear that they routinely had access to some of the best lawyers in the state. Even lawyers who believed that the Chinese were an undesirable element in the state did not hesitate to take them on as clients. John Henry Boalt, a prominent and successful San Francisco lawyer, provides a case in point. Long an opponent of Chinese immigration, in 1877 Boalt published a pamphlet in which he advocated excluding the Chinese because they would never assimilate into California and because they threatened American culture and institutions. Despite such views, Boalt had represented Chinese interests in a bankruptcy suit in 1875. Given the hostility toward the Chinese, their legal advisors also risked public censure. But whereas civil rights cases attracted substantial attention, raising as they did fundamental questions about the status of the Chinese, private civil litigation often went unnoticed. Lawyers like Boalt, for instance, could quietly collect payments for representing Chinese clients while they publicly maintained an aggressive anti-Chinese posture.[6]

In turning to the law for protection, the Chinese were anything but stoic and passive survivors of prejudice. Although civil rights litigation directly responded to a hostile environment, the Chinese who used the courts for private matters are less easily explained. The legal historian Hudson N. Janisch has suggested that the breakdown of arbitration in San Francisco's Chinese community in the 1850s was merely symptomatic of interdistrict association rivalry, underscoring the need for the formation of the Chinese Six Companies. This plausibly explains several instances in which Chinese instigated criminal complaints against one another, but it leaves many other cases unexplained. Moreover, the suits involving Chinese plaintiffs before Hoffman's court demonstrate a pattern of business litigation.[7]

Passenger traffic and trade between Hong Kong and San Francisco gave rise to numerous disputes, some of which found their way into Hoffman's admiralty court. The Chinese community in general and Chinese merchants and sailors in particular showed little reticence in bringing lawsuits ranging from breach of contract of affreightment cases to libels for wages and breach of passenger contracts. As early as 1852, the Chinese agent in San Francisco for the firm of Heung Mow Company libelled the ship *Robert Small* for breach of contract. The ship had been chartered to bring Chinese immigrants to San Francisco, and the suit alleged that the ship captain had refused to release goods and supplies worth $750 left on the vessel by Chinese passengers. Although the parties settled before trial, no objections were raised about the standing of the Chinese plaintiffs to bring the suit against the non-Chinese shipowners. Indeed, throughout Hoffman's tenure, Chinese routinely appeared in court as plaintiffs, defendants, or witnesses in suits against non-Chinese and Chinese alike. With only two exceptions, all the Chinese who brought suits against non-Chinese merchants or shipowners received judgments in their favor or accepted settlements.[8]

Hoffman's bankruptcy docket, initiated with the passage of the federal Bankruptcy Act of 1867, illustrates both the appeal and the availability of his forum to the Chinese community. Under that act, district courts like Hoffman's were constituted courts of bankruptcy. For the next decade Hoffman spent much of his time hearing bankruptcy matters, and although the Chinese formed only a fraction of the total, these cases are significant for what they reveal about Chinese business practices and attitudes toward law. Moreover, the bankruptcy cases show the apparent regularity with which Chinese merchants used the state courts for debt collection before such cases were brought into the federal court.[9]

Under the Bankruptcy Act, individuals and businesses came before Hoffman's court in two ways: voluntarily petitioning for relief on the grounds of insolvency or forced into court by creditors alleging an effort by the insolvent to defraud creditors. Both voluntary and involuntary Chinese bankrupts appeared before Hoffman, and occasionally even Chinese creditors came into court to protect their interest against an insolvent Chinese merchant.

In addition to the normal reasons contributing to bankruptcies, Chinese merchants faced additional economic pressure as a group. From the start of the gold rush, the Chinese in California were relegated to the most tenuous areas of the economy, in jobs and at wages that few others wanted. Some of the few positive characteristics incorporated in an otherwise negative stereotype of the Chinese were their business enterprise, industriousness, and economic tenacity. In fact, their competitiveness in the labor market formed the basis of much of the opposition to their presence in the 1870s and 1880s. Nevertheless, Chinese businesses often operated on a slim margin of profit and hence were more vulnerable to failure.[10]

The first Chinese bankruptcy came from the rural, former gold-rush

county of Butte, some 150 miles northeast of San Francisco. Long Kee, a
merchant in Oroville, voluntarily sought bankruptcy in November 1868. The
bulk of Long Kee's debts was owed to Chinese merchants in San Francisco
(some $10,600), but he owed less than a quarter of his indebtedness (some
$2,400) to non-Chinese merchants in Oroville.[11]

After Long Kee's case, Chinese merchants effectively used the bankruptcy system as a regular part of their business practice, whether as individuals or as members of partnerships. A comparison of the unsecured debts
owed to non-Chinese versus Chinese creditors reveals that the Chinese
who sought voluntary bankruptcy were equally likely to leave both groups
with considerable debts. Ironically, at the peak of the anti-Chinese movement, the Chinese enjoyed the benefits of a bankruptcy system that in
many instances absolved them of substantial financial obligations to white
merchants.[12]

Not only could and did the Chinese use the bankruptcy system, but they
also appear to have received equal treatment, if not protection, at the hands
of Hoffman. The case of *In Re Clifford* (1873) offers one such example. The
Tong Wo Company of San Francisco had sold $10,000 worth of rice to
Clifford, but before the purchase price was paid he declared bankruptcy.
Clifford argued that the rice belonged to him, but Hoffman held that the
Chinese firm still had title to the rice on the grounds that the goods were
still in the U.S. warehouse awaiting payment of duties and thus Clifford
could not claim constructive possession of the rice.[13]

Chinese merchants also used the procedure of involuntary bankruptcy to
protect their financial investments in other Chinese businesses. In 1870, for
instance, the San Francisco merchant Lee Wo Lung petitioned for the involuntary bankruptcy of Hip Yik and Company of Mariposa. Lee Wo Lung,
who had supplied the company with some $1,500 worth of goods and wares,
claimed that in anticipation of bankruptcy, Hip Yik and Company had con-
sented to a debt action in state court brought by yet another creditor, the
San Francisco firm of Wo Kee and Company. On notice of the petition, the
two partners of Hip Yik and Company appeared before Hoffman and con-
sented to an adjudication of bankruptcy.[14]

Although no allegation of collusive lawsuits to defraud creditors was made
in the *Hip Yik and Company* case, it is clear that many Chinese merchants
understood the workings of the bankruptcy system well enough to frustrate
its purpose. In 1875, for instance, non-Chinese creditors of Ah Kee accused

him of arranging for "a pretended creditor," Lee Chung, to institute an action in state court to defraud the real creditors. In yet another case, non-Chinese creditors claimed that a Chinese bankrupt had successfully avoided service of process in a debt-collection suit they had brought in state court until he could confess judgment in yet another state court suit collusively brought by a Chinese "creditor." Such techniques, however, were not used solely against non-Chinese. Chinese creditors too charged that Chinese insolvents initiated collusive suits and wrongfully transferred funds in contemplation of bankruptcy. Indeed, in two cases Chinese merchants forced another Chinese merchant into bankruptcy, the apparent strategy being to force a payment of outstanding debts. In both cases the creditors agreed to a dismissal of the petition of bankruptcy after payment of the money owed them.[15]

Even after the repeal of the Bankruptcy Act in 1878, the Chinese continued to take private disputes into American courts. In 1881, San Francisco's chief of police, Patrick Crowley, and the heads of the Chinese Six Companies disputed for two weeks over the right of the Six Companies to exact a "head tax" on all Chinese who returned to China. Crowley branded the system extortionary. Moreover, wishing to remove barriers to Chinese emigration, he posted circulars throughout Chinatown promising that his officers would insure the departure of any Chinese passenger intent on leaving. Crowley's circulars apparently caused much agitation within the Chinese community, and the Six Companies responded by posting circulars of their own insisting on the contractual duty of all Chinese to pay a "head tax" and vowing that they would seek warrants and arrests against any defaulters "and deliver them over to the American Courts." The incident underscored the extent to which Chinese leaders, as well as individual Chinese, understood and utilized the American legal system by the 1880s.[16]

If Hoffman's court proved a boon to those Chinese engaged in private civil litigation, the experiences of the Chinese as criminal defendants were more mixed. Their belated appearance before Hoffman's court, not until the mid-1860s, contrasted with their early prosecution in the state courts for a variety of criminal offenses. In Hoffman's court most Chinese prosecutions entailed violations of Internal Revenue laws. Although non-Chinese were also prosecuted for similar offenses, one commercial activity in particular dominated by the Chinese—cigar making—was targeted for prosecution. Both the discriminatory nature and the timing of such prosecutions illustrate the discretion enjoyed by U.S. attorneys in criminal matters. In these cases the Chinese received stiffer penalties than non-Chinese defendants charged with similar crimes. On the other hand, when prosecuted for crimes that frequently involved non-Chinese defendants, such as counterfeiting and smuggling, Chinese defendants received comparable sentences if convicted and stood a similar chance of an acquittal or *nolle prosequi* as did non-Chinese defendants. Indeed, given the hostility directed toward them as a group, individual Chinese defendants prevailed in a surprising number of trials—both jury trials and trials in which Hoffman determined the facts as well as law.

In the Chinese-dominated cigar-making industry, however, prosecutions for revenue violations in the northern district assumed a distinctively ethnic cast. Indeed, the aggressive prosecution of the Chinese for revenue violations closely mirrored their entrance into cigar manufacturing in large numbers in the late 1860s and during the peak of anti-Chinese feeling in the late 1870s and early 1880s. Before the Chinese were forced out of the industry in the mid-1880s, they composed at times over 90 percent of the work force engaged in making cigars. By 1866 Chinese owned half of San Francisco's cigar factories and produced goods far more cheaply than could non-Chinese-owned factories that attempted to operate without Chinese labor.[17]

Chinese cigar makers first came before Hoffman's court in the summer of 1865, with three test prosecutions for manufacturing cigars without a federal license. Federal law required individuals to pay a requisite licensing fee or tax for their specific trade or occupation. The results of the first three Chinese prosecutions were mixed. In two cases juries acquitted the Chinese defendants, and the only conviction resulted from a non-jury trial. Even then, the sentence Hoffman imposed was light relative to the discretion allowed him under the criminal statute. That statute gave Hoffman the option of imposing up to two years' imprisonment and up to a $500 fine; instead Hoffman sentenced Ah Fook and Ah Sung to only one month in the county jail, which was still a significantly greater punishment than that normally received by non-Chinese defendants convicted of the same offense.[18]

Despite U.S. Attorney Delos Lake's widespread criminal filings against unlicensed businesses of both Chinese and non-Chinese in 1866, the disposition of cases reveals a discriminatory pattern. In these early prosecutions Chinese defendants accused of selling or making cigars without licenses were routinely brought into court and convicted. Non-Chinese defendants charged with working at occupations without a federal license faced a quite different experience. Prosecutions against non-Chinese stockbrokers, real estate agents, lawyers, civil engineers, building contractors, doctors, and dentists were often abandoned when the U.S. attorney entered a *nolle prosequi*. When Lake did pursue prosecutions against non-Chinese defendants, they routinely pleaded guilty, knowing that they faced only a $1 fine and court costs. Chinese defendants, however, whether they were adjudged or pleaded guilty, received fines of $300 and costs or sentences of twenty days' (and, in one case, four months') imprisonment.[19]

Both Hoffman and Lake thus discriminated against the Chinese in their earliest appearances as criminal defendants before the northern district: the judge by awarding unequal sentences and the U.S. attorney by exercising his discretion to dismiss cases. That each seemed inclined, in this instance, to let federal criminal law fall more heavily on a minority despised by the community is hardly surprising. More unexpected is the fact that after 1867, Hoffman's court accorded Chinese defendants the same procedural and evidentiary rights as non-Chinese defendants and often displayed leniency toward them. For example, despite the sentencing disparity in the early license cases, Hoffman could have imposed considerably stiffer fines and longer prison terms. In addition, Chinese defendants received acquittals from juries and Hoffman as well as *nolle prosequis* from various U.S. attorneys even during the height of the anti-Chinese movement.[20]

The bulk of criminal cases involving Chinese defendants charged with revenue violations and other crimes came in the late 1870s as the anti-Chinese movement gained force. In fact, nearly 70 percent of all the criminal prosecutions for revenue violations filed between 1879 and 1883 involved Chinese defendents. The Chinese in the cigar-making industry became the principal targets in the revenue cases, usually for failing to conform to technical legal requirements designed to insure that all duties and taxes of the manufacture and sale of cigars could be collected by the government. The popular perception that the Chinese widely evaded the revenue laws deepened the resentment of their dominance in the industry. Thus, when the revenue collector and the U.S. attorney prosecuted Chinese cigar makers, they received considerable public support. Moreover, the reward that informers received under the revenue laws encouraged a close scrutiny of Chinese cigar makers, sometimes by their embittered non-Chinese rivals.[21]

By 1879 additional legislation had considerably increased the potential punishment faced by cigar dealers and manufacturers. Whereas in 1864 cigar makers found guilty of revenue violations risked only minimal fines and periods of imprisonment to be imposed at the discretion of federal district judges, subsequent statutes of 1866, 1868, and 1879 established mandatory minimum fines and sentences for violations. The only discretion left to judges was to impose higher fines and longer imprisonments. Moreover, the act of 1868 provided that in addition to any other penalties incurred, convicted cigar manufacturers risked forfeiture of their entire factory, tools, supplies, and even the land on which the factory stood. Although these revenue provisions applied to all cigar manufacturers, they had particular effect on the Chinese in California because of the predominance of the Chinese in the industry and the aggressive prosecution of Chinese violators by the various U.S. attorneys and revenue officials.[22]

One peculiar practice stemmed from the requirement that all cigar manufacturers identify themselves on their boxed product. This ultimately led Chinese cigar makers to use non-Chinese names. Given the popular feeling against the Chinese, non-Chinese cigar manufacturers and dealers who bought Chinese-made cigars had good reason not to advertise that fact. As a consequence, Chinese cigar manufacturers and dealers adopted misleading company names such as Empire, De Soto, Cosmopolitan, and Aetna. This ruse fooled few San Franciscans, but it reflected the ability of Chinese owners to comply with the technical requirements of the law and at the same time accommodate non-Chinese cigar dealers who bought their product for resale locally or for export to the East Coast.[23]

After a hiatus of more than a decade, criminal prosecutions against the Chinese began again in 1879, a fateful time for California's Chinese community. The campaign against their presence had become far more organized and nationally directed. California's second constitutional convention in 1878 vented hostility toward the Chinese, and in a referendum of September 1879 the state's voters overwhelmingly opposed Chinese immigration. To insure that officials in Washington, D.C., understood these feelings, California's governor, William Irwin, sent a copy of the results of the vote on "the Chinese Question" to the U.S. attorney general. In this climate, a new U.S. attorney for the northern district was appointed. Serving from 1878 through 1882, Philip Teare presided over the busiest period of criminal prosecutions against the Chinese and reflected the popular antipathy toward them.[24]

Teare accepted the popular belief that the Chinese had been systematically violating the revenue laws for many years in manufacturing cigars and in their auxiliary business of making matches. In 1881 he complained that Chinese "cunning and alertness in covering up their tracks in these illicit operations" produced "great difficulty . . . in ferreting out and bringing to justice these violators of the law." One measure of the eagerness to successfully prosecute Chinese offenders was the creation of an "Internal Revenue School" presided over by San Francisco's collector of internal revenue. Each Wednesday afternoon clerks and deputies of the collector's office met to review and learn provisions of the revenue laws. With the state and federal officials' raids into Chinatown for suspected violations, the activity of informers, and the aggressive U.S. attorney, the Chinese in San Francisco increasingly found themselves in city and county jails and before state and federal courts as the decade of the 1870s came to an end.[25]

Philip Teare's tenure as the northern district's U.S. attorney not only saw increased prosecution against the Chinese but also indicated how the Chinese fared as criminal defendants. Prosecutions against non-Chinese and Chinese for revenue violations dealing with the sale and manufacture of cigars and matches present a telling comparison. From 1879 through 1882, over 600 cases were filed for such violations. Chinese defendants accounted for nearly 70 percent of that total, not too surprising given their dominance in the cigar trade. In addition, Chinese defendants were convicted more than twice as often as non-Chinese defendants (50 percent to 22 percent) and were far less apt to have a *nolle prosequi* entered in their case (22 percent to 46 percent).[26]

More surprising, however, was the greater willingness of Chinese defendants to go to trial and their higher rate of acquittal by juries. Whereas non-Chinese defendants pleaded guilty 20 percent of the time, Chinese defendants did so approximately half as often. An analysis of the cases vindicates the Chinese choice: the acquittal rate for Chinese defendants was 5 percent higher than for non-Chinese (17 percent to 12 percent). Thus, despite their high conviction rate, going to trial meant that a significant number of Chinese defendants avoided the sentences they would have faced by pleading guilty. Nonetheless, the effort to prosecute the Chinese and their higher acquittal rate suggest that the U.S. attorney may have pursued Chinese defendants even in weak cases. If non-Chinese defendants and their lawyers hoped for more lenient sentences by entering guilty pleas, they were disappointed. Hoffman imposed the same sentence whether the jury returned a verdict of guilty or the defendant pleaded guilty.[27]

In addition, both Chinese and non-Chinese defendants convicted of these crimes received relatively lenient sentences. For both groups, Hoffman's tendency was to impose fines rather than prison; most fines ranged from $50 or $100 to $500, with occasional imprisonment sentences of thirty days or six months. In all cases, Hoffman's sentences were at the low end of the scale for the various revenue violations and usually represented the minimal fines and imprisonment mandated by statute. His stiffest sentence, a $500 fine and an eighteen-month jail sentence, was imposed on a non-Chinese defendant.[28]

Initially, Hoffman sought to encourage the payment of fines, when jail sentences were not mandatory, by imposing the alternative of thirty days in jail. By 1879 Hoffman had abandoned this practice and began imposing the condition that imprisonment would continue until the fine was paid. This device became necessary after many Chinese accepted jail rather than paid fines, as they frequently did when arrested for violations of municipal or state laws directed at them as a group. Thus, the Chinese not only thwarted the revenue-raising objective of the law but forced the government to reimburse local counties for housing federal prisoners. The condition "jail until fine paid" apparently worked and thereafter became part of every revenue sentence Hoffman imposed.

The Chinese indicted by Teare refused to plead guilty more often than non-Chinese defendants. Teare's awareness of the readiness of Chinese defendants to employ legal counsel and use the legal process to vindicate themselves prompted Teare to dismiss more cases involving Chinese defendants than he might otherwise have done. In addition, some Chinese defendants, at least in 1879, managed to arrange plea bargains for their revenue violations. In consideration for dismissing several additional criminal counts, Chinese defendants pled guilty to a single count that usually entailed only a $50 fine. Plea bargaining never involved non-Chinese defendants, perhaps because they were more willing to plead guilty in the first place, and the practice ceased altogether as public opinion hardened against the Chinese in the 1880s.[29]

Despite the willingness of the Chinese to go to court, their higher acquittal rate, and their ability to secure plea bargains, they still suffered mightily under the revenue prosecutions. Considering only the cigar- and match-related convictions during the period when Hoffman imposed imprisonment until fines were paid, the Chinese faced penalties exceeding $53,000. Non-Chinese defendants sentenced for similar offenses during the same period paid less than half that amount, only some $20,000. Substantially greater numbers of Chinese were prosecuted than non-Chinese (420 to 189), and over 60 percent of those Chinese ended up paying fines or serving jail sentences, as opposed to only 42 percent of the non-Chinese defendants.[30]

The statistics for revenue prosecutions appear more dramatic when compared with non-revenue violations. When Chinese were convicted of non-revenue offenses, the sentences they received mirrored those meted out to non-Chinese defendants. For example, Ah Que, convicted of selling liquor to Indians in 1882, received a $20 fine and twenty days in jail for an offense that routinely brought non-Chinese defendants sentenced by Hoffman several months to a year in jail along with an occasional fine of $50 to $100. Likewise, Chinese convicted of counterfeiting or possessing false coins were punished severely, from two to four years' imprisonment, but no more severely than non-Chinese convicted of the same offenses.[31]

Although technically a revenue violation, smuggling opium into San Francisco resulted in a series of prosecutions that might have brought considerable pressure to bear on the Chinese community because the drug was widely associated with the Chinese. Apart from seizing and selling opium on which the required 100 percent duty had not been paid, U.S. attorneys prosecuted those smugglers they could catch. Ultimately, only a fraction of those involved in opium smuggling were caught, but when convicted, Chinese and non-Chinese defendants received similar sentences. In minor cases, sentences might consist of fines of $50 or $75. For more serious smuggling cases, sentences ranged from six months to two years in addition to stiff fines of up to $1,000. The stiffest sentence went to a non-Chinese defendant, James Hacket, who received a $1,000 fine and a two-year prison term in San Quentin. Both Chinese and non-Chinese defendants occasionally were acquitted or had the charges against them dropped. Even though the Chinese were the primary users of the drug, non-Chinese were more

often prosecuted for opium smuggling. Non-Chinese were probably smuggling opium from the early 1860s, when the first seizures were made, and
were often involved with illegal buying and selling within California.[32]

Most criminal prosecutions against opium smugglers were initiated after
1882 when Congress finally responded to anti-Chinese sentiment by enacting a series of laws restricting Chinese immigration. The Chinese became
natural objects of scrutiny and prosecutions. Nonetheless, more than three
times as many non-Chinese as Chinese were prosecuted for opium smuggling, even though the Chinese were routinely linked to the trade. From the
number of prosecutions and the scale of operations uncovered by the U.S.
attorneys, non-Chinese seemingly controlled the illegal trade. Between 1882
and 1891, over sixty cases against non-Chinese were filed and often resulted
in substantial fines and jail terms. Moreover, convicted smugglers saw their
opium forfeited. This procedure encouraged informers and federal authorities alike, since revenue from the sale of condemned opium often brought
handsome, if not fantastic, sums that were shared with those who had made
or helped make the arrests and prosecutions possible.[33]

Predictably, friction developed among the officials who benefited from the
seizures of opium, but the system worked to insure a vigilant detection of
smuggling and its aggressive prosecution. Indeed, as early as 1864 Hoffman
restrained overly eager revenue agents who had seized an unlisted box of
opium on a ship's manifest when the vessel had arrived in San Francisco.
The captain had discovered the omission during the voyage, had instructed
the owner of the opium that duties would have to be paid when the ship
arrived in port, and had placed the drug in the cargo hold with the opium
declared on the manifest. After learning about the opium, customs officers
had told the captain it would be "all right" but subsequently decided to seize
the opium, claiming it had been smuggled. Hoffman dismissed the suit,
holding that no such intention could legally be established and that federal
officers "exercising authority so liable to abuse" were "bound to know the
law." Hoffman reasoned, "[Revenue officers] are justly held to a reasonable
degree of circumspection lest their zeal in executing the Revenue laws,
stimulated, it may be, by the large personal interest they have in every
seizure, betray them into unjustifiable violations of private rights, or unreasonable and vexatious interferences with the operations of trade."[34]

Indeed, the financial incentives for making large seizures and prosecuting
major "rings" probably allowed many Chinese engaged in small-scale smug-

gling to go unmolested. It is unlikely that revenue agents and the U.S. attorney deliberately avoided prosecuting Chinese smugglers, given the economic incentives of revenue statutes and the antipathy toward the Chinese. That less than 30 percent of those prosecuted for opium smuggling were Chinese offers convincing evidence that the larger smuggling operations were financed and operated by non-Chinese.

Although the incentives built into the revenue laws may have worked to the benefit of some Chinese after 1882, when the first Chinese Exclusion Act was passed, events after that date brought Chinese immigration under increasing scrutiny. In particular, Congress passed laws designed to exclude Chinese prostitutes and "coolies." After the mid-1880s, several criminal prosecutions against Chinese convicted of such violations resulted in very stiff fines ($1,000 and $2,000) and imprisonment at San Quentin for four to five years and in one case for ten years. Yet, the prospects of Chinese criminal defendants before Hoffman's court were not as bleak as the public antipathy toward them might suggest. In fact, non-Chinese juries, after two- to five-day trials, found Chinese defendants not guilty twice as often as they convicted Chinese for criminal violations of immigration laws.[35]

These outcomes and what legal success the Chinese enjoyed cannot be attributed to federal judges sympathetic toward the Chinese or their continued immigration. Rather, many judges, Hoffman included, harbored negative views about Chinese immigration. Nonetheless, Hoffman tempered and consciously suppressed such personal feelings as being incompatible with his judicial duty. Indeed, during the 1880s, Hoffman and his court would play a central role in frustrating the anti-Chinese movement.

Along with most white Californians—including most of the lawyers before the court and the other federal judges serving the Far West—Hoffman favored the restriction of Chinese immigration and regarded the Chinese as racial inferiors. Nonetheless, his court gave thousands of Chinese the chance to convince him on an individual basis that they were entitled to enter the country freely. Why Hoffman behaved as he did, given his attitudes toward the Chinese, is best understood in terms of nineteenth-century notions of equality.

A number of scholars have identified a popular ideology of equality that drew from earlier discussions of the nature of Republican government during the American Revolution and that clearly emerged before the Civil War. This commitment to equality cut across party lines, but it reached its fullest expression with the Republicans who drafted the Fourteenth Amendment. A principal drafter of that constitutional amendment neatly captured the persuasive rhetoric of equality when he asserted to fellow lawmakers, "The divinest feature of your Constitution is the recognition of the absolute equality before the law of all persons." If such statements seemed bereft of content, it was precisely this emptiness that gave the concept of equality its powerful appeal, since equality could (and did) mean so many different things to various groups. The coming of the Civil War and the period of Reconstruction that followed brought the status and rights of blacks directly into consideration. Nonetheless, the debates over the fate of freedmen in post–Civil War America foreshadowed issues that federal judges of the Far West would grapple with later in that century in dealing with another racial minority: the Chinese.[36]

One paradox in the nineteenth-century understanding of equality was that it easily accommodated racism. Most of those who embraced the ideal of equality drew a distinction between civil or legal equality and social, economic, or political equality. All people were theoretically entitled to protection of their person, property, and liberty. Consequently, racial distinctions that deprived individuals of their property or their liberty and denied them access to the legal system were eventually perceived as violations of broadly understood notions of equality. Justice Field expressed this view in 1879 when he discussed the equal protection clause of the Fourteenth Amendment. "[It] assure[s] to everyone whilst in the United States, from whatever country he may have come, or whatever race or color he may be . . . that the courts of the country shall be open to him on the same terms as to all others for the security of his person or property, the prevention or redress of wrongs and the enforcement of contracts." On the other hand, such a commitment to equality rarely extended to a belief in social or even political equality—hence the wide support for antimiscegenation laws and constraints on the participation of blacks in the political process. In describing the context of the drafting of the Civil Rights Act of 1866, Justice Joseph Bradley asserted that Congress had not tried "to adjust . . . the social rights of men and races in the community; but only to declare and vindicate those fundamental rights" pertaining to "the essence of citizenship," the "enjoyment or deprivation of which" constituted the "essential distinction between freedom and slavery." Likewise, the legal historian William Nelson has shown that support for racially equal treatment under law by the framers of the Fourteenth Amendment did not mean that they believed that blacks either had or should have the same socioeconomic position as whites. Thus, it was unexceptional for people in the nineteenth century to support legal equality for blacks while regarding "the world as the inheritance of the White man." Justice Field spoke in nearly identical terms when he wrote to a friend in 1882: "You know I belong to the class who repudiate the doctrine that this country was made for the people of all races. On the contrary, I think it is for our race—the Caucasian race."[37]

These distinctions help explain the different experiences of blacks and Chinese before the federal courts in the nineteenth century. Reconstruction floundered, in part, because it clearly implied a significantly enlarged political role for blacks and a radical change in the existing political polity. In contrast, the Chinese posed no such political threat, since they could not become naturalized citizens. Consequently, decisions that upheld legal equality for the Chinese lacked the dangerous prospect of leading to other— for example, political—claims to equality.[38]

Long before the passage of the Chinese Exclusion Act of 1882, the Chinese had become a beleaguered minority in the United States. By the 1870s the complaints about Chinese economic competition merged negative racial stereotypes with an effort to end Chinese immigration and discourage those present from remaining. Although California spearheaded the movement for exclusion, the sources of anti-Chinese sentiment had national origins, so that eventually California found significant support for its position from other sections of the nation. The dominant role California played in the anti-Chinese movement has obscured the significance of the Chinese Exclusion Act of 1882 as an important departure in the history of American immigration: for the first time in the nation's history, an immigrant group would be excluded on the basis of race.[39]

In the 1870s, those opposed to Chinese immigration and a Chinese presence in California confronted their greatest obstacle in the form of the Burlingame Treaty of 1868 between China and the United States. Article Five of the treaty provided for the reciprocal recognition of "the inherent and inalienable right of man to change his home and allegiance" and the "mutual advantage of the free migration and emigration" of people of both nations "for purposes of curiosity, of trade, or as permanent residents."

Article Six of the treaty guaranteed Chinese subjects visiting or residing in the United States "the same privileges, immunities, and exemptions in respect to travel or residence as . . . enjoyed by the citizens or subjects of the most favored nation." [40]

Since the treaty clearly invited Chinese immigration, federal courts invalidated state measures to impose limitations on such immigration. Federal courts also interpreted the "most favored nation" article as implicitly promising the Chinese residents the right to work and earn a living in the United States. Moreover, federal judges held that the Chinese could not be deprived of any "privileges, immunities, and exemptions" enjoyed by other foreigners. As such, the Chinese had the benefit of an additional source of protection for their legal and civil rights, namely the commitment of the United States solemnized in the treaty with China. The importance of the Burlingame Treaty to California's federal judges is clear by their invocation of the treaty during the 1870s in almost every decision that protected Chinese rights. [41]

Although the federal judges who invalidated California's legislative and even constitutional efforts to exclude and discriminate against the Chinese made themselves highly unpopular, they suggested answers to the Chinese "problem." In 1874, for instance, Stephen Field, while presiding over California's federal circuit court, struck down a state law that interfered with Chinese immigration in *In Re Ah Fong*. Field acknowledged and sympathized with the "general feeling" that "the dissimilarity in physical characteristics, in language, in manners, religion and habits," of the Chinese would "always prevent any possible assimilation," but he advised "recourse . . . to the Federal government," which had "the whole power over this subject." [42]

By 1880, the anti-Chinese forces had succeeded in persuading the executive branch of the federal government to renegotiate the Burlingame Treaty. The 1880 treaty represented a compromise between the demands of the West Coast and a deference to existing treaty rights and considerations of trade and commerce with China. The principal blow to free immigration came in the first article. Article One permitted the United States "to regulate, limit or suspend" but not "absolutely prohibit" the immigration of Chinese laborers whenever, in the opinion of the United States, such laborers threatened or endangered the country's "interests" or "good order." Such limitation or suspension, however, should "be reasonable" and should apply only to Chinese immigrating to the United States "as laborers, other classes not being included in the limitations." Moreover, the treaty pledged the United States to protect those Chinese residing in the country from "ill treatment at the hands of any other persons" and "to secure to them the same rights, privileges, immunities, and exemptions as . . . enjoyed by the citizens or subjects of the most favored nation."[43]

Anti-Chinese forces wasted little time in pressuring Congress to take advantage of Article One permitting the "regulation" of immigrating Chinese laborers. In 1882 Congress passed the first Chinese Exclusion Act, which suspended the immigration of all Chinese laborers for ten years but which did not apply to Chinese laborers already in the United States at the new treaty's conclusion—November 17, 1880. Chinese laborers were defined as "both skilled and unskilled laborers and Chinese employed in mining." To allow Chinese laborers already in America by that date to come and go freely, the act set up an identification system. Before resident Chinese laborers could leave the United States, the collector of customs was to issue a so-called return certificate that included "all facts necessary for the identification of each of such Chinese laborers." On the laborer's return to the United States, the collector would compare the certificate issued to the Chinese laborer with a permanent identification record created at the time of the certificate's issuance. If satisfied that the Chinese laborer was entitled to land—since most would be traveling by ship—the collector would file and cancel the return certificate. Under the act, Chinese laborers without legitimate return certificates were denied entry, and any Chinese unlawfully in the country should "be removed therefrom to the country from whence" he had come, "by direction of the President of the United States, and at the cost of the United States, after being brought before some justice, judge, or commissioner of court of the United States and found to be one not lawfully entitled to be or remain in the United States."[44]

Constrained by the terms of the 1880 treaty with China, the act of 1882 sought to insure that Chinese merchants, diplomats, and other nonlaborers (who could still enter under the terms of the treaty) were who they claimed to be. The act required the Chinese government to issue a descriptive certificate (in English) attesting to the status of the holder. These so-called Canton certificates were to serve as *prima facie* evidence of an individual's right to enter the country.

Although the passage of the 1882 act was widely hailed in California, its excessively rigid implementation by San Francisco's collector, ambiguities in the act itself, and the readiness of the Chinese community to contest its implementation quickly dispelled the popular hope that the act would effectively end Chinese immigration. It is little wonder that the anti-Chinese forces, after years of hearing that the authority over Chinese immigration rested with Congress, placed such hopes on the law. Supporters of the anti-Chinese movement, San Francisco customs officials, and California's newspapers sought total Chinese exclusion through the enforcement of the 1882 act. On the other hand, the local federal judges—though favoring the restriction or exclusion of Chinese laborers—would interpret the 1882 act as a limited exception to the treaty with China. Viewed in the light of the 1880 treaty, the 1882 act reaffirmed the U.S. obligation to protect all Chinese already in the country, or those who entered legitimately, and to insure them most-favored-nation status. Those who tended to view Chinese indiscriminately as a problem and who primarily sought to exclude as many Chinese as possible lacked this perspective.[45]

The zealous efforts to enforce the 1882 exclusion law (including subsequent legislation) generated an enormous amount of litigation before the northern district court and before California's federal circuit court, presided over by Lorenzo Sawyer in San Francisco. In Hoffman's court, over 7,000 petitions for writs of habeas corpus were filed by Chinese detained under the exclusion laws during the 1880s, leaving little time for other judicial business. Indeed, as early as September 1882 San Francisco newspapers referred to Hoffman's court as "the habeas corpus mill," and Hoffman and Sawyer soon adopted this nickname to refer to the Chinese writ petitions filed before their courts.[46]

Running these mills would take a physical toll, and both Sawyer and Hoffman received occasional assistance from Nevada's federal district judge, George Sabine. Oregon's federal district judge, Matthew P. Deady, infrequently came down to San Francisco to hold a term of Sawyer's circuit court. As a result, the task of hearing the many thousands of Chinese writ petitions rested primarily with Hoffman and to a lesser extent with Sawyer and Sabine. California's highest-ranking federal judge, Supreme Court Justice Stephen Field, played a minor role in the day-to-day adjudication of the writ cases but played a major role in presiding over a number of the habeas corpus test cases.[47]

Soon after the passage of the 1882 Chinese Exclusion Act, San Francisco's collector of port made it clear that he intended to implement the act as strictly as possible. In so doing, he initiated the federal habeas corpus mills. The collector announced that he intended to exclude any Chinese who had neither a return certificate nor a Canton certificate. This absolutist position led him to detain Ah Sing, one of the first Chinese to arrive in San Francisco after the act of 1882 became law.

Notwithstanding the fact that Ah Sing, a cabin steward on the steamer *Sydney*, had lived in California since 1876, the collector refused him entry for lack of a return certificate. On a writ of habeas corpus to the circuit court, with Justice Field presiding, Ah Sing was discharged. Field made it clear that although he personally favored restriction, the act had never been intended to apply to Ah Sing's situation. In any event, Field noted, since Ah Sing had remained on board the vessel throughout the voyage, he had never technically left U.S. territory.[48]

Undeterred by Field's ruling, the collector proceeded to detain other Chinese sailors on the *Sydney* on the grounds that the sailors, having spent several hours of shore leave in Australia, had lost their claim of remaining continuously within the jurisdiction of the United States. Field again discharged the Chinese petitioners and showed his annoyance at the collector's strained interpretation of the act. He warned that "absurd" applications of the act might lead to its repeal. Instead, Field suggested, "[The] wisdom of its enactment will be better vindicated by a construction less repellent to our sense of justice and right." Nonetheless, Field had to repeat his admonition several months later in a case involving a Chinese merchant, Low Yam Chow.[49]

The significance of *In Re Low Yam Chow* (1882) was its expression, by both Field and Hoffman, of the underlying purpose of the Exclusion Act and the necessity of interpreting the act in the context of the new treaty with China. Low Yam Chow was a Chinese merchant who had done business in South America for many years but was affiliated with a Chinese mercantile firm in San Francisco. After the collector refused to let him land in San Francisco in August 1882, Low Yam Chow sought a writ of habeas corpus from the circuit court composed of Field and Hoffman. Both judges argued that the objective of the treaty of 1880 had been to exclude only certain types of Chinese deemed to pose a threat to the United States. The danger, Hoffman explained, lay in unrestricted immigration of Chinese laborers.

"[Their] presence here in overwhelming numbers was felt by almost all thoughtful persons to bear with great severity upon our laboring classes, and to menace our interest, our safety, and even our civilization." Thus, the treaty and the act were intended to halt undesirable Chinese immigration while still promoting the potentially great benefits of Chinese commerce. Indeed, Field enumerated statistics of the enhanced trade with China since the Burlingame Treaty in a note to his opinion.[50]

Because the 1880 treaty with China gave most-favored-nation status to all Chinese subjects already in the United States, as well as to all those—except for laborers—who immigrated, Field dismissed the claim that Low Yam Chow needed a Canton certificate to come ashore in San Francisco. Such certificates were not indispensable, Field held, but were merely an aid to establishing merchant status; in the absence of such a certificate, Low Yam Chow could introduce oral evidence to establish his right to enter. Requiring the petitioner to return to China to obtain a Canton certificate before entering the United States was "unreasonable" and opposed to the "letter and spirit" of the Exclusion Act. Hoffman concurred with Field's holding and spoke for both when he warned that the collector's overly narrow interpretation of the act threatened to work its repeal. Even after the decision, Hoffman continued to warn that "friends" of the act were being counterproductive in pushing for an unreasonable construction that might bring the law into "odium and disrepute."[51]

Although he later received much abuse for his Chinese decisions, there is little reason to question Hoffman's sincerity in wishing the law well. Several months after the *Low Yam Chow* case, Judge Deady of Oregon rendered a decision that largely followed the reasoning of Field and Hoffman. Deady held that a Chinese actor was not a "laborer" for the purposes of the act and could establish his right to enter without a Canton certificate. Hoffman wrote Deady and expressed his agreement with the result but wondered if Deady's definition of a laborer ("one that hires himself out or is hired out to do physical toil") opened "the door . . . to those classes whom the law intended to exclude." Hoffman pointed out that some Chinese laborers, such as market gardeners, fishermen, and cigar makers, often worked as partners and not for wages. "Indeed, by forming cooperative associations the members to be paid by a share of the profits, they might in all cases take themselves out of the category of 'laborers.'" As a result, Hoffman suggested that

Deady modify his opinion before publication in the official reports. Although Deady did not take Hoffman's advice, the exchange underscores Hoffman's commitment to the objectives of the exclusion acts as long as they were accomplished in the light of the treaty with China.[52]

The significance of the decision in *Low Yam Chow*—beyond Field and Hoffman hearing their first Chinese habeas corpus case together—was that it marked an agreement of opinion that would not be achieved again. Within two years Field reversed his opinion and came close to repudiating the treaty with China in his eagerness to put an end to Chinese immigration. Hoffman, however, remained committed to interpreting exclusion acts within the context of "the solemn pledges of the treaty" despite judicial results that he felt very defensive about and that earned him considerable hostility. Judges Sawyer and Sabine came to share Hoffman's conviction that the laws to implement the treaty were to be guided by the spirit and intention of that treaty. Deeply hurt by newspaper attacks and occasionally responding with decisions that seemed to reflect public pressure, Hoffman nevertheless did not repudiate his opinion in the *Low Yam Chow* case. Although he shared Field's view of the Chinese, Hoffman refused to follow Field's repudiation of the 1880 treaty with China in order to stem Chinese immigration.[53]

After his early interpretation of the Chinese Exclusion Act of 1882, Field left for the East Coast, leaving Hoffman and Sawyer with the task of adjudicating the large number of habeas corpus cases that resulted from vessels arriving in San Francisco with Chinese passengers. Not only was Hoffman's habeas corpus mill kept busy by the collector's continuing refusal to let Chinese land, but the cases also presented novel questions that had not been anticipated by the act itself.

In *In Re Chin Ah On* (1883), Hoffman addressed the question of whether a Chinese laborer who was resident in California at the time the treaty with China was ratified (but who went to China before the passage of the act) was entitled to reenter the country without a return certificate. He conceded that if the terms of the treaty and the act conflicted irreconcilably, then his judicial duty would be to obey the latest expression of legislative will. But since the act sought to restrict only new Chinese laborers from coming into the United States, Hoffman considered Chin Ah On's situation simply a congressional oversight. As such, Hoffman sought guidance from the treaty, Article Two of which guaranteed that Chinese laborers already in the country at the time the treaty was signed could freely leave and reenter the United States. Hoffman thus held that Chin Ah On could not be required to hold a return certificate as a condition of reentering the country.[54]

Hoffman buttressed his reconciliation of the act with the treaty by noting that the collector's superiors in Washington, D.C., had also concluded that Chinese laborers already in the country at the time of the treaty were entitled to reenter even without a return certificate. More important, Hoffman believed that to deny Chin Ah On the right to land would havè been "to attribute to the legislative branch of government a want of good faith and a disregard of solemn national engagements which, unless upon grounds" that left "the court no alternative," would have been "indecent to impute to it."[55]

Hoffman thus voiced a concern—shared by other federal judges—that the nation maintain its honor by faithfully adhering to its treaties. As Oregon's federal judge, Matthew Deady, had said about the Burlingame Treaty in 1879, "An honorable man keeps his word under all circumstances, and an honorable nation abides by its treaty obligations, even to its own disadvantage." For Hoffman, the importance of maintaining treaty obligations was linked to his sense of personal honor. The nation, like an honorable gentleman, would be loath to break a solemn promise. Indeed, according to Hoffman, it was "indecent" to attribute such a motive to Congress unless the intention to break the treaty appeared unequivocally. As such, he felt bound and determined to keep the nation on an honorable course by interpreting the 1882 act in the light of the renegotiated treaty with China two years earlier.[56]

The practical result of Hoffman's decision in *Chin Ah On* was that any Chinese laborer without a return certificate could land in San Francisco after establishing his prior residence. Sawyer and Hoffman later established June 6, 1882, as the date after which all Chinese laborers who left California would not be allowed to reenter without a return certificate. That date marked the first availability of return certificates from the customshouse in San Francisco. Although they established such exemptions according to the spirit of the treaty with China, Hoffman and Sawyer refused to accept any excuses by Chinese laborers for failing to present certificates unless they fell into exempted situations like Chin Ah On's. Nonetheless, the circuit and district courts found their dockets expanding with Chinese habeas corpus cases. Less concerned with judicial reasoning, the newspapers and the general public focused on the fact that the Chinese regularly entered San Francisco through writs granted by the courts.[57]

Thus, the number of Chinese who came into Hoffman's court and over-taxed the northern district resulted in large measure from Hoffman's commitment to judicial due process. By insisting that all Chinese detained by the collector had a right to challenge their detention in habeas corpus proceedings, Hoffman insured himself of a crowded docket. Moreover, in such hearings the Chinese were entitled, as a procedural right, to present any evidence, written or oral, that might establish their unlawful confinement. In Hoffman's view, a denial of access to his court or of the right to testify and present evidence on their own behalf was a violation of basic rights to a fair trial, rights implicitly guaranteed by the treaty of 1880. The determination of whether Chinese were wrongfully denied liberty by the actions of the customshouse officials was emphatically a matter for his court to decide. Hoffman proved unwilling to abdicate such responsibility regardless of the grief it caused him.

The large number of Chinese writ cases concerned Hoffman and his judicial colleagues, as well as the newspapers, because of the drain on the federal courts. In 1884 Hoffman delivered the opinion—actually more of a commentary—in *In Re Chow Goo Pooi*, heard before the circuit court composed of Sawyer, Sabine, and Hoffman. The case involved an attempt by the U.S. attorney to bypass Hoffman's consideration of Chow Goo Pooi's habeas corpus petition in the district court by seeking the permission of Sawyer (as the circuit court judge) to arrest the petitioner as an illegal alien. Speaking for a unanimous court, Hoffman asserted the right of all Chinese detained by the collector to seek their liberty through writs of habeas corpus and the exclusive power of the courts to decide whether a petitioner was entitled to enter the country under the terms of the Exclusion Act. Moreover, Hoffman noted the lack of judicial power, under the act, to detain the vessels that brought Chinese to San Francisco until the numerous investigations and adjudications pertinent to the right of such passengers to land were completed.[58]

Hoffman then turned to what he regarded as the most important question raised under the act: given the flood of habeas corpus petitions, what was to be done with those Chinese passengers in the custody of the federal courts after the vessel that had brought them departed? Hoffman examined the act's "very vague and inexplicit" section that called for the deportation of Chinese. He concluded that the habeas corpus proceedings satisfied the requirements of determining if Chinese were illegal aliens but that Chinese remanded to the custody of the marshal could be held only for a "reasonable time, to await the direction of the president." Drawing an analogy with extradition laws, Hoffman argued that remanded Chinese could be detained for only two months, after which they had to be released in the absence of "just excuse."[59]

Anticipating the public reaction to his opinion, Hoffman warned of the severe strain on the federal courts in San Francisco and called for legislation to relieve the judges from habeas corpus cases. Observing that in his court alone nearly two hundred writ cases remained on the calendar, Hoffman explained: "For five or six weeks, even with night sessions, I have been unable to make any great impression on them. All ordinary business, public and private, of the court is necessarily suspended, or if resumed, these passengers, many of whom may be entitled to their discharge, are left, either in custody or on bail, awaiting the determination of their cases." Hoffman called on Congress to establish a special commissioner who would have final authority to resolve the claims of Chinese passengers.[60]

Hoffman's exhaustion from overwork made far less an impression on the public than the fact that Chinese were walking out of his courtroom and into the streets of San Francisco. Moreover, Hoffman's reputation suffered by comparison with the strong anti-Chinese position of the collector. Customshouse officials were "striving hard" to prevent frauds and the landing of "bogus coolies" but were opposed by "every Chinaman in the city, the Chinese Consulate, dozens of purchased lawyers and untoward circumstances enough to make them sicken of their task." On the other hand, Hoffman, Sawyer, and Sabine were accused of "playing with" and creating "loopholes" in the Exclusion Act. Even worse culprits, according to the press, were the attorneys for the Chinese and the Chinese themselves. It was believed that the Chinese, with the help of counsel and by systematic lying, were succeeding in undermining the Exclusion Act. As early as December 1883, the *Alta California* renamed the law the "Chinese Evasion Act" and "An Act to perfect the art of lying among the Chinese and their white auxiliaries."[61]

In the face of such criticism, Hoffman publicly responded in the case of

In Re Tung Yeong (1884). This opinion, along with a few others, provided the means to discuss the broader issues of the writ litigation. After announcing the discharge of Tung Yeong, Hoffman devoted the bulk of the opinion to vindicating his collective decisions in the habeas corpus cases, decisions that, "though much criticised," he felt had not been "thoroughly understood."[62]

In the *Tung Yeong* opinion Hoffman summarized the three types of Chinese habeas corpus applications: laborers claiming prior residence, applicants seeking to enter on Canton certificates, and children rejoining their parents in San Francisco. Only the first two categories caused problems for Hoffman. In the cases of prior residents lacking return certificates, Hoffman defended his decision, in *In Re Chin Ah On* (1883), to allow them to establish their right to enter as provided by the treaty. He asserted that in the vast majority of such cases, Chinese petitioners had met their burden of proof by documentary evidence or corroboration by testimony sufficient "to satisfy any candid and unbiased mind." Admitting that he may have been deceived in some instances, Hoffman believed the number to be small, "considering that in no case" was a petitioner "allowed to land on the plea of previous residence on unsupported Chinese oral testimony."[63]

The Canton certificate cases, Hoffman admitted, were "exceedingly embarrassing to the court" and had "almost insuperable difficulties." The principal difficulty was that whatever doubts Hoffman had about the reliability of the certificates, they constituted, under the act, *prima facie* evidence of a right to land. Moreover, since the treaty expressly excluded only laborers, Hoffman stated, "The inquiry was not so much whether the person was a merchant as whether he was a 'laborer,' and . . . that inquiry should relate, not to his occupation or *status* in China, but to the occupation in which he was to be engaged in this country; as the intention and object of the law was to protect our own laborers from the competition and rivalry of Chinese laborers here." Since the burden of proof thus rested with the U.S. attorney to rebut the apparent merchant status of immigrants, attorneys for Chinese petitioners routinely introduced a Canton certificate into evidence and then rested their case. Despite the considerable latitude accorded the U.S. attorney in questioning petitioners and Hoffman's own cross-examination, he believed an undetermined number of Chinese had been wrongfully landed simply because the government's attorney had not met his burden of proof.[64]

Lamenting the possible frauds, Hoffman failed to see how they could have been prevented by "any court honestly and fearlessly discharging its duty under the law and evidence." In Hoffman's view:

> By the constitution and laws of the United States, Chinese persons in common with all others, have the right "to the equal protection of the law" and this includes the right "to give evidence" in courts. A Chinese person is therefore a competent witness. To reject his testimony when consistent with itself, and wholly uncontradicted by other proofs, on the sole ground that he is a Chinese person, would be an evasion, or rather violation, of the constitution and law, which every one who sets a just value upon the uprightness and independence of the judiciary, would deeply deplore.

Thus, when the preponderance of proof rested with a Chinese petitioner, Hoffman felt compelled to discharge him despite reservations. Nonetheless, Hoffman sought to deflect criticism by citing customshouse statistics indicating that since 1882, five times more Chinese had left than had arrived in San Francisco. Hoffman never seemed to appreciate that such statistics had far less effect on the public mind than did the reports of the many Chinese he released from detention under decisions of his court.[65]

The Exclusion Act's ambiguities and judicial interpretations that had led Hoffman to decide as he did prompted amendments that were passed into law on July 5, 1884. The principal changes in the second Chinese Exclusion Act made return certificates the only permissible evidence for a laborer to establish a right of reentry. Nonlaborers could enter the country only if they produced Canton certificates that had been verified by American consuls in China. Such Canton certificates were to be the only permissible evidence available to nonlaborers seeking entry, but they still could be challenged by customshouse officials. Although the new act generally made it more difficult for Chinese to establish their right to enter the United States, it did not prove to be a panacea for the anti-Chinese movement. Hoffman and Sawyer continued to interpret the 1884 act in the light of the treaty rights accorded the Chinese, and both judges refused to construe the act in ways that would accomplish total exclusion.[66]

In their earliest opinions interpreting the new act, both Sawyer and Hoffman acknowledged and implemented its tighter requirements, but both reiterated the seemingly obvious point that the 1884 act (as with the 1882 act) was not intended to work retroactively. In other words, they insisted that those Chinese who had left San Francisco before the certificates became available should not be required to show them as a condition of reentry. Hoffman refused to accept an inflexible interpretation of the 1884 act because doing so meant accusing Congress of "gross disingenuousness, and of utter disregard of a treaty stipulation, to the observance of which the national honor was pledged."[67]

Given the mood following the passage of the act of 1884, Hoffman also felt obliged to defend his past record of allowing the Chinese to seek writs of habeas corpus. He explained, "That any human being claiming to be unlawfully restrained of his liberty has a right to demand a judicial investigation into the lawfulness of his imprisonment is not questioned by any one who knows by what constitutional and legal methods the right of liberty is secured and enforced by at least all English-speaking peoples." Hoffman's defense of the rights of the Chinese under the treaty and to writs of habeas corpus hardly altered his low opinion of the Chinese generally. He spoke of their "unscrupulous mendacity" and "fertile ingenuity" as well as "the endless gamut of deceptions" that had "in so many instances wearied and disgusted the court." Yet, despite these misgivings, Hoffman rendered decisions that suggested to the public that he was "engaged in a persistent effort to defeat on technical grounds the operation of the law."[68]

Field returned to the West Coast in September 1884, determined to take a harder line with the Chinese and to correct his misguided colleagues. Presiding over a judicial panel composed of Circuit Judge Sawyer and the two district court judges, Hoffman and Sabine, Field was in a position, as the circuit justice, to control the decision at that stage, even in the face of dissent by his three judicial colleagues. In several early opinions, Field insisted on strictly enforcing the requirements of the 1884 act. Moreover, he resolved a pressing practical question by deciding that the vessels bringing Chinese subsequently remanded by the courts were responsible for returning them to China.[69]

The *Alta California* reacted by suggesting that California had been wrong about Field. Although he had earlier struck down anti-Chinese laws as violating the Burlingame Treaty, Field had, according to the newspaper, suggested the enactment of the first Exclusion Act. In addition, by his most recent opinions, he had closed loopholes through which the Chinese had been getting into the country, and he had swept away "the false and unreliable . . . [oral] testimony of the Chinese." Field's zeal in stopping Chinese immigration, however, took him to extremes from which Sawyer, Hoffman, and Sabine dissented even as the press applauded. The most important test case during Field's September visit raised a question that had already been settled by California's federal courts in accordance with the spirit of interpretation that Field himself had endorsed in 1882.[70]

The habeas corpus petition of Chew Heong became the test case in 1884 that drove a wedge between Field and his judicial colleagues on the West Coast. Chew Heong, a Chinese laborer resident in the United States at the time of the 1880 treaty with China, left California before the 1882 Exclusion Act went into effect. He had thus departed before the return certificates became available. Chew Heong therefore sought to establish his right of reentry in 1884 based on his prior residence.[71]

Estimates of the number of Chinese who had similarly left California before any return certificates existed varied from 12,000 to 15,000. Field showed his determination to exclude the potential return of so many Chinese in a colloquy with one of Chew Heong's attorneys, Thomas D. Riordan, during oral argument before the circuit court. Riordan pointed out that the judges now sitting with Field (Sawyer, Hoffman, and Sabine) had unanimously held that return certificates in such cases as Chew Heong's were not indispensable. The *Alta California* reported the following exchange between Field and Riordan:

Justice Field: The law [Act of 1884] is perfectly plain. It says that the certificate shall be the only evidence. How many Chinamen will try to come in the same way?

Mr. Riordan: About 12,000.

Justice Field: And what shall the Courts do with them? Can it give each one of them a separate trial? Can it let each of them produce evidence of former residence? No; it was because the Courts were overcrowded that the second act was passed. It was to relieve that pressure. Besides, Congress never supposed that Chinamen intended to go back to China and stay several years. If they do not come back at once they should not be allowed to come at all. We can't have them going away and staying as long as they want to.

Mr. Riordan: Then I suppose, your Honor, it is no use arguing the case further.

Justice Field: Not in the least. My mind is made up on the matter. If there is any special hardship, there are other ways of remedying it. Bring the case to the notice of the Chinese Minister at Washington, let him present it to the Secretary of State, with the request that our Minister to China look into the matter and report on it. Or, if you would prefer, appeal the case to the Supreme Court of the United States and have it settled there.

How the other federal judges sitting with Field reacted was not, unfortunately, recorded by the *Alta California*'s reporter. It can safely be assumed, however, that they were not smiling.[72]

In rejecting the earlier opinions of his fellow judges, Field held that the 1882 act had intended by its terms that only those Chinese laborers in the United States at the time the act was passed would be allowed to leave and still return. Those Chinese who left the country before the act took effect were to be excluded, and without a return certificate, no oral evidence could be received to establish reentry. By implication Field suggested that despite their good intentions, Sawyer, Hoffman, and Sabine had, in effect, evaded or misconstrued the Exclusion Act of 1882. Field clearly understood the popular mood of Californians toward their federal judges and the Chinese. He stated: "Oftentimes, indeed, there is a sense of impatience in the public mind with judicial officers for not announcing the law to be what the community at the time wishes it should be. And nowhere has this feeling been more manifested than in California, and on no subject with more intensity than that which touches the immigration of Chinese laborers." Field's opinion could not have been better calculated to appease what he called "impatience in the public mind."[73]

Lorenzo Sawyer, on behalf of himself, Hoffman, and Sabine, filed a lengthy dissent in *Chew Heong* in which he examined the exclusion acts in the light of the treaty with China. Sawyer saw no foundation for the argument that prior Chinese residents should be required to produce certificates they could not have obtained. Moreover, the dissenters disagreed with Field's implication that Chinese laborers who left in good faith with the 1882-type certificates would be required to produce 1884-type certificates.

Primarily, the dissenters argued that Field's decision excluding Chinese laborers came at too high a price: "the plighted faith of the nation." Sawyer argued that the previous decisions of California's federal circuit court not only had observed the treaty but also had been accompanied by a substantial decrease in the number of Chinese in California. As it was, Riordan took Field's advice and appealed the decision to the Supreme Court, where Field's decision was reversed (by a margin of seven to two) for substantially the same reasons as given by the dissenters. Field filed a shrill dissent attacking his circuit and Supreme Court colleagues, claiming they had rendered the 1884 act "nugatory." [74]

When news of the Supreme Court's reversal reached California, it was the three original dissenters' turn to feel vindicated. In a letter headed "Confidential—Destroy" and addressed to Deady, Sawyer confessed, "It is some consolation, after all the lying, abuse, threatening of impeachment etc. as to our construction of the Chinese [exclusion] act, and the grand glorification of brother Field for coming out here and so easily, promptly and thoroughly sitting down on us and setting us right on that subject to find that we are not so widely out of our senses after all." Moreover, Sawyer mentioned a commendation he had received from a stranger in Wisconsin for upholding the rights of Chinese "with courage and energy in opposition to a strong current of popular clamor." He predicted, "Time will bring us out about right." [75]

Despite the vindication of their interpretation and approach to the 1882 and 1884 acts, the three dissenting judges would continue to be plagued by federal officials who strained to exclude the Chinese. In September 1884, John S. Hager, a former U.S. Senator, became the new collector for the port of San Francisco. One U.S. senator remembered that no one exceeded Hager as a "zealous opponent" of Chinese immigration. He was "one of the first" to discover "the Chinese evil." The senator added, "His consistency in opposition to it cannot be questioned." In an interview shortly after his appointment, Hager declared that he would not tolerate any further "interference" by the federal judges and asserted that the Chinese had no right to come before their courts. Even though Hager's stand met with public approval, his efforts to bypass the courts were quickly challenged by Hoffman. [76]

In October 1885, a writ of habeas corpus was sought from Hoffman's court on behalf of two Chinese who had been denied entry because they had

no certificates, even though they claimed to be California residents returning from a trip to China. Under pressure from Hager, U.S. Attorney Samuel
Hilborn challenged the issuance of a writ. Hilborn argued that since the
collector had passed judgment on matters of law and fact, the district court
had no jurisdiction over the case. Hoffman expressed outrage at the pre-
sumptuousness of the government's argument. "The petitioner is a free
man, under our flag, and within the protection of our laws." Hoffman found
the denial of the man's right to land a clear instance of a restriction of liberty.
He reiterated the importance of the writ of habeas corpus to "English-
speaking peoples" as "the most sacred" document of "personal freedom"
and its availability to everyone, "no matter what his race or color." This
ringing assertion of rights due the petitioners, however, did not stop Hoffman from complaining in a letter to a fellow federal judge about "the un-
speakable Chinese" only two months later.[77]

Hoffman also rejected the argument that the Chinese might not be entitled in his court to a full review of the facts surrounding their detention as
an "extraordinary pretention" that sought to make a mere executive decision
"final and conclusive." If the Chinese were entitled to writs of habeas corpus, then requiring "the court in its investigation to be governed by the
decision of an executive officer, acting under instructions from the head of
the department at Washington," would have been "an anomaly wholly without precedent, if not a flagrant absurdity." On appeal, Hoffman's decision
was upheld by the Supreme Court, giving additional force to his conviction,
as he expressed it to a newspaper reporter in 1888, that the right of the
Chinese to land should "be decided by the Courts, and by the Courts
alone."[78]

Hoffman's insistence on the right of the Chinese to come before his court
through writs of habeas corpus and the necessity of applying general principles of evidence in adjudicating their petitions stemmed from his commitment to the equal application of fundamental civil rights irrespective of race.
But although he would not deny the Chinese such rights, his conviction that
many Chinese were giving false testimony led him to endorse procedures
that reflected this bias and discriminated against the Chinese. Specifically,
by 1888 he had allowed Chinese habeas corpus petitioners to be examined
before the U.S. attorney without their own attorneys being present, with
resulting statements admitted later as evidence against the Chinese petitioners in court. According to a Department of Justice official, Hoffman believed

"this 'Star Chamber' proceeding . . . to be absolutely necessary for the successful carrying out of the provisions of the [Exclusion] Act."[79]

Judicial control over Chinese immigration brought additional censure on the federal courts because judges, rather than juries, decided the outcome of habeas corpus petitions. Assistant U.S. Attorney Carrol Cook made a pointed reference to that fact in 1885, during the first criminal prosecution in the northern district of a Chinese defendant accused of falsifying a return certificate. In his opening remarks to the jury, Cook asserted of habeas corpus cases: "[They] have been going on for the last two or three years until the Court, Counsel, and Spectators have become disgusted with the sickening prevarication and perjury that has prevailed in these cases since their inception. Now for the first time we present this kind of testimony to a Jury of Citizens of the State of California." He implied that whether or not Hoffman had been repeatedly duped in the writ cases, the judge bore the responsibility for continued Chinese immigration. Cook added:

> When a Chinaman is refused landing on the ship he attempts to gain an entrance in any way that is possible. He secures sometimes the ablest and most learned counsel and in other cases he secures those who would stoop to anything. He is represented by all the ingenuity that is possible. Every kind of excuse is made, every loop-hole to tear asunder this law [Exclusion Act of 1884], and as I said before, what he cannot swear to is not worth swearing to as a rule.

Cook carried the point, for the jury found the Chinese defendant, Choi Ah Jow, guilty.[80]

Such hyperbole characterized the rhetoric of the federal officials who sought to stop the entry of the Chinese into San Francisco, and their strict policies continued to flood the federal courts with habeas corpus cases even as the relative number of Chinese in the city declined. In May 1887 Sawyer complained that the "zealous customs house officers" rejected the Chinese "without rhyme or reason." Sawyer and Hoffman continued to hear record numbers of writ cases, even with Hoffman in ill health. In January 1888, the *Alta California*, relying on customshouse records, reported that after the exclusion acts had been in operation for almost five years, 87 percent of the almost 4,000 Chinese who had sought writs of habeas corpus from the federal courts had been landed. Although the customshouse records also showed that between 1882 and 1887 Chinese departures had exceeded arrivals by more than 25,000, the habeas corpus cases kept the federal judges before the public eye and subject to continuous criticism.[81]

Little relief seemed imminent from what Sawyer called "an intolerable nuisance." In 1888 he complained, "We are buried out of sight in Chinese habeas corpus cases." Hoffman was at a loss to convince someone "how great" was "the physical distress and mental strain caused by a day's conscientious attention to these Chinese cases." After "weeks and months" of "torture to mind and body," Hoffman was experiencing bouts of illness from which Sawyer thought he might not be able to recover. Temporarily running the habeas corpus mill alone, Sawyer declared himself "utterly discouraged." He explained "The more I do, and the harder and faster I work the more villainously and vigorously I am abused." Hoffman, as well, found that the unremitting prospect of Chinese cases filled him "with dismay and almost with despair," and his frustration spilled over into his written opinions. Eventually the federal judges received some relief in 1888 when Congress gave U.S. commissioners the power to hear habeas corpus petitions filed by Chinese immigrants. Hoffman appointed a special commissioner to take testimony and make recommendations on individual petitions, even though he often differed from the commissioner's report and took additional testimony himself. Further relief took the form of efforts to renegotiate the treaty with China. By May 1888 Sawyer anticipated a respite from the Chinese cases, provided that Congress did not "upset the matter by bungling legislation" to put the treaty into effect.[82]

In the end, it was Congress's eagerness to respond to the anti-Chinese forces during an election year and the Chinese government's reservations about ratifying the new treaty that prompted legislation that truly excluded Chinese laborers. The treaty proposed in 1888 prohibited the immigration of Chinese laborers to the United States for twenty years. Nonetheless, the treaty would have allowed a Chinese laborer in the United States to leave the country and later return if he had a lawful wife, child, or parent in the United States or property or debts due him of at least $1,000. The treaty called for such a laborer to deposit with the collector of customs, before leaving, a full description of his family or property before receiving a return certificate, which had to be used within one year. In September the Chinese minister indicated that his government wanted more discussion on shortening the twenty-year period, lowering the property requirement, and attaining assurances that all Chinese who had been in the United States would be allowed to return. But before negotiation on these matters took place, Congress passed several measures that demonstrated its desire to halt the immigration of Chinese laborers to the United States.[83]

The first measure Congress passed, on September 13, 1888, was entitled an act "to prohibit the coming of Chinese laborers to the United States" and was based on, but exceeded, the proposed treaty. By its terms the act provided for the repeal of the 1882 and 1884 acts with the ratification of the pending treaty with China. As in the proposed treaty, a Chinese laborer already in the United States could reenter the United States after the date the act was passed only if he had "a lawful wife, child, or parent in the United States or property therein of the value of one thousand dollars, or debts of like amount due him and pending settlement." But in addition, return certificates were made indispensable for reentry and constituted the only evidence of a right of reentry for a Chinese laborer. Moreover, the act excluded Chinese laborers for an unlimited period of time. Even before the act received President Grover Cleveland's signature, however, another and much more drastic measure was passed by both houses of Congress.[84]

In early September, Washington learned of a diplomatic dispatch reporting that China had refused to ratify the treaty. Since the act that Congress had just passed was predicated on the ratification of the treaty, a new bill was rushed through Congress without debate. Unlike any of the previous acts dealing with the immigration of Chinese laborers, the act of October 1, 1888, excluded all Chinese laborers for good. The law provided that, as of the date of the act, no Chinese laborer resident in the United States could leave the country and return, nor could Chinese laborers who had formerly lived in the United States return to the country. Moreover, the act declared that all return certificates that had been issued under the 1882 (and by implication the 1884) act were now null and void. The political climate encouraging anti-Chinese legislation and the belief that the treaty with China would not be ratified accounted for the dramatic step of excluding—for the first time in the nation's history—an immigrant group on the basis of race. Within twenty-four hours of President Cleveland's signing the bill into law, the customshouse officials and federal judges in San Francisco were notified by telegram that the October act was to be enforced at once.[85]

The importance of the act of October 1 to both sides resulted in a test case within two weeks of the date the bill became law. The immediate enforcement of the act potentially affected over 30,000 Chinese who had left

China with pre-1888 return certificates but who had not yet returned to California. Chae Chan Ping was one such laborer; he had resided in California from 1875 until 1887, when he had left for China with a return certificate. En route to San Francisco from Hong Kong when the act of October 1, 1888, became law, Chae Chan Ping arrived in the city on October 7 and was refused permission to land on the grounds that the act had annulled the return certificate. Sawyer and Hoffman formed the circuit court that heard arguments in the case, and on October 15 Sawyer sustained the act. Sawyer held that since both treaties and federal laws were "supreme," in any unavoidable conflict (such as that presented by the act of October 1, 1888) the earlier had to give way to the later. The case was appealed to the Supreme Court, where Justice Field delivered the unanimous opinion of the Court and sustained the act in very broad terms.[86]

Although the affirmation of Sawyer's decision ended any challenge to the act itself, it did not mark, as many thought, an effective end to Chinese immigration and the use of the federal courts by the Chinese to establish their right of entry. The anti-Chinese movement might have observed that Sawyer went out of his way to explain that the decision he and Hoffman had reached did not represent a capitulation to popular prejudice. Indeed, Sawyer wrote to Judge Deady in Oregon about the *Chae Chan Ping* decision and confided that he and Hoffman had felt compelled by the terms of the act to decide as they had. Moreover, in the same letter Sawyer announced that he and Hoffman had rejected an overly narrow interpretation of the 1888 act by the collector. Hager had refused to land Chinese laborers traveling from Seattle to San Francisco via Victoria, claiming they had departed from the United States by entering and then leaving British waters. It seemed to Sawyer "as though the Executive departments" were determined to make the U.S. government "as odious to the rest of the world as possible."[87]

Far from cutting off access to the federal courts, the October 1, 1888, act resulted in additional habeas corpus cases well after Hoffman's death in 1891. Beyond not accepting a literal interpretation of the 1888 act, Sawyer and Hoffman also refused to remand automatically those Chinese out on bail and awaiting a decision at the time the act was passed. Although the Supreme Court later approved such a retroactive application of the act in mid-1891, by that time the backlog of cases had been disposed of under the acts of 1882 and 1884. Moreover, many of those Chinese arriving in San Francisco after October 1888 quickly discarded their now useless return certificates and sought entry on such grounds as being "merchants" or "American born citizens." While the newspapers decried the "certain class of lawyers" who abetted the Chinese in "the habeas corpus business," the federal courts continued to land far more petitioners than they remanded. Indeed, in Hoffman's court between October 1, 1888, and December 1, 1890, 1,401 Chinese habeas corpus cases were filed. Of the 620 cases decided by the end of that period, 533, or 86 percent, ended in the discharge of the petitioner, whereas only 87, or 14 percent, of the Chinese were remanded.[88]

The efforts of the Chinese to use the federal courts to ameliorate the effects of exclusion were ultimately a losing battle, especially after the deaths of both Hoffman and Sawyer in 1891. Those two judges had experienced the brunt of public criticism. As one customs inspector put it in 1890, San Francisco's federal courts had been "tarred and feathered." Obviously stung by such disapproval, they nonetheless felt vindicated by the Supreme Court's affirmations. Even in the midst of rendering their popular decision upholding the 1888 act, the judges exhibited the defensive pride that characterized their Chinese habeas corpus cases. Sawyer summed up those decisions in his opinion in the *Chae Chan Ping* case. "We have, heretofore, found it our duty, however unpleasant, at times, to maintain, fearlessly, and steadily, the rights of Chinese laborers under our treaties with China, and the acts of Congress passed to carry them out."[89]

The success the Chinese experienced before Hoffman's court in particular, and the federal judiciary of the Far West generally, hardly resulted from pro-Chinese sympathies. The contemporary press recognized this even when, at its most caustic, it routinely accused the federal judges of being "dupes" of the Chinese rather than their agents. The resistance that Hoffman and other federal judges hearing the Chinese habeas corpus cases showed toward the anti-Chinese movement stemmed both from political concerns and from notions of legal equality that the newspapers did not understand and cursorily dismissed as legal technicalities.

West Coast federal judges shared a deep-seated concern, if not fear, for the lawless and demagogic aspects of the "Chinese-must-go" movement. The judges seemed more concerned about the means used by the movement than they did about the goal of restricting Chinese immigration. Judge

Deady, for one, increasingly viewed the anti-Chinese movement as a conflict "between a shiftless 'mob' on the one hand and public-spirited 'citizens' on the other." In 1886 Judge Sawyer, after issuing a warrant for the arrest of a leader of a mob that had burned the homes of Chinese, recorded that his action had caught the attention of "gubernatorial candidates, politicians, demagogues, Sandlotters, political and social tramps etc." Justice Field, who harbored a "horror of anything that bore the taint of socialism or communism," also worried about "angry menaces against order" finding vent "in loud denunciations." Hoffman's own conservative instincts and reactions to demagogues and extralegal movements squarely placed him in opposition to the terror tactics of the more extreme wing of those who sought to end Chinese immigration.[90]

If many of the federal judges objected to the means by which many in the anti-Chinese movement sought to end Chinese immigration, some of them made their reservations about Chinese immigration explicit. In 1882 Field explained to a correspondent: "The manners, habits, mode of living, and everything connected with the Chinese prevent the possibility of their ever assimilating with our people. They are a different race, and, even if they could assimilate, assimilation would not be desirable." In 1886, in the midst of the Chinese habeas corpus litigation, Lorenzo Sawyer dictated his oral history at the request of the Bancroft Library. In the course of the dictation he explained that he objected to Chinese immigration on the grounds of "the distinction of races." He said: "The Chinese are vastly superior to the negro, but they are a race entirely different from ours and never can assimilate and I don't think it desirable that they should and for that reason I don't think it desirable that they could come here. I think we made a mistake when we opened our door of immigration to them."[91]

But the door of immigration had been opened, the Chinese were in the United States, and a treaty existed giving them special protections. Given this, the shared commitment of Far West federal judges in the 1880s to legal equality and a good-faith interpretation of the treaties with China prompted them to render the decisions they did. Harboring conflicting feelings and pressured by public and political concerns, they only naturally showed signs of these undercurrents in their public comments and opinions.

Unlike most critics of Chinese immigration, Hoffman was forced to deal with the Chinese on a personal, day-to-day basis. Despite his generalized bias toward the Chinese, in his court he did not face "the Chinese" but rather individual Chinese petitioners. The thousands of separate hearings individualized the Chinese, forcing Hoffman to see and hear them as human beings with distinct explanations and histories that had to be appraised. Unlike Field, who heard only test cases in which the Chinese petitioner at hand was largely incidental and symbolic of many others similarly situated, Hoffman and Sawyer could not maintain Field's detachment. Hoffman, for instance, expressed his delight at being able to avoid separating Chinese children from their parents. Likewise, both he and Sawyer admired and respected qualities of Chinese individuals even as they decried the limitations of the race.

The fact that so many Chinese petitioners succeeded in convincing Hoffman and Sawyer that they were legitimately entitled to land underscores the gap between the judges' racial rhetoric and their judicial action. Few critics of the continued immigration of the Chinese could explain why a people, believed to be so notoriously untrustworthy, succeeded time and time again in persuading Hoffman and Sawyer to decide in their favor. The paradox owes much to the fact that, unlike the customshouse officials who were able and certainly willing to implement a bureaucratic procedure that systematically excluded the Chinese, Hoffman witnessed the many examples of individual expression and argument presented by the habeas corpus proceedings. Even though the large number and similarity of many of these cases "bureaucratized" the process in some respects—as Hoffman's and Sawyer's factory-like nickname, the "habeas corpus mill," for their courts suggests—the decisions never became automatic, with predictable results. Having asserted their right to such hearings, Hoffman allowed each Chinese petitioner to present any evidence, testimony, or argument in favor of establishing his liberty. The nature of the judicial process itself thus forced a case-by-case appraisal that entailed decisions affecting one person at a time rather than an entire race or class.

In contrast, Stephen Field tended to speak in sweeping terms about how to deal with "the Chinese problem." His perspective, like that of the collector, did not include the need to look at the Chinese coming before the federal courts as individuals. The collector was quite willing to make an executive decision that would unilaterally affect the Chinese. As a trial judge, Hoffman found himself enmeshed in a far more complicated process. His sense of the importance of maintaining treaty rights and due process in his court resulted in decisions that further estranged him from the forces that sought to end Chinese immigration, even though he agreed with them in principle. Despite his strong desire to be rid of the habeas corpus mill, Hoffman could not avoid that obligation without repudiating his concept of judicial review and duty and the common-law tradition. And this Hoffman was not prepared to do.[92]

Conclusion

Hoffman's Judgeship

When Hoffman reached California in 1850, he did not expect to stay long. A search for new opportunities, health, and a fortune may have drawn him, but the life he cherished and his family and friends tied him to New York. Although California neither made Hoffman rich nor improved his health, it gave him a unique opportunity to leave his mark on that state's federal judiciary. His appointment in 1851 as the northern district's judge was the first and last judicial appointment he would receive; Hoffman could hardly have guessed that he would still be a California federal district judge forty years later. From the start of his judgeship until late in his career, Hoffman yearned for higher federal judicial office, believing that such elevation would give him the recognition his services deserved and would validate his judicial reputation. Toward the end of his life, as decades passed without higher appointment, Hoffman began to realize that his reputation would rest on his forty-year accumulation of decisions.

The judge that Hoffman became reflected, in part, his upbringing and personality. Hoffman's pride and sense of social status became part of his judicial persona. Nonetheless, his most significant judicial characteristics emerged once he confronted situations and circumstances that challenged him to behave judicially. His diligence and conscientiousness, his willingness to listen with an open mind to attorneys and claimants, and his determination to preserve the independence of his court all developed as he became entrenched in his position as a federal judge. Convinced that his court often provided the only hope for relief for litigants and believing that upholding the nation's honor and adhering to judicial due process were central obligations for a federal judge, Hoffman approached his task with a degree of self-sacrifice and hard work that belied his prejudgeship years. Gone were the traces of Hoffman's lackadaisical practice of law before coming to California.

His seriousness of purpose began as an effort to prove himself worthy of the judicial appointment and to establish his reputation. Those motives soon merged with a growing sense of the role that his court played as a national tribunal. The resolution of his early cases, dealing with shipboard brutality and the ill treatment of passengers, required both innovation and a strong assertion of national judicial authority. In those cases, as well as in the early commercial decisions and wage suits for sailors, the isolation of California enhanced Hoffman's understanding of the unique role his court played and the need to come up with novel solutions. Moreover, in the prosecution of filibustering expeditions and vigilante activity and in the vindication of the rights of the Chinese under the Constitution and treaties with China, Hoffman demonstrated that his role as a federal judge prompted him to subordinate many of his personal biases and prejudices.

Hoffman's political outlook also influenced his judgeship. Students of political culture have pointed out that broadly held beliefs and perceptions are often more helpful in understanding reactions and the range of options considered by individuals than they are in explaining specific behavior.[1] This seems particularly true in Hoffman's case. His conservative version of Whig, and later Republican, political culture is primarily helpful in understanding his judicial style and his reaction to people and events. Some political concerns—such as the preservation of the Union and the importance of the nation—were reflected in his belief that his court had a special role to play in maintaining the nation's commitments expressed in treaties. His lifelong attachment to his court and his fierce judicial independence also drew on a political tradition that revered institutions and viewed them as the only means of preserving a state of ordered liberty.

The circumstances under which issues came to Hoffman for resolution also influenced his judicial behavior. Hoffman's legal training and intellectual temperament did not dispose him to ignore or criticize precedent, much less to blaze new doctrinal law. Yet, to a significant degree, that is precisely what he did as a judge. The vulnerability of certain groups of litigants, such as passengers and sailors, and his obligation to monitor activities on the high seas influenced many of the most innovative decisions Hoffman rendered in admiralty cases.

Hoffman adopted a rigid, if not pompous, attitude in isolating his court's business from political influences or the appearance of politics. For Hoffman, politics was distinctly outside the province of the judicial process, and maintaining the appearance of neutrality was such an important goal that he never really considered himself "off the bench." This self-conscious distancing served its purpose well, even if it tended to isolate the judge from his fellows. Yet, when Hoffman believed that principle was involved, he was hardly reticent to engage in politics to defend his court or seek judicial promotion.

Hoffman's attitude of strict judicial independence and his commitment to offer federal justice to all who were legitimately before his court were reflected in a judicial style that lacked a political or even jurisprudential agenda. Unlike some judges who sought self-consciously to advance political objectives or to implement wide-ranging theories of law, Hoffman approached most disputes without the benefit of prior conceptualization. Obviously, he brought his own biases and political predilections into the courtroom, but Hoffman's most pervasive judicial characteristic was his contemplativeness.

This quality of reflection was a source of both compliment and complaint: compliment because Hoffman approached the development of facts and arguments of law with receptivity, and complaint because his reflections bordered on indecisiveness. If parties had confidence that they would get a full and fair hearing before Hoffman, his contemplativeness was less desirable when, as in the San Francisco pueblo case, they wanted a clear indication of how Hoffman would decide the issue. Indeed, Hoffman's earliest judicial opinions, as well as those almost four decades later, illustrate how he agonized over his decisions. The process of judging, for Hoffman, was very much a matter of sifting and weighing evidence, balancing legal arguments and authorities, and ultimately rendering decisions that lacked the absolute certainty that, for instance, marked Justice Stephen Field's opinions.

If Hoffman lacked Field's clarity of an internal vision of how the cases that came before him fit within a broad theoretical scheme, that hardly prevented Hoffman from exercising judicial creativity. The language of Hoffman's opinions, and his actions as a judge, provide a mixed picture that challenges the utility of debates over whether nineteenth-century judges were characterized primarily by formalism or by instrumentalism. A strong believer in precedent, Hoffman, in some of his decisions and opinions, declared in formalistic language that the law compelled him to reach a particular result and that he was merely the "discoverer" and not the "maker" of law. At other times, however, he showed tremendous desire and ingenuity (or what might be called "instrumentalism") in reaching results that he felt were just but that might be frustrated by a strict application of rules and procedures. Such efforts may be deemed an inherent discretion that all common-law judges enjoyed, but the issue is how free nineteenth-century judges felt to exercise such power. In Hoffman's case, his actions as well as his opinions exhibit a range of behavior that belies labeling him a formalist or instrumentalist. At different times he was more like one than the other, but at no time did he feel totally free from the constraints of precedent or totally dominated by prior decisions. Indeed, precedent was only one constraint that limited Hoffman's freedom of decision. Occasionally, his adherence to due process, his allegiance to the sources of law as he perceived them, or his pugnacious reaction to public pressure prompted him to declare that he had no choice and was "bound" to decide in certain ways.[2]

A discussion of who used Hoffman's court and with what effect brings into question scholarship suggesting that law and judges during the nineteenth century played an aggressive and important role in promoting business and commercial interests. Hoffman's tenure suggests that whatever predisposition judges might have had toward the promotion of commerce as a positive good, such an attitude hardly meant that law directly served as the handmaiden to nineteenth-century business or that business interests naturally prevailed in court. In Hoffman's case, his identification with large commercial interests was quite strong. Yet, in the early series of cases that pitted those commercial interests against private individuals, Hoffman consistently ruled against business. Moreover, these adverse rulings did not stop the business community from giving him strong support.

An analysis of Hoffman's commercial litigation indicates that his predictability and impartiality as a judge more than made up for his "anti-commercial" rulings. Far more important to businessmen and their legal advisors was Hoffman's dependability in offering a full hearing followed by clear and consistent rulings. Shipowners could live with adverse decisions—lost profits could be recouped by raising rates, and sea captains who exposed them to liability could be disciplined. What they could tolerate far less were judges who eschewed precedent and who frustrated business planning through their judicial unpredictability.

In fact, even in the tort cases before the district court, Hoffman's decisions demonstrate that he did not regard that branch of law as a means to subsidize business. Hoffman overcame the constraints of precedent with considerable doctrinal ingenuity to insure that injured ship passengers both had a forum for their suits and succeeded in winning judgments against the shipping interests. Moreover, he issued, extraordinarily early, one of the most considered dissents by a common-law judge against the fellow servant rule. That rule—which greatly narrowed the scope of liability of employers—would eventually be overturned after judges riddled it with exceptions in an effort to ameliorate its harsh effects. Hoffman not only registered an early objection to the rule but also questioned its very basis instead of simply suggesting exceptions to the doctrine. Still, his adherence to precedent—the hallmark of his predictability—prompted his reluctant application of the rule even as he demonstrated his independent cast of mind by questioning the logic behind the established law.

In the final analysis, to say that nineteenth-century judges supported commercial growth by rendering "pro-business" decisions may simply be stating a fact about the utility of some of those courts to many classes of litigants. For example, Hoffman's largest docket, admiralty, was overwhelmingly a "plaintiff's court." Plaintiffs prevailed whether they were businessmen, sailors, or ship passengers or whether the matter at hand was commercial or noncommercial.

If Hoffman's development as a judge and the utility of his court provide insights into federal trial courts of the nineteenth century, his experience as a trial judge is more broadly suggestive of the judicial process. It seems likely that beyond Hoffman's background, education, and attitudes, what significantly shaped him as a judge was the fact that he served as a trial judge. The physical presence of and direct interrelationships between parties—witnesses, lawyers, the jury (if any), and the judge—produced a profound difference in the judicial world inhabited by trial judges. The cast of characters—bully sea captains, distraught and injured passengers, wealthy steamship owners, and persistent Chinese immigrants—that came through Hoffman's court produced a vibrant pageantry of life in stark contrast to the more removed atmosphere of appellate arguments and briefs.

This contextual difference, however, went beyond sheer human drama. For trial court judges like Hoffman, the rules of law, public policy, or jurisprudence that became the reasoned basis of their judgments were invoked with the specific circumstances and problems of individual litigants fresh in mind. Traditional common-law judging may well have inclined judges to place "masks" on litigants and ignore human dimensions in favor of applying abstract conceptions of law, but it was far harder to do so when seated across from the aggrieved parties. Not only were trial judges often called on to decide guilt or innocence, but they daily found themselves weighing the probity of witnesses and evidence. Inevitably, the intellectual labors of trial judges were tied to the tempo and demands of people hard to ignore—the litigants before their courts.[3]

The potential for routine litigation was another institutional characteristic of trial courts that influenced Hoffman's judgeship. Invariably, routine cases are not appealed; they are resolved in the trial court or settled before trial. That is not to say that such cases filed in the northern district were unimportant. They were important, especially to the litigants involved and the wider community that relied on Hoffman's court as an effective and valuable forum to resolve disputes. Rather, although those cases validated the institutional worth of Hoffman's court to Californians, the cases lacked the intellectual challenges and wider influence of many cases that were appealed.

Hoffman dealt with the routine, and in retrospect it seems clear that Hoffman's significance as a judge rests as much on his commitment to and resolution of these ordinary cases as it does on his published opinions or extraordinary cases. In the course of hearing many thousands of litigants, Hoffman became deeply enmeshed in what might be called the mechanics of justice. His thorough engagement with the personalities appearing in his court, the procedural aspects of litigation, and the ongoing task of taking notes of witnesses' testimony and lawyers' arguments demanded a kind of attention from which appellate judges were largely immune. The repetitiveness of this activity tended to reinforce an appreciation of procedure and judicial process until these became an integral part of what Hoffman did as a judge. Spending the time that he did overseeing due process and providing procedural guarantees gave Hoffman a strong practical commitment to those judicial ideals. Ultimately, this commitment, internalized in the ongoing performance of his duties as a trial judge, occasionally brought him to decisions that ran directly counter to his personal beliefs and predilections.

It is naive to say that when Hoffman suppressed his racial prejudices or frustrated the economic interests of businessmen friends, he was just doing his job as a judge. Some might say that as a federal judge, Hoffman had no other choice in the Chinese cases but to act as he did. That ignores the fact that Justice Field himself suggested ways the exclusion acts could be interpreted so that Hoffman could reach results more in keeping with public sentiment. Hoffman's assertion that the Chinese were entitled to due process and constitutional rights may well be simply an example of what we expect of judges, but there were numerous judges who fell short of this ideal. The point is that it may be only part of the story to say that individuals of strong and upstanding character who became judges accounted for the judicial impartiality that existed in the nineteenth century. Although strength of character and adherence to judicial ideals certainly promoted such admirable behavior, we need to take into account the way in which the judicial process and the nature of trial judging influenced and molded imperfect men into better judges than they otherwise might have become.

Lastly, nineteenth-century trial judges such as Hoffman experienced an isolated judicial existence. Unlike the multijudge districts of today, nineteenth-century federal district courts were formed by a single judge. Judicial collegiality was largely limited to occasionally sitting with other judges to compose a higher court (the circuit courts) or to have their decisions reviewed by judicial superiors. Thus, in the absence of direct participation in a "court family," federal district judges of Hoffman's era tended naturally to identify with their own courts. Given this, Hoffman eventually subsumed his personal identity into the institution of the court over which he presided. Feeling himself the embodiment of the court, Hoffman perceived criticism or praise directed at the institution as measures of his personal capacity, dignity, and reputation. That close identification prompted Hoffman to understand his role as a federal judge in a way that stressed his independence. In the final analysis, Hoffman's repeated and often stubborn assertions of his judicial independence stemmed neither from innate intellectual self-confidence nor from a predisposition of his personality. Rather, his independence arose from a sense of judicial duty and role that developed in conjunction with his identification with the northern district court.

APPENDIX

TABLE 1. *Cases Filed in All Dockets, 1851–1891*

Docket	Number of Cases Filed	Percent of Total
Private Admiralty		
(Chinese habeas corpus)	7,080	37%
Criminal	2,937	16%
Private Admiralty	2,931	15%
Bankruptcy	2,598	14%
United States Admiralty	1,372	7%
Bond	1,147	6%
Common Law and Equity	486	3%
Private Land Grants	458	2%
Total	19,009	100%

SOURCE: Christian G. Fritz, "A Statistical Summary of Judicial Business: U.S. District Court, Northern District of California, 1851–1891" (MS, U.S. District Court, Northern District of California Archives, San Francisco, 1990).

Table 2 (which follows) represents 2,716 of 2,931 private admiralty cases (excluding miscellaneous and marine tort cases). Tables 3 and 4 represent 470 and 2,333, respectively, of the 2,937 criminal cases (excluding cases of violations of court process).

TABLE 2. *Private Admiralty, Disposition of Litigation, 1851–1891*

Litigants	Decree for Plaintiff	Decree for Defendant	Case Settled	Case Abandoned	Disposition Uncertain	Totals
Seamen*	332 (32%)	89 (9%)	472 (46%)	55 (5%)	87 (8%)	1,035
Businessmen[†]	565 (36%)	185 (12%)	613 (39%)	26 (2%)	167 (11%)	1,556
Passengers[††]	60 (48%)	25 (20%)	31 (24%)	2 (2%)	7 (6%)	125

* Libels for wages.
[†] Commercial litigation was defined to include the following categories of libels: breach of contract of affreightment, libel for supplies, bottomry bonds, money advanced, wharfage, possession, pilotage/towage, salvage, and collision.
[††] Libels for breach of passenger contract.

SOURCE: Christian G. Fritz, "A Statistical Summary of Judicial Business: U.S. District Court, Northern District of California, 1851–1891" (MS, U.S. District Court, Northern District of California Archives, San Francisco, 1990).

TABLE 3 · *Disposition of Crimes within Admiralty, 1851–1891*

Crimes within Admiralty	Acquittal	Conviction	Nolle Prosequi	Total
Beating (of sailors)	67 (34%)	94 (47%)	38 (19%)	199
Assault with dangerous weapon	16 (20%)	44 (54%)	21 (26%)	81
Mutiny (denying captain's authority)	14 (24%)	33 (57%)	11 (19%)	58
Cruel and unusual treatment (of sailors)	19 (43%)	17 (39%)	8 (18%)	44
Desertion	4 (13%)	12 (40%)	14 (47%)	30
Failure to go to sea	5 (24%)	15 (71%)	1 (5%)	21
Larceny/Conversion/Receiving stolen goods	0 (0%)	6 (40%)	9 (60%)	15
Manslaughter	6 (60%)	1 (10%)	3 (30%)	10
Murder	1 (17%)	1 (17%)	4 (67%)	6
Other	1 (17%)	0 (0%)	5 (83%)	6
TOTAL	133 (28%)	223 (47%)	114 (24%)	470 (100%)

SOURCE: Christian G. Fritz, "A Statistical Summary of Judicial Business: U.S. District Court, Northern District of California, 1851–1891" (MS, U.S. District Court, Northern District of California Archives, San Francisco, 1990).

TABLE 4. *Disposition of Crimes under Federal Statutes, 1851–1891*

A.

Maritime matters	Acquittal		Conviction		*Nolle prosequi*		Total
Excess number of passengers	2	(8%)	13	(54%)	9	(38%)	24
Fraudulent ship's registry	0	(0%)	2	(67%)	1	(33%)	3
Excessive steam pressure	1	(100%)	0	(0%)	0	(0%)	1
Other	0	(0%)	1	(100%)	0	(0%)	1
Total	3	(10%)	16	(55%)	10	(35%)	29

B.

Revenue matters	Acquittal		Conviction		*Nolle prosequi*		Total
Failure to pay business tax/license	106	(10%)	548	(51%)	412	(39%)	1,066
Illegal sale/distillation of liquor	9	(3%)	14	(5%)	249	(92%)	272
Smuggling opium	17	(12%)	90	(63%)	35	(25%)	142
Assessor's failure to make returns	1	(6%)	0	(0%)	16	(94%)	17
Fraudulent customs invoice	1	(11%)	0	(0%)	8	(89%)	9
False income returns	3	(33%)	1	(11%)	5	(56%)	9
Impersonating revenue agent	0	(0%)	3	(50%)	3	(50%)	6
Other	0	(0%)	1	(100%)	0	(0%)	1
Total	137	(9%)	657	(43%)	728	(48%)	1,522

TABLE 4. (*continued*)

C.

Violation of other federal statutes	Acquittal		Conviction		*Nolle prosequi*		Total
Sale of naturalization certificates	1	(—)	0	(0%)	200	(100%)*	313
Misuse/robbery of mails	22	(22%)	46	(45%)	34	(33%)	102
Counterfeiting	21	(22%)	55	(57%)	20	(21%)	96
False voter registration	11	(12%)	12	(13%)	71	(76%)	94
Selling liquor to Indians	12	(17%)	44	(62%)	15	(21%)	71
Cutting U.S. timber	2	(4%)	16	(33%)	31	(63%)	49
Other	3	(14%)	5	(23%)	14	(64%)	22
Chinese related[†]	10	(43%)	4	(17%)	9	(39%)	23
Breaking into federal buildings	1	(14%)	6	(86%)	0	(0%)	7
Violation of neutrality laws	1	(20%)	3	(60%)	1	(20%)	5
Total	84	(11%)	191	(24%)	395	(51%)	782

* An additional 112 cases involving naturalization certificates were transferred to the circuit court.

† Importation of prostitutes or false use of entry certificates.

SOURCE: Christian G. Fritz, "A Statistical Summary of Judicial Business: U.S. District Court, Northern District of California, 1851–1891" (MS, U.S. District Court, Northern District of California Archives, San Francisco, 1990).

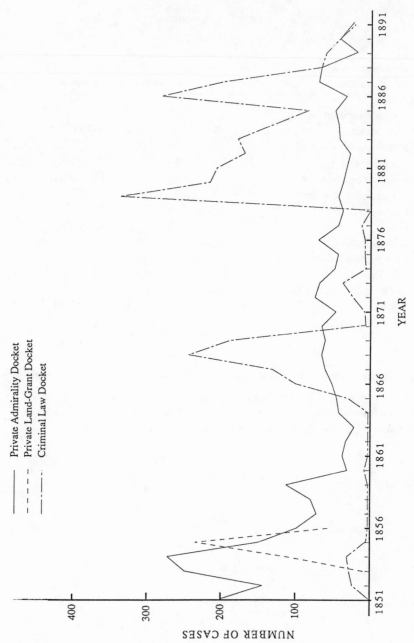

Figure 1. Admiralty, Criminal Law, and Private Land-Grant Cases, 1851–1891

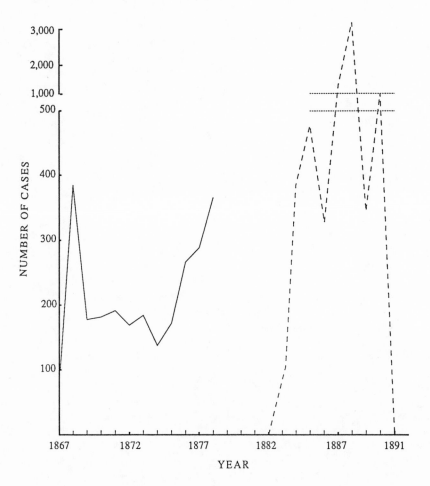

Figure 2. Bankruptcy and Chinese Habeas Corpus Cases, 1867–1891

ABBREVIATIONS

Ad. (Private) Cases	United States District Court, Northern District of California, Admiralty (Private) Case Files, Record Group 21, National Archives
Ad. (U.S.) Cases	United States District Court, Northern District of California, Admiralty (United States) Case Files, Record Group 21, National Archives
AGLR, RG 60, NA	Attorney General's Letters Received, California, 1846–70, Department of Justice, Record Group 60, National Archives
AP, RG 60, NA	Records Relating to the Appointment of Federal Judges, Marshals, and Attorneys, California, 1851–91, Department of Justice, Record Group 60, National Archives
Bank. Cases	United States District Court, Northern District of California, Bankruptcy Case Files, Record Group 21, National Archives
Bidwell Papers	John Bidwell Papers (Sutter Collection)
BL	Bancroft Library, University of California, Berkeley
Black Papers	Jeremiah S. Black Papers
Blair Family Papers	Montgomery Blair Family Papers
CCLC, RG 60, NA	Correspondence on California Land Claims, Department of Justice, Record Group 60, National Archives
CL and Equity Cases	United States District Court, Northern District of California, Common Law and Equity Case Files, Record Group 21, National Archives
Crim. Cases	United States District Court, Northern District of California, Criminal Case Files, Record Group 21, National Archives
CSL	California State Library, Sacramento
Cushing Papers	Caleb Cushing Papers
Deady, *Diary*	*Pharisee Among Philistines: The Diary of Judge Matthew P. Deady*, ed. Malcolm Clark, Jr., 2 vols. (Portland: Oregon Historical Society, 1975)
Deady Papers	Matthew P. Deady Papers
de la Guerra Papers	Pablo de la Guerra Papers
F. Cas.	*The Federal Cases Comprising Cases Argued and Determined in the Circuit and District Courts of the United States*, 30 vols. (St. Paul, Minn., 1894–97)
GLHS	Goshen Library and Historical Society, Goshen, New York

HL	Henry E. Huntington Library and Art Gallery, San Marino, California
HLC	Ogden Hoffman, *Reports of Land Cases Determined in the United States District Court for the Northern District of California* (San Francisco, 1862)
H. Op.	United States District Court, Northern District of California, Unreported Opinions of Ogden Hoffman, Northern District of California Archives, San Francisco
H. Papers	Hoffman Family Papers
HPB Papers	Halleck, Peachy, and Billings Papers
Hunt. Ms.	Huntington Manuscripts
LAR, M-873, RG 59, NA	Letters of Application and Recommendation During the Administrations of James K. Polk, Zachary Taylor, and Millard Fillmore, Microfilm Publication 873, Record Group 59, National Archives
LC	Library of Congress, Washington, D.C.
McCrackan Papers	John McCrackan Papers
Minutes	United States District Court, Northern District of California, *Minutes*, National Archives
NA	National Archives, Washington, D.C., and Regional Branch, San Bruno, California
NYHS	New York Historical Society, New York City
OHS	Oregon Historical Society, Portland
RG	Record Group
2 Sawyer 1	Page one of volume two of L.S.B. Sawyer, *Decisions of the Circuit and District Courts of the United States for the Ninth Circuit*, 14 vols. (San Francisco, 1873–90)
SCF, RG 60, NA	Source Chronology Files, Northern District of California, 1871–84, Department of Justice, Record Group 60, National Archives
SLR(AG), RG 206, NA	Letters Received from the Attorney General, 1822–99, Solicitor of the Treasury, Record Group 206, National Archives
SLR, RG 206, NA	Letters Received from United States Attorneys, Marshals, and Clerks of Court, California, 1851–98, Solicitor of the Treasury, Record Group 206, National Archives
Stearns Papers	Abel Stearns Papers
2 US STAT 1	Page one of volume two of *United States Statutes at Large* (Washington, D.C., 1874–)
VH Coll.	Villiers-Hatton Collection
Wills, *California Titles*	Henry E. Wills, *California Titles*, 19 vols.

NOTES

The source of direct quotations in the text is indicated by an asterisk (*) in the notes in the order they appear in the text. The case files of all the private land grants are in the Bancroft Library. They are cited by the case number assigned by the district court (northern or southern) followed by the case number assigned by the Board of Land Commissioners (for example, 100 N.D., 201 Bd., or 26 S.D., 321 Bd).

PREFACE

1. The title of Karl N. Llewellyn's classic work on the subject suggests this emphasis: *The Common Law Tradition: Deciding Appeals* (Boston: Little, Brown, 1960).

2. See Christian G. Fritz, "A Statistical Summary of Judicial Business: U.S. District Court, Northern District of California, 1851–1891" (manuscript, U.S. District Court, Northern District of California Archives, San Francisco, 1990).

3. In Hoffman's day, admiralty cases heard without a jury formed a good deal of the business of federal district courts. Thus, judges like Hoffman determined issues of both law and fact even more frequently than do their modern counterparts.

4. See in particular Morton J. Horwitz, *The Transformation of American Law, 1780–1860* (Cambridge: Harvard University Press, 1977) and James Willard Hurst, *Law and the Conditions of Freedom in the Nineteenth Century* (Madison: University of Wisconsin Press, 1956).

CHAPTER I

1. Ogden Hoffman, Jr., to Matthew P. Deady, July 11, 1878, Deady Papers, OHS*.

2. Margherita A. Hamm, *Famous Families of New York*, 2 vols. (New York: G. P. Putnam's Sons, 1902), 1:169–85; Eugene A. Hoffman, *Genealogy of the Hoffman Family* (New York, 1899); William W. Hoffman, *Eleven Generations of Hoffmans in New York* (New York: American Historical Co., 1957); Dumas Malone, ed., *Dictionary of American Biography* (New York: Charles Scribner's Sons, 1932), 9:114–15; Donald M. Roper, "The Elite of the New York Bar As Seen from the Bench: James Kent's Necrologies," *New York Historical Society Quarterly* 56 (1972): 227.

3. Dixon Ryan Fox, *The Decline of Aristocracy in the Politics of New York* (New York: Longmans, Green and Co., 1919), pp. 13–14*, 123–24, 128; Josiah Ogden Hoffman to Joseph C. Yates, Jan. 4, 1823, VH Coll., NYHS*.

4. Hamm, *Famous Families*, 1:181–82; Hoffman, *Genealogy*, pp. 279–81; L. B.

Proctor, *The Bench and Bar of New York* (New York, 1870), pp. 1–26; E. M. Ruttenber and L. H. Clark, *History of Orange County, New York* (Philadelphia, 1881); David McAdam, ed., *History of the Bench and Bar of New York*, 2 vols. (New York, 1897), 1:359–60.

5. Emily Burrall Hoffman to Bridget Wickham, March 25, 1827, Jan. 7, Feb. 17*, 1829, VH Coll., NYHS.

6. Ogden Hoffman, Sr., to Hoffman, Jr., May 20, 1833, and Hoffman, Sr., to Bridget Wickham, Oct. 2, 1823, Dec. 13, 1839, VH Coll., NYHS; Elizabeth Sharts, *Land O'Goshen* (Goshen, N.Y.: Bookmill, 1960). For a brief sketch of Samuel L. Southard, see Malone, *Dictionary of American Biography*, 17:411–12.

7. Hoffman, Sr., to William H. Seward, March 5, 1854, William H. Seward Papers, University of Rochester Library, Rochester, New York*; Edward Curtis to Millard Fillmore, Jan. 29, 1851, LAR, M-873, RG 59, NA*; David Walker Howe, *The Political Culture of the American Whigs* (Chicago: University of Chicago Press, 1979); Lee H. Warner, "The Silver Grays: New York State Conservative Whigs, 1846–1856," (Ph.D. diss., University of Wisconsin, 1971); Hendrik Booraem V, *The Formation of the Republican Party in New York* (New York: New York University Press, 1983).

8. Michael Holt, *The Political Crisis of the 1850s* (New York: Wiley and Sons, 1978).

9. Philip Hone, *The Diary of Philip Hone, 1828–1851*, ed. Allan Nevins, 2 vols. (1927; reprint, New York: Kraus Reprint Co., 1969), 1:61*, 283, 288–89, 304–5, 353–54, 457, 498–500, 504, 2:796, 830, 855, 906; Malone, *Dictionary of American Biography*, 9:116*; A. Oakey Hall, "Ogden Hoffman," *Green Bag* 5 (July 1893): 297–300.

10. Howe, *American Whigs*, pp. 23–42, 210–25.

11. On the elite social circles in which Hoffman traveled, see Edward Pessen, "The Wealthiest New Yorkers of the Jacksonian Era: A New List," *New York Historical Society Quarterly* 54 (1970): 145–72; Edward Pessen, "Philip Hone's Set: The Social World of the New York City Elite in the 'Age of Egalitarianism,'" *New York Historical Society Quarterly* 56 (1972): 285–308; Edward K. Spann, *The New Metropolis, New York City, 1840–1857* (New York: Columbia University Press, 1981), pp. 205–41.

12. George Templeton Strong, *The Diary of George Templeton Strong*, ed. Allan Nevins and Milton H. Thomas, 4 vols. (New York: Macmillan Co., 1952), 2:269*; Joseph Hodges Choate to his mother, May 4, 1856, in Edward S. Martin, *Life of Joseph Hodges Choate* (New York: Scribner's, 1920), p. 186*.

13. Hone, *Diary*, 2:526*; Hoffman, Sr., to Hoffman, Jr., June 27, 1842, H. Papers, GLHS*; Hoffman, Sr., to Edward Curtis, March 8, Nov. 28, Dec. 12, 1843, Misc. Legal Papers, and Virginia Southard Hoffman to Bridget Wickham, March 6, 1847*, VH Coll., NYHS.

14. Hoffman, Sr., to Thomas Ewing, March 31, 1849, LAR, M-873, RG 59, NA*.

15. Howe, *American Whigs*, p. 47*.

16. Hoffman, Sr., to William H. Seward, Jan. 11, 1854, William H. Seward Papers*, and Hoffman, Sr., to Thurlow Weed, April 5, 1855, Thurlow Weed Papers*, University of Rochester Library, Rochester, New York.

17. Strong, *Diary*, 2:269; Charles King to Hamilton Fish, May 9, 1856, Hamilton Fish Papers, LC*; Hall, "Ogden Hoffman," p. 300*.

18. Hall, "Ogden Hoffman," p. 297*. On Charles Fenno, see Malone, *Dictionary of American Biography*, 9:110–11.

19. Hoffman, Sr., to Hoffman, Jr., May 20, 1842, H. Papers, GLHS; Charles B. Hoffman to Bridget Wickham, July 29, 1847, VH Coll., NYHS.

20. For example, see Hoffman, Jr., to Bridget Wickham, March 6, Nov. 14, 1842, VH Coll., NYHS, and Wickham to Hoffman, Jr., Dec. 12, 1842, H. Papers, GLHS.

21. Hoffman, Sr., to Bridget Wickham, Dec. 13, 1839*, and Virginia Southard Hoffman to Wickham, n.d. [1842]*, VH Coll., NYHS.

22. Hoffman, Sr., to Bridget Wickham, Oct. 2, 1833, VH Coll., NYHS; Hoffman, Sr., to Hoffman, Jr., May 13, 1842*, and Virginia Southard Hoffman to Charles B. Hoffman, March 23, 1851, H. Papers, GLHS.

23. Hoffman, Jr., to Bridget Wickham, March 17, 1842, and Charles B. Hoffman to Wickham, July 14 and 29, 1847, Dec. 19, 1848, VH Coll., NYHS.

24. R. Kent Newmyer, *Supreme Court Justice Joseph Story: Statesman of the Old Republic* (Chapel Hill: University of North Carolina Press, 1985), pp. 245–46*. See also Charles Warren, *History of the Harvard Law School and of the Early Legal Conditions in America*, 3 vols. (New York: Lewis Publishing Co., 1908), 2:13.

25. Newmyer, *Story*, p. 258*. For the program of legal studies at Harvard during the Story-Greenleaf period, see Newmyer, *Story*, pp. 237–70.

26. Quoted in ibid., p. 266.

27. Hoffman, Sr., to Hoffman, Jr., May 13, 1842, H. Papers, GHLS*. On legal training in this period, see Maxwell Bloomfield, *American Lawyers in a Changing Society, 1776–1876* (Cambridge: Harvard University Press, 1976), and Anton-Hermann Chroust, *The Rise of the Legal Profession in America*, 2 vols. (Norman: University of Oklahoma Press, 1965), vol. 2.

28. Hoffman, Sr., to Hoffman, Jr., Nov. 10, 1842, H. Papers, GLHS*; Hoffman, Jr., to Bridget Wickham, March 17, May 2, Nov. 14, 1842, VH Coll., NYHS.

29. Charles B. Hoffman to Bridget Wickham, July 29, 1847, VH Coll., NYHS.

30. Daniel Lord to Daniel Webster, Jan. 27, 1851*; James A. Dorr to William H. Aspinwall, Jan. 25, 1851; Benjamin D. Silliman to Aspinwall, Jan. 25, 1851; all in LAR, M-873, RG 59, NA.

31. Edward Curtis to Millard Fillmore, Jan. 29, 1851, LAR, M-873, RG 59, NA; Strong, *Diary*, 2:7.

32. Charles H. Harvey to his family, May 28, 1850, Charles H. Harvey Papers, Box 4, LC*.

33. James Rogers to his parents, April 20, 1850, reprinted in Marie Rogers Vail, ed., "Gold Rush Letters of the Reverend James Rogers," *New York Historical Society*

Quarterly 44 (1960): 279*; Hubert H. Bancroft, *History of California*, 7 vols. (1886–90; reprint, Santa Barbara: Walter Hebberd, 1963), 6:239*; John McCrackan to his family, May 8, 1850, McCrackan Papers, BL*.

On life in San Francisco at the time Hoffman arrived, see Bancroft, *History of California*, 6:221–50; J. S. Holliday, *The World Rushed In: The California Gold Rush Experience* (New York: Simon and Schuster, 1981), pp. 297–303, 411–14; and Julia Cooley Altrocchi, *The Spectacular San Franciscans* (New York: Dutton, 1949), pp. 53–62.

34. Joseph B. Crockett to his wife, Nov. 30, 1852, May 20, 1857, Joseph B. Crockett Papers, BL; Oscar L. Shafter, *Life, Diary and Letters of Oscar L. Shafter*, ed. Flora Haines Loughead (San Francisco: Blair-Murdock Co., 1915), pp. 121–22*; William Higby to his father, May 14, 1851, William Higby Papers, Box 218, CSL*; Henry Eno, *Twenty Years on the Pacific Slope: Letters of Henry Eno from California and Nevada, 1848–1871*, ed. W. Turrentine Jackson (New Haven: Yale University Press, 1965), p. 103*.

35. On the ambivalent feelings and disillusionment generated by the gold-rush experience in San Francisco, see Gunther Barth, *Instant Cities, Urbanization and the Rise of San Francisco and Denver* (New York: Oxford University Press, 1975), pp. 128–54; and Kevin Starr, *Americans and the California Dream, 1850–1915* (New York: Oxford University Press, 1973), pp. 49–68. For reactions to California, see John McCrackan to his sisters Lottie and Mary, Feb. 27, 1850, McCrackan Papers, BL*, and Stephen J. Field, *Personal Reminiscences of Early Days in California with Other Sketches* (privately printed, 1880), pp. 12–13*.

36. Hoffman, Jr., to F. H. Delano, May 28, 1850, Delano Family Papers, Box 10, Franklin D. Roosevelt Library, Hyde Park, New York*; R. L. Watson to Wickham Hoffman, May 9, 1850, H. Papers, GLHS*.

37. Joseph Glover Baldwin, *The Flush Times of California*, ed. Richard E. Amacher and George W. Polhemus (Athens: University of Georgia Press, 1966), p. 57*; John McCrackan to his family, Nov. 22, 1850*, Nov. 13, 1852*, McCrackan Papers, BL.

38. Oscar L. Shafter to his wife, Nov. 23, 1854, and Shafter to his father, Jan. 1, 1856, Nov., 1857, in Shafter, *Diary and Letters*, pp. 59–60, 176, 190; Joseph B. Crockett to his wife, Dec. 15, 1852, Jan. 14, April 8 and 30, 1853, Joseph B. Crockett Papers, BL; Henry H. Haight, July 13, 1851, Henry H. Haight Papers, HL; John McCrackan to his family, June 16, Sept. 12, 1850, and McCrackan to his sister Lottie, Nov. 11, 1850, Nov. 8, 1851, Jan. 10, March 13*, 1853, McCrackan Papers, BL.

39. For pressures on gentlemen lawyers, see Ernest De Massey, *Journal of Ernest De Massey*, trans. Maguerite Eyer Wilbur (San Francisco: California Historical Society, 1927), p. 25.

40. John McCrackan to his mother, May 24, 1850, McCrackan Papers, BL*; Joseph B. Crockett to his wife, Dec. 15, 1853, Joseph B. Crockett Papers, BL*.

41. James Rogers to his parents, April 15, 1850, in Vail, "Gold Rush Letters," p. 278*; John McCrackan to his family, May 8, 1850, May 13, 1851, McCrackan Papers, BL; Henry H. Haight to Fletcher M. Haight, Sept. 15, 1853, Henry H. Haight Papers, HL.

42. Joseph B. Crockett to his wife, May 20, 1857, Joseph B. Crockett Papers, BL; Cornelius Cole, *Memoirs of Cornelius Cole* (New York: McLoughlin Bros., 1908), p. 79*; John McCrackan to his sister Lottie, Nov. 24, 1850, McCrackan Papers, BL*.

43. John McCrackan to his sister Lottie, April 16, 1850*, McCrackan Papers, BL; J. D. Borthwick, *The Gold Hunters: A First-Hand Picture of Life in California Mining Camps in the Early Fifties* (New York: Macmillan Co., 1917), p. 76*; Hoffman, Jr., to Matthew P. Deady, March 8, 1883, Deady Papers, OHS* and McCrackan to his sister Mary, Jan. 13, 1852*, McCrackan Papers, BL*.

44. Oscar L. Shafter to James M. Shafter, June 16, 1855, in Shafter, *Diary and Letters*, p. 152; Hoffman, Jr., to F. H. Delano, May 28*, July 31, 1850, Delano Family Papers, Box 10, Franklin D. Roosevelt Library, Hyde Park, New York.

45. Sept. 1850, passim, William Higby Papers, Box 218, CSL; Annis Merrill, "Statement of Recollections on Early Days in San Francisco" (dictation for Bancroft Library, 1878); Eugene Casserly to Pablo de la Guerra, July 28, 1851, de la Guerra Papers, HL; Hamilton Fish to Hoffman, Sr., March 11 and 30, 1850, Hamilton Fish Papers, LC; Joseph B. Crockett to his wife, Nov. 30, 1852, Joseph B. Crockett Papers, BL.

46. William Higby to his father, Dec. 31, 1850, William Higby Papers, Box 218, CSL*; Joseph B. Crockett to his wife, April 22, 1853, Joseph B. Crockett Papers, BL*; John McCrackan to his sister Mary, Feb. 27, 1850, McCrackan Papers, BL*; Oscar L. Shafter to his father, Dec. 14, 1854, in Shafter, *Diary and Letters*, pp. 67–68*. See also Montgomery Blair to his wife, April 2, 1854, Blair Family Papers, Box 41, LC.

The "paltry fees" collected by nineteenth-century New Hampshire lawyers suggest that the contrast of legal fees in San Francisco was as dramatic as correspondents indicated. See John P. Reid, *Chief Justice: The Judicial World of Charles Doe* (Cambridge: Harvard University Press, 1967), pp. 56–57.

47. Hoffman, Jr., to F. H. Delano, July 31, 1850, Delano Family Papers, Box 10, Franklin D. Roosevelt Library, Hyde Park, New York*. On San Francisco's unstable early economy, see Peter R. Decker, *Fortunes and Failures: White Collar Mobility in Nineteenth-Century San Francisco* (Cambridge: Harvard University Press, 1978), and Roger Lotchin, *San Francisco, 1846–1856: From Hamlet to City* (New York: Oxford University Press, 1974), pp. 45–82.

48. Oscar L. Shafter to his father, March 19, 1860, in Shafter, *Diary and Letters*, p. 203*; Decker, *Fortunes and Failures*, pp. 32–59.

49. Hoffman, Jr., to Hoffman, Sr., Feb. 15, 1851, owned by Henry H. Clifford*; *In Memoriam Ogden Hoffman* [San Francisco, 1891], p. 9*.

50. Kermit L. Hall, *The Politics of Justice: Lower Federal Judicial Selection and the Second Party System, 1829–1861* (Lincoln: University of Nebraska Press, 1979), p. 156*.

51. Hall, *Politics of Justice*; Kermit L. Hall, "Mere Party and the Magic Mirror: California's First Lower Federal Judicial Appointments," *Hastings Law Journal* 32 (1981): 819–37*.

52. Hall, "Mere Party and the Magic Mirror," pp. 824–27; Daniel Webster to Millard Fillmore, Oct. 29, 1850, Millard Fillmore Papers, microfilm edition, Reel 22, frames 379–81, Buffalo and Erie County Historical Society, Buffalo, New York; U.S. Cong., *Ex. Jour.* (1850), 8:267.

53. James M. Crane to Millard Fillmore, Aug. 31, 1850, Millard Fillmore Papers, Buffalo and Erie County Historical Society, Buffalo, New York; Truman Smith to John Wilson, Jan. 5, 1851, John Wilson Papers, Box 2, BL; William M. Gwin et al. to Fillmore, Oct. 1, 1850, John Lorimer Graham Papers, HL*; Hall, "Mere Party and the Magic Mirror," p. 830*.

54. Albert H. Dorr to John V. Plume, Jan. 25, 1851; Benjamin D. Silliman to William H. Aspinwall, Jan. 25, 1851; Daniel Lord to Daniel Webster, Jan. 27, 1851; William H. Seward to Webster, Jan. 27, 1851; all in LAR, M-873, RG 59, NA; Marshal O. Roberts et al. to Millard Fillmore, Dec. 14, 1850*, and Aspinwall to Fillmore, Dec. 20, 1850, Millard Fillmore Papers, Buffalo and Erie County Historical Society, Buffalo, New York.

55. Albert H. Dorr to John V. Plume, Jan. 25, 1851, and Plume to Daniel Webster, Jan. 27, 1851, LAR, M-873, RG 59, NA.

56. Benjamin D. Silliman to William H. Aspinwall, Jan. 25, 1851; John V. Plume to Daniel Webster, Jan. 27, 1851; Edward Curtis to Millard Fillmore, Jan. 29, 1851; all in LAR, M-873, RG 59, NA; Daniel Webster to Hoffman, Jr., Feb. 3, 1851, reprinted in Charles R. Boden, "Unpublished Letters from the Files of the Late Ogden Hoffman," *San Francisco Bar* 2 (1938): 6*.

57. Hall, "Mere Party and the Magic Mirror," pp. 832–33; John McCrackan to his sister Lottie, March 24, 1851, McCrackan Papers, BL*; U.S. Cong., Senate *Ex. Jour.* (1850), 8:287, 298.

58. Richard Maxwell Brown, "Violence and Vigilantism in American History," in Lawrence M. Friedman and Harry N. Scheiber, eds., *American Law and the Constitutional Order*, enl. ed. (Cambridge: Harvard University Press, 1988), p. 180. On the vigilante movements in San Francisco generally, see Mary Floyd Williams, *History of the San Francisco Committee of Vigilance of 1851* (1921; reprint, New York: DaCapo Press, 1969); Hubert H. Bancroft, *Popular Tribunals*, 2 vols. (San Francisco, 1887); and Robert M. Senkewicz, *Vigilantes in Gold Rush San Francisco* (Stanford: Stanford University Press, 1985).

59. *Alta California* (San Francisco), March 6, 1851*; Howe, *American Whigs*, pp. 123–49, 181.

For examples of the strong sympathy many leading San Francisco lawyers expressed for the vigilance movements, see Henry H. Haight to Samuel Haight,

Aug. 29, 1851, Henry H. Haight Papers, HL; Speech of Frederic Billings, n.d., HPB Papers, Box 7, BL; Henry Eno to his brother William, Oct. 3, 1856, in Eno, *Twenty Years*, p. 125; and Oscar L. Shafter to his father, Sept. 1, 1856, in Shafter, *Diary and Letters*, p. 181.

60. John McCrackan to his sister Lottie, March 24, 1851, McCrackan Papers, BL*.

61. Hoffman, Jr., to F. H. Delano, July 31, 1850, Delano Family Papers, Box 10, Franklin D. Roosevelt Library, Hyde Park, New York; Hoffman, Jr., to Hoffman, Sr., April 1, 1851, VH Coll., NYHS; John Keteltas Hackett to Hoffman, Jr., Dec. 13, 1857, Hackett Letterbooks, Vol. 1, New York Public Library, New York City; Edwin M. Stanton to Hoffman, Jr., April 1859*, and John J. Astor to Hoffman, Jr., Nov. 7, 1861, Hunt. Ms., HL.

62. *San Francisco Call*, May 31, 1883.

63. Lorenzo Sawyer to Matthew P. Deady, April 28, July 7, 1875, Deady Papers, OHS.

64. Hoffman to Matthew P. Deady, Feb. 23, 1869, Deady Papers, OHS*. (Since Hoffman, Sr., died in 1855, all future references to Hoffman pertain to the California judge unless otherwise indicated.)

65. *Alta California*, Aug. 11, 1852; Holt, *Political Crisis*, pp. 209–15; Joseph H. Parks, *John Bell of Tennessee* (Baton Rouge: Louisiana State University Press, 1950); Peyton Hurt, "The Rise and Fall of the 'Know Nothings' in California," *California Historical Society Quarterly* 9 (1930): 16–49, 99–119.

66. Hoffman to Alexander M. Boteler, Sept. 11, 1860, William R. Perkins Library, Duke University, Durham, North Carolina*; Morton Keller, *Affairs of State: Public Life in Late Nineteenth Century America* (Cambridge: Harvard University Press, 1977), pp. 238–83; William A. Bullough, *The Blind Boss and His City: Christopher Augustine Buckley and Nineteenth-Century San Francisco* (Berkeley: University of California Press, 1979).

67. Hoffman to Archibald C. Peachy, Jan. 10, 1853, quoted in introduction to Ogden Hoffman, *Reports of Land Cases Determined in the United States District Court for the Northern District of California* (1862; reprint, n.p.: Yosemite Collections, 1975)*. The letter is incorrectly given the date Jan. 10, 1858. Statement of William Barber, *In Memoriam Ogden Hoffman*, p. 21*.

68. *Wave* 7 (Aug. 29, 1891) No. 17*.

69. J. Ross Browne, "The Coast Rangers," *Harper's New Monthly Magazine* 23 and 24 (1861–62). The articles were reprinted in J. Ross Browne, *The Coast Rangers* (Balboa, Calif.: Paisano Press, 1959), pp. 45–50*.

70. See chapter 6.

71. *Deed Books*, City of San Francisco, Recorder's Office, 16:580, 20:193, 21:426, 29:352, 31:7, 37:572, 91:550.

72. Hoffman to Matthew P. Deady, Nov. 16, 1871, Deady Papers, OHS*; San Francisco, Board of Supervisors, *Municipal Reports* (San Francisco, 1872–91).

73. Hoffman, Jr., to Hoffman, Sr., April 1, 1851, VH Coll., NYHS; Hoffman to

Matthew P. Deady, Jan. 14, April 8, 1870, Dec. 12, 1885, Deady Papers, OHS; U.S. Cong., *Memorial to the United States Senate,* 32d Cong., 1st sess., 1851, S. Misc. Doc. 5; U.S. Cong., *Resolution of the Legislature of California in Favor of Increasing the Salaries of the United States Judges for that State,* 32d Cong., 1st sess., 1851, S. Misc. Doc. 57. See also Act of June 14, 1860, 12 US STAT 33, Sec. 7; Lorenzo Sawyer to Deady, July 22, 1875, Deady Papers, OHS*.

That Hoffman owned no real property at the time of his death can be inferred from the fact that there is no record of any decree of distribution for his estate within ten years of his death. See *General Deed Books,* City of San Francisco, Recorder's Office, from March 10, 1891 (vol. 149) to Oct. 5, 1901 (vol. 205).

CHAPTER 2

1. Felix Frankfurter and James M. Landis, *The Business of the Supreme Court: A Study in the Federal Judicial System* (New York: Macmillan Co., 1927), pp. 4–102; Act of April 10, 1869, 16 US STAT 44.

2. An Act of June 1, 1872, 17 US STAT 196, provided that whenever a difference of opinion existed among judges sitting as a circuit court, "the opinion of the presiding justice or presiding judge" should prevail and be "considered the opinion of the court for the time being." But on proper certification the case could then be taken to the Supreme Court on a writ of error or an appeal. See Act of June 1, 1872, Sec. 1.

Even though few nationwide changes in the structure of the federal judiciary occurred during Hoffman's judgeship, such changes (and potentially new judgeships) were part of an ongoing debate over judicial reform of federal courts throughout the 1870s and 1880s. Frankfurter and Landis, *Business of the Supreme Court,* pp. 77–102.

3. Quoted in Charles W. McCurdy, "Stephen J. Field and the American Judicial Tradition," *The Fields and the Law* (San Francisco and New York: Northern District Historical Society and Federal Bar Council, 1986), p. 8*; Stephen Field to Matthew P. Deady, May 15, 1884, Deady Papers, OHS*.

4. Hoffman, Jr., to Hoffman, Sr., April 1, 1851, VH Coll., NYHS; *Cong. Globe,* 33d Cong., 2d sess., 1852, pp. 195, 233, 242.

5. *San Francisco Herald,* Feb. 5 and 23, and March 10, 18*, and 29, 1855.

6. *San Francisco Herald,* March 29, 1855; *Alta California,* March 30, 1855; *San Francisco Chronicle,* March 29, 1855; Thomas Gamble, "The McAllisters, 1758–1888" (articles printed in the *Savannah Morning News,* Oct. 5, Nov. 23 and 30, Dec. 14 and 28, 1930, Jan. 4, 11, and 25, 1931, collected in the BL); John McCrackan to his sister Lottie, March 30, 1851, McCrackan Papers, BL*; Hoffman, Jr., to Hoffman, Sr., Dec. 4, 1855, H. Papers, GLHS; Hoffman, Sr., to Hamilton Fish, Nov. 7, 1850, Hamilton Fish Papers, LC.

7. Reverdy Johnson to Hoffman, Jan. 30, 1862, Hunt. Ms., HL*; *San Francisco Examiner,* Aug. 10, 1891.

8. *Dred Scott* v. *Sanford*, 60 U.S. 393 (1857); Henry J. Abraham, *Justices and Presidents: A Political History of Appointments to the Supreme Court*, 2d ed. New York: Oxford University Press, 1985), p. 115; David M. Silver, *Lincoln's Supreme Court* (Urbana: University of Illinois Press, 1956), pp. 83–93; Thompson Campbell to Abraham Lincoln, Feb. 19, 1862, AP, RG 60, NA*; Theodore H. Hittell, *History of California*, 4 vols. (San Francisco: 1885–97), 4:338*; Carl Brent Swisher, *Stephen J. Field* (1930; reprint, Hamden, Conn.: Archon Books, 1963), pp. 116–17; Leland Stanford to William H. Seward, April 10, 1862, AP, RG 60, NA; *Alta California*, Feb. 25, 1863.

9. William Rabe to Abraham Lincoln, Jan. 8, 1862, AP, RG 60, NA; John W. Dwinelle to James Warren Nye, Dec. 31, 1862, James Warren Nye Papers, Box 1, Nevada State Archives, Carson City.

10. *San Francisco Bulletin*, Feb. 24, 1863*.

11. Stephen Field, *Personal Reminiscences of Early Days in California, with Other Sketches* (privately printed, 1880), p. 131*; *Alta California*, Feb. 27, 1863; Letter from Field, Oct. 1897, 168 U.S. 715 (1897)*.

12. Field to Deady, Feb. 14, 1871, Deady Papers, OHS.

13. *U.S.* v. *Greathouse*, 26 F. Cas. 18 (C.C.N.D.Cal. 1863).

14. Field to Deady, March 16, 1874, Deady Papers, OHS*.

15. McCurdy, *The Fields and the Law*, pp. 5* and 8*.

16. Field's political interests and involvements are amply documented in Swisher, *Stephen J. Field* and R. Hal Williams, *The Democratic Party and California Politics, 1880–1896* (Stanford: Stanford University Press, 1973).

17. For example, see Field to Deady, April 8, 1885, Deady Papers, OHS, and Hoffman to Daniel T. Sullivan, Feb. 19, 1885*; Hoffman to Field, Dec. 8, 1885*; Lorenzo Sawyer to Field, Dec. 9, 1885*; all in AP, RG 60, NA.

18. Deady, *Diary*, for instances of Deady's practice of law while on the bench. For monetary gifts and loans he never paid back, see *Diary* entries for Feb. 3, 1872, April 26, 1873, May 5, 1873, Sept. 16, 1876, Sept. 12, 1880, Jan. 23 and Feb. 26, 1881, and Feb. 8, 1882. See also Deady, *Diary*, 2: Appendix A. For Deady's and Field's use of railroad passes, see *Diary* entries for July 2, 1881 and Feb. 8, 1882 and Field to Deady, April 15, 1881, Deady Papers, OHS.

Despite such favors and his willingness to write decisions favoring the railroads, Field made it clear that he felt no obligation to them. See J. E. Gates to Field, April 3, 1891, and Field to Gates, April 4, 1891, Stephen J. Field Papers, BL; Deady, *Diary*, entry for March 21, 1872, 1:72*.

19. Cornelius Cole, *Memoirs of Cornelius Cole: Ex-Senator of the United States from California* (New York: McLoughlin Brothers, 1908), p. 115*; Field to Deady, April 3, 1890, Deady Papers, OHS*.

20. On Deady and his relationship with Field, see Deady Papers and Deady, *Diary*, 1:xxxi–xxxvii.

21. Matthew G. Upton to Deady, April 15, 1873*; George E. Whitney to Deady, Jan. 20, 1889; Field to Deady, Jan. 30, Feb. 9, 1869; all in Deady Papers, OHS.

22. William T. Wallace to Deady, Feb. 3, 1869, ibid.*

23. Act of Feb. 27, 1865, 13 US STAT 440; Field to Deady, March 1, 1865, Deady Papers, OHS; Hoffman to William P. Fessenden, March 2, 1864, Bechtel Collection, California Historical Society, San Francisco*; George E. Whitney to Deady, Jan. 6, 1868, Feb. 4, Dec. 29, 1869, and Hoffman to Deady, Nov. 18, Dec. 21, 1869, Deady Papers, OHS; *San Francisco Examiner*, Dec. 23, 1869.

24. Deady, *Diary*, 1: xxxvi; Field to Deady, Sept. 17, 1866, Aug. 30, 1867, and Jan. 30, 1869*, Deady Papers, OHS.

25. Act of April 10, 1869, 16 US STAT 44.

26. For Sawyer's educational and legal background, see J. Edward Johnson, *History of the Supreme Court Justices of California, 1850–1863*, 2 vols. (San Francisco: Bender-Moss Co., 1963), 1:95–97.

For rumors of his consideration for a cabinet appointment, see *San Francisco Herald*, May 20, 1869 and *San Francisco Bulletin*, Dec. 9, 1869.

27. Hoffman to Deady, Feb. 23*, April 5*, 1869, Deady Papers, OHS.

28. John T. Doyle to William T. Sherman, April 23, 1869, John T. Doyle Letterbooks, vol. 21, BL*; Nathan Porter to Deady, May 27, 1869, Deady Papers, OHS*.

29. Hamilton Fish to Hoffman, Sept. 7, 1869, William T. Sherman Papers, LC; Hoffman to Fish, Sept. 10, 1869, Hamilton Fish Papers, LC*.

30. George E. Whitney to Deady, May 25, 1869*, Deady Papers, OHS.

31. *McCall* v. *McDowell*, 15 F. Cas. 1235 (C.C.D.Ca. 1867); George H. Williams to Deady, Nov. 8, 1869; Henry J. Corbett to Deady, Dec. 1, 1869; Field to George E. Whitney, Dec. 16, 1869; Hoffman to Deady, Dec. 22, 1869*, Jan. 14, 1870; all in Deady Papers, OHS; Hoffman to Fish, March 23, 1870, Hamilton Fish Papers, LC.

32. Henry W. Corbett to Deady, Nov. 15, 1869*, and clipping enclosed in letter from Corbett to Deady, Jan. 2, 1870*, Deady Papers, OHS.

33. Field to George E. Whitney, Dec. 16, 1869, Deady Papers, OHS*; Act of April 10, 1869, 16 US STAT 44, Sec. 3.

34. E. W. McGraw to Deady, Feb. 8, 1870; Sawyer to Deady, Dec. 13, 1869; Hoffman to Deady, Feb. 3, 1869; Dec. 13, 1876, Nov. 26, 1883; all in Deady Papers, OHS.

35. Henry W. Corbett to Deady, April 18, 1869, Deady Papers, OHS*.

36. Samuel F. Butterworth to Deady, Jan. 10, 1870*, and Hoffman to Deady, Jan. 14, 1870*, Deady Papers, OHS; Hoffman to Fish, March 23, 1870, Hamilton Fish Papers, LC*.

37. *Alta California*, Jan. 9 and 11, 1870; *San Francisco Bulletin*, Jan. 10, 1870.

38. Matthew G. Upton to Deady, April 15, 1873*, Deady Papers, OHS; *San Francisco Bulletin*, Dec. 9, 1869*; U.S. Civil Service Commission, *Official Register, 1869* (Washington, D.C., 1870), pp. 300–305; Conkling to Hoffman, Dec. 18, 1869, Hunt. Ms., HL*.

39. Sawyer to Deady, March 14, 1872*, April 28, 1876, Oct. 22, 1879*, Sept. 7, 1881, Jan. 12, 1883, Deady Papers, OHS.

40. The following account of Hoffman's death and funeral draws from the follow-ing sources: Deady, *Diary*, 2:613; *San Francisco Bulletin*, Aug. 10 and 11, 1891; *San Francisco Call*, Aug. 10, 11, and 12, 1891; *San Francisco Chronicle*, Aug. 10, 11, and 12, 1891; *Oakland Enquirer*, Aug. 11, 1891; *San Francisco Examiner*, Aug. 10 and 11, 1891; *San Francisco Daily Report*, Aug. 10 and 11, 1891; *San Francisco Evening Post*, Aug. 15, 1891; *Wave* 7 (July 18, 1891) No. 11, (Aug. 15, 1891) No. 15, (Aug. 22, 1891) No. 16, and (Aug. 29, 1891) No. 17; *In Memoriam Ogden Hoffman*; *Proceedings in the District Court of the United States, District of California* (San Francisco, 1893).

41. *Proceedings in the District Court*, p. 11*.

42. *San Francisco Chronicle*, Aug. 10, 1891*.

43. *Wave* 7 (Aug. 22, 1891) No. 16*.

44. Hoffman to Deady, May 20, 1889, Deady Papers, OHS*.

CHAPTER 3

1. Elbridge Gerry Hall to his wife, June 30, 1849, Elbridge Gerry Hall Papers, BL*; James Rogers to his parents, April 20, 1850, in Vail, "Gold Rush Letters," p. 279*; Decker, *Fortunes and Failures*, p. 30.

For a general definition of the law of admiralty, see Grant Gilmore and Charles L. Black, *The Law of Admiralty*, 2d ed. (Mineola, N.Y.: Foundation Press, 1975), p. 1. For Hoffman's admiralty docket, see Appendix, table 2.

2. John McCrackan to his sister Lottie, Feb. 27*, Oct. 18*, 1850, McCrackan Papers, BL; U.S. Const., art. III, sec. 2.

3. The action *in rem* in English and American law is traced in F. L. Wiswall, *The Development of Admiralty Jurisdiction and Practice Since 1800* (Cambridge: Cambridge University Press, 1970), pp. 155–208.

4. Gilmore and Black, *Law of Admiralty*, pp. 586–89; Paul M. Hebert, "The Origins and Nature of Maritime Liens," *Tulane Law Review* 4 (1930): 381–408.

5. See George Rogers Taylor, *The Transportation Revolution, 1815–1860* (New York: Rinehart, 1951), pp. 32–73, 104–31; Louis C. Hunter, *Steamboats on the West-ern Rivers* (Cambridge: Harvard University Press, 1949), pp. 3–60, 481–519; Carter Goodrich, ed., *Canals and American Economic Development* (New York: Columbia University Press, 1961); Harry N. Scheiber, *Ohio Canal Era: A Case Study of Govern-ment and the Economy, 1820–1861* (Athens: Ohio University Press, 1969), pp. 185–268, 318–52.

6. *Glass* v. *The Sloop Betsey* 3 U.S. 6 (1794); Walter Colton, *Three Years in California* (New York, 1850), pp. 81, 194*.

7. Merrill, "Statement of Recollections," pp. 2–7; Cole, *Memoirs*, p. 82; William Wirt Blume, "California Courts in Historical Perspective," *Hastings Law Journal* 22 (1970): 125–35; *Alta California*, June 7, 1850; case papers for *Bailey* v. *Steamer "New World,"* Halleck, Peachy, and Billings Collection, Box 2, HL.

8. *DeLovio* v. *Boit*, 7 F. Cas. 418 (C.C.D.Mass. 1815)*; *Propeller Genesse Chief* v. *Fitzhugh*, 53 U.S. 443 (1852); *Allen* v. *Newberry*, 62 U.S. 244 (1859).

For the growth of American admiralty jurisdiction, see Note, "From Judicial Grant to Legislative Power: The Admiralty Clause in the Nineteenth Century," *Harvard Law Review*, 67 (1954): 1214–37; David W. Robertson, *Admiralty and Federalism* (Mineola, N.Y.: Foundation Press, 1970), pp. 104–15; and Milton Conover, "The Abandonment of the 'Tidewater' Concept of Admiralty Jurisdiction in the United States," *Oregon Law Review* 38 (1958): 34–53.

9. U.S. Const., art. III, sec. 2*; Act of Sept. 24, 1789, 1 US STAT 73, Sec. 9*; Charles L. Black, "Admiralty Jurisdiction: Critique and Suggestions," *Columbia Law Review* 50 (1950): 259, 263*; 47 U.S. 344 (1849) and 46 U.S. 440 (1848); Robertson, *Admiralty and Federalism*, pp. 123–28.

10. *The Moses Taylor*, 71 U.S. 411 (1867); *The Hine* v. *Trevor*, 71 U.S. 555 (1867).

11. Theodore Minis Etting, *The Admiralty Jurisdiction in America* (Philadelphia, 1879), pp. 83–84*; Alfred Conkling, *The Admiralty Jurisdiction, Law, and Practice of the Courts of the United States*, 2 vols. (Albany, 1857), 1:88–103; Theophilus Parsons, *A Treatise on Maritime Law*, 2 vols. (Boston, 1859), 2:522; Theophilus Parsons, *A Treatise on the Law of Shipping and the Law and Practice of Admiralty*, 2 vols. (Boston, 1869), 2:141–55. Even after Hoffman's court opened, state courts continued to hear *in rem* as well as *in personam* admiralty matters. See Gregory Yale Papers, Box 1, Fldr. 34, BL; Shafter, *Diary and Letters*, Feb. 6, 1855, p. 99; Ad. (Private) Cases [327], Dec. 14, 1852.

12. *The Hine* v. *Trevor*, 71 U.S. 555 at 561*.

13. "The Limits of the Exclusive Jurisdiction of Admiralty in the United States," *American Law Review* 3 (1869): 597*; Gordon M. Bakken, "Admiralty Law in Nineteenth-Century California," *Southern California Quarterly* 58 (1976): 499–514; Parsons, *Treatise on Maritime Law* (2d ed., 1869), 2:155*.

14. *DeLovio* v. *Boit*, 7 F. Cas. 418 at 444*.

15. See Gilmore and Black, *Law of Admiralty*, pp. 3–4, 20–24; Henry B. Brown, "Jurisdiction of the Admiralty in Cases of Tort," *Columbia Law Review* 9 (1909): 1–15; Eberhard P. Deutsch, "Development of the Theory of Admiralty Jurisdiction in the United States," *Tulane Law Review* 35 (1960): 117–28; G. H. Robinson, "An Introduction to American Admiralty," *Cornell Law Quarterly* 21 (1935): 46–83; *New Jersey Steam Navigation Co.* v. *Merchants Bank*, 47 U.S. 344 (1848); *The Moses Taylor*, 71 U.S. 411. See also *The Steamboat New World* v. *King*, 57 U.S. 469 (1854).

16. *The Aberfoyle*, 1 F. Cas. 30 at 35 (D.C.S.D.N.Y. 1848)*; *The Pacific*, 18 F. Cas. 935 (C.C.S.D.N.Y. 1850).

For the *in personam* basis of passenger contract cases before the 1850s, see Alfred Conkling, *The Jurisdiction, Law and Practice of the Courts of the United States in Admiralty and Maritime Causes* (Albany, 1848), pp. 324–26; Andrew Dunlap, *A Treatise on the Admiralty in Civil Causes of Practice of Courts of Maritime Jurisdiction*, 2d ed. New York, 1850), pp. 64–65; and Parsons, *Treatise on Maritime Law* (1859), 1:394.

17. On Dec. 27, 1868, the *Alta California* noted the strategic practice of lawyers representing ship passengers: they pressured shipowners into settling disputes by filing libels shortly before scheduled departures.

18. On water transportation to gold-rush California, see John H. Kemble, *The Panama Route, 1848–1869* (Berkeley: University of California Press, 1943); John H. Kemble, "The Genesis of the Pacific Mail Steamship Company," *California Historical Society Quarterly* 13 (1934): 240–54, 386–406; Oscar Lewis, *Sea Routes to the Gold Fields* (New York: Knopf, 1949); and Ernest A. Wiltsee, *Gold Rush Steamers of the Pacific* (Lawrence, Mass.: Quarterman Publications, 1938).

19. Ad. (Private) Cases [32], [38], [73–75]. The damages awarded the libellants amounted to only $1,935, but Hoffman's decree also imposed on the company the costs of litigation, which exceeded $2,500. See motion filed June 10, 1851, [38].

20. Ad. (U.S.) Cases, 1st Ser., [1183], [1192], [1200], [1207], [1208], [1211], [1212], [1214], [1217], [1218], and [1276]; Calhoun Benham to Solicitor of the Treasury, Oct. 15, 1852, SLR, RG 206, NA*.

21. Ad. (U.S.) Cases, 1st Ser., [1148], [1156], [1184], [1185], [1191], [1193], [1195], [1197], [1199], [1202], [1204], [1206], [1209], [1210], [1213], [1215], [1216], [1219], [1220], [1272–75], and [1277].

22. Ad. (Private) Cases, [192], [218], [363], [403], [408–15], [419], [854], [892], [1079], [1182], [1192], [1269], [1276], [1281], [1282], [1328], [1403], and [1832].

23. Ad. (Private) Cases, [95], [129], [142], [164], [297], [298], [326], [340–48], [357–59], [450], [597], [1092], [1256], [1320], [1473], [1535–36], [1538], [1584], [1624], [1643], [1669], [1696], [1697], [1751], [1925], [2015], and [3466]. Also see Lewis, *Sea Routes*, pp. 47–124.

24. For Hoffman's passenger cases, see Appendix, table 2.

25. *Marshall* v. *Steamship "Tennessee,"* Deposition of John Springer, Ad. (Private) Cases, [32], filed May 31, 1851*.

26. See Ad. (Private) Cases, [73–75], [363], [384], [408–15], [419], [854], [1182], [1192], [1247], [1281], [1473], [1760], and [2287].

27. See Ad. (Private) Cases, [38], [403], [960], [1269], [1276], [1282], [1320], [1328], [1403], [1535–36], [1538], [1669], [1676], [1696], [1697], [1698], [1705], [1751], [1832], [2131], and [3466].

28. *Dowing* v. *Schooner "Golden State,"* Sept. 17, 1858, H. Op.*; *Burke* v. *Steamship "Pacific,"* May 13, 1853, Ad. (Private) Cases, [403].

29. Daily journal, *Poole* v. *Ship "Atlantic,"* [1624]; Hoffman's notes of test., *Smith* v. *Bark "Sir George Grey,"* [1535]*; Ad. (Private) Cases, [403], [1698] and [2131].

30. *Sparks* v. *The Sonora*, 22 F. Cas. 883 at 884 (D.C.N.D.Cal. 1859)*; Hoffman's notes of test., *Gougenheim* v. *Barque "Glimpse,"*Ad. (Private) Cases, [1271], and Feb. 5, 1859, H. Op.; *Bailey* v. *The Sonora*, 2 F. Cas. 383 (D.C.N.D.Cal. 1859)*.

31. Ad. (Private) Cases, [95], [129], [252], [338], [807], [854], and [1223]; Sept. 17, 1858, H. Op*.

32. Conkling, *Admiralty Jurisdiction*, 2:28*. High court costs initially frustrated even the multiple joinder of seamen for their wages. See Ad. (Private) Cases, [4], [9], and [15].

33. *Norris* v. *Steamship "Sonora,"* Jan. 24, 1859, H. Op.; A. P. Needles, comp., *Rules to Regulate the Practice of the Federal, State, and City and County Courts of the City*

and County of San Francisco (San Francisco, 1877), p. 151; Ad. (Private) Cases, [1281], [1320], [1328], [1482], [1527], [1584], [1669], [1676], [1696–97], [1705], [1751], [1763], [1770], [1832], [1833], and [1868]; *Chamberlain* v. *Steamship "Uncle Sam,"* Nov. 15, 1859, H. Op.

34. Dunlap, *Maritime Jurisdiction*, p. 80*; Conkling, *Admiralty Jurisdiction*, 1:47*; Parsons, *Treatise on Maritime Law* (1859), 2:547*.

35. See *Carphin* v. *Ship "Victoria,"* July 31, 1851, *Brig "Decision,"* March 22, 1853, *Hassan* v. *Ship "Tartar,"* Oct. 14, 1856*, H. Op.

36. *Fayet* v. *Ship "Henri,"* Ad. (Private) Cases, [95], filed July 24, 1851.

37. *Fayet* v. *Ship "Henri,"* Sept. 23, 1851, H. Op.*; Ad. (Private) Cases, [129], [134], [142], [164], [276], [450], [672], [950], [960], [1271], [1535–36], [1538], [1584], [1624], [1669], [1676], [1695], [1698], [1704], [1705], [1760], [1763], [1770], [1833], [1870], [2131], [2292], and [3466].

38. *Chamberlain* v. *Chandler*, 5 F. Cas. 413 at 414–15 (C.C.D.Mass. 1823)*.

39. Ad. (Private) Cases, [192]*; *Dupre* v. *Steamer "North America,"* April 3, 1852, H. Op.; Conkling, *Admiralty and Maritime Causes*, 1:324–26; Dunlap, *Maritime Jurisdiction*, pp. 64–65.

40. *Dupre* v. *Steamer "North America,"* April 3, 1852, H. Op.*

41. Ad. (Private) Cases, [218] and [252]*; *Reynolds* v. *Steamship "New World,"* April 17, 1852, H. Op*. See John G. Burke, "Bursting Boilers and the Federal Power," *Technology and Culture* 7 (1966): 1–23 and Act of July 7, 1838, 5 US STAT 304. Appealed to the Supreme Court, Hoffman's decree of $2,500 plus costs for the libellant was affirmed. See *Steamboat New World* v. *King*, 57 U.S. 469 (1854).

42. Conkling, *Admiralty Jurisdiction*, 1:257–61. Passengers filed seven libels for negligence; see Ad. (Private) Cases, [192], [218], [252], [892], [1537], [1636], and [2292].

43. *Nicholson* v. *Ship "John Baring,"* March 23, 1853, H. Op.; Hoffman's notes of argument, *Nicholson* v. *Ship "John Baring,"* Ad. (Private) Cases, [340]*.

44. *Nicholson* v. *Ship "John Baring,"* March 23, 1853, H. Op*.

45. Ibid. Hoffman awarded the libellants nearly $3,000 plus their costs. See Ad. (Private) Cases, [340–48], [357–59].

46. *Bennett* v. *Barque "Pathfinder,"* Dec. 4, 1852, H. Op.* Also see Ad. (Private) Cases, [164], [326], and [450].

47. See Dunlap, *Maritime Jurisdiction*, pp. 295–309.

48. *Pinchbeck* v. *Ship "Hurricane,"* Ad. (Private) Cases, [597]; *Place* v. *Steamship "Golden Gate,"* Sept. 22, 1856, H. Op.

49. *Place* v. *Steamship "Golden Gate,"* Sept. 22, 1856, H. Op*. Hoffman supported his position with a writer's interpretation of the Supreme Court's *in personam* requirement. See Erastus C. Benedict, *The American Admiralty* (New York, 1850), p. 174.

50. *Place* v. *Steamship "Golden Gate,"* Sept. 22, 1856, H. Op.*

51. *McGuire* v. *Steamship "Golden Gate,"* 16 F. Cas. 141 at 142 (C.C.N.D.Cal. 1856)*. In limiting libellants to actual losses, McAllister reduced Hoffman's decree

almost by half. For later passenger cases, see Ad. (Private) Cases, [1256], [1925], and [3466].

52. See *Alta California*, May 9, 1850. Virtually all of the suits based on rudeness and verbal abuse involved women. See Ad. (Private) Cases, [164], [297], [298], [326], [450], [1256], [1925], and [3466].

53. *Morrison* v. *The John L. Stephens*, 17 F. Cas. 838 at 840 (D.C.N.D.Cal. 1861)*; *Richards* v. *Barque "Ethan Allen,"* May 12, 1868, H. Op*.

54. Hoffman's notes of argument, *Henry* v. *Schooner "Selma,"* Ad. (Private) Cases, [1925]*.

55. See Charles Fairman, *Reconstruction and Reunion, 1864–1888: Part Two*, vol. 7 of Paul A. Freund, ed., *The Oliver Wendell Holmes Devise History of the Supreme Court of the United States* (New York: Macmillan Co., 1987), pp. 372–73; Act of Sept. 24, 1789, 1 US STAT 73; Act of March 3, 1875, 18 US STAT 470; and Act of Aug. 1888, 25 US STAT 433.

56. Commercial litigation accounted for more than 50 percent of all libels filed in Hoffman's admiralty court. See Appendix, table 2.

57. Decker, *Fortunes and Failures*, pp. 32–58, 59*, 92.

58. Tony Freyer, *Forums of Order: The Federal Courts and Business in American History* (Greenwich, Conn.: JAI Press, 1979), p. 26*. For Doe, see Reid, *Charles Doe*, pp. 85, 319–31.

59. See *Lower* v. *Brig "Magdalena,"* July 19, 1851, *Carphin* v. *Ship "Victoria,"* July 31, 1851, *Howland* v. *Steamer "Quickstep,"* April 2, 1852, *Stevens* v. *Ship "Isaiah Crowell,"* Sept. 2, 1853, *U.S.* v. *Ship "Charlotte,"* Sept. 26, 1853, *Gill* v. *Schooner "Fashion,"* Feb. 12, 1856, *Goddefroy, Sillem and Company* v. *The "Live Yankee,"* Feb. 18, 1857, *Mason* v. *Barque "Chase,"* March 12, 1857, *Wise* v. *Schooner "Lequellic,"* July 6, 1859, *Soulie* v. *Barque "Pierre,"* March 5, 1861, H. Op. Also see Christian G. Fritz, "Judicial Style in California's Federal Admiralty Court: Ogden Hoffman and the First Ten Years, 1851–1861," *Southern California Quarterly* 64 (1982): 3–4.

60. *Webb* v. *Steamship "Antelope,"* Sept. 22, 1851, H. Op.*, and Ad. (Private) Cases, [73–74].

61. Joseph K. Angell, *A Treatise on the Law of Carriers of Goods and Passengers by Land and by Water* (Boston, 1849), pp. 538* and 160–61*.

62. *Merrill* v. *Bark "Peru,"* Sept. 26, 1851, and *Minturn* v. *Ship "Hornet,"* Nov. 30, 1852, H. Op.

63. *Levy* v. *The "Caroline Reed,"* Dec. 31, 1852, H. Op., and *Adrian* v. *The "Live Yankee,"* 1 F. Cas. 187 (D.C.D.Cal. 1855)*.

64. *Raymond* v. *Bark "Edward,"* Nov. 25, 1851, H. Op*.

65. *James* v. *Ship "Coronation,"* Feb. 15, 1856*, and *Farwell* v. *The "Harvey Buch,"* [n.d.] 1856*, H. Op.; *Brittain* v *The "Alboni,"* 4 F. Cas. 175 (D.C.D.Cal. 1856).

66. *Annan* v. *The "Star of Hope,"* 1 F. Cas. 939 (D.C.D.Cal. 1859)*.

67. See Gilmore and Black, *Law of Admiralty*, pp. 3–4, 24; *Cutler* v. *Rae*, 48 U.S. 729 (1849).

68. *Shepherd* v. *Gardet and Company*, Aug. 28, 1851, H. Op.*; *James* v. *Guy*, May

4, 1855, Ad. (Private) Cases, [919]; *Du Pont de Nemours and Company* v. *Vance*, 60 U.S. 162 (1857).

69. Michael H. Hoeflich, "John Austin and Joseph Story: Two Nineteenth Century Perspectives on the Utility of the Civil Law for the Common Lawyer," *American Journal of Legal History* 29 (1985): 74*; *Gill* v. *Schooner "Fashion,"* Feb. 12, 1856, H. Op. Also see Hoffman, Jr., to Hoffman, Sr., April 1, 1851, VH Coll., NYHS; *Thompson* v. *Ship "Ionian,"* June 13, 1851, H. Op.; *Santiago* v. *Morgan*, 21 F. Cas. 417 (D.C.N.D.Cal. 1851).

70. See *Middleton* v. *Steamer "Gold Hunter,"* [n.d.] 1851, *Dupre* v. *Steamer "North America,"* April 3, 1852, *Kreymel* v. *Grogan*, May 17, 1852, *Stevens* v. *Ship "Isaiah Crowell,"* Sept. 2, 1853, *Fleming* v. *The Proceeds of the Barque "Raymond,"* Aug. 19, 1856, *Farwell* v. *The "Harvey Buch,"* [n.d.] 1856, *West* v. *Steamship "Uncle Sam,"* Feb. 9, 1858, *Hare* v. *The Proceeds of the Schooner "Umpqua,"* May 6, 1858, *Downing* v. *Schooner "Golden State,"* Sept. 17, 1858, *Ferron* v. *Barque "Emily Banning,"* Dec. 29, 1858, *John Norris* v. *Steamship "Sonora,"* Jan. 24, 1859, *Moulin* v. *The "John L. Stephens,"* Oct. 21, 1859, *Chamberlain* v. *Steamship "Uncle Sam,"* Nov. 15, 1859, H. Op.; *Pierce* v. *The "Alberto,"* 19 F. Cas. 631 at 633 (D.C.D.Cal. 1857)*.

71. *Chamberlain* v. *The "Uncle Sam,"* March 9, 1859, H. Op*.

72. See *Poulgram* v. *Lindholm*, Sept. 27, 1851, and *Downing* v. *Schooner "Golden State,"* Sept. 17, 1858, H. Op.; Ad. (Private) Cases, [21], [35], [39], [40], [114], [226], [233], [245], [269], [456], [467], [484], [497], [552], [588], [663], [702], [786], [810], [824], [897], [916], [963], [1020], [1054], [1083], [1104], [1111], [1251], [1446], [1518], [1533], [1632], [1727], [1838], [1944], [2111], [2134], and [2209].

73. For example, see *Horn* v. *Steamer "Martin White,"* Nov. 30, 1855, *Dalton* v. *Schooner "Ellen Adelia,"* Dec. 9, 1864, *George Nauton* v. *Steamer "Oregon,"* March 27, 1867, *Napoleon II Emperor of the French* v. *Ship "Sapphire,"* March 19, 1868, *Simpson* v. *Sprekles*, Aug. 7, 1882, H. Op.; *McFarland* v. *Selby Smelting and Lead Company*, May 28, 1883, 9 Sawyer 53; *Simpson* v. *Steamship "State of California,"* Nov. 27, 1889, 14 Sawyer 346; *Lambert* v. *Freese*, Jan. 22, 1890, 14 Sawyer 380.

74. For example, see *Webb* v. *Steamship "Antelope,"* Sept. 22, 1851, H. Op., and Ad. (Private) Cases, [73–75] (breach of passenger contract); *Merrill* v. *Barque "Peru,"* Sept. 26, 1851, H. Op. and Ad. (Private) Cases, [21] (breach of shipping contract); *Saucelito Water and Steam Tug Company* v. *Ship "Annapolis,"* April 12, 1866, H. Op., and Ad. (Private) Cases, [1621–22] (salvage); *Nauton* v. *Steamer "Oregon,"* March 27, 1867, H. Op., and Ad. (Private) Cases, [1632] (collision); *Johnson* v. *Ship "Industry,"* July 7, 1868, H. Op., and Ad. (Private) Cases, [1727] (salvage).

75. Ad. (Private) Cases, [1215]*; *Alta California*, March 31, 1858*.

76. *Gallagher* v. *The "Yankee,"* 9 F. Cas. 1091 (D.C.N.D.Cal. 1859)*.

77. Ibid.*

78. *Alta California*, Jan. 19, 1859*; *San Francisco Bulletin*, Jan. 18, and 19*, and 21*, 1859.

79. Ad. (Private) Cases, [1411] and [1412]*; *Duane* v. *Pearson*, Dec. 1, 1863, H. Op.; *Pearson* v. *Duane*, 71 U.S. 605 (1867).

80. *Alta California*, March 26, 1864, Jan. 21, 1859*.

81. See James Willard Hurst, *Law and the Conditions of Freedom in the Nineteenth Century United States* (Madison: University of Wisconsin Press, 1956); Horwitz, *Transformation*; Lawrence M. Friedman, *A History of American Law*, 2d ed. New York: Simon and Schuster, 1985).

82. See Appendix, table 2, and Ad. (Private) Cases.

83. Filed mainly by sailors, marine torts, when combined with sailors' wage suits, amounted to 39 percent. Obviously not all those employed were common sailors, or "Jack-tars." For the purpose of this chapter, however, *sailors* and *seamen* will refer to all those working for wages on vessels.

84. *Clauder* v. *Schooner "Eudorus,"* June 28, 1851, H. Op*. The two leading American decisions on maintenance and cure were rendered by Joseph Story in *Harden* v. *Gordon*, 11 F. Cas. 480 (C.C.D.Me 1823) and *Reed* v. *Canfield*, 20 F. Cas. 426 (C.C.D.Mass. 1832). Also see Dunlap, *Maritime Jurisdiction*, pp. 78–79; Parsons, *Treatise on Maritime Law*, 1:441–42.

85. The phrase comes from *Harden* v. *Gordon*, 11 F. Cas. 480 at 485, in which Story observed that sailors were "emphatically the wards of admiralty." See also Dunlap, *Maritime Jurisdiction*, p. 45*.

86. Adolphus Windeler, *The California Gold Rush Diary of a German Sailor*, ed. W. Turrentine Jackson (Berkeley: Howell-North Books, 1969), p. 45*.

87. For example, see Ad. (Private) Cases [4], [34], and [45]. If sailors sometimes suffered in these early cases, businessmen and other commercial creditors suffered even more, since the sailor's lien took priority over all others.

88. Plaintiffs actually succeeded 78 percent of the time, and even that figure is probably low, since a good number of the cases in which the disposition is uncertain were probably settled. Adding the 87 uncertain cases to the settled category increases the plaintiffs' success rate to 86 percent. See Appendix, table 2.

89. See Richard H. Dillon, *Shanghaiing Days* (New York: Coward-McCann, 1961); James Fell, *British Merchant Seamen in San Francisco, 1892–1898* (London, 1899); Lance S. Davidson, "Shanghaied! The Systematic Kidnapping of Sailors in Early San Francisco," *California Historical Society Quarterly* 64 (1985): 10–17.

90. The Reverend William Taylor provided one of the best glimpses of the crimping system in San Francisco in the 1850s, in *Seven Years' Preaching in San Francisco, California* (New York, 1857), pp. 224–41*; *Scott* v. *The "Morning Glory,"* 21 F. Cas. 845 (D.C.N.D.Cal. 1859).

91. "Judge R. F. Peckham, An Eventful Life," *San Jose Pioneer*, July 28, 1877*; De Massey, *Journal*, p. 32; Borthwick, *Gold Hunters*, pp. 73–74; William R. Ryan, *Personal Adventures in Upper and Lower California in 1848–1849*, 2 vols. (London, 1850), 2:149*.

92. *Peterson* v. *The "James C. Perkins,"* June 19, 1851*; *Smith* v. *The "Skylark,"* April 4, 1856, *Petre* v. *The "Horsburgh,"* Dec. 20, 1858, *Humphrey* v. *Ship "Mastiff,"* Sept. 6, 1859, H. Op.

93. *Middleton* v. *Steamer "Gold Hunter,"* [n.d.] 1851, *Pinner* v. *The "Pacific,"* Oct.

9, 1852*, *Sherry* v. *The "Roman,"* July 29, 1853, *Fernandez* v. *The "Emily Banning,"* Aug. 14, 1860, *Kilburn* v. *Ship "Eliza and Ella,"* Sept. 10, 1860, H. Op.

94. See *Dooley* v. *The "Neptune's Car,"* 7 F. Cas. 908 at 909–10 (D.C.N.D.Cal. 1860)*.

95. Ibid. at 911*.

96. *Williams* v. *The "Storm King,"* Jan. 3, 1861, H. Op*.

97. *Ruddy* v. *The "Golden State,"* 20 F. Cas. 1309 (D.C.N.D.Cal. 1861); *Kincaid* v. *Ship "Morning Star,"* May 29, 1861, *Foley* v. *Schooner "J. B. Ford,"* Feb. 4, 1863, *Norton* v. *Ship "Black Prince,"* Oct. 6, 1864, *Baldwin, Executor of John Adams* v. *Barque "Mercury,"* Jan. 16, 1866*, *Maker* v. *Ship "Lagoda,"* Feb. 26, 1866, H. Op.; *Scully* v. *Steamer "Great Republic,"* Feb. 8, 1870, 1 Sawyer 31; *Goodrich* v. *Barque "Domingo,"* June 7, 1879, 1 Sawyer 182 (fishing voyage).

98. *Wickbury* v. *Bark "Rainier,"* Feb. 24, 1868, H. Op*.

99. *Somerville* v. *Brig "Francisco,"* Dec. 1, 1870, 1 Sawyer 390 at 395*.

100. *Scully* v. *Steamer "Great Republic,"* Feb. 8, 1870, 1 Sawyer 31*.

101. Ibid*.

102. *Whitney* v. *Brig "Percy Edwards,"* July 29, 1871, H. Op.*; *The Steamship "S. M. Whipple,"* Feb. 11, 1881, 7 Sawyer 69 at 72*; *U.S.* v. *Hancock,* May 2, 1887, 12 Sawyer 381 at 392*; *Jobson* v. *Brig "Keysing,"* Aug. 2, 1867, H. Op*.

103. *Lindrobe* v. *Dall,* Oct. 5, 1868, H. Op*.

104. *MacDonald* v. *Dall,* Dec. 16, 1868, H. Op*.

105. *Dooley* v. *The "Neptune's Car,"* 7 F. Cas. 908; *Anderson* v. *Ship 'Reuce,"* May 6, 1890, 14 Sawyer 476 at 477*; *Dooley* v. *The "Neptune's Car,"* 7 F. Cas. 908 at 910*; *Pope* v. *Bark "Don Manual Ugarte,"* Feb. 2, 1856*, *Monroe* v. *Schooner "Sea Nymph,"* Oct. 10, 1866, *Bryon* v. *Thomas,* July 25, 1867, *West* v. *Ship "National Eagle,"* Dec. 30, 1867, H. Op.

106. *Monroe* v. *Schooner "Sea Nymph,"* Oct. 10, 1866, *Bryon* v. *Thomas,* July 25, 1867, *Anderson* v. *Ross,* Oct. 10, 1871, H. Op.; *Schooner "Page,"* Nov. 6, 1878, 5 Sawyer 299 at 302.

107. *Anderson* v. *Ross,* Oct. 10, 1871*, *Hassan* v. *The "Tartar,"* Oct. 14, 1856, *MacDonald* v. *Dall,* Dec. 16, 1868, *Lindrobe* v. *Dall,* Oct. 5, 1868*, *Pulgram* v. *Lindholm,* Sept. 27, 1851, *Bryon* v. *Thomas,* July 25, 1867, *West* v. *Ship "National Eagle,"* Dec. 30, 1867, *Haggerty* v. *Lester,* Dec. 7, 1868, H. Op.

108. *MacDonald* v. *Dall,* Dec. 16, 1868, H. Op.*; *Parsons, Treatise on Maritime Law,* 1:464–67; *Anderson* v. *Ross,* Oct. 24, 1871, 2 Sawyer 91 at 94*.

109. The trials got their name from the extremely brutal shipboard conditions and are discussed in chapter 4. Also see Dillon, *Shanghaiing Days,* pp. 66–126, 89*.

110. Parsons, *Treatise on Maritime Law,* 1:458–62; *Strong* v. *The "Columbia,"* June 24, 1853, *Moore* v. *Ship "Roman,"* June 27, 1853, *Anderson* v. *Brig "Ida D. Bogus,"* April 7, 1863, H. Op.

111. *Tomlinson* v. *Hewitt,* April 20, 1869, H. Op.*; *Neilson* v. *Brig "Laura,"* Sept. 12, 1872, 2 Sawyer 242; *Bark "Cambridge,"* May 10, 1877, 4 Sawyer 252; *Raymond* v. *Barque "Ella S. Thayer,"* June 1, 1887, 12 Sawyer 409.

112. See Friedman, *History of American Law*, pp. 301–2; Lawrence M. Friedman and Jack Ladinsky, "Social Change and the Law of Industrial Accidents," *Columbia Law Review* 67 (1967): 51–59; Wex S. Malone, "The Formative Era of Contributory Negligence," *Illinois Law Review* 41 (1946): 151–82.

113. *Dwyer* v. *Steamship "Sierra Nevada,"* Sept. 8, 1864, H. Op.*

114. Ibid.* More than a decade later, Hoffman continued reluctantly to uphold the fellow servant rule because of "copious authority," but he repeated his earlier objections. See *Halverson* v. *Nisen*, March 16, 1876, 3 Sawyer 562.

115. Leonard W. Levy, *The Law of the Commonwealth and Chief Justice Shaw* (Cambridge: Harvard University Press, 1957), p. 171*; Friedman, *History of American Law*, pp. 481–82. Friedman cites cases in 1885 and 1891 as illustrating judicial criticism of the fellow servant rule. Moreover, the California Supreme Court did not begin criticizing the rule until the late 1880s. See Gordon M. Bakken, *The Development of the Law in Frontier California* (Westport, Conn.: Greenwood Press, 1985), pp. 73–83.

116. Horwitz, *Transformation*, pp. 201–10, 209*.

117. See Gary T. Schwartz, "Tort Law and the Economy in Nineteenth-Century America: A Reinterpretation," *Yale Law Journal* 90 (1981): 1717–75.

118. See *McPhain* v. *Bark "Dollart,"* July 31, 1862, *Duane* v. *Goodall*, March 7, 1863, *Heyneman* v. *Ship "Bird of Paradise,"* April 23, 1864, *McAllister* v. *Brig "Anne Sanderson,"* Oct. 24, 1866, and *In Re Isaacs and Cohn*, Dec. 4, 1871, H. Op.

CHAPTER 4

1. James Eisenstein, *Counsel for the United States* (Baltimore: Johns Hopkins University Press, 1978), pp. 9–10; John C. Heinberg, "Centralization in Federal Prosecutions," *Missouri Law Review* 15 (1950): 244–58.

2. See Crim. Cases and Appendix, table 3.

3. See Dillon, *Shanghaiing Days*, pp. 66–126.

4. Starting with the *Waterman* cases in 1851, Hoffman imposed stiff penalties on jurors or witnesses who ignored the summons of his court. See *Minutes*, Dec. 3, 17, 1851, Jan. 6, 27, Feb. 3, June 29, July 7, 9, 13, 19, Dec. 7, 1852, Feb. 11, 16, June 29, and Aug. 3, 22, 1853.

5. Crim. Cases, 1st Ser., [1–21].

6. Act of March 3, 1835, 4 US STAT 775, Sec. 3*.

7. Act of April 30, 1790, 1 US STAT 112, Sec. 8, and Act of May 15, 1820, 3 US STAT 600; *Cong. Globe*, 23d Cong., 2d sess., 1835, p. 265*.

8. Richard Henry Dana, Jr., "Cruelty to Seamen: Case of Nichols and Couch," *American Jurist and Law Magazine* 4 (1839): 92–107.

9. Ibid., pp. 104–5*. Even other judges who were less sanguine about the effects of the 1835 statute expressed a concern for improving the "little confidence" that sailors had in "the justice of superior powers." See *Swain* v. *Howland*, 23 F. Cas. 483 at 484 (D.C.D.Mass. 1858).

10. Dana, "Cruelty to Seamen," p. 102*.

11. Crim. Cases, 1st Ser., [85], [138–52], [261], [267], 2d Ser., [69–74], [202–5], [207], [1522–30], [1774], [1898–99], [2216–17], and [2737].

Whereas the 1835 act provided for a maximum sentence of five years' imprisonment per conviction, multiple trials against the same defendant for different instances of unlawful conduct could result in aggregate prison sentences that exceeded five years.

12. *Harden* v. *Gordon*, 11 F. Cas. 480 at 485 (C.C.D.Me 1823)*.

13. Act of June 11, 1864, 13 US STAT 124*; *Cong. Globe*, 38th Cong., 1st sess., 1864, pp. 153, 553, 1155, 2778, 2796, 2894.

14. Crim. Cases, 1st Ser., [23], [24], [38], [41], [44], [58], [59], [64], [66], [67], [90], [98], [106], [108], [109], [113], [116], [117], [119–26], [133], and [164]; quoted in Dillon, *Shanghaiing Days*, p. 176*.

15. *U.S.* v. *Pendleton*, June 22, 1859, H. Op*.

16. Ibid.*.

17. See, for example, Crim. Cases, 1st Ser., [55] ($350), [131] ($25), [136] ($100), [155A] ($25), [236] ($200), [240] ($75), [242] ($75), [243] ($20), [272] ($50), [281] ($50), 2d Ser., [106] ($200), [112] ($75), [154] ($75), [163] ($25), [171] ($50), [196] ($50), [509] ($50), [524] ($75), [548] ($200), [554] ($100), [559] ($100), and [595] ($30).

18. See Crim. Cases.

19. *U.S.* v. *Pendleton*, June 22, 1859, H. Op.*; Crim. Cases, 1st Ser., [74], [85], 2d Ser. [568–69], [576], [577], [588], [590], [647], [651–52], [661], [670], [688], [1412], [1672], [1893–94], [2322], and [2447].

20. Crim. Cases, 2nd Ser., [564] and [1894]; *U.S.* v. *Curtin*, Proceedings on Motion to Set Cases for Trial, June 17, 1886, Crim. Cases, 2d Ser. [2270]*.

21. Crim. Cases, 1st Ser. [114], [127], [136], [154], [278], 2d Ser., [151], [160], [562], [1389], [1462], [1631], [1903], [2029], and [2312–15]; Joseph Jones to Hoffman, Feb. 21, 1890, Crim. Cases, 2d Ser., [2572].

22. Act of March 3, 1825, 4 US STAT 115 at 121, Sec. 22, and *Revised Statutes of the United States*, 43d Cong., 1st sess., 1874, Title 48, chap. 9; Act of March 3, 1835, 4 US STAT 775, Sec. 1, and *Revised Statutes*, 1874, Title 48, chap. 9.

23. *U.S.* v. *Burtis*, Crim. Cases, 1st Ser. [172]. See also Robert J. Schwendinger, "The Temperate Mutiny," *National Maritime Museum Association Sea Letter*, no. 37 (Spring 1987): 16–21.

24. *U.S.* v *Thompson*, 28 F. Cas. 102 (C.C.D.Mass. 1832) (found not guilty of a mutiny for refusal to obey but guilty of seizing captain and holding him back against the ship's rail); *U.S.* v. *Cassedy*, 25 F. Cas. 321 (C.C.D.Mass. 1837) (guilty of refusal to do further duty); *U.S.* v. *Givings*, 25 F. Cas. 1331 (D.C.D.Mass. 1844) (not guilty of refusing to go to sea and physically resisting captain on grounds vessel unseaworthy); *U.S.* v. *Borden*, 24 F. Cas. 1202 at 1203 (D.C.D.Mass. 1857)*; Act of March 3, 1835, 4 US STAT 775, Sec. 1.

25. Schwendinger, "Mutiny," p. 2*.

26. For relative prosecutions against captains and sailors, see Crim. Cases, 1st and 2d Ser.

27. For captains, see Crim. Cases, 1st Ser., [42], [58], [109],[236–37], [240–41], 2d Ser., [673], [687], [1239–40], [1453], [1807], and [1830]. For first officers, see Crim. Cases, 1st Ser., [55], [64], [141], [243], [261], [269], 2d Ser., [202–4], [509], [671–79], and [1835]. For second officers, see Crim. Cases, 1st Ser., [55], [108], 2d Ser., [1514–22] and [2049].

28. For captains, see Crim. Cases, 1st Ser., [147], 2d Ser., [10], [69], [154], [548], [553–54], [596], [613–615], [683], and [2601]. For first officers, see Crim. Cases, 1st Ser., [142], [144], [147], [149], [155], [272], 2d Ser., [144], [171], [183], [188], [584–85], [594–95], [616–23], [675], [1358], [1483], [1500], [1729], [1809], [1813], [2042], [2250], and [2334]. The heaviest sentence came in 1890 in *U.S. v. Taylor*, Crim. Cases, 2d Ser., [2737]. For second officers, see Crim. Cases, 1st Ser., [273], 2d Ser. [196], [544–46], [580–83], [630–636], [668], [669], [680], [882], [1501], [1828], [1832], [2038], [2358], and [2763]. The harshest penalty of this category occurred in *U.S. v. Mould*, Crim. Cases, 2d Ser., [205–7].

29. *U.S. v. Sparks*, Charge to the Jury, April 21, 1882, Crim. Cases, 2d Ser., [1523]*.

30. Ibid*.

31. *U.S. v. Louns* and *U.S. v. Soule*, Crim. Cases, 1st Ser., [278–79]; *U.S. v. Rock* and *U.S. v. Kelly*, Crim. Cases, 1st Ser., [282–88].

32. *U.S. v. Sparks*, Crim. Cases, 2d Ser., [1523]*.

33. Act of April 20, 1818, 3 US STAT 447.

34. On expansionism generally, see Albert K. Weinberg, *Manifest Destiny* (Baltimore: Johns Hopkins University Press, 1935); Frederick and Lois B. Merk, *Manifest Destiny and Mission in American History* (New York: Knopf, 1963); Robert W. Johannsen, *To the Halls of the Montezumas: The Mexican War in the American Imagination* (New York: Oxford University Press, 1985); and Charles H. Brown, *Agents of Manifest Destiny* (Chapel Hill: University of North Carolina Press, 1980).

35. On William Walker, see William O. Scroggs, *Filibusters and Financiers* (New York.: Macmillan Co., 1916); Albert Z. Carr, *The World and William Walker* (New York: Harper and Row, 1963); Laurence Greene, *The Filibuster: The Career of William Walker* (New York: Bobbs-Merrill Co., 1937); William Walker, *The War in Nicaragua* (Mobile, 1860).

36. On the French filibusters, see Rufus K. Wyllys, *The French in Sonora, 1850–1854* (Berkeley: Univesity of California Press, 1932).

37. Act of April 20, 1818, 3 US STAT 447*. On the difficulty of enforcing the neutrality act, see J. Fred Rippy, *The United States and Mexico* (1926; rev. ed., New York: F.S. Crofts and Co., 1931), pp. 85–105.

38. *Alta California*, Oct. 2, 1853*; Brown, *Agents of Manifest Destiny*, pp. 174–218.

39. Ethan Allan Hitchcock, *Fifty Years in Camp and Field: Diary of Major-General Ethan Allan Hitchcock, U.S.A.*, ed. W. A. Croffut (New York and London: G.P. Putnam's Sons, 1909), pp. 401–2*.

40. David M. Potter, *The Impending Crisis, 1848–1861* (New York: Harper and Row, 1976), p. 180*; "California," *American Review* 16 (1849): 331*; Howe, *American Whigs*, pp. 145–46.

41. *Alta California*, Dec. 9, 1853*, and Feb. 23, 1854*; Brown, *Agents of Manifest Destiny*, pp. 191–97.

42. Jefferson Davis to John E. Wool, Jan. 12, 1854, U.S. Cong., 33d Cong., 2d sess., 1854, S. Ex. Doc. 751, pt. 6:16.*

43. See Jefferson Davis to John E. Wool, April 14, 1854, Wool to Davis, May 30, 1854, Davis to Wool, Dec. 13, 1854, ibid.; Wool to Davis, Jan. 1855, Dec. 4, 1856, U.S. Cong., 35th Cong., 1st sess., 1855–56, H. Ex. Doc. 956, pt. 10:88.

44. Samuel W. Inge to Caleb Cushing, March 16, 1854, AGLR, RG 60, NA; *Alta California*, March 15, 1854*; John E. Wool to Jefferson Davis, March 1, 1854*, U.S. Cong., S. Ex. Doc. 751, pt. 6:16.

45. *Alta California*, March 23, 1854*.

46. Ibid., March 24, 1854*.

47. Ibid*.

48. Ibid., March 25*, April 8* and 11*, 1854.

49. John E. Wool to L. Thomas, March 31, 1854, S. Ex. Doc. 751, pt. 6:16; *Alta California*, April 6, 1854*.

50. *Alta California*, April 19, 1854*.

51. *New York Times*, May 29, 1854*. On Dillon, see A. P. Nasatir, "Guillaume Patrice Dillon," *California Historical Society Quarterly* 35 (1956): 309–23.

52. *Alta California*, April 26, 1854*.

53. Ibid*.

54. Ibid., April 27, 1854*.

55. *In Re Dillon*, April 27, 1854, 7 Sawyer 561 at 563–64*.

56. William L. Marcy to Hoffman, Jr., May 26, 1854, Norris Collection, BL; U.S. Cong., H. Ex. Doc. 956, pt. 10:88.

57. *Alta California*, April 28, 1854*; *New York Times*, May 29, 1854*; *San Francisco Herald*, Aug. 1, 1854; William T. Sherman to Henry S. Turner, [March 2]9, 1855, William T. Sherman Papers, Box 2, Fldr. 2, Ohio Historical Society, Columbus*. I thank Charles Royster for this last reference.

58. *Alta California*, May 30 and Oct. 20, 1854.

59. See Appendix, table 4 and Ad. (U.S.) Cases. Prosecutions by the government from the three separate dockets (Criminal, Admiralty [U.S.], and Bond) amounted to 2,937, 1,372, and 1,147 filings respectively, for a total of 5,456 cases. Of this number, only 903 cases, or 17 percent, dealt with nonrevenue criminal matters.

60. Edward Bates to Edward Johnson, June 22, 1861, and circular from Edward Pierrepont, Aug. 25, 1875, SLR (AG), RG 206, NA; Homer Cummings and Carl McFarland, *Federal Justice: Chapters in the History of Justice and the Federal Executive*

(New York: Macmillan Co., 1937), pp. 142–60, 218–29; Caleb Cushing to Secretary of the Interior McClelland, Oct. 13, 1855, Cushing Papers, Box 241, LC.

61. See CCLC, RG 60, Boxes 1–9, NA.

62. William Blanding to Jeremiah S. Black, July 3 and 20, 1857, AGLR, RG 60, Box 1, NA; David A. Fisher to Augustus H. Garland, May 17, July 26 and 28, 1886, AP, RG 60, Box 81, NA.

63. Lorenzo Sawyer to the Attorney General, March 5, 1879, SCF, RG 60, NA*.

64. *U.S.* v. *Curtin*, Motion, June 17, 1886, Crim. Cases, 2d Ser., [2270]*.

65. David Fisher to Augustus H. Garland, July 28, 1886, AP, RG 60, Box 81, NA*.

66. Royal Fisk to William Evarts, Oct. 5, 1868, SLR (AG), RG 206, NA*.

67. William H. Sharp to Edwards Bates, Feb. 11, 1864; Delos Lake to James Speed, Feb. 9, 1866; Lake to Henry Stanberry, Nov. 19, 1867; all in AGLR, RG 60, Box 1, NA; Samuel W. Inge to Gilbert Rodman, July 15, 1853, SLR, RG 206, NA.

68. William Blanding to the Attorney General, Sept. 17, 1856, AGLR, RG 60, Box 1, NA*. On this case, see John D. Gordan III, *Authorized by No Law* (San Francisco: Ninth Circuit Historical Society and Northern District Court Historical Society, 1987).

69. For the proceedings against the Chapman privateers, see chapter 6. Public attitudes during the Civil War in California are examined in Robert J. Chandler, "The Press and Civil Liberties in California During the Civil War, 1861–1865" (Ph.D. diss., University of California, Riverside, 1978).

For prosecutions of the Chinese, see Philip Teare to Attorney General, Dec. 10, 1881, SCF, RG 60, NA; Hudson N. Janisch, "The Chinese, the Courts, and the Constitution: A Study of the Legal Issues Raised by Chinese Immigration to the United States, 1850–1902" (J.S.D. diss., University of Chicago, 1971).

For examples of dissatisfaction that U.S. attorneys were not doing more to prosecute the Chinese, see Manuel Eyre to Elijah Halford, Jan. 11, 1890, John Caldwell Pembroke to Attorney General, Aug. 13, 1885, Aug. 13, Oct. 15, 1886, J. P. Dameron to Grover Cleveland, June 15, 1886, J. E. Prewett to Cleveland, Feb. 20, 1886, AP, RG 60, Box 81, NA.

70. See Act of Sept. 24, 1789, 1 US STAT 73; Felix Grundy to Solicitor of the Treasury, April 12, 1839, SLR (AG), RG 206, NA*.

71. Lorenzo D. Latimer to George H. Williams, April 20, 1872, SCF, RG 60, NA*.

72. Ibid.*; Samuel W. Inge to Caleb Cushing, Feb. 26, 1854, Delos Lake to James Speed, Feb. 9, 1866, Lake to Henry Stanberry, Nov. 19, 1867, AGLR, RG 60, NA; Walter Van Dyke to Attorney General, April 14, 1876, SCF, RG 60, NA*.

73. On potential abuses of the fee system, see Larry D. Ball, *The United States Marshals of New Mexico and Arizona Territories, 1846–1912* (Albuquerque: University of New Mexico Press, 1978), p. 6 n. 18.

74. See Act of Sept. 28, 1850, 9 US STAT 521.

75. See Act of Feb. 26, 1853, 10 US STAT 161.

76. Ibid*.

77. Ibid*.

78. Samuel W. Inge to Gilbert Rodman, July 15, 1853, SLR, RG 206, NA*. See "Common Law and Equity, United States Cases," U.S.D.C., Northern District of Calif., Docket Books, vols. 1–2 (Northern District Court Archives, San Francisco); CL and Equity Cases, [1–1147].

79. Ad. (U.S.) Cases, 1st Ser. [1149–55], [1157–74], [1177–81], and [1183]. The estimate of fees is conservative because the fees collected were not indicated in every case.

80. William H. Sharp to Edwards Bates, Feb. 11, 1864, Alfred Briggs to James Speed, Feb. 2, 1865, AGLR, RG 60, NA; Philip Teare to Charles Devens, March 4, 1881, SCF, RG 60, NA; Wayne MacVeagh to Philip Teare, May 4, 1881, SLR (AG), RG 206, NA. See Ad. (U.S.) Cases, 1st and 2d Ser.

81. See Ad. (U.S.) Cases, 1st Ser.

82. See Appendix, figure 1, and Ad. (U.S.) Cases, 1st Ser.

83. See Appendix, figure 1, and Crim. Cases.

84. For Chinese defendants, see Crim. Cases, 1st Ser., [168B], [169A], [169B], [170A], [170B], [190B], [191A], and [226]. For non-Chinese defendants, see Crim. Cases, 1st Ser., [175B], [176B], [180B], [181A], [182B], [184B], [187A], [188B], [189A], [196], and [204].

CHAPTER 5

1. *U.S.* v. *Kingsley*, 37 U.S. 476 (1838); *U.S.* v. *Boisdore*, 52 U.S. 62 (1851); *U.S.* v. *Fremont* , 58 U.S. 541 (1855); *U.S.* v. *Cervantes*, 59 U.S. 553 (1856).

2. *U.S.* v. *Teschmaker*, 63 U.S. 392 (1860).

3. 9 US STAT 922 at 929 (1848), Art. VIII*.

4. Act of March 3, 1851, 9 US STAT 631. Although Paul W. Gates defends the 1851 act, many of its scholarly critics are listed in his article: "The California Land Act of 1851," *California Historical Society Quarterly* 50 (1971): 404–5, n. 28. See Henry W. Halleck to Pablo de la Guerra, March 1, 1852, de la Guerra Papers, HL*.

5. On the political maneuvering behind the act of 1851, see Paul W. Gates, "Adjudication of Spanish-Mexican Land Claims in California," *Huntington Library Quarterly* 21 (1958): 213–36.

6. U.S. Cong., Henry W. Halleck, *Report on the Laws and Regulations Relative to Grants or Sales of Public Lands in California*, 31st Cong., 1st sess., 1850, H. Ex. Doc. 17; William Carey Jones, *Report on the Subject of Land Titles in California* (Washington, D.C., 1850); Halleck, *Report*, pp. 118, 129–30*.

7. Jones, *Report*, pp. 26–27, 38–39*; Paul W. Gates, "The Frémont-Jones Scramble for California Land Claims," *Southern California Quarterly* 56 (1974): 21–22*.

8. Paul W. Gates, "Carpetbaggers Join the Rush for California Land," *California Historical Society Quarterly* 56 (1977): 115, nn. 80–81; Halleck, *Report*, p. 122*.

9. Halleck, *Report*, p. 124*.

10. Paul W. Gates, *History of Public Land Law Development* (Washington, D.C.: Zenger Publishing Company, 1968), pp. 87–114; Henry L. Coles, Jr., "The Confirmation of Foreign Land Titles in Louisiana," *Louisiana Historical Quarterly* 38 (1955): 1–22; Gates, "California Land Act," pp. 411–21; John Conness to J. S. Wilson, July 17, 1868, CCLC, RG 60, Box 4, NA.

11. Act of March 3, 1851, 9 US STAT 631 at 632, Sec. 8*.

12. John Sutter to John Bidwell, Feb. 13, 1855, Bidwell Papers, Box 349, CSL*; William N. Walton to John Center, July 16, 1855, John Center Collection, Box 1, HL*.

13. D.C.S.D.Cal., *Minutes*, vol. 3, June 3, 4, 8, 1857, June 14, 16, 17, 1858 (Film), California State Archives, Sacramento; "Southern District of California," Misc. Case Papers, 1851–61, Order to dismiss appeals, Feb. 24, 1857, Feb. 1 and March 4, 1858, RG 21, Box 1, NA; Frederick Billings to Henry W. Halleck and Archibald Peachy, Jan. 8 and 26, 1857, HPB Papers, Box 1, BL; Land Grant Cases, 100 Southern District (S.D.), 566 Board of Land Commissioners (Bd.), 207–17, BL. But compare David Hornbeck, "The Patenting of California's Private Land Claims, 1851–1885," *Geographical Review* 59 (1979): 440.

14. Act of March 3, 1851, 9 US STAT 631 at 633, Sec. 11*.

15. Jacob N. Bowman, "Index of the Spanish-Mexican Land Grant Records and Cases in California" (typescript, 1958), BL.

16. David Hornbeck, "Land Tenure and Rancho Expansion in Alta California, 1784–1846," *Journal of Historical Geography* 4 (1978): 383–84.

17. William W. Morrow, *Spanish and Mexican Private Land Grants* (San Francisco: Bancroft-Whitney Co., 1923); Malcolm Ebright, "Spanish and Mexican Land Grants and the Law," *Journal of the West* 27 (1988): 3–11; Iris H. W. Engstrand, "An Enduring Legacy: California Ranchos in Historical Perspective," *Journal of the West* 27 (1988): 36–47; Maud Adamson, "The Land Grant System of Governor Juan B. Alvarado" (Master's thesis, University of Southern California, 1931); Robert H. Becker, *Diseños of California Ranchos* (San Francisco: Book Club of California, 1964), pp. ix–xxii.

18. Pablo de la Guerra, Speech, n.d., de la Guerra Papers, HL*; Henry W. Halleck to Abel Stearns, April 14, 1852, Stearns Papers, Box 33, HL; William W. Robinson, *Land in California* (Berkeley: University of California Press, 1948), p. 103; Robert Glass Cleland, *The Cattle on a Thousand Hills: Southern California, 1850–1880* (1941; reprint, San Marino, Calif.: Huntington Library, 1975), p. 55.

19. Joseph W. McCorkle to John Bidwell, Dec. 11, 1851, Bidwell Papers, Fldr 29, CSL*.

20. R. O. McMurray to Henry W. Halleck, Aug. 8, Sept. 9, 1851, March 9, Oct. 4, 1852, Halleck, Peachy, Billings Collection, Box 1, Special Collections, University of California, Los Angeles; Idwal Jones, *Ark of Empire* (Garden City, New York: Doubleday, 1951); Halleck to Pablo de la Guerra, Jan. 18*, April 2*, 1852, March 5, 1853, de la Guerra Papers, HL.

21. *Organization, Acts and Regulations of the United States Land Commissioners for California* (San Francisco, 1852) and *Instructions of the Department of the Interior to the Commissioners* (San Francisco, 1852), both in Wills, *California Titles*, vol. 11, HL.

22. Henry W. Halleck to Pablo de la Guerra, March 17, 1852*, March 1, 1852*, de la Guerra Papers, HL; Richard Somerset Den to Abel Stearns, July 14, 1852, Stearns Papers, Box 20, HL*.

23. Land Grant Cases, 3 N.D., 56 Bd. and 1 N.D., 1 Bd., BL.

24. HLC, 10*. For an English translation of the 1828 regulations, see Frederic Hall, *The Laws of Mexico: A Compilation and Treatise* (San Francisco, 1885).

25. Henry W. Halleck to Pablo de la Guerra, March 1, 17, and 27*, 1852, de la Guerra Papers, HL.

26. Paul W. Gates, "California's Embattled Settlers," *California Historical Society Quarterly* 41 (1962): 99–130; Henry W. Halleck to Pablo de la Guerra, Jan. 29, 1852, de la Guerra Papers, HL; Thomas Douglas to Caleb Cushing, May 15, 1854, CCLC, RG 60, Box 1, NA*.

27. Gates, "California Land Act," pp. 401–2; Henry W. Halleck to Pablo de la Guerra, April 23*, Aug. 25, 1853, de la Guerra Papers, HL; Elisha O. Crosby to John Bidwell, July 20, 1853, Bidwell Papers, Box 128, CSL*; Elisha Oscar Crosby, *Memoirs of Elisha Oscar Crosby*, ed. Charles Albro Barker (San Marino, Calif.: Huntington Library, 1945), p. 70*.

28. Samuel W. Inge to Caleb Cushing, Nov. 1, 1853, CCLC, RG 60, Box 7, NA*; Henry W. Halleck to John Youtz, Nov. 27, 1853, HPB Papers, Box 1, BL*; Archibald C. Peachy to J. L. Folsom, Aug. 14, 1853, William A. Leidesdorff Papers, Box 6, HL*; Halleck to Pablo de la Guerra, Nov. 22, 1853, de la Guerra Papers, HL*; Larkin to John Bidwell, Oct. 30*, Nov. 18*, 1853, Bidwell Papers, Box 132, CSL.

29. *U.S.* v. *Cervantes*, HLC, 9 at 12*; Samuel W. Inge to Cushing, Nov. 1, 1853, CCLC, RG 60, Box 7, NA*.

30. *U.S.* v. *Cervantes*, HLC, 16*; *Cervantes* v. *U.S.*, 57 U.S. 619 (1854).

Hoffman, sitting with McAllister, subsequently confirmed Cervantes' claim, relying on the Supreme Court's decision in the *Fremont* case. When the government then appealed to the Supreme Court, Hoffman and McAllister's decision was affirmed. See *U.S.* v. *Cervantes*, 59 U.S. 553.

31. *U.S.* v. *Fremont*, 58 U.S. 541; Montgomery Blair to Mrs. Montgomery Blair, April 17–30, July 9, 1854, Blair Family Papers, Box 41, LC; Dwight L. Clarke, *William Tecumseh Sherman: Gold Rush Banker* (San Francisco: California Historical Society, 1969), pp. 25 and 366, n. 44; Mary Lee Spence, "David Hoffman: Frémont's Mariposa Agent in London," *Southern California Quarterly* 60 (1978): 379–403.

32. Joseph S. Wilson to Cushing, Oct. 30, 1853, CCLC, RG 60, Box 1, NA*.

33. Montgomery Blair to Mrs. Montgomery Blair, April 9* and 22*, 1854, Blair Family Papers, Box 41, LC.

34. Carl Brent Swisher, *The Taney Period, 1836–1864*, vol. 5 of Freund, ed., *Holmes Devise History*, pp. 779–80; *U.S.* v. *Fremont*, 58 U.S. 541 at 552 (1855)*; Allan Nevins, *Frémont: Pathmarker of the West* (1939; new ed., New York: Longmans,

Green, 1955); Montgomery Blair to Mrs. Montgomery Blair, April 18, 1854, Blair Family Papers, Box 41, LC*.

35. Charles G. Crampton, "The Opening of the Mariposa Mining Region, 1849–1859, with Particular Reference to the Mexican Land Grant of John Charles Frémont" (Ph.D. diss., University of California, Berkeley, 1941); *Biddle Boggs* v. *Merced Mining Company*, 14 Cal. 279 (1859); *Moore* v. *Smaw* and *Fremont* v. *Flower*, 17 Cal. 199 (1861).

36. See *U.S.* v. *Boisdore*, 52 U.S. 62 (1851); *Glenn* v. *U.S.*, 54 U.S. 250 (1852); *Heirs of Don Carlos de Vilemont* v. *U.S.*, 54 U.S. 260 (1852).

37. Brief for the United States, *U.S.* v. *Cervantes* (Dec. term, 1853), in Wills *California Titles*, vol. 11, HL*; *Frémont* v. *U.S.*, 58 U.S. 541 at 563*.

38. *U.S.* v. *Fremont*, 58 U.S. 541 at 572*.

39. *Arguello* v. *U.S.*, 59 U.S. 539 at 552 (1856)*.

40. Ibid., 550, 553*.

41. On attitudes of the justices, in particular Taney, Catron, and Daniel, see Leon Friedman and Fred L. Israel, eds., *The Justices of the United States Supreme Court, 1789–1979*, 5 vols. (New York and London: Chelsea House Publishers, 1969), 1:635–54, 737–49, 795–805, and Swisher, *Taney Period*, p. 748. The first three California land grants were *U.S.* v. *Fremont*, 58 U.S. 541; *U.S.* v. *Ritchie*, 58 U.S. 524 (1855); *U.S.* v. *Reading*, 59 U.S. 1 (1856).

42. *U.S.* v. *Reading*, 59 U.S. 1 at 15*.

43. *Teschmaker* v. *U.S.*, HLC, 28 at 29*. Where the board had rejected claims, see HLC, 28, 37, 43, 66, 69, 87, 107, 113, 116, 130, 142, 162, 173, 188, 191, and 248. Where the board had confirmed claims, see HLC, 41, 49, 68, 72, 74, 75–76, 77, 79, 79–80, 80–81, 83–84, 84–85, 86–87, 89, 92–94, 96, 99, 101, 103, 109, 124, 126, 129, 137, 138, 141, 171, 172, and 176.

44. HLC, 219, 230, and 249 were rejected on their merits; the other two cases were HLC, 272 and 273. On the government's lack of argument, see HLC, 86–87 and 161. Compare Gates, "Spanish-Mexican Land Claims," p. 226, and Gates, "California Land Act," pp. 402–4.

For the problems faced by the U.S. attorney's office, see Samuel W. Inge to Cushing, Feb. 26, 1854, Feb. 4, April 1, 1856, AGLR, RG 60, Box 1, NA; Inge to Cushing, Oct. 15, 1853, CCLC, RG 60, Box 7, NA; Inge to Gilbert Rodman, July 15, 1853, SLR, RG 206, NA.

The cases in which the government offered no argument were HLC, 41, 49, 68, 72, 74, 74–75, 75–76, 76–77, 77, 79*, 79–80, 80–81, 81, 82, 82–83, 83–84, 86–87, 89, 92–94, 94–95, 96, 97, 99, 99–100, 101, 103, 105, 109, 110, 111, 124, 126, 137, 138, 139, 141, 142*, 154, 155, 162, 170, 171, and 191.

45. HLC, 43, 68, 72, 74, 76, 77, 80–81, 82, 83–84, 109, and 142.

46. HLC, 116 at 117*.

47. Ibid. at 123–24*.

48. HLC, 191 at 195*. Even the sharpest critics of the land adjudication acknowledged that relatively few claims had been rejected by 1857. Most criticism centered

on the length of time it was taking to settle titles and the consequences of delay for land claimants.

For Hoffman's doubts in confirming land grants, see HLC, 86–87, 90–92, 125, 161–62, 170, 177, and 188 at 190*.

49. See, for example, *U.S.* v. *Pico*, 64 U.S. 321 (1860); *U.S.* v. *Osio*, 64 U.S. 273 (1860); and *U.S.* v. *Neleigh*, 66 U.S. 298 (1862).

50. Eisenstein, *Counsel*, pp. 9–10; Albert Langeluttig, *The Department of Justice of the United States* (Baltimore: Johns Hopkins University Press, 1927), pp. 1–17; Cummings and McFarland, *Federal Justice*, pp. 142–60.

51. James F. Stuart to Cushing, Jan. 19, 1857, CCLC, RG 60, Box 2, NA*; William M. Gwin and Milton S. Latham to Cushing, Dec. 1, 1853; John B. Weller to Cushing, Dec. 2, 1853; Gwin to Cushing, March 5, 1856; all in CCLC, RG 60, Box 1, NA.

52. Cushing to William M. Gwin, Dec. 3, 1853, CCLC, RG 60, Box 1, NA*.

53. Act of March 3, 1851, 9 *US STAT* 631, Sec. 12; Act of August 31, 1852, 10 *US STAT* 76, Sec. 12.

54. Cushing to Milton S. Latham, Dec. 13, 1854, CCLC, RG 60, Box 1, NA*; Cushing to Franklin Pierce, March 4, 1857, Box 242, and A. Anderson to Cushing, Feb. 16, 1857, Box 245, Cushing Papers, LC; Act of Aug. 18, 1856, 11 *US STAT* 102.

55. Cushing to Thomas Douglas, Sept. 29, 1854; Cushing to Thomas M. J. Denhen, March 28, 1855; Cushing to Louis Jarvis, Feb. 9, 1856; Cushing to J. B. Crockett, April 30, 1856; Cushing to E. Stanley, Jan. 31, 1857; all in CCLC, RG 60, Box 1, NA. Samuel W. Inge to Cushing, Oct. 15, Nov. 14, 1853, Feb. 1, March 15, May 1, July 15, 1854; A. Glassell to Cushing, March 30, Nov. 30, 1855; William Blanding to Cushing, Sept. 19, Oct. 14, Dec. 17, 1856, Jan. 19, 31, Feb. 3, 23, March 4, 12 and 14, 1857; all in CCLC, RG 60, Box 7, NA. Cushing to A. Glassell, Jan. 3, 1856; Cushing to Samuel W. Inge, May 17, 1856; Cushing to William Blanding, Dec. 10, 1856, June 17, 1857; all in CCLC, RG 60, Box 8, NA. Cushing to Franklin Pierce, March 4, 1857, Cushing Papers, Box 242, LC.

56. James F. Stuart to Cushing, Jan. 19, 1857*, and Cushing to M. Farmer, Jan. 14, 1857*, CCLC, RG 60, Box 2, NA.

57. Cushing to James A. Bayard, Jr., March 15, 1856, CCLC, RG 60, Box 1, NA*.

58. Opinions of the Attorney General, Sept. 18, Oct. 15, 1855, May 29, 1856, Jan. 6, 1857, and Cushing to Franklin Pierce, March 4, 1857, Cushing Papers, Box 242, LC; Cushing to Secretary of the Interior, Sept. 18, 1855, Cushing Papers, Box 241, LC.

59. Halleck, Peachy, and Billings to Cushing, Feb. 8, 1855, CCLC, RG 60, Box 1, NA*.

60. Act of Sept. 28, 1850, 9 *US STAT* 521; Act of Aug. 31, 1852, 10 *US STAT* 76 at 84; Hoffman, Sr., to Hamilton Fish, Feb. 22, 1853, Hamilton Fish Papers, LC*; Hoffman, Jr., to Cushing, Oct. 15, 1853, AGLR, RG 60, Box 1, NA*; and *Minutes*, Oct. 17, 1853.

61. Samuel W. Inge to Cushing, July 15, 1854, Box 7*, and Alpheus Felch to Cushing, July 13, 1854, Box 6, CCLC, RG 60, NA.

62. Act of Feb. 13, 1801, 2 *US STAT* 89. Cushing's proposal for changes in the structure of the federal judiciary appear in U.S. Cong., 33d Cong., 1st sess., 1854, S. Ex. Doc. 41. For the debates in 1855, see *Cong. Globe*, 33d Cong., 2d sess., 1855, pp. 195, 203, 233, 242, 340, 357, 358, 605, 970–71; Cushing to Milton S. Latham, Dec. 13, 1854, CCLC, RG 60, Box 1, NA.

63. *Cong. Globe*, 33d Cong., 2d sess., 1855, pp. 583, 604, 605*, 606–7, 681; Act of March 2, 1855, 10 *US STAT* 631 at 632, Sec. 6*.

64. Gamble, "The McAllisters, 1758–1888," BL; Douglas S. Watson, "The San Francisco McAllisters," *California Historical Society Quarterly* 11 (1932): 124–28; Hall, *Politics of Justice*, p. 224 n. 55; *Alta California*, March 18, 1855.

65. Act of April 30, 1856, 11 *US STAT* 6, Sec. 2*; C.C.C.Cal., *Minutes*, I–II, July 2, 1855, to June 29, 1863, BL; D.C.N.D.Cal., Decree Book, June 5, 1851 to Feb. 15, 1858, BL; HLC; Gamble, "The McAllisters, 1758–1888," p. 120, BL*.

66. Henry W. Halleck to Pablo de la Guerra, Sept. 9, 1856, de la Guerra Papers, HL; Cushing to W. Bigler, Jan. 14, 1857, CCLC, RG 60, Box 1, NA; Cushing, Circular of Attorney General's Office, April 2, 1856, Cushing Papers, Box 242, LC*. The two cases were *Frémont* v. *U.S.*, 58 U.S. 541 and *U.S.* v. *Ritchie*, 58 U.S. 524.

67. William Carey Jones to Cushing, March 28, July 16, 1855, and Cushing to James A. Bayard, March 15, 1856, CCLC, RG 60, Box 1, NA; Jones to Jeremiah S. Black, March 18, 1857, CCLC, RG 60, Box 2, NA; Cushing, Circular, Cushing Papers, Box 242, LC*.

68. John A. Sutter to John Bidwell, May 6, 1854, Bidwell Papers, Box 349, CSL; Samuel A. Morrison to Cushing, July 1, 1855, CCLC, RG 60, Box 1, NA; James F. Stuart to Cushing, Jan. 19, 1857, CCLC, RG 60, Box 2, NA; Jones to Cushing, March 28, 1855, CCLC, RG 60, Box 1, NA*; William Carey Jones, *Condition of Real Property in California* (San Francisco, 1855), p. 2*; Cushing, Circular, Cushing Papers, Box 242, LC; Cushing to Louis Worcester, May 3, 1856, CCLC, RG 60, Box 9, NA.

69. Cushing to Franklin Pierce, March 4, 1857, Cushing Papers, Box 242, LC.

70. C. Peter Magrath, *Yazoo: Law and Politics in the New Republic, the Case of Fletcher v. Peck* (Providence, R.I.: Brown University Press, 1966); Cummings and McFarland, *Federal Justice*, pp. 120–28; Gates, *Public Land Law*.

71. S. K. Norse to Cushing, March 31, 1856; Settlers petition to Cushing, June 25, 1856; A. Keefer to Cushing, Dec. 19, 1855; Printed petition [1855]*; all in CCLC, RG 60, Box 1, NA.

72. William Carey Jones to J. W. Denver, Aug. 5, 1856, in Wills, *California Titles*, vol. 13, HL*.

73. Land Grant Cases, 548 N.D., 424 Bd.; 549 N.D., 429 Bd.; 715 N.D., 315 Bd.; 780 N.D., 317 Bd.; 781 S.D., 311 Bd.; 782 S.D., 314 Bd.; 783 S.D., 321 Bd.; 784 N.D., 307 Bd.; all in BL; Billings to J. L. Folsom, Feb. 15, 1853, William A. Leidesdorff Papers, Box 6, HL*.

74. Cushing to Samuel W. Inge, May 17, 1856, CCLC, RG 60, Box 8, NA; Cushing to Franklin Pierce, May 24, 1856*, Cushing Papers, Box 242, LC; J. B. Crockett to Caroline Matilda Crockett, Nov. 30, 1852, Joseph B. Crockett Papers, BL; Crockett to James Gadsen, Dec. 30, 1853, CCLC, RG 60, Box 1, NA.

75. Joseph B. Crockett to James Gadsen, Dec. 30, 1853, CCLC, RG 60, Box 1, NA*; John S. Hittell, *A Brief Statement of the Moral and Legal Merits of the Claim Made by José Y. Limantour* (San Francisco, 1857), in Wills, *California Titles*, vol. 19, HL; Treasury Agent J. Ross Browne to James Guthrie, April 5, 1856, CCLC, RG 60, Box 4, NA*.

76. Peter Della Torre to Jeremiah S. Black, Dec. 4, 1857, CCLC, RG 60, Box 7, NA*.

77. Peter Della Torre to John B. Floyd, July 20, 1857, CCLC, RG 60, Box 7, NA*.

78. E. F. Northam to Jeremiah S. Black, July 4, 1857, CCLC, RG 60, Box 2, NA*; Benjamin P. Thomas and Harold M. Hyman, *Stanton* (New York: Knopf, 1962), pp. 42–67; U.S. Cong., Jeremiah S. Black, *Report on California Land Claims to the House of Representatives*, 36th Cong., 1st sess., 1860, H. Ex. Doc. 84*; George C. Gorham, *Life and Public Services of Edwin M. Stanton*, 2 vols. (Boston, 1899), 1:55–56*.

79. E. F. Northam to Cushing, July 31, 1856, CCLC, RG 60, Box 1, NA; Auguste Youan to Jeremiah S. Black, April 19, 1857, vol. 5, and Youan to Black, May 18, 1857, vol. 7, Black Papers, LC; Black to Northam and H. W. Whitmore, June 17, 1857, CCLC, RG 60, Box 2, NA; Peter Della Torre to Black, June 16, 1857, vol. 8, Black Papers, LC*.

80. Peter Della Torre to Jeremiah S. Black, July 20, 1857, CCLC, RG 60, Box 7, NA*; Larkin to Jacob Leese, Jan. 3, 1857, Mariano Guadalupe Vallejo Papers, Box 4, HL*; Leonard Pitt, *The Decline of the Californios: A Social History of the Spanish-Speaking Californians, 1846–1890,* (Berkeley: University of California Press, 1970), pp. 26–82. For conflicts between Anglos and Hispanics in terms of their cultural expectations of law in California in the period prior to American conquest, see David J. Langum, *Law and Community on the Mexican California Frontier: Anglo-American Expatriates and the Clash of Legal Traditions, 1821–1846* (Norman: University of Oklahoma Press, 1987).

81. Speech of Pablo de la Guerra in the California Senate criticizing the operation of the act of 1851 and the actions of the board and the federal courts, n.d., 2–9, de la Guerra Papers, HL; Pitt, *Californios*, pp. 83–119; Cleland, *Cattle on a Thousand Hills*, pp. 39–46, 238–43. Paul W. Gates has shown that a substantial number of claimants before the board were non-Hispanics (some 42%), who either had been granted the land originally (16%) or had subsequently acquired it (26%), and that numerous other grants passed to non-Hispanics before they were ultimately patented. See Gates, "California Land Act," pp. 408–10. Although the causes of this shift in land ownership may be debated, its occurrence could not help but shape Hispanic attitudes toward the land litigation process. For de Puig's characterization, see de Puig to Pablo de la Guerra, April 12, 1857, de la Guerra Collection (film), California Historical Survey Comm., Item 691, HL*.

82. Peter Della Torre to Jeremiah S. Black, July 20, 1857, CCLC, RG 60, Box 7, NA*.

83. Jeremiah S. Black to Isaac N. Thorne, July 17, 1858, vol. 18, Black Papers, LC*; Peter Della Torre to Black, Jan. 19, 1858, CCLC, RG 60, Box 7, NA*; Edwin M. Stanton to Black, April 16*, Aug. 1*, 1858, vol. 17, Black Papers, LC.

84. Employment contract, Feb. 17, 1858, vol. 16, Black Papers, LC; Edwin M. Stanton, Daily Journal, April 13, 17, 19, 21, 23, 28, May 20, 22, June 13, July 14, 1858, CSL.

85. Edwin M. Stanton to Peter H. Watson, April 2, 1858, quoted in Thomas and Hyman, *Stanton*, p. 77*; Stanton to Jeremiah S. Black, April 16, 1858, vol. 17, Black Papers, LC*; Stanton, Daily Journal, April 21, 22, 27, 1858, CSL; Stanton to unknown correspondent, Sept. 5, 1858, quoted in Gorham, *Edwin M. Stanton*, 1:65*.

86. See Peter Della Torre to Jeremiah S. Black, July 3, 1858, CCLC, RG 60, Box 7, NA. For the expense involved, see *Expenditures on Account of Private Land Claims in California*, 36th Cong., 1st sess., 1859–60, H. Exec. Doc. No. 84.

87. HLC, 389 at 451*.

88. D.C.N.D.Cal., *U.S.* v. *Limantour*, Misc. Small Collections, LC. As Carl B. Swisher put it, "The Court was being educated" (*Taney Period*, p. 782). See also Jeremiah S. Black to R. C. Hopkins, Aug. 6, Nov. 19, 1859, and Hopkins to Black, Sept. 19, 1859, CCLC, RG 60, Box 9, NA.

89. Black, *Report*, p. 31*; Peter Della Torre to John B. Floyd, July 20, 1857, CCLC, RG 60, Box 7, NA; John Wilson to Edward Bates, March 23, 1861, CCLC, RG 60, Box 3, NA; Henry W. Halleck to Milton S. Latham, March 26, 1860, and Halleck to G. W. Cooley, April 1, 1852, HPB Papers, Box 1, BL; R. C. Hopkins to Stephen J. Field, Oct. 19, 1863, Stephen J. Field Papers, BL.

90. Black, *Report*, p. 32*.

91. Jeremiah S. Black to Count de Sar Tiges, Feb. 14, 1859, CCLC, RG 60, Box 5, NA*.

92. Peter Della Torre to Jeremiah S. Black, July 20*, Dec. 4, 1857, Jan. 19, 1858, CCLC, RG 60, Box 7, NA; Edwin M. Stanton to Black, April 16, 1858, vol. 17, Black Papers, LC*.

93. E. F. Northam to Jeremiah S. Black, July 18, 1857, CCLC, RG 60, Box 2, NA*; Peter Della Torre to Black, Aug. 4, 1857; CCLC, RG 60, Box 7, NA*. John Clarken to Black, Dec. 3, 1857; Thompson and Campbell to Black, Dec. 18, 1857; Senica Ewer to Black, March 7, 1858; E. L. Gould to Black, March 20, 1858; Black to Louis Blanding, June 16, 1858; Blanding to Black, July 19, 1858; Memorial to Congress, Feb. 2, 1859; Gould to Black, June 17, 1859; William Carey Jones to Black, June 13, 1859; Louis Janin to Black, Sept. 1, 1859; all in CCLC, RG 60, Box 2, NA. Obed Short to Black, July 2, 1860, Box 3; Edmund Randolph to Black, Oct. 17, 1859, Box 6; Della Torre to Black, July 3, Aug. 4, Oct. 19, 1858, Box 7; Black to Della Torre, March 3 and 17, 1859, and I.S.K. Ogier to Black, Jan. 26, 1860, Box 8; Black to John S. Phelps, Dec. 18, 1858, Box 1*; all in CCLC, RG 60, NA.

94. HLC, 191 at 193*, 197 at 200*, and 389 at 412*. For inconsistencies detected

by Hoffman, see HLC, 188–90, 191–96, 197–203, 249–72, 284–98, 305–12, 345–73, and 389–451.

95. HLC, 50–65 and 290, both dealing with non-Hispanics.

96. Ibid., 284–88* and 389 at 395*.

97. Halleck to Pablo de la Guerra, March 1, 1852*, and Feb. 24, 1854*, de la Guerra Papers, HL.

98. J. L. Folsom to John Bidwell, June 12, 1854, Box 129, and Thomas O. Larkin to Bidwell, Oct. 10, 1853, Box 132, Bidwell Papers, CSL; Henry W. Halleck to Pablo de la Guerra, Feb. 24, 1854, de la Guerra Papers, HL. Sidney L. Johnson to Joseph P. Thompson, Oct. 10, 1859, Box 35; Charles R. Johnson to Abel Stearns, Sept. 4, 1862, Box 36; Larkin to Stearns, June 17, 1854, Box 40; Thompson to Stearns, April 28, 1854, June 27, 1861, Box 66; all in Stearns Papers, HL. Pitt, *Californios*, pp. 89–91; Halleck to Pablo de la Guerra, May 23*, Nov. 10*, 1853, de la Guerra Papers, HL.

99. HLC, 50, 86–87, 90–92, 125, 161, 170, 177, 219, 230, 249, 284, 305, 313, 345, and 389.

100. *U.S.* v. *Cambuston*, 61 U.S. 59 (1858); 15 Lawyers Ed. 828 at 829*; HLC, 86–87.

101. *U.S.* v. *Cambuston*, 61 U.S. 59 at 64* and 65*.

102. HLC, 284 at 298*. Also see HLC, 305, 313, and 345.

103. *U.S.* v. *Cambuston*, 25 F. Cas. 266 (D.C.D.Cal. 1859)*; Gates, "California Land Act," pp. 424–25 n. 27.

104. *U.S.* v. *Cambuston*, 61 U.S. 59; *U.S.* v. *Fossat*, 61 U.S. 413 (1858); *U.S.* v. *Sutter*, 62 U.S. 170 (1859); *U.S.* v. *Nye*, 62 U.S. 408 (1859); *U.S.* v. *Bassett*, 62 U.S. 412 (1859); *U.S.* v. *Fossatt [sic]*, 62 U.S. 445 (1859); *U.S.* v. *Rose*, 64 U.S. 262 (1860); *U.S.* v. *Widow and Heirs of West*, 63 U.S. 315 (1860); *U.S.* v. *Alviso*, 64 U.S. 318 (1860); *U.S.* v. *Bennitz*, 64 U.S. 255 (1860); *U.S.* v. *Teschmaker*, 63 U.S. 392 (1860); *U.S.* v. *Pico*, 63 U.S. 406 (1860); *U.S.* v. *Vallejo*, 63 U.S. 416 (1860); *U.S.* v. *Murphy* and *U.S.* v. *Pratt*, 64 U.S. 476 (1860); *U.S.* v. *Pico*, 64 U.S. 321 (1860); *U.S.* v. *Osio*, 64 U.S. 273 (1860); *U.S.* v. *Pacheco*, 63 U.S. 225 (1860); *Yturbide's Executors* v. *U.S.*, 63 U.S. 290 (1860); *U.S.* v. *Noe*, 64 U.S. 312 (1860); *Yontz* v. *U.S.*, 64 U.S. 495 (1860); *U.S.* v. *Widow, Heirs, and Executors of Hartnell*, 63 U.S. 286 (1860); *U.S.* v. *Garcia*, 63 U.S. 274 (1860); *Gonzales* v. *U.S.*, 63 U.S. 161 (1860); *U.S.* v. *Galbraith*, 63 U.S. 89 (1860); *U.S.* v. *Widow and Heirs of Berreyesa*, 64 U.S. 499 (1860); *U.S.* v. *Heirs of De Haro*, 63 U.S. 293 (1860); *U.S.* v. *Castillero*, 64 U.S. 464 (1860); *Fuentes* v. *U.S.*, 63 U.S. 443 (1860); *Luco* v. *U.S.*, 64 U.S. 515 (1860); *U.S.* v. *Gomez*, 64 U.S. 326 (1860); *U.S.* v. *Bolton*, 64 U.S. 341 (1860); *Castro* v. *Hendricks*, 64 U.S. 438 (1860); *U.S.* v. *White*, 64 U.S. 249 (1860).

105. See, for example, *U.S.* v. *Noe*, 64 U.S. 312.

106. *U.S.* v. *Teschmaker*, 63 U.S. 392; *Fuentes* v. *U.S.*, 63 U.S. 443; *U.S.* v. *Castro*, 65 U.S. 346 (1861); *Romero* v. *U.S.*, 68 U.S. 721 (1864).

107. *U.S.* v. *Teschmaker*, 63 U.S. 392*; HLC, 28.

108. *Luco* v. *U.S.*, 64 U.S. 515, and *U.S.* v. *Osio*, 64 U.S. 273.

Justice Field's opinion in *Hornsby* v. *U.S.*, 77 U.S. 224 (1870), epitomizes the return to the liberality of *Fremont*. See Fairman, *Reconstruction and Reunion*, vol. 7 of Freund, ed., *Holmes Devise History*, pp. 619–20.

CHAPTER 6

1. The Act of 1851 allowed authorities of California towns to present their claims for pueblo lands. See Act of March 3, 1851, 9 US STAT 631, Sec. 14; preemption was a preferential right given to actual settlers on government land to purchase up to 160 acres of land they occupied at minimum prices. The federal preemption act of 1841 was extended to California in 1853. See Robinson, *Land in California*, pp. 163–75.

2. Between 1846 and 1850, the Mexican office of *alcalde* was continued, but was largely filled by non-Hispanics, giving rise to the term *American* alcalde *grants*. See Alfred Wheeler et al., *Report on the Condition of the Real Estate Within the Limits of the City of San Francisco* (San Francisco, 1851); Bancroft, *History of California*, 5:652–55, 6:195–96, 755.

3. Bancroft, *History of California*, 6:192; Zoeth Skinner Eldredge, *The Beginnings of San Francisco*, 2 vols. (San Francisco: Z. S. Eldredge, 1912), 2:565–67; Bruno Fritzsche, "San Francisco, 1846–1848: The Coming of the Land Speculator," *California Historical Society Quarterly* 51 (1972): 17–34; Gates, "Carpetbaggers," pp. 99–127; Argument of R. A. Wilson, *Woodworth* v. *Fulton*, 1 Cal. 295 at 303 (1850); William T. Sherman, *Memoirs of General William T. Sherman*, 2 vols. (New York, 1875), 1:33*.

4. Lotchin, *San Francisco*, p. 63; Shafter, *Diary and Letters*, July 20, 1855, p. 160*; John McCrackan to his sister Mary, Oct. 14, 1850, McCrackan Papers, BL; C. B. Strode to Abel Stearns, Nov. 18, 1854, Box 64, and Joseph P. Thompson to Stearns, Feb. 12, 1855, Box 66, Stearns Papers, HL. For the reference to "mushroom" millionaires, see Oscar L. Shafter to his wife, in Shafter, *Diary and Letters*, Feb. 23, 1855, pp. 113–14.

5. See Hittell, *History of California*, 2:634–37, 656, 658, 737–38, 3:370–73, 380–84, 388–89, 394–96, 400–402; John S. Hittell, *A History of the City of San Francisco* (San Francisco, 1878), pp. 113, 116–17; Bancroft, *History of California*, 5:652–54, 6:193, 755–57; Kenneth M. Johnson, "The Judges Colton," *Southern California Quarterly* 57 (1975): 355–60; Bernard Moses, *The Establishment of Municipal Government in San Francisco* (Baltimore, 1889), pp. 56–60; *San Francisco Herald*, Feb. 25, 1852; Henry H. Haight to Fletcher M. Haight, July 17, 1850, Henry H. Haight Papers, HL*; John McCrackan to his sister Mary, Aug. 18, 1850, McCrackan Papers, BL*.

6. Henry H. Haight to Joseph B. Wells, April 22, 1854, Henry H. Haight Papers, HL; McCrackan to his sister Lottie, Feb. 27, 1850, and McCrackan to his mother, May 24, 1850* (water lot), McCrackan Papers, BL; Francis L. Aud to John Wilson,

Dec. 23, 1851, John Wilson Papers, Box 1, BL; Joseph B. Crockett to Mrs. Joseph B. Crockett, Feb. 28, Aug. 16, 1853, Joseph B. Crockett Papers and Deed Portfolio, BL; Elbert P. Jones, Portfolio (water lots purchased in 1847), BL.

7. On these execution sales, see Molly Selvin, "'This Tender and Delicate Business': The Public Trust Doctrine in American Law and Economic Policy, 1789–1920" (Ph.D. diss., University of California, San Diego, 1978), pp. 183–90; "Evidence of the Amount of Lands held in San Francisco Against 'Peter Smith Deeds' and Explanations of the 'Peter Smith Map'" (1859), in *Pamphlets on San Francisco Lands* n.d., II, no. 2, BL; Herbert William Drummond, "Squatter Activity in San Francisco, 1847–1854" (Master's thesis, University of California, Berkeley, 1952), p. 22; Lotchin, *San Francisco*, pp. 136–63.

8. Joseph Folsom to Peachy, Jan. 1852*; John B. Weller to Folsom, June 18, 1852; Peachy to Folsom, Jan. 31, Feb. 24, April 16, May 31, 1853; all in William A. Leidesdorff Papers, Box 6, HL.

9. "The Land Litigation on the Confines of the City," *Weekly Law Review* 1 (July 19, 1855), in Wills, *California Titles*, vol. 12; Oscar T. Shuck, *History of the Bench and Bar of California*, (Los Angeles: Commercial Printing House, 1901), pp. 417–21, 454–56; Thomas G. Barnes, *Hastings College of the Law: The First Century* (San Francisco: Hastings College of the Law Press, 1978), pp. 1–42; McAllister Scrapbooks, 2:88–93, Society of California Pioneers Library, San Francisco; J. L. Folsom to A. C. Peachy, Jan. 1852, William A. Leidesdorff Papers, Box 6, HL; Hittell, *History of California*, 3:400; David A. Williams, *David C. Broderick: A Political Portrait* (San Marino, Calif.: Huntington Library, 1969), pp. 28–29.

10. "Judge R. F. Peckham, An Eventful Life," *San Jose Pioneer*, July 28, 1877*.

11. On squatter activity, see Drummond, "Squatter Activity"; Oscar L. Shafter to his father, in Shafter, *Diary and Letters*, Dec. 14, 1854, p. 67; Montgomery Blair to Mrs. Montgomery Blair, June 11, July 9, 1854, Blair Family Papers, Box 41, LC; Elisha O. Crosby to John Bidwell, July 20, 1853, Bidwell Papers, Box 128, CSL; Henry W. Halleck to Pablo de la Guerra, Jan. 29, 1852, Oct. 19, 1853, de la Guerra Papers, HL; David Spence to Pablo de la Guerra, Feb. 2, 1857, de la Guerra Papers (Film), HL; Thomas O. Larkin to Abel Stearns, March 12, April 24, 1856, Stearns Papers, Box 41, HL; Hittell, *History of California*, 3:677–78, 681–85; *Alta California*, Feb. 25, 1852, June 10, July 22, 1853, May 31, June 2, 6, 7, and 10, 1854; *San Francisco Herald*, Feb. 25, 1852, May 28, 1854.

For legal and judicial support for squatterism, see Gates, "Settlers," pp. 99–130; Richard R. Powell, *Compromises of Conflicting Claims: A Century of California Law, 1760 to 1860* (Dobbs Ferry, New York: Oceana Publications, 1977), pp. 168–72; Harry N. Scheiber and Charles W. McCurdy, "Eminent Domain Law and Western Agriculture," *Agricultural History* 49 (1975): 112–30; Charles W. McCurdy, "Stephen J. Field and Public Land Law Development in California, 1850–1866," *Law and Society Review* 10 (1976): 235–66; Hittell, *History of California*, 3:685–87; Act of April 20, 1852, *Cal. Stat.* (3rd sess., 1852), 158; Act of April 11, 1855, *Cal. Stat.*

(6th sess., 1855), 109; Act of March 3, 1853, 9 *US STAT* 631; Act of March 3, 1853, 10 *US STAT* 244.

12. Hittell, *History of California*, 3:679; *Alta California*, July 22, 1853*.

13. *Alta California*, June 10, 1853*, Aug. 4, 1853*.

14. Wheeler, *Report; Alta California*, Oct. 15, 1853, June 2, 16, 18, 21, and 25, July 1, 1854, March 11, 1858; *San Francisco Herald*, May 28, 1854; William Carey Jones, *The "Pueblo Question" Solved, in a Plain Statement of Facts and Law* (San Francisco, 1860), BL; San Francisco, Board of Supervisors, *Municipal Reports*, Report of the City and County Attorney, 1859–60 (San Francisco, 1860); William J. Shaw and Nathaniel Bennett, *Land Titles in San Francisco* (San Francisco, 1862), in *Pamphlets on San Francisco Land*, V, no. 9, BL; *Alta California*, May 30, 1865; Bancroft, *History of California*, 6:565–70; Selvin, "Public Trust Doctrine," chap. 3.

15. *Woodworth v. Fulton*, 1 Cal. 295 at 307* and 312–22 (1850).

16. *Cohas v. Raisin*, 3 Cal. 443 (1853). There is some evidence to suggest that the change in the court's composition, made possible by Bennett's resignation in 1851, was deliberately induced by those who sought to see *Woolworth v. Fulton* reversed. See Johnson, *Supreme Court Justices*, 1:40.

17. *Welch v. Sullivan*, 8 Cal. 165 at 201* (1857).

18. *Hart v. Burnett*, 15 Cal. 530 (1860). For the background of the case and its legal significance, see Selvin, "Public Trust Doctrine," chap. 3.

19. *Hart v. Burnett*, 15 Cal. 530 at 540* and 573*.

20. *San Francisco v. U.S.*, 21 F. Cas. 365 (C.C.N.D.Cal. 1864); *Townsend v. Greeley*, 72 U.S. 326 (1867); *Grisar v. McDowell*, 73 U.S. 363 (1868); *Hart v. Burnett*, 15 Cal. 530 at 610* and 612*.

21. Field, *Personal Reminiscences*, pp. 149*, 159*; Swisher, *Stephen J. Field*, pp. 35, 70–71, 82–90, 97; McCurdy, "Field and Public Land Law."

22. John W. Dwinelle, *The Colonial History: City of San Francisco* (4th ed., 1867; reprint, Ross Valley Book Co., 1978), addenda nos. 112*, 146; "The Land Litigation," in Wills, *California Titles*, vol. 12; Hittell, *Moral and Legal Merits*, in Wills, *California Titles*, vol. 19. South of the intersection at Market Street, Larkin Street was called Johnson Street but today is called Ninth Street.

23. Kenneth M. Johnson, *José Yves Limantour v. the United States* (Los Angeles: Dawson's Book Shop, 1961); Francis J. Corbett, "The Public Domain and Mexican Land Grants in California" (Master's thesis, University of California, Berkeley, 1959), pp. 62–63.

24. Claim for Mission Dolores, 338 N.D., 81 Bd.

25. William Kelly, *An Excursion to California*, 2 vols. (London, 1851), 2:33*; William T. Sherman to Henry Smith Turner, June 15, 1855, quoted in Clarke, *Gold Rush Banker*, p. 148*.

26. William N. Walton to John Center, July 16, 1855, John Center Papers, Box 1, HL; San Francisco Land Association, *Articles of Association and Agreement of the San Francisco Land Association* (Philadelphia, 1855), p. 5; "Memorial to Congress," Feb. 2, 1859, CCLC, RG 60, Box 2, NA; Black, *Report*.

27. "Memorial to Congress," Feb. 2, 1859, CCLC, RG 60, Box 2, NA.

28. F. Fraley to Jeremiah S. Black, Feb. 2, 1858, XV; George F. Campbell to Black, April 8, XVII; Isaac N. Thorne to Black, June 19, 1858, XVII; R. L. Roman to Roger B. Taney, July 1, XVIII; Black to Throne, July 17 1858, XVIII*; Fraley to Black, Dec. 23, 1858, XX; Nathaniel Bennett to Black, Jan. 16, 1860, XXVII; all in Black Papers, LC; Black to Peter Della Torre, March 3, 1859, Box 8, and Black to J. W. Mandeville, Jan. 16, 1860, Box 9, CCLC, RG 60, NA; *U.S.* v. *Bolton*, 64 U.S. 341 at 352* (1860).

29. *U.S.* v. *Sherrebeck*, 27 F. Cas. 1062 (D.C.N.D.Cal. 1859); Black, *Report**; HLC, 106 appendix.

30. *Minutes*, March 30, 1857; San Francisco, Board, *Municipal Reports*, Report of the City, p. 173. The brief prepared by John W. Dwinelle was later published as *The Colonial History: City of San Francisco.*

31. Hoffman sought strict compliance with conditions, such as land habitation and land improvements, found in some grants. For example, see *U.S.* v. *Cervantes*, HLC, 2.

32. *U.S.* v. *Greathouse*, 26 F. Cas. 18 (C.C.N.D.Cal. 1863).

33. See James G. Randall, *Constitutional Problems under Lincoln* (1926; rev. ed., Urbana: University of Illinois Press, 1951), pp. 74–95; Act of July 17, 1862, 12 US STAT 589; Swisher, *The Taney Period*, pp. 951–60.

34. On the Chapman incident, see Benjamin F. Gilbert, "Kentucky Privateers in California," *Kentucky State Historical Society Register* 38 (1940): 256–66; William M. Robinson, Jr., *The Confederate Privateers* (New Haven: Yale University Press, 1928), pp. 279–89; Asbury Harpending, *The Great Diamond Hoax*, ed. James H. Wilkins (Norman: University of Oklahoma Press, 1958), pp. 48–64; Robert J. Chandler, "The Release of the *Chapman* Pirates: A California Sidelight on Lincoln's Amnesty Policy," *Civil War History* 23 (1977): 129–43.

On the specific details of the Chapman incident and trial, see *Alta California*, March 16–21, 26–28, 30, April 5, 18, May 27, Aug. 11–13, Sept. 2, 7–10, 26, 29–30, Oct. 1, 3–8, 13, 15–18, 23, 1863; C.C.D.Cal., *Minutes*, Aug. 31, Sept. 7–9, 21–25, 28–30, Oct. 1–3, 5–10, 12–17, 1863, Jan. 26, Feb. 1, 15–16, March 7, 1864, RG 21, NA.

35. Proclamation, Dec. 8, 1863, 13 US STAT 737*; Abraham Lincoln, *The Collected Works of Abraham Lincoln*, ed. Roy P. Basler, 8 vols. (New Brunswick, N.J.: Rutgers University Press, 1953–55), 7:53–56, 67–68*; Swisher, *Taney Period*, pp. 959–60; Chandler, "Release of the *Chapman* Pirates," pp. 134–35.

36. Lincoln, *Works*, 7:67–68*; *In Re Greathouse*, 10 F. Cas. 1057 (C.C.N.D.Cal. 1864); *Alta California*, Feb. 16, 1864*; *San Francisco Bulletin*, Feb. 15, 1864; *Suisun Solano Herald*, Feb. 20, 1864; *Missouri Democrat*, Feb. 23, 1864*; *Nevada Gazette*, March 16, 1864; *Sacramento Union*, Feb. 20, 1864*. Joseph W. Drew to Deady, March 5, 1864, Deady Papers, OHS.

37. *San Francisco Bulletin*, March 24, 1864*; "Judge Hoffman and Senator Conness," in "Bancroft Scraps: Educated Men of California," 30:11, BL; John Astor, Jr.,

to Hoffman, Nov. 7, 1861; Joseph Hooker to Hoffman, May 21, 1862; Hoffman to Hooker, Dec. 19, 1862*; all in Hunt. Ms., HL; Hoffman to William P. Fessenden, March 2, 1864, Bechtel Collection, California Historical Society, San Francisco*.

38. One San Franciscan noted the general impression that Conness was "moved by personal hostility to Judge Hoffman and the desire to have one of his own friends appointed in his place." See William Norris to Montgomery Blair, March 22, 1864, Blair Family Papers, Box 7, LC.

39. John B. Williams to Hoffman, May 12, 1864*, Hunt. Ms., HL; *Alta California*, March 17, 1864; *San Francisco Bulletin*, March 17, 23, April 18, July 6, 1864; *Sacramento Union*, April 16, 1864; *Cong. Globe*, 38th Cong., 1st sess., 1864, p. 582*; Hoffman to William P. Fessenden, March 2, 1864, Bechtel Collection, California Historical Society*; Act of Feb. 17, 1864, 13 US STAT 4.

40. Act of July 1, 1864, 13 US STAT 332, Sec. 3; John B. Williams to Hoffman, May 12, 1864, Hunt. Ms., HL*.

41. Field, *Personal Reminiscences*, pp. 161–62; Act of July 1, 1864, 13 US STAT 332, Sec. 4* and 5.

42. *Cong. Globe*, 38th Cong., 1st sess., 1864, p. 786*; *Sacramento Union*, March 18, 1864*; Hoffman to William P. Fessenden, March 2, 1864, Bechtel Collection, California Historical Society*.

43. Williams to Hoffman, May 12, 1864, Hunt. Ms., HL*. See also *Sacramento Union*, April 30, 1867, and *Colusa Sun*, May 11, 1867, for land title undercurrents in Hoffman's differences with Field and Conness.

44. *Alta California*, March 17* and 26*, 1864.

45. *Alta California*, April 14, 1864*; William Norris to Montgomery Blair, March 22, 1864, Blair Family Papers, Box 7, LC.

46. Lafayette S. Foster to Hoffman, April 14, 1864, Hunt. Ms., HL; *Alta California*, April 6, 14, June 28, 1864; *San Francisco Bulletin*, April 5, 1864; *New York Tribune*, March 25, 1864; *Sacramento Union*, April 15 and 16, May 19, 1864; Hoffman to Fessenden, March 2, 1864, Bechtel Collection, California Historical Society*.

47. *San Francisco Bulletin*, March 23, 1864; *Alta California*, March 24, 1864.

48. *Cong. Globe*, 38th Cong., 1st sess., 1864, pp. 1311–12*.

49. Ibid., p. 1312*.

50. Ibid.*; 13 US STAT 332. Some thought Field's legislative involvement highly inappropriate. See *San Francisco Bulletin*, March 23, 1864; Charles E. Pickett, *Land-Gambling Versus Mining-Gambling*, 2d ed. (San Francisco, 1879), p. 7; Bancroft, *History of California*, 7:231.

51. *Alta California*, Sept. 6, 1864*. As was discussed in chapter 1, the San Francisco records indicate that Hoffman was a city-lot holder in the 1850s, but there is no evidence to suggest any conflict of interest in the 1860s.

52. *Alta California*, Sept. 6, 1864*, Sept. 1, 1867.

53. San Francisco, Board of Supervisors, *Municipal Reports*, Report of the City and County Attorney (San Francisco, 1864), pp. 171–72.

54. John B. Williams to Titian J. Coffey, June 21, 1862; James F. Shunk to

Edwin M. Stanton, Jan. 17, 1861; Williams to Edward Bates, April 10, 1861; Williams to James Speed, June 2, 1865; all in CCLC, RG 60, Box 6, NA; Reverdy Johnson to Williams, May 10, 1864, and Williams to Hoffman, May 12, 1864, Hunt. Ms., HL.

55. Delos Lake to William M. Steward, Dec. 31, 1864, CCLC, RG 60, Box 1, NA.* According to Attorney General James Speed, Lake's actions had run counter to specific instructions from the U.S. attorney general's office. See Delos Lake to James Speed, May 18, June 3, 1865, CCLC, RG 60, Box 7, NA.

56. *San Francisco* v. *U.S.,* 21 F. Cas. 365 at 368* (C.C.N.D.Cal. 1864).

57. Ibid.* and at 370*; John W. Dwinelle to Frank McCoppin and Monroe Asbury, Feb. 9, 1867, Chipman-Dwinelle Collection, Box 2, HL.

58. *Alta California,* Nov. 3, 1864; Dwinelle, *Colonial History,* addenda nos. 118–20, 121*, 122; Swisher, *Taney Period,* p. 808 n. 168.

59. Dwinelle, *Colonial History,* addenda no. 123; Conness to Speed, April 5, 1865, CCLC, RG 60, Box 1, NA; *Alta California,* Sept. 2, 1867.

60. Dwinelle, *Colonial History,* addenda no. 128*.

61. *Alta California,* Nov. 3, 1864*; *U.S.* v. *Circuit Judges* 70 U.S. 673 (1866).

62. *U.S.* v. *Circuit Judges* 70 U.S. 673 at 677* and 681*.

63. Act of March 8, 1866, 14 US STAT 4*. As a result of the act, the appeal before the Supreme Court was dismissed. See *Townsend* v. *Greeley,* 72 U.S. 326 (1867). The litigation and conflict surrounding the disposition of San Francisco's confirmed pueblo was not over, but the key issues of the existence of a pueblo and the trust nature of the tenure under which the lands were held dictated the narrow terms within which the remaining disputes were resolved. See *Appendix to the Journals of the Senate and Assembly,* 17th sess., vol. 3 (Sacramento, 1868), *Report of the Judiciary Committee in Relation to Pueblo Lands in San Francisco,* pp. 3–8; San Francisco, Board of Supervisors, *Municipal Reports,* Report of the City and County Attorney (San Francisco, 1867–69).

64. For appraisals of the 1851 act, see William H. Ellison, *A Self-Governing Dominion: California, 1849–1860* (Berkeley: University of California Press, 1950), pp. 121–22; Robinson, *Land in California,* pp. 107, 109; Pitt, *Californios,* especially pp. 83–119; Cleland, *Cattle on a Thousand Hills,* pp. 33–50; Hornbeck, "California's Private Land Claims," pp. 438–40; Swisher, *Taney Period,* p. 809; Joseph Ellison, *California and the Nation* (Berkeley: University of California Press, 1927), pp. 23–24; John W. Caughey, *California,* 2d ed. (New York: Prentice-Hall, 1953), pp. 306–7. But compare Gates, "California Land Act," pp. 395–430.

65. *Alta California,* June 25, 1854*. Those who claimed land in San Francisco on the basis of possession were not necessarily simple settlers. The preemption claim in *Hart* v. *Burnett* was presented by Beideman, "a merchant and minor politician as well as real estate investor." See Selvin, "Public Trust Doctrine," pp. 185, 259.

66. *Hart* v. *Burnett,* 15 Cal. 530 at 610 (1860).

67. Eldredge, *Beginnings of San Francisco,* 2:567*; "Judge R. F. Peckham, An Eventful Life," *San Jose Pioneer,* July 28, 1877; John McCrackan to his mother,

Aug. 18, 1850, and McCrackan to his sister Mary, Aug. 18, 1850, McCrackan Papers, BL.

68. Field, *Personal Reminiscences*, pp. 160–61.

69. McCurdy, "Field and Public Land Law," p. 266*; Carl A. Pierce, "A Vacancy on the Supreme Court: The Politics of Judicial Appointment, 1893–1894," *Tennessee Law Review* 39 (1972): 558–62.

70. Field's resolution of the pueblo case brought not only criticism but also an attack on his life. See Field, *Personal Reminiscences*, pp. 164–68, 243–45.

CHAPTER 7

1. Most studies of the Chinese in nineteenth-century America have not emphasized the legal issues generated by their presence. For example, see Gunther Barth, *Bitter Strength: A History of the Chinese in the United States, 1850–1870* (Cambridge: Harvard University Press, 1964); Stuart C. Miller, *The Unwelcome Immigrant* (Berkeley: University of California Press, 1969); Shih-Shan Henry Tsai, *The Chinese Experience in America* (Bloomington: Indiana University Press, 1986); Alexander Saxton, *The Indispensable Enemy* (Berkeley: University of California Press, 1971); and Sucheng Chan, *This Bitter-Sweet Soil: The Chinese in California Agriculture, 1860–1910* (Berkeley: University of California Press, 1986).

2. To the extent that legal issues dealing with the Chinese experience in California have been studied, scholars have tended to focus on civil rights cases raising constitutional issues. For example, see Elmer C. Sandmeyer, *The Anti Chinese Movement in California* (Urbana: University of Illinois Press, 1939); Milton R. Konvitz, *The Alien and the Asiatic in American Law* (Ithaca: Cornell University Press, 1946); John R. Wunder, "The Chinese and the Courts in the Pacific Northwest: Justice Denied?" *Pacific Historical Review* 52 (1983): 191–211; John R. Wunder, "Chinese in Trouble: Criminal Law and Race on the Trans-Mississippi West Frontier," *Western Historical Quarterly* 17 (1986): 25–41; Charles J. McClain, Jr., "The Chinese Struggle for Civil Rights in 19th Century America: The Unusual Case of *Baldwin* v. *Franks*," *Law and History Review* 3 (1985): 349–73; and Charles J. McClain, Jr., "The Chinese Struggle for Civil Rights in Nineteenth Century America: The First Phase, 1850–1870," *California Law Review* 72 (1984): 529–68.

Two notable exceptions that discuss the habeas corpus writ litigation are Janisch, "The Chinese, the Courts, and the Constitution," and Nelson G. Dong, "The Chinese and the Anti-Chinese Movement: The Judicial Response in California, 1850–1886" (Seminar paper, Yale Law School, 1974).

3. Act of April 16, 1850, Ch. 99, Sec. 14, *Cal. Stat.* (1st sess., 1850), 229, 230 (criminal cases), and the Civil Practice Act of 1851, Ch. 5, Sec. 394(3), *Cal. Stat.* (2d sess., 1851), 51, 114 (civil cases); *People* v. *Hall*, 4 Cal. 399 (1854), and *Speer* v. *See Yup Company*, 13 Cal. 73 (1859); Act of March 18, 1863, Ch. 70, *Cal. Stat.* (14th

sess., 1863), 69, repealed by omission from codification California Penal Code Sec. 1321 (1872), and Act of March 16, 1863, Ch. 68, *Cal. Stat.* (14th sess., 1863), 60, repealed by omission from codification California Civ. Pro. Code Secs. 8, 1880 (1872).

In 1865, Lorenzo Sawyer, as an associate justice of the California Supreme Court, wrote an opinion for the court sustaining the testimony ban against the Chinese but modified it by allowing Chinese testimony in criminal cases where the defendant was Chinese. See *People* v. *Awa*, 27 Cal. 638 (1865).

4. *Minutes*, July 3, 1851; *Alta California*, Jan. 28, 1871.

5. Tsai, *Chinese Experience*, pp. 45–55; William Hoy, *The Chinese Six Companies* (San Francisco: Chinese Consolidated Benevolent Association, 1942), p. 8*; Barth, *Bitter Strength*, pp. 77–100; Victor G. Nee and Brett de Bary Nee, *Longtime Californ': A Documentary Study of an American Chinatown* (New York: Pantheon Books, 1973), pp. 65–67; Augustus Ward Loomis, "The Six Chinese Companies," *Overland Monthly* 1 (1868): 221–27.

6. John H. Boalt, *The Chinese Question* (San Francisco, 1877); Bank. Cases, *In Re Chung Luck and Ching Eide* [1631], May 18, 1875.

7. Janisch, "The Chinese, the Courts, and the Constitution," pp. 50–52, 77–80, 114–17, 283, 285–88, 310–11.

8. Ad. (Private) Cases, *Chou Ateen* v. *Ship "Robert Small,"* [250], May 24, 1852; CL and Equity Cases, [29], [70], [161], and [251–53]; Ad. (Private) Cases, [253], [775], [797], [804–8], [819], [828], [1087], [1103], [1432], [1675], [2078], [2120], [2124], [2195], [2277], [2367], [2457], [2485], [2500–2502], and [2505]; CL and Equity Cases, [161].

In the remainder of this chapter, *non-Chinese* will be used when it is not possible to identify the litigant or defendant as "white" from the court records. Nonetheless, it is unlikely that such persons were not white.

9. Act of March 2, 1867, 14 US STAT 517. Only 21 of the 2,598 bankruptcy cases Hoffman heard between July 8, 1867 and Aug. 31, 1878, involved Chinese bankrupts. For a history of this act and its operation nationally, see Charles Warren, *Bankruptcy in United States History* (Cambridge: Harvard University Press, 1935); Bank. Cases, [725], [1019], [1429], [1551], [1645], [2239], and [2486]. See also *Lloyd* v. *Hoo Sue*, 15 F. Cas. 718 (D.C.D.Cal. 1878).

10. Ping Chiu, *Chinese Labor in California, 1850–1880* (Madison: State Historical Society of Wisconsin, 1963); Jack Chen, *The Chinese of America* (New York: Harper and Row, 1981), pp. 65–116; Miller, *Unwelcome Immigrant*, pp. 145–90; Saxton, *Indispensable Enemy*; Janisch, "The Chinese, the Courts, and the Constitution."

11. Bank. Cases, *In Re Long Kee*, Schedule A [368], Nov. 21, 1868.

12. Bank. Cases, *In Re Lang Tuig and Ah Chow* [1429] [Non-Chinese creditors $1,788; Chinese creditors $829]; *In Re Kim Wing* [1441] [Non-Chinese creditors $4,835; Chinese creditors $600]; *In Re Kee Yung and Long Lum* [1670] [Non-Chinese creditors $1,361; Chinese creditors $0]; *In Re Cheang Guau Woo and Company* [1686] [Non-Chinese creditors $4,179; Chinese creditors $735]; *In Re Young You, Ah Yet,*

and Wong Bun [2131] [Non-Chinese creditors $195; Chinese creditors $2,823]; *In Re Sin Hop and Company* [2403] [Non-Chinese creditors $2,483; Chinese creditors $26,639].

13. *In Re Clifford*, 5 F. Cas. 1050 (D.C.D.Cal. 1873).

14. Bank. Cases, *In Re Hip Yik and Company* [725]. See also *In Re Yuen Wo and Company* [1551] and *In Re Lang Wo and Company* [2239].

15. Bank. Cases, *In Re Ah Kee* [1645]*, *In Re Lee Gow and Lee Kee* [2486]*, *In Re Chung* [2467], *In Re Sang Wo and Company* [2239], *In Re Him Lung* [2367], *In Re Chung Luck and Ching Eide* [1631].

16. *Alta California*, Jan. 21, 1881*, July 27, 1882.

17. Chiu, *Chinese Labor*, pp. 119–28; Willis N. Baer, *The Economic Development of the Cigar Industry in the United States* (Lancaster, Pa.: Art Printing Co., 1933); Saxton, *The Indispensable Enemy*, p. 213.

18. Crim. Cases, 1st Ser., [159], [162], and [163]; Act of June 30, 1864, 13 US STAT 223, 249, Sec. 73.

19. Crim. Cases, 1st Ser., [162B], [168B], [169A], [169B], [170A], [170B], [175B], [176B], [180B], [181A], [182B], [184B], [187A], [188B], [189A], [190B], [191A], [196], [204], and [226].

One might wonder why the U.S. attorney would bring prosecutions in the first place if he was inclined to dismiss such suits. One possible reason is that he received some compensation for prosecuting these suits even if they did not result in convictions (see chapter 4).

20. *Alta California*, Oct. 30, 1879, Aug. 5 and 7, 1880, July 24, 1883.

21. Ibid., Aug. 26, 1880.

22. Compare Act of June 30, 1864, 13 US STAT 223 at 263 and 270–71 with Act of July 13, 1866, 14 US STAT 98 at 125–26; Act of July 20, 1868, 15 US STAT 125 at 160–63; Act of March 1, 1879, 20 US STAT 327 at 345–49; *Alta California*, May 20, July 29, Aug. 27, 1880.

23. Act of July 20, 1868, 15 US STAT 125 at 162; Bank. Cases, [1019], [1322], [1429], [1487], [1631], [1645], and [1670]; *Alta California*, Aug. 26 and 27, 1880.

24. Sandmeyer, *Anti Chinese Movement*, pp. 57–77; *Alta California*, Aug. 18, 1880, Feb. 18, May 11, 1882; William Irwin to Charles Denvens, Dec. 1879, SCF, RG 60, NA*.

25. Philip Teare to Charles Denvens, Dec. 10, 1881, SCF, RG 60, NA*; *Alta California*, Aug. 18, 1880*.

26. See Ad. (U.S.) Cases, 2d Ser.

27. See Crim. Cases, 2d Ser., [689–1649].

28. Crim. Cases, 2d Ser., [1301].

29. Crim. Cases, 2d Ser., [698], [701], [722], [724–25], [730], [865], [912], [915], [962], [967], and [969].

30. Crim. Cases, 2d Ser., [689–1649].

31. For non-revenue prosecutions, see Crim. Cases, 2d Ser., *U.S.* v. *Ah Que* [1556]. For examples of non-Chinese sentenced for the same offense, see [1441]

($50 and 5 months), [1503] (45 days), [1504] (70 days), [1566] ($100 and 1 year), [1568] ($100 and 1 year), [1577] (3 months), and [1578] (6 months). For counterfeiting, see Crim. Cases, 2d Ser., [873], [1375], and [1377]. For the range of sentences meted out to non-Chinese defendants, see chapter 4.

32. On prosecutions directed at the opium trade, see Robert McClellan, *The Heathen Chinee: A Study of American Attitudes Towards China, 1890–1905* (Columbus: Ohio State University Press, 1971), pp. 38–39; Miller, *Unwelcome Immigrant*, pp. 147–49, 182–83, and Ad. (U.S.) Cases, 1st Ser., *U.S.* v. *10 Boxes of Opium*, Notes of Testimony, July 19, 1865, and Ad. (U.S.) Cases, 2d Ser., *U.S.* v. *22 Boxes of Opium*, Charge to the Jury, Nov. 24, 1869 [636].

For examples of minor opium cases, see Crim. Cases, 2d Ser., [1626] (Chinese, $50), [1680] (Non-Chinese, $50), [1683] (Non-Chinese, $75), and [1685] (Chinese, $75). For examples of more serious opium cases, see Crim. Cases, 2d Ser., [1702] (Chinese, 6 months and $1,000), [2365] (Non-Chinese, 18 months), [2464–65] (Chinese, 1 year), [2655] (Non-Chinese, 18 months and $500), and [2751] (Non-Chinese, 1 year). For the stiffest sentence, see Crim. Cases, 2d Ser., [2345] and for examples of acquittals, see Crim. Cases, 1st Ser., [289] (Chinese, not guilty), 2d Ser., [1596] (Non-Chinese, *nolle prosequi*), [1597] (Chinese, *nolle prosequi*), [1946] (Non-Chinese, not guilty), and [2688] (Chinese, *nolle prosequi*). For evidence of non-Chinese smuggling, see Ad. (U.S.) Cases, 2d Ser., *U.S.* v. *20 Boxes Containing Each 5 Taels Opium*, Notes of Testimony and Hoffman's Jury Charge [636].

33. For Chinese prosecutions, see Crim. Cases, 2d Ser., [1626], [1685–87], [1814], [2268], [2330–32], [2368], [2444], [2450], [2464–65], [2535], [2542], [2637], and [2688]. For non-Chinese prosecutions, see Crim. Cases, 2d Ser., [1596], [1680], [1702], [1711–12], [1768], [1782–83], [1818], [1865], [1867], [1875], [1889], [1900–1901], [1946], [2011], [2027], [2028], [2251], [2261], [2266–67], [2287], [2303], [2321], [2325–27], [2336–37], [2345], [2348], [2365], [2369], [2412], [2463], [2495], [2518], [2541], [2605], [2610], [2615–16], [2624–27], [2630], [2643–44], [2655–57], [2662], [2685], [2687], [2719], [2720], [2751], [2755], [2760], and [2771–72]. For condemnation of opium, see Ad. (U.S.) Cases, 1st Ser., [1270], [1374], [1377], [1421–22], [1445–49], [1452], [1465], [1467], [1477], [1483], [1550], [1565], and [1631–42], 2d Ser., [564], [580–99], [636], [851–52], [902–4], [913], and [1079–85]. In 1882 one case involved the seizure of well over $600,000 worth of opium, but it is unclear whether the drug was auctioned off. See 2d Ser., [1882].

34. *U.S.* v. *1 Case of Opium*, Jan. 13, 1864, H. Op*.

35. Crim. Cases, 2d Ser., [1821], [1886], [2021], [2054–55], [2267], [2350], [2493], [2527], [2531], [2534], [2538], [2581], [2688], and [2732].

36. Quoted in William E. Nelson, *The Fourteenth Amendment: From Political Principle to Judicial Doctrine* (Cambridge: Harvard University Press, 1988), p. 73*; Eric Foner, *Free Soil, Free Labor, Free Men: The Ideology of the Republican Party before the Civil War* (New York: Oxford University Press, 1970); Rush Welter, *The Mind of*

America, 1820–1860 (New York: Columbia University Press, 1975), pp. 77–104; Holt, *Political Crisis*.

37. Harold M. Hyman and William M. Wiecek, *Equal Justice Under Law: Constitutional Development, 1835–1875* (New York: Harper and Row, 1982), pp. 395–438; Foner, *Free Soil*; *Ho Ah Kow* v. *Nunan*, 12 F. Cas. 252 at 256 (C.C.Cal. 1879)*; *Civil Rights Cases*, 109 U.S. 3 at 22 (1883)*; Nelson, *Fourteenth Amendment*; Edmund Randolph to Hoffman, Jan. 17, 1861, Hunt. Ms., HL*; Stephen Field to John N. Pomeroy, April 14, 1882, Stephen J. Field Papers, BL*; Keller, *Affairs of State*, pp. 49, 63, 65, 122, 143–45, 209, 227, 230, 447–49, 451–54, 559.

In addressing the University of Oregon's first graduating class, Judge Deady decried the age's "insane rage for equality." "Democracy being necessarily founded on political equality, many of the members of such a society are easily led to think that this includes social equality as well." Address by Matthew Deady, June 21, 1878, quoted in Ralph James Mooney, "Matthew Deady and the Federal Judicial Response to Racism in the Early West," *Oregon Law Review* 63 (1984): 634*.

38. Linda Przybyszewski has noted the different claims that blacks and the Chinese were making, but she explains Circuit Judge Lorenzo Sawyer's decisions favorable to the Chinese in terms of his "rare sympathy" for and "non-racist" view of the Chinese. See Linda C. A. Przybyszewski, "Judge Lorenzo Sawyer and the Chinese: Civil Rights Decisions in the Ninth Circuit," *Western Legal History* 1 (1988): 23–56, 23*, 32 n. 29.

39. Miller, *Unwelcome Immigrant*; Saxton, *The Indispensable Enemy*; Sandmeyer, *Anti Chinese Movement*; Mary Roberts Coolidge, *Chinese Immigration* (New York: H. Holt and Co., 1909); William J. Courtney, *San Francisco's Anti Chinese Ordinances, 1850–1900* (San Francisco: Rand E. Research Associates, 1974); Leigh Dana Johnsen, "Equal Rights and the 'Heathen Chinee': Black Activism in San Francisco, 1865–1875," *Western Historical Quarterly* 11 (1980): 57–66; Edward P. Hutchinson, *Legislative History of American Immigration Policy, 1798–1965* (Philadelphia: University of Pennsylvania Press, 1981).

40. Proclamation, July 28, 1868, 16 US STAT 739*.

41. *In Re Ah Fong*, 1 F. Cas. 213 (C.C.D.Cal. 1874); *Baker* v. *Portland*, 2 F. Cas. 472 (C.C.D.Or. 1879); *In Re Tiburcio Parrot*, 1 F. 481 (C.C.D.Cal. 1880); *In Re Quong Woo*, 13 F. 229 (C.C.D.Cal. 1882); Dong, "The Chinese and the Anti-Chinese Movement," pp. 226–391.

42. *In Re Ah Fong*, 1 F. Cas. 213 at 217 (C.C.D.Cal. 1874)*.

43. Treaty of Nov. 17, 1880, 22 US STAT 826, 827*; David L. Anderson, "The Diplomacy of Discrimination: Chinese Exclusion, 1876–1882," *California History* 57 (1978): 32–45.

44. Act of May 6, 1882, 22 US STAT 58*; U.S. Cong., Senate, Letter from the Secretary of the Treasury, 49th Cong., 1st sess., 1885, Ex. Doc. No. 103.

45. On the tenacity of customs officials in enforcing the exclusion laws, see Robert J. Schwendinger, *Ocean of Bitter Dreams: Maritime Relations Between China and the United States, 1850–1915* (Tucson: Westernlore Press, 1988), pp. 103–20.

46. Ad. (Private) Cases; *Alta California*, Sept. 16, 1882*; *San Francisco Chronicle*, Aug. 17, 1886; Lorenzo Sawyer to Matthew Deady, Feb. 18, Oct. 13, 1884, Deady Papers, OHS.

47. Since no southern district court for California existed between 1866 and 1886, Hoffman served as California's only federal district judge during this period. Moreover, Hoffman received little help from Oregon's Judge Deady, who was kept busy during this period with his own dockets. Between 1885 and 1893 Deady released some 150 Chinese on habeas corpus petitions. In comparison, Hoffman released 533 Chinese between 1888 and 1890 alone, and from 1882 to 1890 over 7,000 Chinese habeas corpus petitions were filed in Hoffman's court. See Mooney, "Deady and the Federal Judicial Response"; Appendix, figure 2; *Minutes*, D.C.D.Or., Sept. 12, 1859, to July 1, 1893, RG 21, NA.

48. *In Re Ah Sing*, 13 F. 286 (C.C.D.Cal. 1882).

49. *In Re Ah Tie*, 13 F. 291 at 294–95 (C.C.D.Cal. 1882)*; *In Re Low Yam Chow*, 13 F. 605 (C.C.D.Cal. 1882).

50. *In Re Low Yam Chow*, 13 F. 605 at 615*.

51. Ibid., 609*; *Alta California*, Sept. 13, 1882.

52. *In Re Ho King*, 14 F. 724 (D.C.D.Or. 1883); Hoffman to Matthew Deady, Feb. 1, 1883, Deady Papers, OHS*.

53. See *In Re Ah Lung*, 18 F. 28 (C.C.D.Cal. 1883); *In Re Cheen* [*sic*] *Heong*, 21 F. 791 (C.C.D.Cal. 1884); Field's dissent in *Chew Heong* v. *U.S.*, 112 U.S. 536 (1884); *In Re Low Yam Chow*, 13 F. 605 at 617 (C.C.D.Cal. 1882)*; *In Re Shong Toon*, 21 F. 386 (D.C.D.Cal. 1884); *In Re Chin Ah Sooey*, 21 F. 393 (D.C.D.Cal. 1884).

54. *In Re Chin Ah On*, 18 F. 506 (D.C.D.Cal. 1883).

55. Ibid., 507–8*.

56. *Baker* v. *City of Portland*, 123 F. Cas. 472 at 473 (C.C.D. Or. 1879)*.

57. *In Re Leong Yick Dew*, 19 F. 490 (C.C.D.Cal. 1884); *In Re Tong Ah Chee*, 23 F. 441 (D.C.D.Cal. 1883); *In Re Shong Toon*, 21 F. 386; *In Re Ah Kee*, 21 F. 701 (C.C.D.Cal. 1884); *In Re Kew Ock*, 21 F. 789 (C.C.D.Cal. 1884).

58. *In Re Chow Goo Pooi*, 25 F. 77 (C.C.D.Cal. 1884).

59. Ibid. at 81*; Act of July 5, 1884, 23 US STAT 115, Sec. 12.

60. *In Re Chow Goo Pooi*, 25 F. 77 at 82*.

61. *Alta California*, Dec. 18, 1883*, Jan. 5 and 17*, Feb. 12, 1884; *San Francisco Chronicle*, Aug. 17, 1886, July 14, 1887.

62. *In Re Tung Yeong*, 19 F. 184 at 185, 190–91 (D.C.D.Cal. 1884)*.

63. Ibid., 187*.

64. Ibid., 187–88*.

65. Ibid., 190*. For the different standards used by the courts and the collector in assessing Chinese testimony, see Lucy Salyer, "Captives of Law: Judicial Enforcement of the Chinese Exclusion Laws, 1891–1905," *Journal of American History* 76 (1989): 104–9.

66. Act of July 5, 1884, 23 US STAT 115, Sec. 4 and 6.

67. *In Re Shong Toon*, 21 F. 386 at 389*; *In Re Ah Quan*, 21 F. 182 (C.C.D.Cal. 1884).

68. *In Re Chin Ah Sooey*, 21 F. 393, 395 (D.C.D.Cal. 1884)*; *In Re Shong Toon*, 21 F. 386 at 392.

69. Act of June 1, 1872, 17 US STAT 196, Sec. 1, provided that whenever a difference of opinion existed among judges sitting as a circuit court, "the opinion of the presiding justice or presiding judge" should prevail and be "considered the opinion of the court," but the act allowed the review of such a case by the Supreme Court. *In Re Ah Kee*, 21 F. 701 (C.C.D.Cal. 1884); *In Re Ah Moy*, 21 F. 785 (C.C.D.Cal. 1884); *In Re Kew Ock*, 21 F. 789 (C.C.D.Cal. 1884).

70. *Alta California*, Sept. 25, 1884*.

71. *In Re Cheen* [*sic*] *Heong*, 21 F. 791.

72. *Alta California*, Sept. 27, 1884*; Coolidge, *Chinese Immigration*, p. 498.

73. *In Re Cheen* [*sic*] *Heong*, 21 F. 791 at 793*; *Alta California*, Sept. 27, 1884. Field's earlier Chinese decisions had played a significant role in frustrating his political ambitions, and public reaction to them may well account for his turnabout in the *Chew Heong* case. Long harboring presidential aspirations, Field lost Californian support in his 1880 presidential candidacy—due in part to a disenchantment with Field over the Chinese cases he had decided even before the passage of the first Exclusion Act. See Swisher, *Stephen J. Field*, pp. 288 and 283. Four years later Field explicitly blamed his failure to receive the nomination of the Democratic party in 1884 on the fact that his own party in California had repudiated him. See Field to John N. Pomeroy, July 28, 1884, Stephen J. Field Papers, BL.

Although rendered two months after he lost his bid for the 1884 presidency, Field's widely praised opinion in *Chew Heong* may have been influenced by his political ambitions. Field's claims that his political quest was over with the defeat in 1884 cannot be taken at face value because similar protestations after his unsuccessful bid for the presidency in 1880 had not stopped him from seeking that office in 1884. See Swisher, *Stephen J. Field*, p. 298.

In any event, such considerations might well have motivated Field because his decision in *Chew Heong* could scarcely be reconciled with his interpretation of the Exclusion Act two years earlier.

74. *In Re Cheen* [*sic*] *Heong*, 21 F. 791 at 808*; *Chew Heong* v. *U.S.*, 112 U.S. 536 at 561 (1884)*.

75. Lorenzo Sawyer to Matthew Deady, Dec. 22, 1884, Deady Papers, OHS*.

76. *Cong. Record*, 50th Cong., 1st sess., 1887–88, p. 7304*; *Alta California*, Sept. 23, 1885*; *San Francisco Chronicle*, Aug. 17, 1886, July 14, 1887.

77. *In Re Jung Ah Lung*, 25 F. 141 (D.C.D.Cal. 1885)*; Hoffman to Matthew Deady, Dec. 12, 1885, Deady Papers, OHS*.

78. *In Re Jung Ah Lung*, 25 F. 141 at 142–43*; *U.S.* v. *Jung Ah Lung*, 124 U.S. 621 (1888); *Alta California*, March 23, 1888*.

79. Quoted in Salyer, "Chinese Exclusion Laws," p. 103*. For the centrality of

the writ of habeas corpus in Anglo-American law, see William F. Duker, *A Constitutional History of Habeas Corpus* (Westport, Conn.: Greenwood Press, 1980).

80. Crim. Cases, 2d Ser., *U.S.* v. *Choi Ah Jow*, Bill of Exceptions, 9 [2021]*.

81. Lorenzo Sawyer to Matthew Deady, May 25, 1887, Deady Papers, OHS*; *Alta California*, Jan. 25, 1888; U.S. Cong., *Letter of Collector J. S. Hager, Giving Statistics of the Number of Arrivals and Departures of Chinese at the Port of San Francisco*, 50th Cong., 1st sess., 1887–88, S. Misc. Doc. 90.

82. Lorenzo Sawyer to Matthew Deady, May 25, 1887*, March 4*, May 23*, 1888, Deady Papers, OHS; *Alta California*, March 8, 1888*; Hoffman to Charles N. Felton, Jan. 1888, in *Cong. Record*, 50th Cong., 1st sess., 1888, p. 6569*; U.S. Cong., Select Committee on Immigration and Naturalization, "Chinese Immigration," 51st Cong., 2d sess., March 2, 1891, pp. 315–19.

83. For the political context surrounding the attempts to renegotiate the treaty with China and the congressional legislation of 1888, see Sandmeyer, *The Anti Chinese Movement*, pp. 99–102.

84. Act of Sept. 13, 1888, 25 US STAT 476*.

85. Act of Oct. 1, 1888, 25 US STAT 504; Hutchinson, *American Immigration Policy*; *Alta California*, Oct. 3, 1888; *San Francisco Chronicle*, Oct. 3, 1888.

86. *In Re Chae Chan Ping*, 36 F. 431 (C.C.N.D.Cal. 1888)*; *Alta California*, Oct. 3 and 14, 1888; *Chae Chan Ping* v. *U.S.*, 130 U.S. 581 (1889).

87. *In Re Chae Chan Ping*, 36 F. 431 at 436–37; Lorenzo Sawyer to Matthew Deady, Oct. 18, 1888, Deady Papers, OHS*; *In Re Tong Wah Sick*, 36 F. 440 (C.C.N.D.Cal. 1888); *In Re Jack Sen*, 36 F. 441 (C.C.N.D.Cal. 1888).

88. See Ad. (Private) Dockets, vols. 14–18, 1890–1906; *Wan Shing* v. *U.S.*, 140 U.S. 424 (1891); *Alta California*, Oct. 20*, 24, Nov. 26, 1888; *San Francisco Chronicle*, Oct. 21, Nov. 13, 1888; U.S. Cong., Joint Select Committee on Immigration and Naturalization, 51st Cong., 2d sess., 1890, H. Rept., no. 4048, p. 412.

89. See Janisch, "The Chinese, the Courts, and the Constitution," pp. 903–1087; Testimony of S. J. Ruddell in Select Committee on Immigration and Naturalization, "Chinese Immigration," p. 278*; *In Re Chae Chan Ping*, 36 F. 431 at 436*; Salyer, "Chinese Exclusion Laws."

90. Mooney, "Deady," p. 606*; Lorenzo Sawyer to Matthew Deady, April 2, 1886, quoted in Przybyszewski, "Sawyer," p. 49*; Swisher, *Stephen J. Field*, p. 383*; Keller, *Affairs of State*, p. 367*. For concern about social disruption, see Keller, *Affairs of State*, pp. 188–91.

91. *In Re Low Yam Chow*, 13 F. Cas. 605 at 615 (C.C.D.Cal. 1882); Stephen J. Field to John N. Pomeroy, April 14, 1882, Stephen J. Field Papers, BL*; Sawyer Dictations, Folder C-D 321:1, Sept. 22, 1886, BL*. See also Keller, *Affairs of State*, pp. 439–47.

92. Field's Chinese opinions were part of his effort to integrate his broad theories about the Fourteenth Amendment into the existing corpus of constitutional law. See McCurdy, *The Fields and the Law*, pp. 5–18, and Charles W. McCurdy, "Justice

Field and the Jurisprudence of Government-Business Relations: Some Parameters of Laissez Faire Constitutionalism, 1863–1897," *Journal of American History* 61 (1975): 970–1005.

CONCLUSION

1. See, for example, Howe, *American Whigs*, pp. 1–10.

2. Stephen B. Presser's study of John Thompson Nixon, U.S. district court judge for New Jersey between 1870 and 1889, also suggests a degree of judicial creativity that defies the conventional wisdom that the late nineteenth century was a time of rigid and formalistic jurisprudence. See his *Studies in the History of the United States Courts of the Third Circuit, 1790–1980* (Washington, D.C.: Bicentennial Committee of the Judicial Conference of the United States, 1982), pp. 69–127.

On the more complex nature of judicial decision-making in the late nineteenth century, see Harry N. Scheiber, "Instrumentalism and Property Rights: A Reconsideration of American 'Styles of Judicial Reasoning' in the Nineteenth Century," *Wisconsin Law Review* (1975), pp. 1–18.

3. On the tendency of common-law judging to distill human beings and their conduct into abstractions, see John T. Noonan, Jr., *Persons and Masks of the Law: Cardozo, Holmes, Jefferson, and Wythe as Makers of the Masks* (New York: Farrar, Straus, and Giroux, 1976).

INDEX

Admiralty law: and bottomry bonds, 72; breach of contract in, 76–77; and commercial litigation, 84–85; damages in, 72, 75–77, 94–96; and deferral to higher judges, 72; definitions for, 52; and general average claims, 78–79; *in personam* and *in rem* suits under, 52, 55–58, 64, 66–70; jurisdiction in, 52–57, 60–61, 64–65, 88; liability in, 57–58, 68–70, 75–76; liens in, 52–53, 58; multiple joinder in, 63–64; and passenger contracts, 60–61, 65–72; and sailors, 85–92, 94–98; and standards of care for passengers, 62–63, 66, 68–71; and support from business, 73–76, 78–79, 81, 83–84; testimony in, 92–94; and vigilantes, 81–83

Ah Fook, 216
Ah Kee, 214
Ah Que, 221
Ah Sing, 229
Ah Sung, 216
Alvarado, Juan B., 149–50
American Jurist and Law Magazine, 103
Andres Pico. See *U.S. v. Pico*
Arguello v. U.S. (1855), 151–52
Arroyo Seco (rancho), 154
Aspinwall, William H., 19–20, 59. *See also* Pacific Mail Steamship Co.
Attorneys General, U.S. *See* Black, Jeremiah Sullivan (1857–60); Cushing, Caleb (1853–57); Hoar, Ebenezer (1869–70); Speed, James (1864–66)

Baja California, Mexico, 114–15
Baker, Edward D., 119
Baldwin, Joseph, 189–90, 206

Bankruptcy, 213–15
Baring case. See *Nicholson v. Ship "John Baring"*
Bayard, James A., Jr., 158–59
Bell, John, 24
Benedict, Erastus C., 70
Benham, Calhoun, 59–60, 126, 129
Benjamin, Judah P., 18–19
Bennett, Nathaniel, 187
Benton, Thomas Hart, 137
Bidwell, John, 173
Billings, Frederick, 166
Black, Jeremiah Sullivan: archival documentation of, 169–72, 177, 179, 191; on *Bolton* and *Sherrebeck* claims, 191–93; compared to Cushing, 155–56, 163–65; on fraud, 163–65, 169, 172; legacy of, 135, 155–56; and San Francisco's pueblo title, 187–93, 202; staff accomplishments, 167–72; in *U.S. v. Cambuston*, 176
Blacks, 211, 224–25, 247
Blair, Montgomery, 149
Blanding, William, 124, 126
Boalt, John Henry, 212
Board of Land Commissioners: appeal process of, 130, 139–40; establishment of, 139; first (1851–53), 143–48, 150, 157; function of, 139–41; members of, 141–43, 145; second (1853–56), 141–42, 145–46, 166
Bolton, James R., 191–93
Bolton claim, 191–93, 208
Bond cases, 129–30
Boyd, James T., 17, 80
Bradley, Joseph, 224–25
Broderick, David C., 185
Browne, J. Ross, 26
Buckley, "Blind Boss" Christopher, 25

Burgoyne and Co., 20
Burlingame Treaty. *See* Treaties
Burnett, Peter, 188
Burrall, Emily. *See* Hoffman, Emily
Burrall (family), 2

California: anti-Chinese legislation
  in, 211, 218; circuit judgeship of,
  30–31, 34, 36, 40–41; politics, 19,
  38, 44, 218; prosquatter support in,
  186. *See also* Supreme Court (Calif.);
  Vigilance committees
California Civil Practice Act, 211
California Land Act (1851), 136; adju-
  dication of, 157, 159; as departure
  from previous land-title resolution,
  139–40; and Mexican law, 142; and
  San Francisco's pueblo, 202, 204
California Land Act (1852), 157, 162
Campbell, John, 151–52
Campbell, Thompson, 34, 145
Canadaigua (Ontario Co., N.Y.), 9–10
Catron, John, 151–53
Chae Chan Ping. See *In Re Chae Chan
  Ping*
Chamberlain v. *Chandler* (1823), 66, 69
Chew Heong. See *In Re Chew Heong*
China, 43, 225–28, 230–32, 235–39,
  243–44, 246–47. *See also* Treaties:
  Burlingame
Chinese, in California: attitudes toward,
  211, 216–19, 221, 223, 225, 228; in
  bankruptcy cases, 213–15; and Canton and return certificates, 227,
  230–32, 235–39, 244–45; criminal
  prosecutions of, 131–32, 216–23;
  discriminatory enforcement against,
  131–32, 216–21; economic vulnerability of, 213; and head tax, 215; immigration and *habeas corpus* cases of,
  228–46; and legal equality, 225; in
  local jails, 216, 219, 220–21; and
  opium smuggling, 221–23; and
  pay-or-jail system, 220; and plea-
  bargaining, 220; and prosecutions
  under Exclusion Acts, (of 1882)
  228–36, 239–40, (of 1884) 236–43,

(of 1888) 244–46; revenue violations
  of, 216–23; sentencing of, 213,
  216–21, 223, 246; testimony of, 211,
  236; trial by jury for, 217, 223; use of
  lawyers by, 212
Chinese Six Companies, 211–12, 215
Choi Ah Jow, 242
Circuit courts. *See* U.S. Ninth Circuit
  court
Civil Rights Act of 1866, 224–25
Clay, Henry, 24
Clayton, John M., 102
Cleveland, Grover, 244
Coast Rangers, 26
Cohas v. *Raisin and Legris* (1853),
  187–88
Cole, Cornelius, 40, 44
Collector of the Port. *See* Customs,
  U.S., in San Francisco
Colonization Act of 1824, 140–41, 150
Columbia College, 2, 4, 8
Common law, 52–53, 55, 68, 79–80,
  134
Confederates, 36, 194–95. *See also*
  Greathouse, Ridgely
Congress, U.S.: appoints northern dis-
  trict judge, 20–21; on circuit judge-
  ship, 36; creates special circuit court,
  33, 161; enacts Calif. Land Act
  (1851), 138–39; Hoffman to Senate
  Finance Committee of, 199; and
  powers of U.S. commissioners, 243;
  Senate Judiciary committee of, 44;
  sets judicial fees and salaries, 27, 128
Conkling, Roscoe P., 44, 47
Conness, John, 181, 194–96; and puni-
  tive legislation against Hoffman,
  197–201; on San Francisco's pueblo
  claim, 201–4, 207–8
Constitutional law. *See* U.S. district
  court (N.D.): habeas corpus
Constitutional-Union party, 24, 35
Cook, Carrol, 242
Cope, Warner, 189
Copperhead, 195
Court of First Instance (Monterey,
  Calif.), 54

Criminal law: under 1818 Act, 112–22; under 1835 Act, 102–4, 106; under 1864 Act, 105–6; fees for U.S. attorneys and others, 126–30; Hellship cases, 95–96, 101–2, 104, 111–12; Hoffman inherits circuit court docket, 131; Hoffman on duties of court in, 106–7, 111; mutiny trial (1866), 108–9; and prosecution of Chinese, 131–32, 215–23; and prosecution of ships' officers, 109–10; sentencing, 104–8, 110–11; and sources of cases in, 101, 122–23; statutory limits for, 108; testimony, 105, 110–11; and trial without jury, 105; and U.S. attorneys' independence, 123–32
Crockett, Joseph B., 11, 13–14
Crosby, Elisha O., 145–46
Crowley, Patrick, 215
Curry, John, 20
Cushing, Caleb: in *Cervantes* case, 150–51; on circuit court expansion, 160; compared to Black, 155–56, 163–65; on fraud, 164–66; in *Fremont* case, 148–49; and land claims, 156–59, 162–63; legacy of, 135, 155–57; staff accomplishments, 157–58
Customs, U.S., in San Francisco, 127, 130, 217, 222–23; and Chinese immigration, 227–31, 234, 240, 243
Cutler v. *Rae* (1849), 78
Cutting, Francis B., 19

Dana, Richard Henry, Jr., 103–4
Daniel, Peter, 151–53
Davis, David, 31
Davis, Jefferson, 116
Deady, Matthew P.: on Chinese, 230–31, 247; on judicial behavior, 39–40; in *McCall* v. *McDowell*, 44–45; as member of the Ninth Circuit, 30, 32, 44–45, 228; as protégé of Field, 31, 40–41; social origins of, 40; support for circuit judgeship, 40–46

De la Guerra, Pablo, 142, 173, 175
Delano, F. H., 15
Delano (family), 15
Della Torre, Peter, 165, 167–69, 172
Delovio v. *Boit* (1815), 54
del Valle, Luis Maria, 113, 116, 118–21
Democratic party, 3, 5, 34, 196, 199; in California, 19, 38, 161
Departmental Assembly (Mexico), 151, 154, 177
de Young, M. H., 49
Dillon, Guillaume Patrice, 116, 118–22. See also *In Re Dillon*
District courts, 29–30, 46–47. *See also* U.S. district court (N.D.); U.S. district court (S.D.)
Doe, Charles, 74
Dooley v. *Ship "Neptune's Car"* (1860), 89–90
Douglass, James, 101–2
Downing v. *the Schooner "Golden State"* (1858), 63
Dred Scott v. *Sanford* (1857), 34

El Rincon claim, 192
Emory, Frederick, 116, 118
Eno, Henry, 11
Equality, ideology of, 223–25
Everett, Edward, 24
Exclusion Acts: general, 76; (of 1882), 223, 225, 227–40, 244; (of 1884), 236–40, 242, 244; (of 1888), 242, 244–46. *See also* Chinese, in Calif.

Fair, James G., 49
Farwell, Seth B., 145
Fayet v. *Ship "Henri"* (1851), 64–65
Federalism, 54, 180–81, 205
Federalists, 1
Felch, Alpheus, 145
Fellow servant rule, 96–98
Fessenden, William P., 199
Field, David Dudley, 34–35
Field, Stephen J.: as *alcalde*, 38, 189; arrival in San Francisco of, 12; bid for U.S. Chief Justice, 37; on

Field, Stephen J. (*continued*)
Chinese, 226, 231, 238–39, 247;
competition with Hoffman for circuit
judgeship, 34–36; with Conness on
legislating against Hoffman, 196–98;
as judge, 30–32, 39, 131; judicial
philosophy and role of, 31, 37–38,
181, 208; judicial style of, 181; as
member and Chief Justice, Calif. Supreme Court, 181, 189; personality
of, 31–32, 36–40; political affilia-
tions of, 34–35, 38–39; and pragma-
tism regarding land grants, 35; relationship with Hoffman, 23, 36–37,
41, 45–46, 193; on San Francisco
pueblo title settlement, 202–4,
206–8; support of Deady, 40–45;
views on equality, 224–25
Fillmore, Millard L., 24, 114, 141, 143;
appoints Hoffman as northern district
judge, 18–21
Fish, Hamilton, 44, 46, 159
Florida land grants, 139, 148, 150
Folsom, Joseph L., 182–84
France, 64–65, 116, 118–19
Frémont, John C., 137, 148–50. See
also *Fremont* v. *U.S.*
Fremont v. *U.S.* (1855), 146, 176–79;
significance of, 134–35, 148–55
Freyer, Tony, 74

Gadsden Treaty, 116
Gallagher v. *James Smith* (1859), 81–83
General Land Office, 197, 200
Georgia land frauds, 164
Goodrich, Charles B., 19
Gorham, George C., 203
Goshen (Orange Co., N.Y.), 2–3, 5, 8
Grant, Ulysses S., 42–46
Gray, Horace, 31
Greathouse, Ridgely, 194–95. See also
U.S. v. *Greathouse*; *In Re Greathouse*
Greenleaf, Simon, 8–9
Grier, Robert C., 204
Gwin, William M.: on expansion of
circuit court system, 160–61; on
Hoffman's appointment to the north-

ern district, 19–21; as prosettler,
137–40, 145, 156–57; as sponsor of
California Land Act (1851), 138–40

Habeas corpus. *See* U.S. district court
(N.D.): habeas corpus
Hacket, James, 221
Hager, John S., 240, 245
Haight, Henry, 13, 183
Hall, Hiland, 143
Halleck, Henry W., 173, 195; on Land
Boards, 143–46; on land issues,
137–39; on testimony of Californios,
174–75
Halleck, Peachy and Billings, 143
Hamilton, Alexander, 4
Harlan, James, 200
Harrison, William H., 5
Hart v. *Burnett* (1860), 35–36, 188–90,
193, 203, 205–7
Harvard Law School, 8–9, 56
Hastings, Serranus Clinton, 184
Healy, John Plummer, 18–19
Hendricks, Thomas A., 200
Heung Mow Co., 212
Heydenfelt, Solomon, 188
Hilborn, Samuel G., 124, 241
Hip Yik. See *In Re Hip Yik*
Hip Yik and Co., 214
Hispanics, 149, 165; attitudes regarding
Anglos, 168–69; as government offi-
cials, 149, 173, 175, 177; in land
grant cases, 136, 142, 144, 149–51,
154; testimony of, 142–43, 152, 169,
173–75, 178
Hitchcock, Ethan Allan, 114–16, 126
Hittell, John S., 166
Hoar, Ebenezer, 45
Hoffman, Charles, 2–3, 6–7
Hoffman, Charles Fenno, 7
Hoffman, Emily (née Burrall), 2–3, 7
Hoffman, Josiah Ogden, 1–2
Hoffman, Murray, 4
Hoffman, Ogden, Jr.: appointment as
district court judge, 17–21; arrival in
San Francisco, 10–11, 71; childhood
and youth in New York, 2–3, 6–8;

and China mission, 43; on Chinese, 223, 229–30, 236–37, 241, 247–48; death of, 48–49; education, 8–9; eulogy for Clay, 24; European tour, 10; family of, 1–10, 12, 23, 48; finances of, 7, 10, 15, 17, 27–28, 47; friends and social life, 10, 17, 48, 80, 92, 195; health of, 8, 160–61, 242; and honor, 6–7, 25; judicial philosophy and role, 25–26, 181, 208–9; judicial style, 29, 181, 209; legal analysis of, 74–75, 79; legal clerkships, 9–10; personality of, 6–8, 10, 32, 36–40; politics of, 21, 24–25, 35, 38–39; relationship with Field, 23, 32, 36–39, 41, 45–46, 181, 193–94; residence in Pacific-Union Club, 22–23; rivalry for judicial offices, 31, 34, 40–47; San Francisco law practice, 14–17; support for Fillmore (1856), 24; support from business, 73–76, 78–79, 198–99; support from New York, 10, 15, 18–20, 44. *See also* U.S. district court (N.D.)
Hoffman, Ogden, Sr. (father): death of, 6; education, 2; efforts for his son, 9–10, 15, 20, 159; family and social connections of, 1–5, 7; finances of, 3–7; as friend of Webster and Seward, 18–20; in the navy, 2; New York City criminal prosecutions, 2; and party politics, 6; political appointments, 2–3, 5; and political offices held, 2–3, 6; personality of, 4–6; as Whig orator, 3–4
Hoffman, Southard, 23, 48
Hoffman, Virginia (née Southard), 3, 6–8
Hoffman, Wickham, 12
Honor (national), 25, 111, 115, 117; and treaties, 122, 232, 237
Hooker, Joseph, 195
Horwitz, Morton, 98
Howe, David Walker, 6
Humboldt Ring, 124

Immigration and racial exclusion, 225, 244. *See also* Exclusion Acts

Indians, 113, 122, 151, 211
Inge, Samuel W.: on bond cases, 129; on del Valle incident, 119, 121 (*See also* del Valle, Luis Maria); and land-cases report, 160; in Walker cases, 114, 116–17, 126
In Re Ah Fong (1874), 226
In Re Chae Chan Ping (1888), 245–46
In Re Chew Heong (1884), 238–40
In Re Chin Ah On (1883), 231–32, 235
In Re Chow Goo Pooi (1884), 233
In Re Clifford (1873), 214
In Re Dillon (1854), 120. *See also* Dillon, Guillaume Patrice
In Re Greathouse (1864), 195.
In Re Hip Yik and Company (1870), 214
In Re Low Yam Chow (1882), 229–31
In Re Tung Yeong (1884), 235–36
Interior Department, 123–24, 137, 143–44
Internal Revenue School. *See* Treasury Department
Irving, Washington, 7
Irwin, William, 218

Janisch, Hudson N., 212
Jay, John, 1
Johnson, Reverdy, 34, 200
Jones, William Carey, 137, 152, 162–63, 165; and *Cervantes* case, 144, 147–48; and *Fremont* case, 149, 151
Jouan, Auguste, 168
Judiciary, congressional committees of, 44
Judiciary (federal), 17–18, 25, 47. *See also* U.S. statutes
Judiciary Act (1789), 55, 100
Justice Department, 100

Kearny, Stephen W., 54
Kent, William, 19
Knickerbocker Magazine, 7

Lake, Delos, 131–32, 201–3, 216–17
Land grants: allegations of fraud in, 156, 164–65, 167–72, 175–78; and

Land grants (*continued*)
appeals to district court, 130–31,
139–40, 153, 159; and archival
documentation, 170–71, 176–77,
178–79; and circuit court, 160–61;
congressional resolution of, in Louisiana and Florida, 139, 147, 150;
reports of Halleck and Jones on,
137–38; role of U.S. attorneys general in, 135, 156; role of U.S. circuit
judge McAllister in, 135; in San
Francisco, 138, 165–67 (*See also*
San Francisco land); shifts in Supreme Court rulings on, 134–35,
176–79; and squatters, 145–46, 183,
185–86, 189–91; testimony concerning, 142–43, 152, 156, 173–77
Larkin, Thomas O., 146, 168
Las Mariposas (rancho): in *Fremont*
case, 137, 144, 146, 148–51; original
sale price and later value of, 136, 149
Las Pulgas land grant, 145
Latham, Milton S., 34
Latimer, Lorenzo D., 127
Lee Chung, 215
Lee Wo Lung, 214
Legal education, 8–9
Limantour, José Y., 155–56, 165–73
Lincoln, Abraham, 34–36, 202; and
Greathouse case, 194–95
Long Kee, 214
Lord, Daniel, 10, 19
Louisiana land grants, 139, 147–48,
150, 164

McAllister, Hall, 33, 184
McAllister, Matthew Hall, 33–34, 36;
on admiralty cases, 70–72; as special
circuit judge, 30, 40–41, 135, 161–
62, 184
McCall v. *McDowell* (1867), 44–45
McCracken, John, 12–15, 20, 52, 183
McDougal, John, 185
Manifest Destiny, 112–13, 115
Maxwell, Hugh, 2
Mexico: and Gadsden Treaty, 116; il-
legal incursions into, 112–14, 116,

118; officials of, in land cases, 149,
166, 168–70, 174–75, 177. *See also*
Treaty of Guadalupe Hidalgo
Mexico, land grant law of: Board of
Land Commissioners' interpretations
of, 141–48, 150–51; reports by
Halleck and Jones on, 137–39; shifts
in Hoffman's view of, 134–36, 173,
176–78; and terms and procedures
of, 140–41; U.S. Supreme Court on,
150–52, 154, 176, 178–79
Micheltorena, Manuel, 149, 174
Miller, Samuel, 55, 204
Milpitas (rancho), 145
Missions, secularization of, 141
Missouri Compromise, 3
Monopolies, Jacksonian attitude toward,
152
Morrow, William W., 49
Murray, Hugh, 188

National Republicans, 3. *See also* Whigs
Nelson, Samuel, 176
Nelson, William, 225
Neutrality laws, 112–18, 121–22
New Jersey Steam Navigation Co. v. *Mer-
chants Bank* (1849), 55
New York (city), 1–5, 10, 19, 22
New York (state), 1–10, 15; support for
Hoffman in, 10, 15, 18–20, 44. *See
also* Pacific Mail Steamship Co.
New York *Times*, 121
Nicaragua, 116
Nicholson v. *Ship "John Baring"* (1853),
68–69
Ninth Circuit. *See* U.S. Ninth Circuit
court.
Nisi prius judges, 47
Noche Buena (rancho), 168
Nunez v. *U.S.* (1857), 173

Opium, 130, 221–23
Orange County (N.Y.), 2
Oregon. *See* Deady; U.S. Ninth Circuit
court: members

Pacific Club, 22–23

Pacific Mail Steamship Co., 19, 59–61, 69, 75, 96–97
Pacific-Union Club, 23, 48–49
Palmer, Cook and Co., 148
Parsons, Theophilus, 56
Peachy, Archibald C., 146, 184
Peckham, Robert F., 185
Peter Smith deeds, 184–85, 188–90, 205–7
Peyton, Bernard, 168
Philadelphia, 191–92
Pico, Pio, 175, 177
Pico v. *U.S.* (1856), 154, 173
Pierce, Franklin, 115–16, 141–42, 145–46, 161, 163
Pillsbury, E. J., 49
Place v. *Steamship "Golden Gate"* (1856), 69–70
Plume, John V., 20
Polk, James K., 5
Postmaster General, 123
Preemption claims, 185–86
Property law. *See* Land grants; San Francisco land
Public trust doctrine, 188–89. See also *Hart* v. *Burnett*

Racism, 224. *See also* Equality
Railroad regulation, 73, 97
Randolph, Edmund, 117
Raousset-Boulbon, Count Gaston de, 113, 116
Republican party, 25, 44, 224
Reynolds v. *New World* (1852), 54, 67–68
Riordan, Thomas D., 238–40

Sabine, George, 228, 231, 234, 238–39
Sacramento Union, 195
Sanchez, Francisco, 174
San Francisco: Boss politics in, 25; business support for Hoffman in, 73–76, 79, 81, 83–84, 198–99; chief of police, 215; Chinese (*see* Chinese, in California); cigar-making industry, 216, 218; club life in, 22–23, 48–49; early law practice in,

11–17; early settlement of, 11; federal courts in (*see* U.S. district court; U.S. Ninth Circuit court); French community of, 64–65, 112–13, 116, 118–21; port and customs officials in (*see* Customs, U.S., in San Francisco); pueblo dispute, 190, 193, 202–3 (*see also* San Francisco land); real estate speculation in, 182–83; revenue prosecutions in, 129–30, 219–23; and shipping industry, 51, 88–89; Superior Court of, 114, 184
San Francisco *Alta California*: on Chinese, 211, 234, 237–38, 242; endorsement of Deady, 46; on *Gallagher* case, 82–84; on *In Re Greathouse* case, 198–99; on Neutrality Act, 114–16, 118, 121; on San Francisco pueblo case, 201, 204, 206; on squatters, 186
San Francisco Bulletin, 47; on *Gallagher* case, 83; on *In Re Greathouse* case, 195; publication of legal notices, 46; on San Francisco's pueblo title, 35–36
San Francisco Chamber of Commerce, 199
San Francisco Chronicle, 45, 49
San Francisco Herald, 121
San Francisco land: and *alcalde* grants, 182; and beach and water lots, 182–83; and *Bolton* claim, 191–93, 208; business community and, 186, 199; effect of inflation on, 182; execution sales of, 184, 188; fraud allegations, 183, 191–92; Limantour claim to, 165–66, 190–91; and Peter Smith deeds, 184–85, 188–90, 205–7; preemption claims to, 185–86; and property owners, 186; and public trust doctrine in *Hart*, 188–89; and pueblo issue, 180–81, 187–93, 201–8; and *Sherrebeck* claim, 191, 193, 208; speculation in, 182–83; and squatters, 183, 185–86, 189–91; and Van Ness ordinance, 190, 197

San Francisco Land Association, 191–92
San Francisco v. *United States* (1864), 202–4
San Joaquin (rancho), 144
San Luis Rey and Pala tract, 138
Saratoga Springs (N.Y.), 8
Sawyer, Lorenzo: on Chinese, 239–40, 242–43, 245–47; conflict with Field, 39–40, 240; as member, Ninth Circuit, 30, 32; relations with Ninth Circuit judges, 47; relinquishment of criminal docket to Hoffman, 124, 131; support for appointment to Ninth Circuit, 42–47
Scully v. *Steamer "Great Republic"* (1870), 91
Secretary of State, 5, 18, 121
Secretary of the Interior, 123, 127, 159
Secretary of the Treasury, 123
Secretary of War, 116, 123
Seward, William Henry, 19
Shafter, Oscar L., 11, 13, 16
Sherman, William T., 42–43, 121, 182
Sherrebeck claim, 191–93, 208
Sibley, Mark, 9–10
Silliman, Benjamin D., 19
Solicitor General, 124
Solicitor of the Treasury, 60, 123
Somerville v. *Brig "Francisco"* (1870), 91
Sonora, Mexico, 112–14, 116
Southard, Samuel L., 3
Southard, Virginia. *See* Hoffman, Virginia
Speed, James, 203–4
Sprague, Pelig, 108
Stanford, Leland S., 35
Stanton, Edwin S., 165, 167–72
State Department, 121
Story, Joseph: as Hoffman's law professor, 8–9; interpretation of 1835 Act, 103–4; views and opinions of, 54, 56–57, 65–66, 79, 103–4
Sullivan, Daniel T., 92
Supplemental Regulations, 1828 (Mexico), 140–41, 144, 147, 150
Supreme Court (Calif.): on admiralty jurisdiction, 56; in *Cohas* v. *Raisin*, 187–88; Field as member of, 181; and *Fremont* case, 150; in *Hart* v. *Burnett*, 188–90; on San Francisco land cases, 187–90; Sawyer as member of, 42; in *Welch* v. *Sullivan*, 188; in *Woodworth* v. *Fulton*, 187
Supreme Court (U.S.): on admiralty jurisdiction, 54–57; in *Arguello*, 151–52; in *Bolton*, 192–93; California representative on, 33; in *Cambuston*, 176–78; in *Cervantes*, 148, 150–51; circuit duties of, 30, 41; in *Cutler* v. *Rae*, 78; in *Dred Scott* v. *Sanford*, 34; Field's contribution to, 37–38; in *Fremont*, 148–51; on land cases, 134–35; in *New Jersey Steam Navigation Co.* v. *Merchants Bank*, 55; proposed expansion of, 36; in *Reynolds*, 68; in *San Francisco* v. *U.S*, 202–3; in *Sherrebeck*, 193; in *U.S.* v. *Boisdore*, 134; in *U.S.* v. *Circuit Judges*, 204; in *U.S.* v. *Kingsley*, 134; in *U.S* v. *Teschmaker*, 135, 178; in *Waring* v. *Clarke*, 55
Surveyor General, 140, 170, 196
Sutter, John A., 139, 164, 173
Swayne, Noah H., 42

Taney, Roger B., 149–50, 152, 171
Taylor, Zachary, 5, 34
Teare, Philip, 130, 219–20
Testimony. *See by docket, e.g.*, Admiralty law: testimony
Thomas, Robert A., 145
Thornton, Harry I., 143
Tong Wo Co., 214
Tort law, 96–98
Treason, statutory, 194. See also *U.S.* v. *Greathouse*
Treasury Department, 101; and Collector of Internal Revenue, 215, 219
Treaties: Burlingame (1868), 122, 225–26, 230, 232; 1880 treaty with China, 226–31, 233, 235; with France, 119; Gadsden, 116; and national honor, 122, 232, 237; and U.S.

Constitution, 119. *See also* Treaty of Guadalupe Hidalgo
Treaty of Guadalupe Hidalgo: Black's attitude toward, 163, 172; in *Cervantes*, 144–45; in *Fremont*, 149; obligations under, 144–45; as source of law for Land Boards, 140; terms of, 136
Two Years Before the Mast (Dana), 103

Union Club (N.Y.), 5
Union Club (San Francisco), 22
U.S. Army, 114. *See also* Folsom, Joseph L.; Halleck, Henry W.; Hitchcock, Ethan Allan; Sherman, William T.; Wool, John E.
U.S. attorney (N.D., Calif.). *See* Benham, Calhoun (1850–53, 1860–61); Blanding, William (1856–58); Della Torre, Peter (1858–60); Hilborn, Samuel G. (1882–86); Inge, Samuel W. (1853–56); Lake, Delos (1865–69); Latimer, Lorenzo D. (1869–73); Sharp, William (1861–65); Teare, Philip (1878–82)
U.S. attorney (S.D., N.Y.), 5, 128
U.S. attorneys in California: advocacy in land cases, 153; discretion in prosecution, 123–32, 216–23; Hoffman's relations with, 124–25; independence from U.S. Attorney General, 101, 123–25, 156; pressures on, 126; prosecution of Chinese by, 125, 131–32, 216–23, 228–46; removal of, 123–24; and revenue, 126–30; in the southern district, 18, 32. *See also* U.S attorney (N.D., Calif.)
U.S. Circuit Judge Act (1869), 42
U.S. Congress. *See* Congress, U.S.
U.S. Constitution: and Commerce clause, 54; and conflict with treaties, 120; and Equal Protection clause, 224; Fourteenth Amendment of, 224–25; Sixth Amendment of, 119
U.S. Customs. *See* Customs, U.S., in San Francisco
U.S. district court (N.D., Calif.): ad-

ministration of, 41; admiralty cases, 59–99; admiralty law innovations and, 56, 58, 60–73, 75–77; appointment to and establishment of, 20–21, 32; and bankruptcy cases, 213–15; and bond cases, 129–30; Chinese testimony admitted in, 211; clerk of court for, 41; criminal cases, 101–2, 104–22, 125–26, 130–32, 215–23; and criminal docket from Sawyer, 124, 131; and habeas corpus cases of Chinese, 228–46; and jurisdiction and consolidation bill, 197–99; jurisdiction of, 30–33, 148, 159; jurisdiction over surveys, 197–200; and land cases, 146–63, 165–70, 172–79, 190–93, 201–2; workload, 80; workload in admiralty cases, 51, 60–61, 64, 83–85, 130; workload in bankruptcy cases, 213; workload in bond cases, 129; workload in criminal cases, 101, 122–23, 125, 129–31; workload in criminal cases against Chinese, 215–23; workload in habeas corpus cases, 210, 228, 234, 242–43, 245–46; workload in land cases, 135–36, 159
U.S. district court (S.D., Calif.): establishment of, 32–33, 159–60; jurisdiction of, 148, 197–98; in land cases, 139–40
U.S. Navy, 2–3
U.S. Ninth Circuit court: on anti-Chinese movement, 246–47; conflict with Justice Field, 31–32; court clerk of, 203; jurisdiction of, 30–32, 161; McAllister's qualifications for, 33–34; members of, 30, 228; as preferred business forum, 74; and special circuit court, 30, 160–61. *See also* Deady, Matthew P.; Field, Stephen J.; Hoffman, Ogden, Jr.; McAllister, Matthew Hall; Sabine, George; Sawyer, Lorenzo
U.S. statutes: Judiciary Act (1789), 55, 100; Criminal Punishment Act (1790), 102; Judiciary Act (1801),

U.S. statutes (*continued*)
  160; Neutrality Act (1818), 112–18,
  121–22; Revolt and Mutiny Act
  (1835), 102–6; California Land Act
  (1851), 136–40, 142, 157, 159, 202,
  204–5; Civil and Diplomatic Expenses Act (1852), 157; Uniform Fee
  Act (1853), 128–29; Survey Act
  (1860), 197, 200; Survey Act (1864),
  201, 204; Summary Trial Act (1864),
  105–6; Bankruptcy Act (1867), 213,
  215; Circuit Judge Act (1869), 42;
  Administration of Justice Act (1872),
  31; Exclusion Act (1882), 223, 225–
  35; Exclusion Act (1884), 237–43;
  Exclusion Acts (1888), 244–46
U.S. Supreme Court. *See* Supreme
  Court (U.S.)
U.S. v.: Boisdore (1861), 134; *Bolton*
  (1860), 191–93, 208; *Burtis* (1866),
  108–9; *Cambuston* (1858), 176–78;
  Cervantes (1856), 134–35, 144,
  146–49, 151; *Circuit Judges* (1865),
  204; *Fremont*, 134–35; *Greathouse*,
  36–37, 41, 194–96; *Kingsley* (1838),
  134; *Limantour* (1858), 165–74;
  Nichols (1839), 103–4; *Pico* (1860),
  154, 173; *Sherrebeck* (1859), 192–93;
  Teschmaker (1860), 135, 178; *Watkins*
  (1854), 116–18

Vallejo, Juan A., 178
Vallejo, Salvador, 178
Van Ness ordinance, 190, 197, 205–6
Vigilance committees: of 1851, 21–22,

81, 101; of 1856, 21, 81–83, 100,
  124, 126

Waite, Morrison, 37
Walker, William, 113–17, 121
Waring v. *Clarke* (1848), 55
Waterman, Robert H., 95–96, 101–2,
  126
Watkins, Henry P., 116–18, 121–22
Watson, R. L., 12
Webster, Daniel, 4, 18–20
Weed, Thurlow, 6
Welch v. *Sullivan* (1857), 188
Weller, John B., 145, 160
Whigs, 3–6, 17, 21, 38, 115; and ap-
  pointment of Hoffman, 18–20, 22; in
  California, 19; Hoffman's father as
  member of, 3–4; in New York, 5–6,
  9, 19
Wickham, Bridget, 3, 7–8
Wickham, George, 3, 8
Wickham (family), 2–3
Williams, John B., 198, 201–3
Wilson, James, 143
Wilson, Joseph, 148
Windeler, Adolphus, 86–87
Wo Kee and Co., 214
Women: in Hoffman family, 2–3, 6–8;
  as passengers, 61, 69, 71; as plain-
  tiffs, 72, 223
Woodworth v. *Fulton* (1850), 187–88
Wool, John E., 115–16, 118–19, 126

Yates, Joseph, 2
Yerba Buena (pueblo), 187, 192